Classical Debates for the 21st Century

Classical Debates for the 21st Century
Rethinking Political Thought

Thomas O. Hueglin

broadview press

Library and Archives Canada Cataloguing in Publication

Hueglin, Thomas O. (Thomas Otto), 1946–

   Classical debates for the 21st century : rethinking political thought / Thomas O. Hueglin.

Includes bibliographical references and index.
ISBN 978-1-55111-847-5

   1. Political science — History — 21st century. 2. World politics — 21st century. I. Title.
JA66.H84 2008   320.9'0511   C2007-907123-6

Broadview Press is an independent, international publishing house, incorporated in 1985. Broadview believes in shared ownership, both with its employees and with the general public; since the year 2000 Broadview shares have traded publicly on the Toronto Venture Exchange under the symbol BDP.

We welcome comments and suggestions regarding any aspect of our publications — please feel free to contact us at the addresses below or at broadview@broadviewpress.com.

North America
PO Box 1243, Peterborough, Ontario, Canada K9J 7H5
2215 Kenmore Avenue, Buffalo, NY, USA 14207
Tel: (705) 743-8990; Fax: (705) 743-8353
email: customerservice@broadviewpress.com

UK, Ireland, and continental Europe
NBN International, Estover Road, Plymouth, UK PL6 7PY
Tel: 44 (0) 1752 202300; Fax: 44 (0) 1752 202330
email: enquiries@nbninternational.com

Australia and New Zealand
UNIREPS, University of New South Wales
Sydney, NSW, Australia 2052
Tel: 61 2 9664 0999; Fax: 61 2 9664 5420
email: info.press@unsw.edu.au

· **www.broadviewpress.com**

This book is printed on paper containing 100% post-consumer fibre.

Copy-edited by Kirsten Craven.

Designed by Chris Rowat Design, Daiva Villa

PRINTED IN CANADA

For my teacher Alois Riklin.

Contents

Acknowledgments   ix

CHAPTER 1   **Time to Rethink**   1

2   **Method of Inquiry**
Descartes v. Vico   15

3   **Nature of the Political**
Plato v. Aristotle   29

4   **Governance**
Thomas v. Marsilius   49

5   **Class Politics**
Machiavelli's Prince *v.* The Discourses   73

6   **Sovereignty**
Hobbes v. Althusius   93

7   **State and Society**
Locke v. Montesquieu   119

8   **Power of the Majority**
Rousseau v. Tocqueville   147

9   **Human Rights**
Burke (and Rousseau) v. Wollstonecraft   177

10   **Modernity and Beyond**
Nietzsche v. Marx   203

Notes   232
Bibliography   269
Index   283

Acknowledgments

I want to thank my students in PO 235/236 at Wilfrid Laurier University on whom I first tried out the interpretations in this book. I am proud to be a Broadview Press author for the second time. Greg Yantz listened to my ideas for a book on the history of political thought before the previous book on federalism was even finished. Michael Harrison came up with a much better title. As usual, the production process was in the competent hands of Judith Earnshaw. Particular thanks are owed to Kirsten Craven, who copy-edited the manuscript with great care and patience. Her many queries greatly improved clarity and style. Whatever remains unclear or clumsy is entirely my own fault.

Time to Rethink

Scientific globalization industries are hammering home a message of world transformation. At the universities, new global studies programs are established, students are fed with global transformation readers, and research projects are devoted to searches for global democracy. Yet, we continue to take for granted, and teach our students, the classical canon of political thought without raising the question whether this classical canon is of much further use in a radically changing world.

From Plato to Hobbes, Rousseau, and Marx, the march through the history of political thought is characterized by a search for one best solution: the absolute truth of the philosopher-king, the absolute sovereignty of one government over one territory, the unerring general will of one society, and even the end of history as the victory of one social formation over all others. Yet again the real world we live in appears to be characterized much more by a plurality of competing ideas, visions, identities, and solutions.

To a large extent, the conventional history of political thought can be seen as a retrospective justification for the assumptions of modern statehood. It provides little heuristic value for a globalization debate focussing on a world of overlapping legal domains, debordered authority, pluralized societal contexts, and competing normative visions. As long as heuristic guidance from the history of political thought is still desirable, it seems necessary and appropriate to rethink the continued relevance of some of its main theories and assumptions.

The idea for this book came to me when I taught an advanced seminar on globalization theories alongside an introductory course on the history of political thought. More precisely, it hit me when we started discussing social contract theory and had arrived at the point where Locke declares that a "Body Politick" is created when "any number of Men have so consented to make one Community or Government ... wherein the Majority have a Right to act and to conclude the rest."[1] The underlying assumptions for this theory were as false then as they are now because neither Scottish, Welsh, nor Irish men had been asked. It is indeed astounding that such a theory should still be of significant appeal to, say, Canadian political science students living in a country with a serious secessionist movement at one end, a no less serious case of regional alienation at the other, and some 600 bands of Aboriginal Peoples struggling for means of autonomous survival in between. It is even more astounding that such a theory should remain an unchallenged part of the classical canon in a globalizing world in which "the extensive penetration of civil society by transnational forces has altered its form and dynamics" and the "exclusive link between territory and political power has been broken."[2]

No attempt will be made to get into the globalization debate, however. This is the question as to whether we now live in a new and post-Westphalian world in which nation-states are no longer in full command of the kind of exclusive state sovereignty traditionally attributed to them. What matters is that the discourse has changed. Instead of talking about government, we are now talking about governance, the dispersal of the act of governing among a plurality of public and private actors within and across nation-state boundaries. Whether this is really new or only a new and belated realization of a reality that never quite lived up to the Westphalian model is not the primary issue here. What is, however, inviting a critical re-evaluation of the history of political thought is the fact that our concepts of political institutions and processes are now less attached to the idea of one society and one government than they have been throughout most of their history.

An issue closely related to the globalization debate is the alleged transition from a modern to a postmodern world. For our purposes, it does not matter whether value changes, new information technologies, social movements, and the pluralization of identities and citizenship more generally have in fact begun to deconstruct the conventional world of states and societies, or whether, once again, this kind of deconstruction and reconstruction has been part and parcel of modernity all along.[3] But there can be no doubt that we have become more reluctant to tell the story of the world as some grand narrative of all-encompassing truth and progress. Instead, we let the plurality and diversity of social phenomena tell their own stories and we hope that the result will not be chaos but some new form of interconnectedness on the basis of autonomy and mutual respect.

Only the kind of liberal triumphalism that raised its parochial head after the demise of its main ideological rival, communist internationalism, continues to insist that there must be a universal solution to the world's manifold problems and yearnings. And the more such universalism proves disastrous in practice as much as it is rejected in theory, the more also it becomes problematic to rely on the old models and patterns of thinking. Those are the patterns and models committed to the logic of universal causality and the certainty of absolute truth. Not just for the champions of postmodernism it would seem is such logic, in the words of the incomparable Nietzsche, "unbearable like wasps" (*unerträglich wie Wespen*).[4]

The plan for this critical re-evaluation of the classical canon in the history of political thought seemed clear, then. I would separate "good" theories and ideas, emphasizing plurality, diversity, and open-endedness, from "bad" ones committed to a search for absolute truth, universality, and homogeneity. In doing so, I would create a new canon of political thought by entirely leaving out some of the classical authors that seemed no longer relevant in an age of globalization and adding new authors that had thus far been neglected because their ideas did not gel with the dominant paradigms of nation-state, individual liberalism, and universal citizenship.

During my sabbatical year in 2005-06, I reread the classical canon all the way from Plato to Marx and Nietzsche, mostly sitting in a deck chair overlooking the shores of Lake Huron. It was a most pleasant undertaking, reconnecting me with old friends, as well as discovering new ones. The last time I had seriously studied the history of political thought had been 30 years earlier as a Ph.D. student in Switzerland. In the meantime, much of my work had focussed on comparative federalism, often a rather dry and tedious subject matter, even though it had been the idea of federalism as organized plurality that had convinced me that a fresh look at the history of political thought was a worthwhile project in the first place. However, while falling in love with the classical canon of political thought all over again, I soon realized that my initial plan for the book would not work.

The great theorists of universal truth and order, Plato, St. Thomas Aquinas, Hobbes, Locke, and Rousseau, are great for a reason. Take Rousseau, for example. His formula of a universal "general will" (*volonté générale*) as a computation of the "will of all" (*volonté de tous*) minus "the pluses and minuses which cancel each other out" (*les plus et les moins qui s'entre-détruisent*) may not strike us any more as a particularly relevant or useful expression of "the common interest" (*l'intérêt commun*).[5] But his insistence on the existence of such a common interest in principle as the ultimate and universal yardstick for the organization of civil society, any civil society, not only inspired the French Revolution and its *Declaration of the Rights of Man and of the Citizen*, it also stands as the timeless expression of a humanity of equals. (Mary Wollstonecraft, of course, would criticize Rousseau a few decades later for not having included women in that humanity.)

For these and many other and similar reasons, the book has taken a shape different from the one originally intended. Most of the classical authors are still there, and only a few more neglected voices have been added. Among the latter, Marsilius, Montesquieu, and Tocqueville tend to appear in the classical canon only on occasion although they are well known and well studied. Wollstonecraft, on the other hand, finally seems to have gained permanent status as a classic among her male colleagues. Only the inclusion of Althusius marks a significant departure from convention — although the great early-modern theorist of organized plurality and shared sovereignty once figured quite prominently in what is arguably still the most famous book on the history of political thought, George Sabine's *A History of Political Theory*.[6]

More importantly, instead of presenting a revised history of political thought in terms of good or bad, useful or useless, the argument will be presented as a kind of profit and loss account, noting the increasing or decreasing relevance of certain concepts and theories rather than endorsing or rejecting them altogether. To make such an obvious concession is not as ridiculous as it sounds. When a friend of mine taught a course in the history of political thought, also some 30 years ago, at the University of Konstanz in Germany, he tried to convey to his students this sense of dialectical ambiguity, of on-the-one-hand-and-on-the-other, of theory and practice, idealism and realism. He first presented Plato in glowing terms as the timeless theorist in search of ultimate truth, and then, by turning the argument around, denounced him as a dangerous theorist of an autocratic, hierarchical, and closed society. As he proceeded, he noticed how a sulky silence had fallen across the entire room until, from the last bench, a lonely voice cried out: "Write on the blackboard which it is!"

For the sake of instructive purposes that are not entirely illegitimate, it is much easier to paint a stark picture of right and wrong, good and evil, than to advance a more differentiated view of lingering uncertainty, "beyond good and evil," as Nietzsche demanded. For this reason, the book still proceeds as originally intended and in the same way I have taught the course on the history of political thought ever since — as a series of classical debates. With one exception, two political thinkers are confronted with one another in each chapter. These debates, however, do not proceed in strictly chronological order or linear fashion. This requires some additional explanation.

The history of political thought is conventionally constructed in chronological order. This makes sense not only because of the chronology of history itself but also because the great political thinkers and philosophers often learned from one another. As a result of this chronological ordering, the classical canon is typically presented as a history of perpetual and linear progress. Where one thinker has left off, the next one will continue. Thus, Hobbes first conceptualized absolute state authority as a rational way of achieving public security; Locke then protected property rights by making state authority accountable to those who paid taxes; Rousseau proceeded to extend citizenship to all men; Wollstonecraft demanded the inclusion of women; Marx insisted that political equality had to be presupposed by socioeconomic equality; and, voilà, the enlightened end of history is near.

Postmodern political thought would beg to differ, of course, and reject this grand narrative of linear intellectual progress, postulating instead that we need to replace the old search for finality with a new sense of open-ended uncertainty. But such paradigmatic change, like the one from state government to governance beyond the state, still remains generally committed to a chronological order of intellectual development. Thus, in the history of political thought as much as in the globalization debate there is a tendency to distinguish premodern, modern, and postmodern periods of theory and practice: before the state, with the state, and after the state. This means that a qualitative assessment of political thought in each period is already made before the analysis of individual authors and theories has even begun. The heuristic value of the history of political thought as a vast reservoir of concepts and ideas remains underexplored.

In order to make a fuller and more thorough use of that reservoir, it might be helpful to cut through the maze of political thought in a way that is different from the conventional one. Instead of making latitudinal cuts distinguishing premodern, modern, and postmodern slices of intellectual development, we might want to make longitudinal cuts distinguishing alternative segments. This would allow us to recognize the diversity of political concepts and traditions across the boundaries of time and circumstance.

In this book I am suggesting such a different approach by distinguishing two different methods of inquiry according to which the history of political thought can be sorted into two camps, one committed to abstract reason, and the other to historical learning. In Chapter 2, therefore, Descartes's insistence that knowledge must be "clear and certain" (*evidens et certum*)[7] will be compared to Vico's suggestion that human affairs can only be deciphered by a "common sense" (*senso commune*) of shared collective experience.[8] This classical debate on method sets the stage for all of the remaining chapters.

Thus, in Chapter 3 Plato's quest for an imaginary best state will be confronted with Aristotle's more pragmatic search for political reconciliation among a plurality of social claims. In Chapter 4, the uneasy truce between reason and faith in the hierarchical universalism of Aquinas will be contrasted with Marsilius's endorsement of a human legislator deriving legitimacy from the active involvement of the different social parts of a political community. In a departure from the two-author pattern, in Chapter 5 Machiavelli's brief turn to pure power politics in *The Prince* will be framed by his own analysis of the social conditions of liberty in a mixed polity. In Chapter 6, Hobbes's unitary construction of state and society will be compared to the retention of organized social plurality in Althusius's theory of federalism. In Chapter 7, Locke's abstract individual liberalism will be juxta-posed to Montesquieu's retention of social difference as the inevitable sociolog-ical starting point for all practical political theory. And Rousseau's celebration of the general will's moral superiority over all particular interests will be exposed to Tocqueville's critical account of majority rule in action in Chapter 8.

The last two chapters connect with some of the issues of modernity that appear far from resolved. In Chapter 9, both Burke's conservative obfusca-tion of historical fact and Rousseau's naive yearning for a simpler world will be confronted with the intellectual rigour of Wollstonecraft's vindication of the rights of men and women. Mary Wollstonecrfaft is not only the first important feminist thinker in the classical canon. She is also a merciless ana-lyst of traditional prescriptions of inequality, and an ardent believer in the liberating forces of a modernity harnessed by reason. And finally, in the con-cluding chapter, Chapter 10, the seductive appeal of Nietzsche's archaic escapism into a culture of nihilism will be confronted with Marx's timeless analysis of modernity as a relentless process of creation and destruction.

The idea of "historical learning" also provides the cue for the interpreta-tive approach to the history of political thought more generally. There is widespread disagreement about how this history should be studied.[9] For some, the masterpieces of political philosophy must be appreciated as free-standing monuments of intellectual achievement regardless of time and cir-cumstance. For them, the classical texts are classical precisely because they address issues of political order and justice that remain the same throughout history. In order to understand what Plato means by justice, for instance, one does not need to know that he developed it during a time of crisis in Athens.

For others, however, the meaning and importance of these classical texts can only be unfolded fully in their historical context. They would not deny, of course, that there are perennial issues such as order and justice, nor that the classical authors have addressed them in a significant way. But they would argue that these contributions cannot be fully appreciated unless they are placed within the time and circumstances that gave rise to them. The gen-eral significance of Machiavelli's ideas for ruthless princely rule, to use another example, cannot be gauged adequately outside the context of politi-cal corruption in Medici Florence.

A related problem is that of reconstruction and relevance. In the words of J.G.A. Pocock, are we interested in finding out "what *eigentlich* was meant" by particular political thinkers in their time, or is our primary interest to explore what we "can make it mean" for our own time?[10] By the untranslat-able German expression *eigentlich*, Pocock, one of the pre-eminent historians of political thought, means to indicate a search for true historical meaning in its own right. But *letztlich* (in the last instance, or ultimately), such a separation of true historical meaning from interpretation biased by the preconceived meanings of a later time is impossible. It would be like trying to play the works of, say, Mozart, as they were meant to be played in Mozart's own time. We can use original instruments, and maybe we can even wear powdered wigs, but we cannot entirely untrain our ears from twenty-first-century acoustic expectations.

This is not to say that we should not try to come as close as possible to an authentic understanding of what was meant. Precisely because our aim is to make use of the history of political thought as a reservoir of ideas and theories for a better understanding of our own time, we need to get right what those ideas and theories were in the first place. And in order to do that we need to study them in their own historical context even though what we are ultimately after is their timeless substance. Without such substance we could hardly use them for comparative purposes across time and circumstance.

The methodological truth of the matter, in other words, lies somewhere in the middle, in a prudent application of different approaches: trying to understand each thinker's contribution to perennial issues of order and justice through careful textual and contextual analysis, and to make meaningful comparisons across time and circumstance on that basis. In line with this intended plurality of approaches, I will also ignore another matter of considerable contention if not confusion: whether what we are after is a history of "political thought," "theory," or "philosophy."[11]

To my mind, political thought identifies the field most generally and includes everything revolving around political issues such as order and justice, power, organized forms and processes of collective decision-making, criteria of citizenship, and inclusion and diversity. Political theory then constitutes attempts of thinking about these issues systematically in a comprehensive and logically interrelated way. For example: If citizenship is defined as including political rights of diversity and plural identity, then it follows that majority rule alone does not suffice as a legitimate means of reaching collective decisions. Political philosophy in turn addresses broader questions and issues of human nature, ethical standards, and normative positions of right and wrong in which more specific political theories and thoughts are embedded. For example: Democratic political theories are embedded in the philosophical assumption that all human beings are equal by nature. Most classical authors combine all aspects of political thinking by addressing particular issues, formulating theories, and by embedding these in some larger philosophical context.

There is one particular matter which is often neglected even though it poses some of the most intricate problems of reconstruction and interpretation: translation. When I studied Plato for the first time as an undergraduate student in Germany, the German title of his main work of political philosophy was *Der Staat* (*The State*). When I came to North America, the same work was titled *The Republic*. These are loaded terms and they are both wrong, of course, and they already constitute the first step of a possibly inadequate interpretation. The title of Plato's work is *Politeia*, which means that it deals with the *polis*, the Greek city state that Plato was familiar with.

But this is not yet where it ends. All through my German academic life, I thought that the core of Plato's political philosophy was his *Ideenlehre* (theory or doctrine of "ideas"). Once I began to open Plato's works in English, however, it had transmuted into a theory or doctrine of "forms." At the heart of the discrepancy seems to lie the ambivalence of the Greek word *eidos*, which literally means the original image or essence of something. If you read competent translations and interpretations of Plato carefully, it can all amount to pretty much the same thing in the end, of course. But it is also possible that Plato's *politeia* turns out to be about the idea of the state in one instance, and about the republican form in the other.

Similar tales could be told just about every other major work of political thought that we read in translation. One of the more absurd cases occurred in Germany as well. Montesquieu, in the foreword to his major work on political thought, *The Spirit of the Laws*, describes his methodological intention by writing that he believed that men, despite the infinite diversity of their laws and customs, "were not led by their fancies alone" (*n'étaient pas uniquement conduits par leurs fantaisies*).[12] For a long time the only available standard German translation left out the "not" and thus insinuated that the great French sociological observer did not believe in basic or common patterns of human behaviour.

This omission may have been an unfortunate fluke, but it demonstrates vividly that our understandings of those classical texts not written originally in English — or even modern English — inevitably come to us in an altered form. In this book, therefore, I have made sure to provide all direct citations in both English and the original language. With one unfortunate but unavoidable omission, though: While I can read classical texts in English, German, French, Italian, and Latin, I have never learned ancient Greek. This inconsistency is lessened, however, by the fact that the core interpretative problems of translation usually revolve around well-known words such as *eidos* or *polis*, and that the secondary literature usually provides helpful glossaries and explanations. Also, in the case of Aquinas, I provide the Latin original only for formulations of particular importance and significance.

Presenting the original and the translation side by side can clarify, but it can also confuse further. Sometimes it may amount to reading two different texts. Throughout almost all of my Canadian academic life, for example, I have been familiar with Tocqueville's scathing verdict on the phony kind of liberalism that existed in nineteenth-century English class society: "Particularly noteworthy is the skill with which the English nobility, in order to safeguard their position, were quite ready, whenever it seemed advisable, to fraternize with the common people and to profess to regard them as equals." This is the most commonly available translation found in most North American libraries. When I finally looked up the French original, I could hardly recognize it: "*Il est curieux de voir comment la noblesse anglaise, poussée par son ambition même, a su, quand cela lui paraissait nécessaire, se mêler familièrement à ses inférieurs et feindre de les considérer comme ses égaux.*"[13] Nobody is fraternizing here. Equality is not professed but only pretended. And the driving force turns out to be ambition, not safeguarding necessity. Fortunately, there is now a new and more precise translation: "It is interesting to see how the English nobility, pushed by its own ambition, has known how to mingle on familiar terms with its inferiors when necessary, and pretend to consider them its equals."[14]

What's the fuss, you may think. The bottom line of the argument as rendered in these different versions is quite similar. But if this kind of inaccuracy permeates an entire text, the end result may be that different students using editions based on different translations come to different conclusions. The point, however, is not to be overly pedantic about the translator's need to transform meaning rather than to translate words. It is only to suggest caution. Translation itself is a serious issue of interpretation.

We are not the first ones to be confronted with this issue. When the works of Aristotle were rediscovered towards the end of the Middle Ages, for example, most if not all commentators and scholars read him in the Latin translation rather than in the Greek original. Thus, the Aristotle used by Aquinas, Marsilius, or Althusius had certain late medieval connotations alien to his original intentions, a fact we have become aware of only much more recently when classical Greek scholarship reverted to using the original language.

Again, the point is not that the history of political thought can only be presented legitimately through its original language. Precisely because we are as much interested in what the classical texts can be made to mean for our own time as we are interested in their true original meaning, there is nothing wrong in following an already existing and well-established path of translated meaning and interpretation. But we need to be aware of possible distortions and confusions arising from the process of translation.

An altogether different matter is how to deal with the errors, contradictions, and inconsistencies arising from the text itself. The current climate of scientific exactitude demands that nearly nothing must be put on paper that cannot be supported by an ample supply of footnoted evidence of fact or previous argument. By comparison, the great political thinkers of the past were also great because they did not shy away from bold postulations that sometimes belied their own evidence. Althusius, for example, asserted that a right to govern could only be "granted by the people" (*a populo est concessa*),[15] yet later had to admit that provincial rulers in fact received their governing rights from imperial privilege. And John Locke based the origin of the social contract upon consent among "any number of men,"[16] but then conceded to time and circumstance that political rights would be weighted in accordance with property or taxpaying capacities.[17]

I would like to contend that it is at these seams between theoretical ambition and practical concession that the history of political thought becomes most interesting and most instructive. Does a particular political thinker go beyond what is conventional in theory and practice at the time? Do the limiting concessions to time and circumstance in a particular political theory invalidate its claims to universality, or does the generality of its underlying principles allow their application to a wider circle of inclusion later on?

Answers to such questions are seldom easy or straightforward. A relatively clear case is that of Aristotle, who defined citizenship as to govern and to be governed.[18] Even though the Greek philosopher took for granted that women, slaves, and even most of the working population would be excluded from citizenship thus defined, it seems obvious that the principle could eventually be extended to include all of humanity, and that this extension would even be in line with Aristotle's own suggestion that social and political stability has to be found among the many who make up the middle of society.

The case of Locke, by comparison, is not so clear. On the one hand, one can argue that property or tax qualifications only pose a contemporaneous and hence removable restriction to the universality of his social contract theory. On the other hand, however, one can understand these restrictions much more fundamentally as a requirement of common interest and social homogeneity without which the entire social contract construction collapses. Under conditions of class division or other forms of deep-seated diversity, the assumption that "any number of men" will consent to representative governance by majority rule cannot be sustained.

Locke, of course, is a particularly controversial case. For some he is the rational constructor of a "classic theory of individual popular sovereignty."[19] For others the significance of his theory is "almost the opposite," a logical and moral justification for the unlimited appropriation of private property and social inequality in Locke's outgoing eighteenth century.[20] If I tend to side with the latter interpretation rather than the former, the reason is not that I wish to present Locke as an early apologist of bourgeois class society — or even an early-modern capitalist villain — but that I find generally unconvincing any attempts at presenting great political thinkers as entirely driven by abstract reason.

Political thought at its best always constitutes both an abstraction from, and a reflection of social reality.[21] The great classical authors of political thought wanted to transcend time and circumstance as much as they wanted to be read and understood within that time. Yet, the juxtaposition of abstraction and reflection almost inevitably leads to contradictions. To explore these, I believe, is one of the most fruitful and rewarding approaches to the study of the history of political thought.

Context, of course, goes a long way in explaining where the classical authors took their material from, why and how they thought about it, and what conclusions they arrived at. But it also explains a lot about why and how books on the history of political thought like this one are written. In my particular case, the most important source of influence and stimulation has always been books. In a fast-paced age of information and communication, scholarship significantly and critically has come to rely on journal articles and chapter contributions to edited volumes. But it is books that continue to provide, in this world of "spaciotemporal accellerations,"[22] old-fashioned repositories of sustained argument and meaning.

One of the first books that had a great influence upon my own formation as a student of political thought was Habermas's *Theorie und Praxis* (*Theory and Practice*).[23] From the pages of the early Habermas I learned to distinguish between those political thinkers whose method of inquiry is driven by a technical-rational interest aimed at the discovery of objective truths and single solutions, and those other political thinkers committed to a practical-historical interest aimed at the discovery and accommodation of a plurality of possible truths and solutions.

Macpherson's *The Political Theory of Possessive Individualism* was perhaps the book that influenced my own thinking about the history of political thought more than any other I ever read.[24] But it was not the rigorous textual deconstruction of seventeenth-century as much as contemporary liberalism that impressed me so much. As may be well known, Macpherson attacked liberalism as theoretically confused and, precisely because of that confusion, practically appealing.[25] It was the irreverent way in which Macpherson approached the majestic temple of classical political thought. It taught me not only that getting immersed in that daunting pile of theories and ideas can be fun but also that such irreverence yields the best possible outcome of learning: the realization that even the greatest political philosophers cannot resolve with any degree of rational finality the problem of a just human order.

Although I share to a considerable degree the postmodern "incredulity toward metanarratives,"[26] I have also retained a fascination for sweeping accounts of grand history. Charles Tilly's edited volume, *The Formation of National States in Western Europe*, is such an account, but its macrohistorical theorizations are convincing precisely because they are embedded in an enormous wealth and plurality of well-researched smaller stories.[27] Veit Valentin's *Weltgeschichte (World History)*, by comparison, one of my favourite history books of all time, for the most part abstains from theorization.[28] Valentin was a German radical democrat and pacifist who lost his academic position twice, and under two different political regimes, in 1917 and again in 1933. His account of world history as a perpetual struggle for freedom of religion, arts, and sciences, and for political self-determination first impressed me as a high school student even though it is compelling for its subtlety of evaluation rather than its rashness of judgment.

Valentin's central message was that political and diplomatic history cannot be divorced from social and popular history. Contrary to those who want to turn the entire world into a war museum,[29] Valentin insisted that in order to understand the world, equal weight must be accorded to political, cultural, and social history, or any other kind of history that records how men and women make themselves "at home in a constantly changing world."[30]

Of the many books on the history of political thought I will single out only two. One is Robert Nisbet's slim volume, *The Social Philosophers*.[31] Instead of following the trodden path of distinguishing different epochs of political thought in chronological order — classical, medieval, early-modern, and modern — Nisbet grouped the classical canon into four visions of community: political, religious, ecological, and revolutionary. Even though I did not want to subscribe to all of this "conservative" sociologist's interpretations and conclusions, Nisbet's book struck me as an open-minded and innovative way of looking at the history of political thought.[32]

The other book is Sheldon Wolin's much weightier tome, *Politics and Vision*.[33] Originally published in 1960, the greatly expanded 2004 version contains seven new chapters alongside the original 10. What impressed me most about this book was how Wolin managed to sustain the core of his argument over a period of more than 40 years. In his first interpretative chapter, which was on Plato, he pointed out the dialectical tension between the philosophical yearning for "political fixity"[34] and the empirical acknowledgment of the "random movements"[35] in real politics. Still, in his newly added chapter on Rawlsian liberalism, Wolin noted that it struck him as outright "quixotic" to assume that there could be one political culture based on universally shared "basic values" in an age of "multiculturalism, ethnic diversity, and porous borders."[36] He ended his book with the observation that the "central challenge at this moment is not about reconciliation but about dissonance, not about democracy's supplying legitimacy to totality but about nurturing a discordant democracy."[37]

In my own effort to rethink the history of political thought, I have tried to follow the rationale of contrasting the "quixotic" search for political "fixity" with a more pragmatic investigation of societal complexity and its political accommodation by means of balance and compromise. This works fairly well for the comparison between Plato and Aristotle, Aquinas and Marsilius, Machiavelli's *Prince* and the *Discourses*, Hobbes and Althusius, Locke and Montesquieu, and Rousseau and Tocqueville. It does not work so well for Burke and Wollstonecraft or Nietzsche and Marx.

In the case of Burke and Wollstonecraft, it is of course the radical feminist who champions enlightened reason and universal progress, whereas the conservative politician points out that "the objects of society are of the greatest possible complexity" and therefore cannot be put on a trajectory of universal or linear progress.[38] However, in the end, Burke, as all conservatives, has only one prescription and solution: to maintain the status quo no matter what. Wollstonecraft, on the other hand, may believe in universal progress, but such progress need not end up in universal uniformity. When she demands representation for women in legislative assemblies, for example, the reason is not just universal inclusion in an undifferentiated collective body of citizens but the advancement of specific women's issues.

With Nietzsche and Marx, a case of monism v. pluralism is even harder, if not outright impossible, to make. Marx is the one who not only wants to reduce all social and political phenomena to one explanatory agent (the class antagonism between bourgeoisie and proletariat), he moreover believes that the eventual victory of the proletariat will result in communism as "the riddle of history solved" (*das aufgelöste Rätsel der Geschichte*).[39] Nietzsche, by comparison, preaches to live with a consciousness of uncertainty, and he attacks the uniformity of modern mass culture at every turn. But then again, it is Marx's steadfast focus on political economy analysis that uncovers not only the exploitative character of capitalist relations of production but also brings to light the complex and fluid nature of modern capitalism. Precisely because Marx understands and describes the nature of capitalist modernity as one of relentless destruction and reconstruction, the door remains open for a plurality of options. By comparison again, Nietzsche's nihilist attack on moral certainty, in his own words, "aims at nothing and achieves nothing" (*dass... nichts erzielt, nichts erreicht wird*).[40] Nietzsche's call for the destruction of all cultural and moral values associated with the search for stability and security does not open any new doors.

There is one last issue of classification that needs to be sorted out. It concerns the distinction between conservative and progressive or emancipative political thought. The latter is usually associated with demands for universality and centralization. This has to do with the French Revolution, which swept away the particularism of the old feudal order and replaced it with the centralized Jacobin state as the only and logical dispenser of universal civic and social rights. As a consequence, political thinkers who emphasize plurality and decentralization, such as Althusius, Montesquieu, and Tocqueville, are usually classified as conservative, or at least as more conservative than the great universal simplifiers of politics, Hobbes, Locke, and Rousseau.

To my mind, however, this classification is the result of a circular argument. First, in the name of universal progress, plurality and particularity are tossed aside as important principles of social and political order, thus leaving them to those, like Burke, who indeed want to use them for conservative purposes. And then these principles themselves are redefined as conservative principles, which means that their progressive potential for the rethinking and restructuring of a modern world of diversity is entirely lost. To put it differently, by paraphrasing the late Canadian Prime Minister Pierre Trudeau: It is not because the reactionaries have in the main endorsed decentralization that socialists should necessarily dismiss it.[41] It seems to me that in an age of complex plurality and interdependence, progressive and radical democrats have to reoccupy the ground they abandoned.

CHAPTER 2

Method of Inquiry

Descartes v. Vico

How does one construct a classical canon in the history of political thought? Until the so-called Age of Enlightenment consciously began to raise the question of tradition and progress, the old masters had been studied as undisputed and timeless sources of wisdom and intellectual authority. Scholastic arguments were garnished with ubiquitous references to the great thinkers of the past. But there were few explicit attempts at improving or overcoming the positions they held.

Radical change first came from the two great intellectual and spiritual movements commonly associated with the final transition from the Middle Ages to the early-modern world: the Renaissance and Reformation. While the Renaissance rediscovered the classical heritage of antiquity with a new critical consciousness, the Reformation marked the beginning of a new age of individual conscience. Such a new age, so it seemed to many, also needed a new approach to science, philosophy, and politics. To put it into the words that Marx would use much later about a different age: The entire scholastic heritage of "ancient and venerable prejudices and opinions" had to be "swept away."[1] Not everybody agreed. And from that disagreement sprang the two methods of modern political thinking that are still the dominant ones today:

1. a method of pure or technical reasoning, insistent on "getting it right" once and for all, either entirely abstract and speculative, or based on the objectivity of strict empirical observation;
2. a method of historical or practical reasoning, committed merely to "getting along," based on common experience and a tradition of shared values.[2]

Each led to diametrically opposed assumptions about the ultimate driving forces behind human conditionality and progress: scientific exactitude and

15

rational choice in the one case, and the collective exercise of common sense through historical learning in the other.

Context

In 1536 the French logician Pierre de La Ramée (1515-72) burst upon the scene with a master's thesis claiming that everything that Aristotle had taught was false.[3] During the same century, the Copernican postulation of a heliocentric world system began to question previous scientific assumptions about the world and universe. But it was not until the following seventeenth century that the power of tradition would be challenged more seriously. After the invention of the microscope and telescope, it became possible to see the universe as a calculable entity from the infinitesimal to the infinite.

The new scientists lived dangerously not so much because of what they discovered about the earth or stars but because of the implications this had for the established order. In 1600 the Neapolitan philosopher Giordano Bruno (1548-1600) was publicly burnt at the stake by the Inquisition, naked, hung upside down, and with a gag on his tongue. He had led an itinerant life, escaping from city to city and country to country, and he had endured seven years of incarceration prior to his trial and conviction of heresy all because the new understanding of the world and universe had led him to believe that man was a microcosm of that universe and that God was present in all of its parts. This in turn implied that the church as intermediator was no longer needed. More famous, of course, is the case of Galileo Galilei (1564-1642), who probably escaped death, or at least lasting imprisonment, because he recanted his belief in the Copernican system in 1633 and was therefore "only" put under house arrest for the rest of his life.

As a natural scientist, Galileo was not particularly interested in the social or political ramifications of his work. He probably recanted not only because he was old and ill but also because he did not care what the church thought about him and his work as long as he could continue to do it. Replacing the cosmological world view with mathematical calculation based on exact empirical observation, he refuted the Aristotelian tradition of natural science, and of physics in particular. The philosopher's views on politics as the art of practical wisdom were of little if any concern to him.

But it was only a matter of time until the new natural scientism would also infect the liberal arts and, therefore, politics. Thomas Hobbes visited Galileo in 1637, and shortly thereafter in 1642 published his first work of politics, *On the Citizen* (*De Cive*), in which every reference to Aristotle would be negative. And in 1651 in *Leviathan* Hobbes would speak of the "vain and erroneous Philosophy of the Greeks, especially of Aristotle."[4]

In order to appreciate the epochal battle between the classical traditionalists and the modernists, we need to take a brief look at the Aristotelian method of inquiry. On the basis of a strict separation of theoretical sciences such as physics from practical sciences such as ethics and politics, Aristotle held that "precision cannot be expected in the treatment of all subjects alike." Indeed, he continued that "a well-schooled man is one who searches for that degree of precision in each kind of study which the nature of the subject at hand admits: it is obviously just as foolish to accept arguments of probability from a mathematician as to demand strict demonstrations from an orator."[5] In his *Topics*, Aristotle elaborated on how knowledge can be achieved in the practical sciences: through dialectical reasoning, taking into consideration what is held by most or the best, by including everything that mirrors a plurality of opinion, and, in doing so, by generating a suitable catalogue of topics (*topoi*) pertinent to a particular problem. These topics must then be examined systematically by securing reasonable propositions, investigating a variety of expressions, and by distinguishing similarity and difference.[6] In other words, practical science or philosophy was for Aristotle the art of critical examination and formulation of reasonable assumptions.

Fascinated and overwhelmed by the new scientific exactitude, the modernists of the seventeenth century rejected such imprecision. If man was a microcosm of a universe increasingly understood as matter in motion, just as the world revolving around the sun and the stars following their calculable trajectories, then human behaviour had to follow predictable scientific patterns also.

In due course, the conviction took hold that political order was a matter of mathematical calculation as well. The search for such calculations also no longer required the argumentative environment of an entire academy. As Descartes reported in his *Discourse*, the new method came to him in the solitude of a stove-heated room somewhere in wintery Germany where he was occupied with nothing more than his own thoughts.[7]

René Descartes (1596-1650)

Born near the city of Tours in west-central France, Descartes was first educated in a Jesuit college and then took a law degree at the University of Poitiers. At the age of 22, and ostensibly because he wanted to travel and see the world, he joined various armies in Holland and in Germany, where the Thirty Years War had just begun. When he had his wintery methodological vision in 1619, he was on his way back from Frankfurt, where he had attended the coronation of Emperor Ferdinand II, returning to the army of Duke Maximilian of Bavaria.[8]

His aristocratic background supplied him with sufficient means for a comfortable life, and in 1628 he settled in Holland as a private scholar. It had been in Holland that he had first become exposed to the new science of the age. With some interruptions and travels, and the frequent changing of his address for whatever reason, security or privacy, he remained in Holland until 1649 when he accepted an invitation by Queen Christina of Sweden to become her private tutor in philosophy. He died in Stockholm the following year.

Descartes's philosophical-scientific ambition was enormous, and he pursued it with the kind of rigour of someone who knew exactly what he was aiming for. Upon his return from Germany, he put his mind to the composition, in Latin, of *Rules for the Direction of the Mind* (*Regulae ad Directionem Ingenii*), in which he first conceptualized the outlines of a universal scientific system entirely based on the mathematical logic of "the indubitable conception of a clear and attentive mind, which proceeds solely from the light of reason" (*mentis purae et attentae non dubium conceptum, qui a sola ratione lucis nascitur*). What is thus "clear and certain" (*evidens et certum*) has to be distinguished from "ordinary philosophy" (*philosophia vulgaris*) with its assertions merely based on "probable conjectures" (*probabilibus tantum conjecturis*).[9] The *Rules* remained uncompleted and were not published during his lifetime.

Descartes then worked on an ambitious work on cosmology and physics, written in French and titled, *The World* (*Le Monde*). It cautiously and hypothetically raised the issue of a heliocentric world system and ended with a short treatise on man as a mechanism driven by the same forces as the universe. *The World* was completed in 1633, but Descartes abstained from publication after he had heard about Galileo's condemnation. In a letter to a friend he wrote: "I desire to live in peace."[10]

Next came *Discourse on the Method*, Descartes's first published work, published in 1637 together with three essays on meteorology, optics, and geometry. Written in French again, it was meant to appeal to a more general audience of readers who were even admonished at the outset to read it in portions rather than in one sitting. More forcefully than the *Rules*, the *Discourse* was also meant as a manifesto laying down the principles for Descartes's entire scientific quest. Programmatically, this found expression in the lengthy title, "Discourse on the Method of Rightly Conducting One's Reason and Seeking the Truth in the Sciences" (*Discours de la méthode pour bien conduire sa raison et chercher la vérité dans les sciences*).[11]

The *Discourse* not only contained the aforementioned autobiographical wintery episode in Germany but also Descartes's most famous statement: "I am thinking, therefore I exist" (*je pense, donc je suis*), or, as it became better known from the later Latin edition, "*cogito, ergo sum.*"[12] At a deeper philosophical level this assertion was quite problematic because, as Descartes continued, it meant that the essence of human existence was the capacity to think and reflect, and this existence was manifest "entirely distinct from the body" (*entièrement distincte du corps*).[13] In other words, despite the fact that Descartes had earlier defined man as a mechanism driven entirely by physical forces, he now argued that his existence was nevertheless comprised in his entirely immaterial capacity to think. At a much simpler level, however, and with much more far-reaching practical consequences, Descartes's famous formulation brought on its way a new philosophy of pure reason detached from historical learning and experience.

The *Discourse* was followed by *Meditations on First Philosophy* (*Meditationes de prima Philosophia*, 1641).[14] Here, Descartes returned to writing in Latin, and, as the dedicatory letter to the "most learned and distinguished men, the Dean and Doctors of the sacred Faculty of Theology at Paris" shows, the purpose was to convince the scholarly establishment of his new method. And since he knew well that criticism was to come, he included in the publication a collection of solicited responses as well as his own replies to them.[15] And just in case the scholarly establishment might find his extended reasoning too alien or cumbersome, he also provided a short "Preface to the Reader" as well as a "Synopsis" of the main arguments. As the title indicates, the narrative was presented as a series of meditations by which Descartes meant to suggest that each reader could put himself in the place of the meditator.[16]

The *Meditations* reiterate and deepen the argument of the *Discourse*. A framing theme is the question of the existence of God, perhaps not surprising in a publication meant to impress a faculty of theology — which, apparently, it did not. In essence, Descartes's argument revolves around the assertion that God must exist because perfect knowledge, which is possible, can only come from a perfect source, which is God. As he sums up the argument at the end of the Fifth Meditation, "the certainty and truth of all knowledge depends uniquely on my awareness of the true God" (*omnis scientiae certitudinem & veritatem ab unâ veri Dei cognitione pendere*).

Two major works were still to follow. The first, *Principia philosophiae*, 1644, was written in traditional textbook style as a series of short enumerated articles.[17] It contained four parts: on the methodology of human knowledge, on physics, on the laws of the universe, and on the earth. It was a compilation and extension of all previous work meant to replace in its entirety the Aristotelian tradition of scholarly inquiry and learning.[18] In his last completed major work, *The Passions of the Soul* (*Les Passions de l'âme*, 1649), Descartes finally turned to questions of love, hatred, joy, and sadness. At the outset he accused the ancients of having neglected passion as a topic of particular interest,[19] but then came to a rather traditional conclusion nevertheless, and well in line with what the ancients had already said: From the passions arise the sweetest pleasures (*le plus de douceur*), as well as the bitterest moments in life (*le plus d'amertume*), whence it is the principal goal and task of wisdom to gain control of passion (*la sagesse...à s'en rendre tellement maître*).[20]

Descartes turned to the question of passions mainly at the insistence of Princess Elizabeth of Bohemia with whom he had been corresponding for some time, and he also appears to have sent an earlier short draft to Queen Christina of Sweden who reportedly read it while hunting.[21] The decision to accept Christina's invitation to move to Stockholm would prove bitter for Descartes. Not taking well to the harsh northern climate and to the imposition of meeting the queen for her tutorials at five o'clock in the morning, he fell ill and died of pneumonia a few months after his arrival. There is a final irony in this. During his early years of learning at the Jesuit College of La Flèche in Anjou, he had been excused from morning classes because of his poor health. According to anecdote, he later told another famous mathematician and philosopher, Pascal, that good mathematics could never be done in the morning.[22]

This brief and very cursory summary of the work and philosophy of one of the greatest thinkers of all time is only meant to serve one particular purpose: to demonstrate Descartes's colossal ambition of throwing overboard all that had previously been thought and taught, and of inventing a new universal system of thought and knowledge that would arise solely from the one and only truth the philosopher was sure of – that he existed, and was therefore thinking. There was an enormous arrogance in this endeavour, and particularly in the way in which Descartes dismissed all previous tradition. In his reply to one of the objections that had been raised against his *Meditations*, he wrote: "I make no mystery of the fact that I trust Aristotle less than my reason," and he even belittled Galileo's earlier critique of Aristotle with the remark: "Galileo is eloquent in refuting Aristotle; but it is not so difficult to do so."[23]

But while the new achievements in mathematics, astronomy, and physics had indeed led to the refutation of much of what Aristotle had held to be true about the world and universe, Descartes's dismissal not so much focussed on what was demonstrably wrong as on the traditional method of inquiry. And he was wary about studying the old masters more generally because he feared that their mistakes would infect his own thinking (*errorum maculae contractae*).[24] There was no place for historical learning or gradual progress here.

In the *Rules*, Descartes is still relatively appreciative of past achievements. "We ought to read the writings of the ancients," he notes, "in order to learn what truths have already been discovered" (*quae jam olim recte inventa sunt*).[25] But then he immediately offers a number of reservations about such historical open-mindedness: Not only will these ancients try to convince us of their point of view by ensnaring us with their most "subtle arguments" (*subtilissimis argumentis*), they will also "begrudge us the plain truth" (*nobis invident apertam veritatem*) because "hardly anything is said by one writer the contrary of which is not asserted by some other" (*quicquam ab uno dictum est, cujus contrarium ab aliquo alio non afferatur*).[26]

Descartes obviously did not like the kind of arguments that make up the methodological core of traditional philosophy. In fact, as he points out mockingly at the beginning of the *Discourse*, such philosophy is only useful because it "gives us the means of speaking plausibly about any subject and of winning the admiration of the less learned" (*que la philosophie donne moyen de parler vraisemblablement de toutes choses, et se faire admirer des moins savants*).[27] He then comes to the point: "Diverse opinions" (*diverses opinions*) are merely expressions of what is "probable" (*vraisemblable*) and therefore "false" (*faux*).[28] This is the moment when Descartes tells us about his (wintery German) methodological road to Damascus. He also provides a telling example of what is wrong, in his opinion, with traditional imprecision. Compared to the kind of "orderly towns which planners lay out as they fancy on level ground" (*ces places régulières qu'un ingénieur trace à sa fantaisie dans une plaine*), ancient cities are usually "ill-proportioned" (*mal compassées*) with "streets crooked and irregular" (*rues courbées et inégales*).[29]

This example is telling because it reveals, with anticipatory brilliance, modernism's relentless commitment to scientific certitude and progress. During the nineteenth century, straight boulevards would be blasted through the old crooked neighbourhoods of most major cities, creating new commercial "arteries in an urban circulatory system" through which, at the same time, "troops and artillery could move effectively against future barricades and popular insurrections."[30] A century later, even one of the last vestiges of "traditional imprecision," the production of wine, had come under attack when scientific manipulation increasingly replaced attention to *terroir* and local custom under the dictates of a global marketplace.[31]

For Descartes, the source of knowledge and progress was no longer the community, school, or even books, but the individual master thinker or master builder. The kind of book knowledge "amassed little by little from the opinions of many different persons" (*grossies peu à peu des opinions de plusieurs diverses personnes*) is never as close to the truth as the "simple reasoning" (*les simples raisonnements*) undertaken by a "man of good sense" (*un homme de bon sens*).[32] In fact, since Descartes is entirely concerned with finding out for himself what is true and not at all with what might get him along in practical life, leave alone politics, he can easily assert that "a majority vote is worthless as a proof of truths that are at all difficult to discover" (*la pluralité des voix n'est pas une preuve qui vaille rien, pour les vérités un peu malaisées à découvrir*).³³ And this is so, because Descartes is convinced, nay, he *knows* that "there is only one truth concerning any matter" (*n'y ayant qu'une vérité de chaque chose*).³⁴

Here we have it, then: the unsurpassable arrogance of a new age, committed to nothing and indebted to nobody. In the preface to the French edition of what he thought would be the textbook for that new age, *Principles of Philosophy*, Descartes wrote unabashedly that "the truths contained in these principles, because they are very clear and very certain, will eliminate all ground for dispute" (*les vérités qu'ils contiennent, étant très claires et très certaines, oteront tous sujets de dispute*).³⁵ And, as he added, the new certitude would thus "dispose people's minds to gentleness and harmony" (*ainsi disposeront les esprits à la douceur et à la concorde*).³⁶

All of this was not meant to be the end of history, though, at least not yet. Nor did it find immediate acceptance. At the same time as the Glorious Revolution in England (1688) established constitutional limits upon traditional monarchical rule, a literary *querelle des anciens et des modernes* (quarrel between ancients and moderns) broke out in Paris. At stake was the question to what extent—if at all—the teachings and traditions of the past should be considered as authoritative guidelines in the construction of future progress. From this debate emerged, eventually and gradually, the Enlightenment conviction that the destiny of man was marked by linear progress towards rational and scientific perfection.

The same quarrel also dominated intellectual life in Italy, albeit under much more difficult circumstances. As we remember, Bruno had been burnt at the stake for his endorsement of the new science in 1600, and Galileo had chosen to recant in order to escape incarceration in 1633. Still, in 1691 the Inquisition put on trial four men who had professed to believe that the universe was composed of atoms (admittedly, they had also held that Christ was an impostor).³⁷ This happened in Naples, a thriving metropolis in the southern Mediterranean but also a stronghold of orthodox Catholicism. As prohibition often begets the opposite of its intentions, so did the suppression of the new science fan the flames of intellectual radicalism. The works of Galileo, Descartes, and others, such as the great English empiricist Francis Bacon, or the new champion of the law of nations, Hugo Grotius, were eagerly studied in Neapolitan intellectual circles.

Among the members of these circles was Giambattista Vico. Initially as enthusiastic about the new science as his friends, Vico would eventually develop a rather cautious view of its merits, making up, in the formulation of Jürgen Habermas, a kind of "profit and loss account."³⁸ As this satisfied neither his friends nor his enemies, Vico would remain, in his own words, "a foreigner in his own country" (*straniero nella sua patria*).³⁹ Only later, after his death, would the recognition grow that this Neapolitan professor had in fact formulated the most enlightened alternative to Cartesian rationalism, a method of historical inquiry based on collective learning and common sense. Inadvertently, it would also bring on its way the beginnings of a modern philosophy of history.

Giovanni Battista (Giambattista) Vico (1668-1744)

As the sixth of eight children, Vico was born into the family of a poor book dealer. Like Descartes, he was first educated by Jesuits and eventually ended up with a law degree. However, he never seems to have been satisfied with what school and university had to offer. He drifted in and out of these institutions and mainly educated himself as an autodidact. Despite his enthusiasm for the new science and methodology, Vico never lost sight of the classics. Next to Bacon and Grotius, he counted Plato and the Roman historian Tacitus among the authors he felt most indebted to.[40]

In 1697 Vico was appointed professor of rhetoric at the University of Naples. One of his tasks in this position was to deliver annual orations or lectures at the beginning of the academic year. The first of these to be published, in 1709, was *On the Study Methods of Our Time* (*De nostri temporis studiorum ratione*).[41] For our methodological discussion, this is Vico's most important work. It was entirely meant as a response to, and critique of, Descartes's rational methodology. Vico did not so much reject or deny the scientific validity of this method as he argued that it leaves out as much as it adds, by focussing only on what can be demonstrated with certainty, and by neglecting the entire realm of probability and historical experience.

The *Study Methods* are primarily concerned with education. "The greatest drawback of our educational methods (*incommodum nostrae studiorum rationis maximum*), Vico tells his academic audience, is the excessive study of natural science (*naturalibus doctrinis impensissime studeamus*) at the expense of ethics (*moralem non tanti facimus*). As a consequence, he exhorts, "a noble and important branch of studies, i.e., the science of politics, lies almost abandoned and untended" (*amplissima praestantissimaque de republica doctrina nobis deserta ferme et inculta iacet*).[42] To be sure, he points out, the new scientists have "freed us from the burdensome task of speculating on nature" (*tanto negocio naturae ultra contemplandae liberarunt*).[43] But, and here he comes to his central methodological point, "it is impossible to assess human affairs by the inflexible standards of abstract right" (*non ex ista recta mentis regula, quae rigida est, hominum facta aestimari possunt*).[44]

The difference between abstract scientific knowledge and prudence in human affairs, Vico continues to explain, is this: While science aims at "reducing a large multitude of physical effects to a single cause" (*unam caussam, per quam plurima naturae effecta perducunt*), prudence operates by investigating "the greatest possible number of causes which may have produced a single event" (*unius facti quam plurimas caussas vestigant*) — and only then will it "conjecture" which of these may be the "true" one (*quae sit vera, coniiciant*).[45] Earlier, Vico had already revealed the classical source from which such prudence of investigation derives its inspiration: It is "the art of topics" (*topica*), which the new critical science had relegated to near oblivion.[46]

With an increasingly sharper tone of voice, Vico declares that it simply is an "error to apply to the prudent conduct of life the abstract criterion of reasoning" (*non recte ... iudicandi rationem, qua utitur scientia, in prudentiae usum transferunt*). And then comes the programmatic sentence that encapsulates Vico's entire methodological endeavour:

> Satisfied with abstract truth alone, and not being gifted with common sense, unused to following probability, those doctrinaires do not bother to find out whether their opinion is held by the generality and whether the things that are truths to them are also such to other people. (*Et cum sensum communem non excoluerint, nec verisimilia unquam secuti sint, uno vero contenti, quid porro de eo homines communiter sentiant, et an iis quoque vera videantur, nequicquam pendunt.*)[47]

Here, in a nutshell, are all the themes that Vico will develop more fully in his later works: abstract reasoning and scientific demonstration cannot be applied to ethics and politics; the moderns neglect and therefore lack experience with the probabilities of human affairs; truth is a relative concept that means different things to different people. This is Vico's profit and loss account: To the extent that the new science derives rational explanations from exact demonstrations, it loses the capacity of the old science to provide rules for the prudent conduct of human affairs. Because these rules are the result of mere probabilities, they fall outside the range of scientific interest and inquiry.[48]

In his next published work, *On the Most Ancient Wisdom of the Italians* (*De antiquissima Italorum sapientia*, 1710), Vico added a historical dimension to his critique of the new science.[49] Truth not only may mean different things to different people. It also and most definitely means different things for different ages. In deliberate juxtaposition to the Cartesian *cogito, ergo sum*, Vico postulates that *verum esse ipsum factum*, that "what is true is the same as what is made."[50]

The historicity of Vico's central methodological maxim is not readily evident and will come fully to the fore only in his master opus, the *New Science (Scienza nuova)* of 1744.[51] But the argument goes like this: Contrary to the Cartesian quest for the universality of "clear and certain" knowledge through abstract reasoning, Vico claims that knowledge of any matter is only possible through the making and operation of that matter. Only God, therefore, possesses universal knowledge because he made the universe. Men can only have knowledge of the human history they made. This is even so in the case of geometry: We know that it is true, not because God implanted in us a universal capacity for abstract truth, but because we "made it."[52]

Abstract reasoning committed to the discovery of "one truth concerning any matter" will result in general rules of conduct and order that are independent of time and circumstance.[53] Reasoning derived from the process of making history will result in differentiation and plurality of what is true. In what he programmatically called his *New Science*, Vico set out to place knowledge into a human geometry of historical and sociological differentiation. The *New Science* is a baroque maze of thoughts and digressions, and it may well be, as has been remarked with a good degree of Old-World conceit, that it cannot be fully appreciated in its "deeper meaning" when it is merely used as a "quarry" of ideas, "as is particularly common in American Vico research."[54]

But a quarry it is, and no attempt will be made within the narrow confines of this preliminary methodological chapter to do justice to a work of which James Joyce once remarked that it made his imagination grow "as it doesn't when I read Freud or Jung."[55] However, on the basis of what we already know, it seems possible to distil from its 1,411 paragraphs a few central passages that bring to the fore the core of Vico's methodological intent.[56]

In sharp contrast to Descartes's abstract reason, Vico postulates that "human choice, by its nature most uncertain, is made certain and determined by the common sense of men with respect to human needs or utilities" (*L'umano arbitrio, di sua natura incertissimo, egli si accerta e determina col senso commune degli uomini d'intorno alle umane necessità o utilità*).[57] We remember that Vico had already introduced the idea of "common sense" in his *Study Methods* as a kind of collective prudence or wisdom that alone can help to decipher the probabilities in a plural world of human affairs.[58] He now defines it as "judgment without reflection, shared by an entire class, an entire people, an entire nation, or the entire human race" (*Il senso comune è un giudizio senz'alcuna riflessione, comunemente sentito da tutto un ordine, da tutto un popolo, da tutta una nazione o da tutto il gener umano*).[59] And from here he proceeds to formulate the essence of his understanding of the nexus between knowledge and history: "Theories must take their beginning from the times which bring forth the material of which they treat" (*Le dottrine debbono cominciare da quando cominciano le materie che trattano*).[60]

What is this "material," and what is the meaning of "judgment without reflection"? Read superficially, it could mean that we should simply take as material the world we live in now, and that we should try to understand it without recourse to eternal or universal truths that are beyond our comprehension. But elsewhere, Vico argues against this kind of day-to-day pragmatism by claiming for his *New Science* the same kind of general validity that is provided by geometry.[61]

This science, however, is not to be based on "the conceit of the nations, each believing itself to have been the first in the world" (*la boria delle nazioni, d'essere stata ogniuna la prima del mondo*).[62] That would mean giving way to unprincipled empiricism. Neither is it to be based on "the conceit of the scholars, who will have it that what they know must have been eminently understood from the beginning of the world" (*la boria de' dotti, i quali vogliono ciò ch'essi sanno essere stato eminentemente inteso fin dal principio del mondo*).[63] That would mean indulging in abstract generalization. Instead, and this is Vico's synthesis of old and new, it is to be based on the kind of principled historical reflection that can only spring from human comprehension of a world made by humans (*verum ipsum factum*):

> But in the night of thick darkness enveloping the earliest antiquity, so remote from ourselves, there shines the eternal and never failing light of a truth beyond all question: that the world of civil society has certainly been made by men, and that its principles are therefore found within the modifications of our own human mind. (*Ma, in tal densa notte di tenebre ond'è coverta la prima da noi lontanissima antichità, apparisce questo lume eterno, che non tramonta, di questa verità, la quale non si può a patto alcuno chiamar in dubbio: che questo mondo civile egli certamente è stato fatto dagli uomini, onde se possono, perché se ne debbono, ritruovare i principi dentro le modificazioni della nostra medesima mente umana.*)[64]

This, if a heliocentric pun is allowed, is the light of knowledge around which Vico's world revolves. On its basis, Vico develops a theory of three historical ages: an age of the gods based on divine authority, a heroic age based on aristocratic superiority, and an age of men based on the recognition of natural equality.[65] More importantly, the *verum/factum* principle leads Vico to understand the dynamic of human development in both its practical-political and intellectual-reflective dimension. It is not a dynamic guided by the discovery of abstract and timeless principles. Its driving force is the dialectical and man-made friction between different levels of civic consciousness.

Vico explains the emancipative quality of this dialectical process with his favourite object of historical learning: In classical Rome, the plebeians became suspicious of the aristocrats' heroic pretensions, and when they began to understand themselves to be "of equal human nature with the nobles" (*d'ugual natura umana co' nobili*), class struggle, "the struggle of plebs with nobility" (*le plebi ... gareggiassero con la nobilità*), led to the age of men as an age of "civil sovereignty" (*i popoli ad esser sovrani*).[66] Class struggle as the ultimate source of human progress: No wonder that the Neapolitan professor has for the most part remained on the sidelines of the classical canon in political thought.

It does not matter that Vico provides us with a rather foreshortened view of Roman history.[67] After all, a good deal of Descartes's scientific assumptions would have to be as much revised over time as would Vico's views of history. What matters is that the *verum/factum* principle "was turning Descartes on his head."[68] Where the Frenchman had argued that the truth of the matter lay in abstract mathematical principles and that therefore the study of history "was a waste of time,"[69] the Italian insisted that history, because it was man-made, provided a more reliable access to knowledge. To be sure, it would be a knowledge of probabilities rather than certainties. But it would be more reliable precisely because these probabilities were spread over time, as well as over a diversity of classes, peoples, and nations.

Critical Evaluation

Both Descartes and Vico have secured their places in the pantheon of intellectual achievement. However, it is important to bear in mind the different implications that the methodological approach of each has for the history of political thought in particular, and for the understanding of politics more generally.

There is a direct path from Descartes's faith in abstract reasoning to the universalist claims inherent in the modern social contract tradition. Hobbes and Rousseau can take their cues directly from Descartes. If there is only "one truth concerning any matter," there must obviously be one and only one solution for political order. Man will be declared to be of one particular nature, "man's wolf" or "born free," and from this nature will spring one and only one construction of state and society. In fact, the power of reason dictates that each individual comes to the same conclusion by his or her own intellectual effort: to surrender their will to the collective security of the sovereign state, as in Hobbes's *Leviathan*, or to become part of the general will, as in Rousseau's *Social Contract*.[70]

Moreover, that solution will be purely technical, occasioned by systemic constraints alone, as a later age would put it, and void of all traditional adherence to historical experience or ethical responsibility. What matters alone is the desired effect, security in the one case or freedom in the other. There is an almost eerie resemblance between Descartes's confident pronouncement of a truth that is "clear and certain," and, as first preformulated by a 1919 US Supreme Court decision, the conjecture of "a clear and present danger" that allows curtailment of constitutional civil rights.[71]

The renunciation of tradition and reverence in the name of technical progress and mastery of nature, as well as social order, would ultimately lead to the opposite of what its advocates had hoped for. Instead of producing "gentleness and harmony," as Descartes had dreamed, the ultimate consequence of the Age of Reason would be Nietzsche's nihilist world of chaos in which nobody would any longer be committed to anything or anyone.

The other methodological path leads from Vico's historical common sense to the kind of sociological appreciation of diversity across time and circumstance that we commonly associate with the much more conservative political thought of Montesquieu or Tocqueville. But Vico's separation of the eternal truth of the universe from the historical probabilities of man-made human affairs — in other words, the separation of science from politics and ethics — would also be noticed by Karl Marx. Obviously attracted by Vico's understanding of history as a history of developmental stages and class struggle, Marx, in a rare direct reference to Vico, remarked that it was the weakness of the merely abstract materialism in the natural sciences that it "excluded history and its process."[72]

To lump together Montesquieu, Tocqueville, and Marx may come as a surprise. What these thinkers share with Vico, however, is the conviction that the riddle of human affairs and politics cannot be governed or resolved by abstract principles of universal rationality. There is no abstract or best model of harmony in human affairs. Those who claim that such a model exists usually only promote what is in their own interest. Politics, in other words, is the ongoing search for common sense among a plurality of human beings who gain their diverse understanding and consciousness from the material world which they produce. Marx, of course, would not leave it at that. He went on to postulate that communism would do away with differences of interest, and that therefore the interests of each would become the common sense of all.

Vico criticized the new science of rationalism for its neglect of politics. By rejecting the critical discourse among different opinions as a basis of knowledge, Descartes had deprived the study of human affairs of its classical core: topical or problem-oriented reasoning for the purpose of finding common sense or common ground. As we shall see in the next chapter, this debate about the method of inquiry is as old as the study of politics itself.

CHAPTER 3

Nature of the Political

Plato v. Aristotle

A ll histories of Western political thought begin in ancient Greece. More precisely, they begin in the Athenian city state (*polis*) where, over a period of little more than a hundred years, politics was invented as citizens' active participation in public life, and political leadership came to depend on public opinion and public approval.

Context

At the beginning of the sixth century BCE, the lawgiver Solon ended a period of economic crisis and social conflict between the aristocracy and peasants by introducing a political constitution that effectively ended traditional aristocratic rule. Citizenship became more inclusive with the creation of four different political classes with differentiated sets of rights according to wealth. All male adult citizens had access to the general popular assembly (*ekklesia*). Also attributed to Solon was the introduction of a representative council of 400 (*boule*) as the actual governing body, and a people's jury-court (*heliaia*).

At the end of the sixth century, and again in response to economic crisis and political instability, the reforms of Cleisthenes marked what is generally regarded as the real beginning of Greek democracy. Cleisthenes created the first constitutional order based on the principle of territorial representation. He distinguished three regions in the city state that corresponded to its main economic interests: the city proper as the location of trading and merchant interests, the surrounding agricultural land, and the coastal area with its naval interests. He then divided the city state into 10 new tribes or political units, each comprising a part of the city, land, and coast. Each composite tribe sent a delegation of 50 representatives to a new council of 500, determined by lot and for one year only. Each delegation presided over the council business for one-tenth of the year, while the actual "president" or leader of the council changed daily.

This reorganization of political life and citizenship broke down the traditional fault lines between city aristocracy and peasants, and it strengthened the influence of coastal dwellers and sailors, who generally belonged to the poorest class of citizens but on whom the wealth and security of Athens as a naval empire depended. Cleisthenes probably also established the famous annual practice of ostracism whereby the general assembly of citizens could vote to exile for 10 years a citizen whom the majority deemed a threat to democracy.

Halfway through the next and fifth century, which is the one usually associated with Greek democracy, further reforms under Ephialtes and Pericles completed the Athenian democratic experiment. Voting by majority, the general assembly of citizens assumed legislative sovereignty. The council of 500 as the agenda-setting political executive became accountable to regular reviews by the assembly. The popular jury-courts punished those who were deemed to have violated the popular will. The holders of most public offices were determined by lot and could serve only once. All public officials were paid, and the poor received daily allowances (diets) in order to enable their participation in council and jury-courts. In other words, fifth-century Athenian democracy was based on the rule of law, on accountability, and on an extraordinary level of direct public participation.[1]

Athenian democracy remained a fragile construction. The great reformers had been political arbitrators, between traditional aristocratic power presumptions, the peasants' need for debt relief — which in turn also benefited the city elites because it ended economic paralysis — and the expectations of the poorest citizens to be rewarded for their services in the military and navy. The aristocratic elites always remained powerful and manipulative, but they acquiesced to the democratic turn of events as long as it was accompanied by economic and military success. Most of the political leaders championing democracy were in fact aristocrats themselves who would use their superior skills as orators for public support in their rivalries with other aristocratic factions.

Athenian democracy was far more based on its utility for practical purposes than on lofty ideals of justice and equality. When Pericles declared in his famous funeral oration on the eve of the Peloponnesian War in 431 that "our constitution ... favours the many instead of the few," and that "if a man is able to serve the state, he is not hindered by the obscurity of his condition," this was at least as much meant to rally the troops as it was a genuine celebration of democracy.[2]

Democracy was a means to a particular end, which was the creation of the broadest possible support on the home front. Elsewhere, in foreign affairs, for instance, other ends would justify different means. Later on, in that

fateful Peloponnesian War in 416, the Athenians showed no hesitation in justifying their unprovoked and strategically unnecessary attack upon the tiny
island city of Melos by declaring: "of men we know, that by a necessary law
of their nature they rule wherever they can."[3]

Athenians practised democracy because it served their purposes and interests and not because they were a priori committed to some universal principle of justice. And it most certainly did not occur to them that democracy at
home might be jeopardized or corrupted by a decisively undemocratic behaviour in foreign affairs — only the German idealist philosopher Immanuel
Kant would much later make such a suggestion.[4] On the contrary, democracy, the involvement of the majority of ordinary citizens in public affairs,
may have been the price the Athenian elites had to pay for the willingness of
those citizens to fight and die for Athens. Nevertheless, considering how the
rightless masses were herded into battle elsewhere, and for a long time to
come, this was nothing short of a democratic miracle.

Certainly, the rise of democracy in Athens coincided with the city state's
military success and economic expansionism. The Athenian navy had defeated
the Persians in the sea battle of Salamis (480). Shortly thereafter, Athens
gained pre-eminence among Greek city states by forging a maritime league in
the eastern Mediterranean. Its members either committed themselves to participate with Athens in further military campaigns against the Persians, or,
more likely, to make tributary payments which greatly enhanced the economic wealth of Athens and allowed it to expand and strengthen its own
fleet. That point was not lost on those ordinary citizens whose livelihood
depended on the navy or on employment in the shipyards.

When military and economic success faltered, however, so did democracy.
The Peloponnesian War against Sparta (431-404) was fought over pre-eminence on the Greek peninsula itself. Already in the spring of 411, after a disastrous military campaign in Sicily, antidemocratic sentiments had become
so strong that the council of 500 was briefly replaced by an oligarchic council of 400 on the basis of property qualifications rather than democratic
allotment. One of the key recommendations made by a hastily convoked
constitutional commission was to end "receipt of pay" for all office holders[5]
in order to eliminate those from politics who, in the words of one of the oligarchic leaders, "on account of their poverty would sell their city for a
drachma."[6]

When Sparta finally defeated Athens, with the help of Persian ships and
money, democracy was overthrown and a brutal oligarchic regime of terror
was established (Tyranny of the Thirty). It only lasted for 10 months, but
even though the democratic constitution was essentially re-established in
403, the democratic spirit of unity was broken. Despite an amnesty that

spared the lives of most collaborators, the division between those who had arranged themselves with the tyranny and those who had fought against it "had become an inescapable fact of circumstances."[7]

Nothing illustrates better these circumstances of factious division than Socrates's trial and condemnation to death by hemlock in 399. Although he declared himself at his own trial to be the wisest of men, many Athenians regarded him as being only a deranged philosophical fool. How could such a fool become the number one public enemy?

The official accusation against Socrates was impiety and corruption of the young. That Critias, the bloodthirstiest among the Thirty, had once been a member of Socrates's regular group of companions probably played a role in his condemnation. Behind the official facade, however, loomed a much more general conflict between the restored democratic regime and Socrates as the most notorious exponent of an intellectual elite calling into question democracy's capacity to lead Athenians to the good life. Socrates had not been a supporter of the Thirty, but his self-righteous contempt for all political leaders and public figures was understood as contempt for public authority in general, democratic or otherwise. At a moment in time when the restoration of democratic authority was at stake, this arrogance was deemed dangerous to public stability.

It was this fatal clash between the "incorrigible elitist"[8] and the idea of democracy as a regime of collective wisdom that triggered the most profound outburst of political thought in the work of Plato. But it was an outburst almost entirely committed to the denouncing of the very idea that had sustained democracy for over a hundred years: the idea of politics as a system of broad participation and active involvement in public affairs. It was not an accident that Socrates would figure most prominently in Plato's quest for absolute truth and justice.

Plato (427-347 BCE)

As a young man of noble birth, Plato lived through war, defeat, tyranny (Critias was a second-degree uncle), and, above all, the trial and death of his admired teacher Socrates. In the famous *Seventh Letter*, Plato explains how these events drove him towards philosophy and away from a planned political career. He had despised the terror of the Thirty, but he was even more appalled when it was democracy that put Socrates to death. His conclusion was that "all existing states are badly governed," and that betterment could only come from a truly philosophical understanding of justice and its application to human affairs.[9] Around 385 he founded his own school of philosophy, the legendary Academy. It existed without interruption until the Roman emperor Justinian had it closed in the fifth century CE.

Presumably, Plato wrote this autobiographical account towards the end of a long life as a philosopher and teacher that left to the world an extraordinary body of work comprising 35 dialogues and other writings, such as the *Letters*.[10] The best-known and most often cited centrepiece of this work is *Politeia*, which comprises 10 books about justice and the best state.[11] Without suggesting any particular — and ultimately uncertain — chronology, it seems plausible to distinguish a group of earlier works such as *Protagoras* and *Gorgias*, which can be interpreted as setting the stage for the discussion in *Politeia*, from a set of later works such as *Politikos* (Statesman) and *Nomoi* (Laws), which appear to offer modifications to the central arguments of *Politeia*. And this is the order in which I will proceed with my own interpretation of Plato's political thought.

In *Protagoras*, Plato still appears relatively sympathetic to the democratic idea of active citizenship. This is a dialogue between Socrates and Protagoras, one of the leading *sophists* or teachers of civic virtue. At stake is the question of whether such civic virtue can be taught. Protagoras argues that it can (after all, this is how he makes his living) by distinguishing civic virtue from other and more specialized skills. While architecture, for example, requires a specialized excellence only found in the few, "political excellence, which must proceed entirely from justice and temperance" requires a particular civic virtue, which is "shared by all, or there wouldn't be cities."[12]

Socrates appears to agree that virtue can be taught. But he nevertheless succeeds in casting doubt on the validity of Protagoras's argument. He gets him to admit that it must be wrong to associate justice and temperance with a particular virtue (available to all) because all types of excellence require knowledge and therefore are the same.[13] Knowledge, however precise as the "art of measurement," can perhaps be taught, but not by those who will base their arguments only on the "power of appearance."[14]

In *Gorgias*, Plato then reveals what Socrates really thinks about sophists. First, he has Gorgias himself describe his craft as "the ability to persuade by speeches judges in a law court, councillors in a council meeting, and assemblymen in an assembly or in any other political gathering that might take place."[15] Persuasion, of course, Socrates will point out, is nothing other than using the power of appearance to tell the people "what it wants to hear."[16] The crucial difference is that he, Socrates, loves philosophical truth regardless of the consequences,[17] whereas sophists seek personal gain by endearing themselves to the people in order to "have great power in the city."[18]

To this point, Plato's analysis offers a devastating critique of democratic Athens. Far from the Periclean idyll of a city prudently governed by the many, he sees a city in which the ignorant masses are manipulated and ruined by men exactly like Pericles who "made the Athenians idle and cowardly, chatterers and money-grubbers, since he was the first to institute wages for them."[19] In *Politeia*, Plato will complete the picture by describing Athens as a feverish city of pigs, fattened and pampered by "all sorts of delicacies, perfumed oils, incense, prostitutes and pastries," surrendered to the "endless acquisition of money," driven to territorial expansion, and, therefore, ultimately, into war.[20]

While squarely laying the blame at the feet of the sophists and other political leaders who "make" the people what they are, Plato's real concerns are the ignorance and malleability of the people. He could have suggested that true philosophers should instruct the people instead of sophists but he fears that the people would neither listen nor understand. Instead, he offers a solution in *Politeia* that aims at the most rigorous selection of the best as philosopher-kings and rulers and the exclusion of everyone else from political participation.

He offers his solution in three steps. First, right after the discussion of the city of pigs, he argues that a city bent on expansion and war obviously needs soldiers, and that "warfare is a profession" like any other in a city whose well-being depends on a specialized division of labour.[21] Later, however, this horizontal division of labour is turned into a vertical division of rank. This is the dialectical pattern Plato employs throughout the dialogue. He first has others give expression to the conventional point of view, and then has Socrates tell them what the real truth is.

Plato is aware, of course, that a hierarchy of rank is not something the people will recognize and accept as in their best interest, and he therefore has Socrates suggest the employment of a founding myth, which he calls a "noble" lie or falsehood:[22]

> All of you in the city are brothers, we'll say to them in telling our story, but the god who made you mixed some gold into those who are adequately equipped to rule, because they are most valuable. He put silver in those who are auxiliaries and iron and bronze in the farmers and other craftsmen.[23]

Socrates continues by pointing out that the most important task for the ruler will be to select and educate the young by means of their metal quality because "the city will be ruined if it ever has an iron or bronze guardian."

Plato's resorting to myth for the sake of social engineering is by no means unprecedented, and it may have been a reaction to recent events. The Thirty had tried to rid Athens of its democratic practices by appeals to "ancient truths." While these were officially promulgated, public debate was stifled by a law banning instruction in the art of debate.[24] The leaders of the democratic restoration afterwards understood this very well in their own appeals to "ancestral practices" (*kata ta patria*). However, by turning to "written statutes" (*nomoi*) as the ultimate source of authority, they dealt a "blow to the aristocratic tradition that held that authoritative expertise was an expression of personal excellence, or *arete*."[25]

In the second step to his solution, Plato turns to the idea of justice as the most important virtue in a city — as we already know from *Protagoras*. Again, justice is described first in conventional popular terms as "to give to each what is owed to him."[26] Contracts should be honoured, and friends should be rewarded for their support. But Plato then slips in a political version of the definition: As democracies make democratic laws, and tyrannies make tyrannical laws, justice means "the same in all cities, the advantage of the established rule."[27] Justice, in other words, is presented as a political concept, and what is owed to whom depends on who makes the rules.

Yet, in line with the dialectical method of reasoning, the meaning of justice is changed once again. It is now defined as "doing one's own work"[28] and not "meddling with what isn't one's own."[29] It no longer describes a relationship among partners or friends but instead denotes an absolute category of lawful civic behaviour. No longer shall a "craftsman or some other kind of money-maker," who is "puffed up with wealth," or in command of a "majority of votes" aspire to enter the class of soldiers, judges, or guardians.[30] Justice, in other words, is the concept that puts the noble lie into a fixed political form.

In his third step, Plato develops a grandiose if terrifying vision of how such a fixed political form would have to be achieved.[31] We already know that there would have to be a strict separation of classes. The craftsmen and money-makers would enjoy property and wealth but would be denied all political rights in order to prevent corruption and governance by persuasion or self-interest. For the same reason, the guardians (auxiliaries and potential rulers) would be deprived of personal property. They would be selected to receive the most rigorous education and training. Because Plato sees no reason why the true qualities of a philosopher-ruler cannot be found in men and women alike,[32] and in order to assure that both will receive the same education and training, guardians would also have to be denied traditional family life: women and children would be held in common. The selection of the ruling philosopher-king, finally, would be based on excellence in science (the objective art of "measurement"), as well as in dialectical reasoning as the pure philosophy of knowledge (*episteme*). Guided entirely by knowledge based on objective truth, such a philosopher-king would not be bound by law.

In *Politikos*, Plato retreats from his utopian vision and seems to make peace with the legalistic turn of events in Athens after 403. That "ideal rule may exist even without laws," he admits, "was something harder for a hearer to accept."[33] He reiterates, however, that the mass of people can never govern a city with intelligence, and therefore suggests, as his second-best option, a regime based on strict adherence to the laws: "No one in the city should dare to do anything contrary to the laws."[34]

At this point, Plato delves into a lengthy discussion of what he had already begun in *Politeia*,[35] a two-fold distinction of different regime types or forms of government. He begins with the traditional distinction of whether a government is based on the rule of one, the few, or the many. He then adds a second distinction. Each of the three principal forms can be either just and lawful or unjust and lawless. Thus, the rule of one can be either a lawful monarchy or a lawless tyranny. The rule of the few can be a lawful aristocracy or a lawless oligarchy. For the rule of the many, finally, Plato retains the democracy label regardless of whether it is lawful or lawless.

So far this is a rather conventional discussion of different regime types well known to all Greeks. What makes it interesting is Plato's ranking order. Of course, all lawful regimes are better than all the lawless ones. Given his disdain for democracy as unintelligent mob rule, however, one would further expect its ranking to come last among both lawful and lawless regimes. But it does not. Instead, it is the rule of one that is both best and worst: best when it is a lawful monarchy and worst when it is a lawless tyranny. And while aristocracy and oligarchy occupy a middle ground in terms of good and bad, democracy is declared to be the least effective of all regimes. It is the weakest form of government when it is lawful, but it is also the least harmful when it is lawless. It is in fact the most liveable among the lawless regimes because "under it offices are distributed in small portions among many people."[36]

This ranking or classification of democracy is remarkable. It is also ambiguous. On the one hand, the paramount characteristic of democracy for Plato will always be that it is based on the rule of the many who are not intelligent. It almost does not seem to matter whether it is based on the rule of law or not. On the other hand, Plato concedes that the dispersal of power in a democracy makes it liveable even under conditions of lawlessness. If we add to this that for Plato all government is ultimately imperfect and corrupt unless it is in the hands of a true philosopher-king, we may almost come to the conclusion that the great philosopher is making his peace with "really existing" democracy, here. If all imperfect regimes are ultimately prone to degenerate into corrupted lawlessness, so we may extrapolate Plato's train of thought, the dispersal of power under a democracy might not be so bad after all.

Politikos can be interpreted as a bridge between the radical idealism of *Politeia* and the resigned pessimism of Plato's last work, *Nomoi*: "The organization of a state is almost bound to fall short of the ideal,"[37] he regretfully admits, and, before entering into a lengthy and detailed discussion of crime and punishment, he draws up as his second-best state a bizarre vision of a polity limited to 5,040 households with four property classes in which "the greatest possible unity"[38] is enforced by laws that must never be changed.

There is something desperate about Plato's desire to avoid change at all cost. The education of children, he suggests, should be controlled so that they "always play the same games under the same rules and in the same conditions" and with the "same toys" because only in this way the "conventions of adulthood" will remain unaltered. To instill in them a desire for novelty will only result in the "biggest disaster any state can suffer."[39] Plato has long since parted company with that deranged philosophical fool Socrates who would rather drink hemlock than comply with impositions of the state, any state.

One can cast judgment on Plato's political philosophy in almost any number of ways, but one cannot but admire the enormity of the task he accomplished: By insisting that each part of a city or polis is related to every other part, he put into the world the idea of "political society as a functioning system."[40] For all times to come, this would remain one of the principal yardsticks for political thought. There is a difference, however, between political philosophy that inquires about the abstract nature of society, of what is good and evil, just and unjust, and political theory that asks what happens when political society is organized and acts in one way or another, and what can be done about it. From the philosophical perspective, Plato's vision can rightly be celebrated as the fulfilment of human yearning:

> All of Western man's aspirations to justice and the good life are given expression and fulfilment in Socrates' proposals for a city. This is a regime where men's faculties are not denied their exercise by poverty, birth, or sex, where the accidental attachments of family and city do not limit a man's understanding and pursuit of the good.[41]

Yet, it is those "accidental attachments" that make up the real world of politics. To deprive an entire class of citizens, the vast majority, of the right to argue and deliberate about how they want to live, in the name of "absolute truth and beauty," is to take out of politics what Greek democracy had just put into it.[42] Plato's political philosophy, in other words, denies the nature of the political that the Greeks had defined in practice as active participation in public affairs. Only after Plato's death would his most famous pupil dare to disagree.

Aristotle (384-322 BCE)

Aristotle came to study at Plato's Academy as a 17-year-old in 367. He was not born in Athens and therefore would never have citizenship rights. He stayed at the Academy for 20 years and only left when Plato died. After a few itinerant years in Asia Minor (where he joined the school of a friend) and on the island of Lesbos (where he founded a school of his own), he was called to become the tutor of Alexander (later known as Alexander the Great), the 13-year-old son of Philip II of Macedonia, in 343-42 BCE. Dismissed from this job in 340, Aristotle retreated to Stagira (or Stageira), his city of birth, which had been captured and destroyed by the Macedonians eight years earlier but would be rebuilt in his honour by Philip and Alexander. In 335 Aristotle returned to Athens where he founded his own school of philosophy at the Lyceum. As a foreign-born noncitizen, he could not own property, but arrangements were made so he could lease the premises.

In the meantime, Philip had conquered all of Greece, and Athens had become a member of his Corinthian League. In 336 Philip was murdered and his son Alexander became the Macedonian king. When Alexander suddenly died himself, in 323, an anti-Macedonian rebellion broke out in Athens. Aristotle, who was well known for his connections to Alexander, fled the city after an indictment of impiety had been brought against him — the same charge of which Socrates had been found guilty 76 years earlier. According to anecdote, Aristotle remarked that he left Athens so that the Athenians could not commit a second crime against philosophy. He died a year later at the age of 62.[43]

If Plato was the eminent master philosopher in search of eternal truth, Aristotle came to be the consummate analytical scientist. Presumably mostly written during his short 12 years at the helm of his school at the Lyceum, Aristotle produced works on just about everything deemed worthy of systematic inquiry: physics, meteorology, animals, colours, plants, mechanics, economics, and, yes, the "master science" of politics,[44] alongside various treatments of logic (such as in *Topics*), metaphysics, and ethics. He also had carried out an encyclopaedic comparative study of 158 known constitutions in Greece and elsewhere which he meant to turn into a grand theory of politics. But all that has come down to us of this comparative collection is the *Constitution of Athens*, perhaps the most important document providing information about the city's constitutional history from its ancient beginnings down to the restoration of democracy after the Peloponnesian War.[45]

As a teacher, Aristotle agreed with Plato that education was the fundamental basis for the establishment and stability of a *polis*, and he shared with him his disdain for the sophists who he felt engage in empty rhetoric without really knowing what they are talking about.[46] But in several crucial aspects, Aristotle differed fundamentally from his great teacher. The reason why the sophists are not qualified to teach politics, he held, is not that they do not possess true knowledge. It is that they lack practical political experience.[47]

Experience (rather than a golden or silver predisposition) also accounts for the ability to learn and understand. "A young man," the Lyceum professor exclaimed in exasperation, "is not equipped to be a student of politics; for he has no experience in the actions which life demands of him, and these actions form the basis and subject matter of the discussion."[48] And, finally, while Aristotle shared with Plato his basic ideas about education, there is none of the paranoid fear of novelty.[49]

Aristotle mainly developed his political thought in his *Nicomachean Ethics* (*Ethika*) and *Politics* (*Politika*).[50] As is the case with most of his works, these constitute lecture notes rather than finished works intended for publication. They were gathered and put in order by his successors at the Lyceum, or by later editors, which explains the somewhat scattered or *peripatetic* character of the argument.[51] Aristotle himself would, of course, revise and add to the lecture notes. Thus, for example, parts of his earlier *Eudemian Ethics* reappear in the later *Nicomachean Ethics* which allows us to view the later work as fully comprehensive with regard to Aristotle's mature thinking about ethics.[52] The *Politics* can probably be appreciated best as fragmentary evidence of a much grander and more systematic political theory that Aristotle meant to develop from his comparative constitutional studies. It nevertheless constitutes the very beginning of political science.

Ethics and politics belong together. They are both part of the practical sciences or arts that provide knowledge about how to live the good life. For Aristotle, this is only possible in the context of the *polis*. Man is *zoon politikon*, a political animal.[53] Literally, this means that man is meant by nature to live in a *polis*. In more broadly interpretative terms, it means that man is by nature a community-building animal who cannot achieve the good life in isolation. Politics is about how to organize the good life in a city. Such organization, however, requires individual citizens who know how to, and want to, live and act well. This is the kind of knowledge that the art of ethics provides. And in this way, politics is the "master science" because it comprises ethics as the moral foundation for the organized good life in the city.

The *Nicomachean Ethics* can also be read as a methodological introduction to political theory. Especially in Book I, Aristotle lays out his views on politics as a practical art or science, and there is no doubt that it is here that he draws a sharp line of distinction between his understanding of politics and that of his teacher Plato. "Precision cannot be expected," he declares, because the problems that political science examines "present so much variety and irregularity."[54] And if that is not clear enough, he adds a little later: "The term 'good' has as many meanings as the word 'is' ... It is clear, therefore, that the good cannot be something universal."[55]

In other words, political science as a practical art does not aim at universal truth or knowledge (*episteme*) but instead relies on "practical wisdom" (*phronesis*) which pertains to "acting in matters involving what is good for man."[56] Far from leaving this capacity with a philosopher-king, Aristotle declares that "in general, a man of practical wisdom is he who has the ability to deliberate."[57]

In general, practical wisdom means deliberating, or using one's sense of judgment, with regard to all human activities from household management to politics. Aristotle distinguishes this from a more specific "political wisdom" (*politike*), which comprises legislation, the enactment of decrees, and judicial activities. In the same passage, however, Aristotle separates the "supreme" art of legislation from politics, which is said to include deliberative and judicial activities.[58] The point of reference, here, is obviously the Athenian democratic constitution. Deliberation takes place in the assembly and results in the promulgation of decrees administered by the council. Judicial activities take place in the jury-courts. By legislation, Aristotle seems to mean the constitutional framework as the supreme part of political wisdom which is not open to deliberation.[59]

The purpose or end of these political activities is collective action "in matters involving what is good for man." Since there are many understandings of what is good, however, presumably varying from man to man and citizen to citizen, Aristotle introduces political justice as a balancing principle: "In associations that are based on mutual exchange, the just [which holds the association together] is reciprocity in terms of a proportion and not in terms of exact equality in the return. For it is the reciprocal return of what is proportional that holds the state together."[60]

Proportional reciprocity sounds similar to Plato's definition of justice: obligations and rewards are distributed not on the basis of absolute equality but according to the metal quality of each. Aristotle immediately distances himself from this understanding of justice by pointing out that there is a difference between justice in an "unqualified sense" (i.e., based on a universal principle of what is just, as in "doing one's own work") and justice in "political matters" which is justice among "free and equal."[61] And foreshadowing his famous definition of citizenship in the *Politics*, Aristotle then defines political justice as a principle of lawfulness that "applies to people who have a natural capacity for law, that is people who have the requisite equality in ruling and being ruled."[62]

In the *Nicomachean Ethics*, Aristotle develops a concept of political justice with many qualifiers. Reciprocity stands for mutual exchange and benefit. Any political arrangement that serves only the interests of some at the exclusion of others cannot be just. Proportionality in turn requires at least some degree of distributive fairness. Most importantly, however, both reciprocity and proportionality are anchored in a system of law among free and equal citizens.

Thus equipped with an understanding of the nature of political justice, Aristotle suggests at the end of the *Nicomachean Ethics* that we can turn to the *Politics* as a general investigation into the constitution of a state (*polis*) and "complete as best as we can our philosophy of human affairs."[63] In his *Politics*, then, Aristotle will resort to the traditional Greek way of discussing political affairs by comparing different regimes: democracy, oligarchy, aristocracy, and tyranny, as already championed by Plato. Like Plato, he will be critical of democracy, and he will suggest as his best state a mixed polity based on proportional equality among rich and poor.[64]

But, unlike Plato, Aristotle will not reinvestigate the nature of political justice and redefine it by means of deduction from his idea of the ideal *polis*. Instead, he will conversely arrive at his idea of the mixed polity by means of induction from his observations of political justice as the result of deliberation among free and equal citizens equipped with practical wisdom. This is why the *Nicomachean Ethics* is the key to the understanding of the *Politics*.

Although the *Politics* is in many ways a direct and critical response to Plato's *Politeia*, Aristotle does not even bother to mention the idea of the philosopher-king. Of course, it is legitimate to ask what government is best, but the "excellent ideas" of those political writers "who would have none but the most perfect" are for the most part "unpractical." Based on real "political insight" (*phronesis*), the task of political science is to investigate what is "attainable" under different conditions and circumstances, and to gain from this analysis an understanding of "the form of government which is best suited to states in general."[65]

This practical and analytical approach is embedded in Aristotle's sociology: "A state is not only made up of so many men, but of different kinds of men."[66] With reference to his *Ethics*, Aristotle reiterates that it is under these conditions of plurality that the principle of "reciprocity" will be the "salvation of states" more generally.[67] Reciprocity, as we already know, refers to social balance, and therefore, with reference to the *Ethics* again, the "best state" (*polis*) will be one in which virtue or "excellence is a mean," and life "is in a mean, and in a mean attainable by everyone."[68]

This is how we can understand Aristotle's definition of justice, already laid down in the *Nicomachean Ethics* as well, according to which the excellence of a good citizen is comprised in his ability to govern and to be governed well.[69] And from here we gain an understanding of what Aristotle means when he declares, out of the blue and in the middle of his discussion of different regimes, that the generic name for constitutional government is polity (*politeia*), and that under this form of constitutional government, "the many administer the state for the common interest."[70]

41

The stage is set, but by no means for democracy. Aristotle rejects the entire conventional classification of different regimes according to the rule of one, few, or many. Adding a political economic perspective to his sociological approach, he declares that what really sets democracy and oligarchy apart is poverty and wealth.[71] And according to common sense, there are only these two regimes or forms of government. Either the *polis* is governed by the rich, who are few, and it is an oligarchy, or it is governed by the poor, who are many, and it is then a democracy.[72]

This argument contains two remarkable deviations from the Platonic view. First, Aristotle seems to dismiss the juxtaposition of true and perverted regimes.[73] His assumption is that the few will always rule in their own interest rather than for the common good, and so will the many. Hence, there is only oligarchy and democracy as self-interested rule of the few and many, respectively. Secondly, in his brief presentation of the conventional juxtaposition of good and bad regimes, he pairs democracy as the self-interested rule of the many with *politeia*, which he had just earlier defined as rule of the many for the common good.[74]

How can Aristotle explain this idea of constitutional government, polity, or *politeia*, which is not the same as democracy but nevertheless rule of the many? Here, we are finally coming to the epicentre of his political thought, the idea of the mixed polity. It is this idea that established Aristotle as one of the most influential political theorists of all time — even though not necessarily in his own time. It also established his reputation as a conservative thinker, who did not seek to radically overcome the precarious predicaments of time and circumstance like his teacher Plato. Instead, his idea of the mixed polity aimed at a pragmatic (reciprocal and proportional) political compromise among the two dominant factions in Athenian politics.

Constitutional government, Aristotle declares, "may be described generally as a fusion of oligarchy and democracy."[75] This compromise is the only way a polity can be governed without a permanent threat to its stability because it is the only way that both sides will accept the constitutional framework. There are "two parts of good government," he reminds his readers: the laws must not only be good in and of themselves, they must also be accepted and obeyed.[76] At this point, Aristotle also explains why he tends to ignore the idea of aristocracy, the rule of the few with virtue or excellence: "The fusion goes no further than the attempt to unite the freedom of the poor and the wealth of the rich, who commonly take the place of the noble."[77] Only such a constitution will be balanced, "in the mean."[78]

We remember that Aristotle had criticized Plato for his "unpractical" idea of a best state or *polis*. But he has not said anything yet as to how his own best state, the mixed polity, might be attainable as a political partnership (*politike koinonia*).[79] Aristotle thinks that partnership is most likely among "equals and similars."[80] The search for the best possible polity must therefore focus on a way of life and form of government that are not "above ordinary persons."[81] And this insight leads him to propose constitutional government or polity as a regime based on a large middle class. There are in fact three elements in all polities, he affirms: the rich, the poor, and those somewhere in the middle,[82] and "the best political community is formed by citizens of the middle class."[83]

Aristotle's idea of middle class rule is one of arbitration. The "rich and poor will never consent to rule in turn, because they mistrust one another."[84] The middle class, being the most numerous part of the city, will act as a buffer in what appears to be a regime of legislation based on compromise by making sure that democratic laws do not become too democratic, nor oligarchic laws too oligarchic. Aristotle is aware that this sounds like driving all legislation down to the lowest common denominator. But make no mistake, he cautions, by desiring governance based on aristocratic excellence instead. This would not only give "too much power to the rich" but would also and more importantly "cheat the people." It would turn a "false good" into a "true evil, since the encroachments of the rich are more destructive to the constitution than those of the people."[85]

Nowhere does Aristotle develop a theory or economic plan of how exactly a large middle class is supposed to come into existence, and he even seems to abandon the idea later when he talks about justice and equality as a class-based system of voting among rich and poor.[86] He does mention that the poor should be led into "lasting prosperity" by redistributive public policies, and we can assume that again he derived his ideas from observing the Athenian example.[87] While the democratic constitution of Athens never entirely escaped from oligarchic machinations, the rule of the many proved remarkably stable and resilient as long as economic prosperity prevailed and a larger middle class in fact existed.

This interpretation of Aristotle as a social and economic thinker is further supported by Aristotle's views on citizenship and education. As is well known and often criticized, he recommended that workers and artisans be excluded from citizenship because they would not have the leisure "for the development of excellence and the performance of political duties."[88] One can read this as an endorsement of aristocracy through the back door, but, without denying the limitations of Aristotle's view of political inclusion, one can also read it as a cautionary tale about the conditions under which the rule of the many is possible.

"There are three things which make men good and excellent," Aristotle affirms, and these are "nature, habit [and] reason."[89] If, then, political excellence depends on genes, socialization, and education, a life of drudgery will hardly allow for the labouring classes to acquire such excellence. "These men's opportunities of knowledge and inquiry," as Locke would put it so incomparably much later on, "are commonly as narrow as their fortunes."[90] Yet, while Locke goes on to say that "a great part of mankind are, by the natural and unalterable state of affairs, unavoidably given over to invincible ignorance,"[91] the Aristotelian vision of a middle-class society at least makes questionable whether political inclusion and exclusion are absolutes. Leisure, in this vision, is not an absolute end in itself but leisure for a purpose, the development of political skills. For Aristotle, that goal is obviously attainable for the many. In fact, in what is perhaps his most astonishing statement, he expresses confidence in the soundness of collective practical wisdom: "For the many, of whom each individual is not a good man, when they meet together may be better than the few good, if regarded not individually but collectively."[92] This endorsement has sustained the idea of democracy ever since.

Critical Evaluation

In one way, comparing Plato and Aristotle is like comparing the incomparable. Plato is the philosopher's philosopher searching for truth. To find this truth requires abstract rational demonstration removed from the corrupted incidences of reality.[93] In fact, for Plato, only this abstract knowledge is reality. Aristotle is a political scientist committed to a different reality. He is searching for attainable goals in practice. For him, this is a matter of probability rather than strict demonstration.[94] What separates these two thinkers most fundamentally, therefore, is their methodological understanding of science.

For Plato, there is only one science, the science of truth (*episteme*), which holds the key to the understanding of all phenomena. For Aristotle, the world of phenomena is one of plurality and diversity, and such a world can only be understood by a plurality of scientific approaches. The kind of rational precision appropriate in mathematics, for instance, is entirely inappropriate for politics, the nature of which can only be understood by practical and therefore, inevitably, imprecise wisdom (*phronesis*). As we already know, this debate will resurface at the beginning of the modern age, with Vico's rejection of Descartes's abstract rationalism.

We could leave it at that and simply appreciate the fundamental importance of both thinkers in putting onto the trajectory of history two different manifestations of reasoning. After all, nobody would deny that each has its ongoing place in the history of philosophy and science. However, in the context of the history of political thought, we cannot leave it at that.

Plato's political philosophy has consequences. By definition, it is extremely hostile to political participation. It takes out of politics what the

Greek tradition had just put into it so formidably and convincingly: that the good life among men can only result from active participation in public affairs. Moreover, the idea of the philosopher-king, while thought about in abstraction and even rejected in practice in the end, opens the door to the legitimization of absolute power, from the divine rule of popes and kings to the dictatorship of the vanguard party.

All that these later usurpers of absolute power had to do for the purpose of self-legitimization was to impose upon society their particular and self-interested definition of wisdom or truth. Plato, of course, would not admit that there is more than one definition. But it is precisely this insistence on one truth and rationality that makes it impossible to understand—and organize—the world according to what Aristotle held to be the plurality of human nature. To put it differently: Plato was mistaken in thinking that unity was "synonymous with uniformity," and his idea that such unity required an "imposed vision" was "dangerously arrogant."[95]

Aristotle's political thought has consequences, too. By singling out the particular quality of rule among free and equal citizens, his political thought accompanies much more congenially the unique contribution of ancient Greece to world civilization. But in doing so, it also separates what is just in the *polis* from what is just outside the *polis*, in the private sphere of the household (*oikos*) where not only slaves but also women, on the assumption of their natural inferiority, remain subjected to inequality and excluded from participation in public life. By comparison, Plato's abstract rationalism acknowledges, at least in principle, that women of "golden" quality can lead as much as men—although one may well wonder what chance they have as the communal property of the guardians.[96]

The same goes for Aristotle's uncritical acceptance of rich and poor as sociologically given. This must strike us as so much more conservative than Plato's radical insistence on excellence regardless of birth, gender, or economic status. However, it is precisely this sociological and political realism permeating his *Politics* that places Aristotle at the beginning of a political science tradition committed to the examination of power relationships as they exist in real societies. After all, if there is one sociological fact that has remained constant throughout the more than 2,000 years of human history after Aristotle, including all experiments in modern democracy to date, then it is what Charles Tilly has called "durable inequality," categorical differences among groups of citizens and their impact on the inequality of welfare.[97]

While Plato's meritocratic illusions foreshadow the modern liberal delusion about equality of opportunity, Aristotle assigns to political science the difficult but timeless task of squaring the circle between inequality of social condition and equality of citizenship. And in doing so, Aristotle brings to the fore what is the essence of the political art: balanced "reconciliation of a wide range of valid claims" through a process of public deliberation.[98] From Plato's elitist arrogance there is no path towards a modern understanding of politics as a process of collective decision-making on the basis of equal rights and mutual respect. To Aristotle we owe the comforting assurance that collective action can result in reasonable and fair outcomes even though self-interest, of individuals as well as among social groups, remains the principal force motivating human action.

To Aristotle also we owe a more uncomfortable insight: that the rule of the many may require a middle-class society capable of the kind of leisure that is the prerequisite for the development of political skills. In a world of "durable inequality," this has rather ominous implications. It may in fact help explain the elusiveness of stable democracy in Third-World countries, as well as the fallacy of the Marxist dream about proletarian revolution. It most certainly would seem to disavow the facile equation of "free" elections with substantive democracy.

As it turns out, it was to be Plato's vision that would dominate the next thousand years, and when Aristotle was finally rediscovered, it was almost too late. Two historical developments account for this. The first was the rise of the Roman Empire as the dominant source of power and influence in the Western world. Rome was initially a republic not dissimilar to the kind of mixed regime that Aristotle had declared to be best in practice. The philosophy and culture of the conquered Greeks were absorbed quite eagerly by the victorious Romans. But the ever-expanding Empire required unity of law and uniformity of administration, and it was Roman law that passed on to the Middle Ages the "fundamental assumption of a world organized under a single emperor on whose supreme authority the validity of the system depended."[99] In such a system, political participation and deliberation no longer were central categories of political thought.

The second historical development was Medieval Christian Platonism. The Christian religion had become the official religion of the Roman Empire in CE 381. But that Empire was decaying, and the new church was in danger of losing its worldly protection. In 410 Rome was sacked by the Visigoth Alarich. Shortly thereafter, St. Augustine began to write the most influential work of the Middle Ages, *The City of God* (413-26), which effectively told Christians to turn away from the idea of a just world on earth and to seek salvation in the otherworldly realm of faith. At about the same time, availing itself of neo-Platonic ideas of hierarchy, the papacy began to assert its claim of supremacy.

Christian thinkers concerning themselves with the problem of worldly justice tended to pursue the Platonic idea of an ideal or best state. In such an intellectual climate, the study of politics could only mean "finding the best constitution and reforming existing states in the light of it, not examining the works of man as a source of greater enlightenment."[100] Aristotle's project of practical politics as the organization of plurality was for the most part forgotten or "remained on file."[101]

The real world of Medieval politics, however, was a feudal world of fragmentation and plurality. While pope and emperor battled for supremacy, ordinary people continued to live in small communities and under overlapping circles of power and authority, being governed simultaneously by city councils, princes, bishops, and kings. Precarious stability only existed when these various parties came to an agreement. Thus, when Aristotle was "rediscovered" towards the end of the Middle Ages, as we shall see in the next chapter, his political ideas fell on fertile ground and could not be ignored by the masters of Medieval Christian scholasticism.

However again, the early-modern "Renaissance" of Aristotelian political thought was short-lived. When the Reformation destroyed the ideological bond of universal Christian unity and religious wars devastated Europe, a "new political science" returned to the idea of organized unity — no longer in an ideal Christian empire across the territorial boundaries of princely governance, but internalized as the rational organization of sovereignty by a plurality of territorial states.

This idea and concept of the exclusive allocation of power in the sovereign territorial state has dominated political thought throughout the modern epoch. But it has been challenged by perceptions of "globalization," in theory and practice, that began to permeate political thought towards the end of the twentieth century. Indeed, the alleged or real emergence of a new and postmodern epoch has been likened to a neomedieval order of fragmentation and plurality.[102] It is into this context that our critical evaluation of Plato and Aristotle as the two founders of political philosophy and thought needs to be placed.

CHAPTER 4

Governance
Thomas v. Marsilius

Judging retrospectively from the modern perspective on individual liberalism, the Middle Ages, with their feudal system of loyalties owed to seigneurs and lords, must appear like the Dark Ages. And in a way they were in the sense that Plato's noble lie reigned supreme. As Augustine had put it authoritatively: "Order is the disposition of equal and unequal things in such a way as to give each its proper place."[1]

But as in the case of Plato, the idea of tranquillity in a fixed universal order was not much more than wishful thinking. Such thinking could become an imposed vision for the masses of ignorant peasants who had nothing but their Christian faith to rely on, but it entirely failed to impress pope and emperor, as well as kings, princes, and bishops who were in a constant battle, with words as much as with arms, over where the divine disposition was supposed to have placed them. During the eleventh and twelfth centuries, their power quests were complemented by those of the cities which, beginning in upper Italy, were increasingly successful in casting off the feudal yoke. The rediscovery of Aristotle's more realistic sense of justice and social order a century later triggered a thorough reassessment of theory and practice, faith and reason, which already contained the seeds of humanism that would eventually bring the Middle Ages to an end.

Context
As a crisis system, the medieval order can be described in terms of three interrelated issues that commanded considerable attention among legal scholars and political thinkers. First and foremost among these was the rivalry between pope and emperor. This was something entirely new in the world of politics. Greeks and Romans had worshipped their gods, but political direction, divine or worldly, had come from but one source of authority. The reasons why there came to be two powers with aspirations of supremacy

during the Middle Ages are complex and need not be retold here. Suffice it to say that both pope and emperor claimed to be the rightful inheritors of imperial Rome's authority. A doctrine of *two swords* developed giving expression to the existence of separate spiritual and secular powers. For centuries, popes and emperors each claimed in turn that they held both but, as such a claim proved untenable, they battled for supremacy of one over the other.

The second issue was the relationship between the emperor and the other kings and princes. Ever since Pope Leo III had crowned the Frankonian King Charles (Charlemagne) as the first medieval "Roman" emperor and official protector of the church, on Christmas Day CE 800, the other Christian rulers had contested his and his German successors' supremacy claims. Eventually, around 1200, the formula of *rex imperator in regno suo* was developed according to which each king was to have as much power and authority in his own realm as the emperor had over the whole empire.[2] This formula only confirmed the reality of an overlapping plurality of rule in medieval Europe.

The third issue pertained to the mode of decision-making in such a system of plural authority. In order to contain permanent conflicts of power concurrency, a formula for arbitration and agreement was needed, and it was found in the old adage of Roman law according to which *quod tangit omnes, ab omnibus approbetur*: what concerns all must be approved by all. Emperor Frederic II may have used it first, in a 1244 invitation to other imperial princes for a council in the Italian city of Verona.[3] But the formula only gave expression to a political practice that had existed for some time. The emperor could only make law and hope for its acceptance, if he first consulted with all the other important and concurrent authorities and reached an agreement. Governance in medieval Europe, if it didn't resort to the power of the sword, very much depended on deliberation and consent.

Emperor Frederic II was the same Frederic (1194-1250) who had been born by his mother *en route* in an upper Italian town square in order to provide a public record of his status as legitimate heir to the throne. Frederic grew up in Sicily as an orphan with the pope as his legal guardian. He spoke Arabic, gathered pre-eminent Christian and Muslim scholars at his court in Sicily (where he was also suspected of maintaining a harem), wrote a book about falcon hunting, gave Sicily Europe's first codified system of public administration, and led the fifth crusade to Jerusalem where he did not fire a shot but secured free access to the holy Christian sites by means of a treaty with the Islamic sultan. In 1224 he also founded one of the earliest universities, the University of Naples. At least for some time to come, as an imperial institution, it remained free from church supervision and intervention.

It was in Frederic's cosmopolitan empire that an enormous intellectual transformation began to take shape with the rediscovery of Aristotle. Until the end of the twelfth century, only a few Latin fragments of Aristotle's work had survived in medieval Europe. In the Arabic world, however, an Aristotelian renaissance had already taken place, and many of his important works had been commented on by Muslim scholars. The most influential among these was Ibn Rushd (in Latin: Averroes, 1126-98), whose commentary on Aristotle's *Nicomachean Ethics* was available in Latin by the mid-1200s. Dissipating into Frederic's empire, mostly from Muslim Spain, and often via his court in Sicily, these commentaries would finally lead to successive Latin translations of Aristotle's entire works from the original Greek. A new generation of scholars would begin referring to Aristotle simply as "the philosopher," and to Averroes as "the commentator."

As a result, the entire question of the relationship between faith and reason, spirituality and politics, which had largely been left untouched since Augustine's tale of the two cities, had to be rethought. Averroes had gone as far as to postulate the superiority of philosophy over theology since true knowledge could only be exacted from rational demonstration.[4] What must have come like a bombshell to the scholastic establishment had reverberations for centuries. In Raffaello's famous fresco of *The School of Athens*, painted centuries later at the beginning of the sixteenth century, Averroes is given a place of honour among the immortals of Greek philosophy. The works of Aristotle were duly banned by the church, but the question of social justice, established by human reasoning, could no longer be ignored.

As has been pointed out, this transformation was not so much a revolution as it was a new focus.[5] For the real world of politics, which had long since employed purely secular doctrines and formulae for the conduct of its complex affairs, Aristotelian political thought provided a new and more precise language, and it re-established political science as a subject matter in its own right.

It was in the church-free environment of Frederic's university at Naples where Thomas Aquinas first studied Aristotle at a time when this was restricted by the church at the three papal universities of Bologna, Paris, and Oxford.

Thomas Aquinas (1225-74)

As the son of the count of Aquino in Frederic's Neapolitan/Sicilian kingdom, Thomas was destined for an illustrious public career. His education began at the age of five in the monastic school of Montecassino. He was only 14 when he enrolled in the general arts program at the University of Naples. Against the wishes of his family, however, he entered the new "beggars' order" of the Dominicans in 1243, thus renouncing worldly power and wealth. In 1245 he became a student of Albertus Magnus (Albert the Great, 1200-80) in Paris and Cologne. In 1252 he began to teach at the University of Paris. He returned to Naples some time after 1259, and for the rest of his life worked, taught, and wrote at various Italian institutions, as well as back in Paris. He died shortly after a final return to Naples, probably from exhaustion.

At Naples, his curriculum of studies included Aristotelian logic. It is likely that he also became exposed, for the first time, to Aristotle's so-called natural philosophy (as opposed to the official church philosophy of predestination), as well as to the writings of Averroes. His main intellectual formation, however, would take place later under the tutelage of Albertus, one of the most ency-clopaedic minds of the time. It was Albertus who had first sought to reconcile Aristotle with church doctrine. In doing so, he had rejected the Averroist posi-tion according to which natural philosophy and faith were irreconcilable.

But it was Thomas's own synthesis of faith and reason that would become the timeless bedrock of church doctrine. Already in 1323 he was canonized as saint, and in 1567 he was named teacher of the church (*doctor ecclesiae*). In 1879 Pope Leo XIII effectively declared "Thomism" the official church philosophy. From a political science perspective, that alone should arouse some suspicion, although it would be unfair to hold Thomas — or any other political thinker — responsible for the way he was received and used by later interpreters of his work.

His enormous work, collected in more than 30 volumes, is of course not primarily dedicated to political philosophy or thought.[6] Yet, it is permeated with Aristotelian language and with the unwavering conviction that the kind of scientific reason that Aristotle had employed to explain human affairs was not in contradiction to Christian faith and most importantly could never supersede it. Thomas even hurried back to Paris in order to defend this con-viction both against the anti-Aristotelian church establishment (his views would be censured alongside the proscription of Aristotle's natural philoso-phy in 1277) and the radical Averroists.

During this last stint in Paris (1268-72), Thomas also wrote a commen-tary on Aristotle's *Ethics*. But the essence of his political thought is usually associated with two other works, the *Summa Theologiae*[7] (*Sum of Theology*), probably written between 1266 and 1273, and a short treatise, *De Regimine Principium* (*On Kingship*, probably 1267). The *Summa* contains the culmi-nation and final synthesis of Thomas's entire theological philosophy. It is more than 3,000 pages long and yet remained unfinished in the end. Students of political thought usually rely on the compiled extraction of relevant pas-sages. The treatise on kingship contains a more conventional treatment of politics. Only Book I and the first six and a half chapters of Book II were in fact written by Thomas. The rest was added by a pupil.[8]

Thomas's contributions to political thought are best discussed in two steps. First, we will turn to his thoughts on state, law, and the common good. It is here that he is closest to the Aristotelian tradition. Second, we will turn to his more abstract thoughts on the nature of order and rule. Here is where he most significantly departs from the philosopher.

Aristotle's political philosophy was seen as "natural" because it knew nothing about Christian providence. Man, the philosopher had defined, was a political animal by nature. In examining whether this was a view compatible with the Christian faith, Thomas had to reformulate the question: Before the Fall, when the original sin had not yet been committed and men lived in a state of paradise or innocence, would there have been any kind of organized social life that included "dominion," the rule of one man over another? Referring to Aristotle as an authority who was no longer disputed, Thomas's answer was yes, because man is a "social animal" (*animal sociale*) by nature and therefore "in the state of innocence would have lived a social life."[9]

But what kind of social life? Here it becomes necessary to distinguish between *De Regimine Principium*, probably written earlier and a clear endorsement of monarchy, and the *Summa Theologiae*, in which Thomas adopted a much more Aristotelian and balanced argument that did not exclude popular and mixed regimes.

In the treatise on kingship, written much like a traditional "princely mirror," presumably for a king of Cyprus and abandoned when that king died, Thomas sets out a string of arguments in favour of monarchy. A plurality of rulers will not achieve unity,[10] he argues, and "goodness arises in things from one perfect cause."[11] Monarchy, he appears to be convinced, "is the best form of government"[12] because "wherever things are organized into a unity, something is found that rules all the rest."[13]

Thomas was aware of the fact that monarchs tend to become selfish and tyrannical. He refers to Rome, which got rid of its kings for that very reason, as did the Jews in biblical Israel. He even refers to republican Rome as an example of a mixed polity that "prospered under the government of many."[14] But then, in the following chapter, he nevertheless insists, and this time without providing any historical examples or evidence, that tyranny is much more likely to arise from the rule of the many than from the rule of one. He even suggests that in order to avoid a greater evil, a tyrant should be obeyed as long as his tyranny does not become "excessive." This was all probably meant to convince the king of Cyprus that he, Thomas, was not out to question his position and power. After that assurance has been put on paper, the remainder of the treatise proceeds by admonishing and advising the king as to what he ought to do in order to be a good king. And, ultimately, "by a wondrous dispensation of Divine providence," this means that the "kings must be subject to priests."[15]

In the *Summa*, Thomas's argument becomes both more sophisticated and abstract. At the centre of his political thought is the discussion of law. Agreeing with the philosopher, he first states that law is "the guiding principle in all matters of action," and that, therefore, it is "something belonging to reason."[16] He then affirms that because the purpose of all human reasoning is to achieve "common happiness ... every law is directed to the common good."[17] Finally, he advances the thought that "the common good consists of many things, and so the law must take many things into account, having regard to persons and matters and times" (*secundum personas, et secundum negotia, et secundum tempora*).[18]

What Thomas means by persons, matters, and times becomes clear when he takes on the question as to whether human law is immutable or subject to change. In one of the most remarkable passages of the *Summa*,[19] and one that is most at odds with the Augustinian sense of order (or the Platonic fear of novelty), he entertains the thought that a law might be useless and therefore ought to be changed if it does not reflect the "custom of the country" (*consuetudo patriae*). Custom, he points out, is not whimsical: "When something is done again and again, it seems to proceed from the deliberate judgment of reason." This can easily be misread as a conservative endorsement of keeping things as they are. But what Thomas has in mind, clearly, are changing circumstances in a society which require adaptation of the law. Accordingly, "custom has the force of law, abolishes law, and is the interpreter of law." Thus, when he continues to say that custom is "one of the conditions of law" because "it is difficult to set aside the custom of a whole community" (*difficile enim est consuetudinem multitudinis removere*), he does not have in mind "old prejudices" of the kind Burke cherishes but instead seems to point to legislation as an ongoing process that accompanies the evolution of society.[20]

Nowhere does Thomas come closer to accepting the Aristotelian idea that a combination of reason and plurality seems possible. And it is because of this acceptance that he acknowledges the legitimacy of a variety of forms of government (*diversa regimina civitatum*).[21] In particular, he admits that the common good can also result from law made by "the whole community," or by "someone acting on behalf of the whole community" (*vel totius multitudinis, vel alcuius gerentis vicem totius multitudinis*).[22]

With reference to the philosopher again, he also expounds on the nature of just laws in a perfect community, which must adapt to happiness and its parts by means of political communication (*politica communicatione*).[23] He consequently endorses the Aristotelian idea of the best polity as a mixed regime (*optima politia, bene commixta*), not without quickly noting, again with reference to the tribes of Israel, that this is also the best regime according to divine law.[24] Thomas also alludes to the overlapping plurality of rule in medieval Europe by pointing out that the law in a particular community may be superseded by the law of a higher authority, and that the law may more generally vary from city to city and kingdom to kingdom.[25] This is as close as he ever comes to reflecting on practical politics.

However, Thomas would not be the *doctor ecclesiae* if he did not put a firm lid on any unrestrained endorsement of plurality. In fact, as a political thinker, he is perhaps best known for his proposition of a hierarchy of laws.[26] He distinguishes the kind of human law which does allow for considerable variance in obtaining happiness or the common good from eternal and natural law, which frames and supersedes it, and from divine law, which is different altogether. Nothing that guides the "rational pattern of the government of things"[27] (*ratio gubernationis rerum*) can be outside eternal law, which is given by divine providence, or natural law, which is nothing but the "participation of the rational creature in the eternal law."[28]

Thomas even grants that human reason will be able to distinguish from civil law, which provides "specific applications," a more general law of nations (*ius gentium*), which is part of natural law because it lays down those general principles "without which men cannot live together."[29] In the medieval context, this is all astonishingly modern, because, ultimately, it seems that Thomas is content to leave to human reasoning the discernment of a moral code of general law.

But then finally there is divine law, not open to reason at all but instead providing infallible direction for all human action. As Thomas elaborates, divine direction was not needed "if the only end appointed for mankind were one which did not exceed the capacity of man's natural faculty."[30] One can still read this simply as an acknowledgment that there are things beyond human comprehension, and that faith is the only way of accommodating the fears arising from that incomprehension.

Elsewhere, however, in his earlier commentaries on Peter Lombard's *Four Books of Sentences*,[31] Thomas reveals that he may have in mind a more direct and political role for divine law. Alluding to the *two swords* of spiritual and secular power, he first refers to Matthew 22:21 ("render to Caesar the things that are Caesar's") in order to point out that "in those things which pertain to the civil good, the secular power should be obeyed before the spiritual." This sounds much like Luther's later attempt at distancing himself from the questioning of secular authority during the peasant uprisings in his name.[32] Ultimately, we may draw the conclusion that law and order are more important than conscience. However, Thomas goes one decisive step further. This separation of the two swords is only valid as long as someone does not hold both powers, "that is, the spiritual and the secular, through the disposition of Him Who is both priest and king." That someone is the pope who "holds the summit of both powers."

Admittedly, Thomas may have written this when he was perhaps no more than 27 years of age. But there does not appear to be anything in the *Summa* of the more mature *doctor ecclesiae* that would seem to exclude this view according to which divine authority as represented by the pope is the ultimate arbiter in human affairs. In the Thomist reception of Aristotle, it seems, Plato's philosopher-king creeps back in through the back door of Christian revelation. Indeed, when we turn to Thomas's more abstract thoughts on power and authority, we find that by attempting to synthesize the political thought of the philosopher with the unwavering commitment to a hierarchical Christian order, there is no hesitation in compromising the former for the sake of the latter.

Thomas translates *zoon politikon* as *animal sociale*. Man is a social, not a political, animal.[33] As first pointed out by Hannah Arendt, this "unconscious substitution of the social for the political" betrays the essence of Greek political thought because, there, "the human capacity for political organization is not only different but stands in direct opposition to that natural association whose centre is the home (*oikia*) and the family."[34] As Jürgen Habermas will elaborate later, by relinquishing this crucial difference, Thomas transforms the science of politics into a science of social order.[35] Dominion (*dominium*) no longer just denotes the rule of the *paterfamilias* in the household. Instead, it is generalized as the essence of rule everywhere.

Indeed, Thomas begins his answer to the question of whether there would have been dominion or rule in the state of innocence (see above) by stating that "dominion is understood as referring in a general way to [the rule of] any kind of subject whatsoever; and in this sense even he who has the office of governing and directing free men can be called a master" (*gubernandi et dirigendi liberos, dominus dici potest*). And, in what constitutes a deliberate rather than an unconscious misrepresentation of the very essence of the philosopher's political thought, he uses a passage from Aristotle's discussion of household management[36] to assert that "wherever many things are directed to one end, there is always found one at the head, directing them" (*semper invenit unum ut principale et dirigens*).[37]

Nowhere does Thomas acknowledge that the Aristotelian essence of political rule is "to govern and to be governed." He does mention that for the sake of popular peace (*pax populi*) the many ought to have some input into public affairs (*ut omnes aliquam partem in principatu habeant*), and this leads to his endorsement of the mixed regime, by which he means that kings are to be elected (like the emperor) and that they should rely on the advice of their princes (as in the formula of *quod omnes tangit* ...).[38] But neither does this take back his insistence on the universal nature of rule as dominion, nor is it meant to allow any notion of reciprocity, leave alone popular governance, into his hierarchical construction of law and order.

Even the most sympathetic interpretation of Thomas's Aristotelian-Christian synthesis must come to the conclusion that it is, ultimately, "intellectually dishonest."[39] The angelic doctor has no qualms about making a travesty of the philosopher's understanding of politics. Aristotle had defined that "in general, a man of practical wisdom [i.e., *phronesis* or political prudence] is he who has the ability to deliberate."[40] Thomas defines political prudence quite differently. "The kind of prudence associated with politics" (*species prudentiae quae politica vocatur*), he asserts, can be defined as that kind of "rectitude" among "men who are slaves or subjects in any sense" by which they "direct themselves in obeying their superiors" (*rectitudo regiminis per quam seipsos dirigant in obediendo principatibus*).[41]

Thomas's entire grandiose edifice erected in the *Summa* serves the one purpose of making the newly discovered Aristotelian language of political science compatible with church-imposed hierarchy. With or without the direct interference of the pope, it is faith which instructs kings, and kings which govern their subjects on behalf of that faith. "In human affairs," Thomas exclaims, "the higher must move the lower by their will in virtue of a divinely established authority" (*superiores moveant inferiores per suam voluntatem, ex vi auctoritatis divinitus ordinatae*).[42] In the end, it is the grace of God alone which moves the world: "Among men the orders are distinguished according to the gratuitous gift only, and not according to nature" (*in hominibus distinguuntur ordines secundum dona gratuita tantum, et non secundum naturam*).[43]

In 1272 Thomas had left Paris for the last time. At that time, it was not clear at all whether his attempt at harnessing Aristotle's philosophy of reason to the Christian cause would be successful. According to some sources, Thomas did not stop working on the *Summa* in 1273 because he was sick or too exhausted but because he had doubts that it had accomplished anything.

In 1313 the record shows that Marsilius, a former physician from Padua, had become rector of the University of Paris. Another nine years later Marsilius would claim that the sole cause of discord in the city and state was the "pernicious pestilence" of papal meddling in political affairs. A lot had happened during the intervening half-century.

Marsilius of Padua (1275-1342)

Very little is known about Marsilius's life,[44] and he seems to be the only one among the luminaries in the history of political thought of whom we do not even possess a single contemporaneous image.[45] Marsilius was born into a prominent Paduan family. His father was a notary at the University of Padua.

Probably at Padua, he was trained as a physician. The university was one of the leading medical schools in Europe. At some point he must have turned to theology (he even became ordained as a priest) and philosophy, pursuing both further during his tenure in Paris, but why and when we do not know.

Marsilius probably was simply a man of diverse interests. There exists an undated and rhymed epistle addressed to him by a Paduan civic leader, friend, and mentor, who chides him for his fickleness for turning "from the path of sacred study to the unspeakable acts of men."[46] That was probably a reference to Marsilius's lifelong involvement in the politics of the day in the service of upper Italian city rulers in Verona and Milan and eventually at the court of the German king and emperor to whom the same epistle referred as the "German sword."

But it was not just fickleness that drove Marsilius away from the university and into the arms of politics. He had published his main work, *Defensor Pacis (Defender of Peace)*, anonymously in 1324.[47] This was the work that attacked the pope as a "pernicious pestilence" (*perniciosa pestis*).[48] When Marsilius's authorship became known two years later, he had to flee Paris and seek refuge at the court of Ludwig of Bavaria, himself at the time engaged in an epic battle with the pope over his recognition as German king and holy Roman emperor.

We need to backtrack a few steps. When Thomas left Paris, the papal church had been at the zenith of its power. In 1077 the German emperor Henry IV had been forced to do humiliating penance before Pope Gregory VII at Canossa in order to have the papal excommunication lifted that threatened his throne.[49] Still in 1302, the Bull *Unam Sanctam* of Boniface VIII declared that the papacy held both swords over the spiritual realm, as well as over the material world.

But reality would catch up to the papal claim five years later when, under French pressure, the next pope, Clemens V, was crowned in Lyon, stayed in France, and eventually settled in Avignon, which would remain the seat of the papacy, with some interruptions, until 1376. The French king had a natural interest in strengthening the papacy as a political weapon against his own main rival, the German king and emperor. It should not come as a surprise that the antipapist Marsilius fled from Paris and into Ludwig's Bavarian sanctuary.

Marsilius was part of Ludwig's entourage during a momentous journey to Italy in 1327. After shoring up support in upper Italy (here, Marsilius's connections to Verona and Milan probably came in handy), Ludwig continued on to Rome where he had himself crowned emperor by a representative of the Roman people. He also declared the pope (in Avignon) deposed and appointed an antipope. None of this came to very much in the end, though.

Still in the same year, Ludwig left Rome and Italy, and, Marsilius still in tow, returned to Germany.

It is tempting to see Marsilius's hand in all these machinations. But in fact there is no hard evidence of this, and next to nothing is known as to what became of him after 1328. Presumably, he lived in Munich and perhaps worked again as a physician, likely having fallen out with Ludwig. Towards the end of his life, he wrote another treatise, *Defensor Minor* (*Minor Defender*), a summary and extension of his earlier work.[50] From a passing reference in a papal document we know that he was dead by April 1343.[51] The usually assumed year of his death is 1342.

Thomas became the undisputed church philosopher only in the nineteenth century at a time when the papacy once again tried to assert its pre-eminence in human affairs, this time directed against the formation and rise of the sovereign territorial nation-state in Italy and elsewhere.[52] Marsilius's belated fame had to wait a little longer still, until 1956, when Alan Gewirth published the first complete vernacular translation of the *Defensor Pacis* in English.[53] This quickly spawned a more thorough interest in the Paduan than the (mostly) occasional learned references to him in earlier literature on political thought. But Marsilius is still by no means a regular in the classical canon.[54]

This neglect is probably owed to several reasons. One is that there was not much room left for anyone else after it became generally accepted that it was Thomas's towering accomplishment that lastingly transformed medieval political thought and that therefore prepared the grounds for a new age. Another is that Marsilius had been celebrated, here and there, as a medieval advocate of democratic radicalism.[55] When more critical scholarship found the textual evidence wanting, he was quickly dismissed as altogether unimportant and lacking a voice of his own. Finally, even more well-meaning scholars detected in his political thought the same fickleness he had been accused of in life.[56] Finding it difficult to discern whether Marsilius actually defended a mixed regime of civic governance, backed the imperial claims of Ludwig, or even sympathized with the authoritarian princely rulers of Verona and Milan, his political theory was dismissed as inconsistent and lacking principle.

As we shall see, the relative neglect Marsilius's political thought has suffered is both unwarranted and unfortunate. Marsilius stands at the European beginning of secular political theory. In that alone, his adaptation of the Aristotelian heritage is much more genuine than that of Thomas. And if there is a path of demystification,[57] from the otherworldly Christian Middle Ages to the here and now in the Machiavellian world of *realpolitik*, then that path begins with Marsilius's treatment of plurality in a complex political world. It is time to take a look at the text.

The formal composition of that text, the *Defensor Pacis*, already reveals its secularist intention.[58] Contrary to conventional practice, the discussion of church and state governance is strictly separated. Discourse (*Dictio*) I contains the treatment of secular governance and Discourse II then turns to church governance. A third discourse contains a brief summary of the main arguments. It also reveals that, despite their separate treatment, the two principal questions about governance in state and church are in reality closely interconnected.

Throughout the *Defensor*, Marsilius never loses sight of his overriding polemical intention of identifying — and then removing — the "singular cause which has hitherto produced discord" (*singularem civilis discordie ... assignavimus causam*): the "Roman bishop and his clerical coterie" (*Romanus episcopus et suorum cetus clericorum*) in their desire "to seize secular rulerships and to possess excessive temporal wealth" (*ad seculares tendunt principatus et temporalia possidenda superflue*).[59]

In this single-minded intention, the *Defensor* can almost be appreciated as a deliberate sequel to Aristotle's *Politics* because, as Marsilius points out at the beginning, "neither Aristotle nor any other philosopher of his time" could have known this singular cause of discord.[60] His solution (the removal of the cause of discord) will be twofold. In Discourse I, Marsilius essentially puts forward an Averroist position according to which matters of faith have nothing to do with civil governance, and that priests are in fact subject to civil legislation. This is meant to remove church authority from secular affairs. In Discourse II, Marsilius then puts forward a theory of conciliar supremacy according to which it is the general council of church members, priests as well as lay persons, that has the last word on church governance. This is meant to break the hierarchical authority of the papacy.

Marsilius supports these positions with a number of arguments that completely fly in the face of convention and particularly renounce the Thomist position that faith and reason can be fused in such a way as to leave the hierarchy of the Christian order untouched. When it comes to the establishment of government, he snickers, it may well be that this was in some distant past the matter of a "divine will" (*divina voluntas*), possibly even transmitted through a "determinate oracle" (*oraculo determinato*). It may also well be that God is always behind all human action, as a "remote cause" (*causa remota*), so to speak. But if so, Marsilius continues with resolve, [God] does not always act immediately; indeed, in most cases, nearly everywhere, he establishes governments by means of human minds, to which he has granted the discretionary will for such establishments (*tamen no est immediate semper, quinimo ut in pluribus et ubique quasi hos statuit per hominum mentes, quibus talis institucionis concessit arbitrium*).[61]

From this postulation of the human mind as the fundamental and independent cause of governance, Marsilius can move on to a whole series of arguments in favour of his secularist position. Instead of endorsing a hierarchy of law, as had Thomas,[62] there are for him only two kinds of law: human law, which sets standards of right and wrong as well as punishes transgressors in the present world; and divine law, which likewise contains behavioural standards for the present world but can only inflict punishment in a future world which is out of reach of reason and demonstration.[63] As but one part of a state that is willed by human law alone, priests receive their authority from that law only.[64] And because their coercive power can only inflict punishment in a future world, they can teach and admonish sinners, but they have no coercive power over them in this present world.[65]

What goes for individual priests, applies no less to the pope. Not only is he declared to be merely the first among equals and subject to the collective authority of a general council comprising priests and ordinary believers,[66] he is moreover subject to human law as much as any ordinary priest and is therefore to be installed either by such a general council or by the faithful human legislator. And, since he is the bishop of Rome, it may well be the city of Rome to whom this task behoves (*auctoritas instituendi ... modem Romane urbi*).[67] One can easily see why the ultimately speculative suggestion is so compelling that Marsilius had a direct hand in Ludwig of Bavaria's 1328 coronation by a representative of the city of Rome and the subsequent imperial appointment of an antipope.

If this was all that the Paduan physician had to say, it would be remarkable enough. His fierce secularism, his condemnation of the papacy's greed for power and wealth, his endorsement of a strict distinction between faith and demonstrable reason, and finally his subjection of the priesthood to secular supervision all had reverberations for centuries to come, from the pagan humanism of the Renaissance to Luther's Reformation and the breakaway of the Church of England under Henry VIII shortly thereafter. Thomas Cromwell, Henry's principal architect of the new state church, supported an abridged English translation of the *Defensor* in 1535.[68]

However, Marsilius had much more to say. What elevates him to the rank of one of the undisputed original masters in the history of political thought is not his polemical rant against the pope and church but his adaptation of Aristotle to a secular theory of politics. This is what lends to his anticlerical stance its logical (and hence: demonstrable) foundation. While falling way short of anything like a modern theory of democracy, it nevertheless reintroduces medieval Europe to classical concepts of citizenship and governance that proscribe anyone's claim to power and authority by divine or hereditary right. With good reason, one of the chapters left out in the English edition of

1535 was the one in which Marsilius declares that rulers must be punished for serious repeated transgressions of the law.[69]

Marsilius's basic presentation of the nature and purpose of politics is quintessentially Aristotelian.[70] He does not cite directly the most famous of all Aristotelian contributions to political thought, the definition of man as a political animal (*zoon politikon*). But Discourse I is nevertheless permeated with the exact same idea of man fulfilling his nature as part of a political community. In fact, Marsilius cites Aristotle's own interpretation of what *zoon politikon* means, from the same chapter and passage in *Politics*: "All men are driven toward such an association by natural impulse" (*secundum nature impetum*).[71]

Marsilius also faithfully reproduces, still from the same chapter in the *Politics*, that "the perfect community ... came into existence for the sake of living, but exists for the sake of living well" (*perfecta communitas ... vivendi gracia facta, existens autem gracia bene vivendi*).[72] But then he seems to depart from the Aristotelian notion of the good life by declaring that without such a civil community a "sufficient life cannot be obtained" (*vivere hoc sufficiens obtineri non potest*).[73] How can a "sufficient life" and "living well" contain one and the same idea? It may be only a matter of translation. Like Thomas, Marsilius relied on Moerbeke's Latin translation of Aristotle. It was Moerbeke who had translated the Greek word "autarchy" (*autarkeia*) as "sufficiency." Autarchy means not to be dependent on others. It does not necessarily entail an appeal to frugality or mere living in an existential sense. The Paduan physician had no problems with living well. Sufficient is simply whatever is "useful and necessary for the harmonious exercise of social life," as Althusius would later interpret and give meaning to the same Aristotelian passage.[74]

There is nothing in Marsilius that would contradict this meaning of sufficiency. He not only defines, again very much in Aristotelian fashion, that "living and living well" (*vivere et bene vivere*) includes "having leisure for those liberal functions in which are exercised the virtues of both the practical and the theoretic soul" (*qualia sunt virtutum tam practice, quam speculative anime*).[75] He also reiterates, again with direct reference to Aristotle, that to "live and live well" means receiving fulfilment "through art and reason" (*ab arte ac racione*).[76] This fulfilment is the purpose of the entire complex organization of society into different parts, groups, or classes, or arts, virtues, and offices. While some derive their existence "from necessity" (*ex necessitate*), others aim at "pleasure and living well" (*ad delicias et bene vivere*).[77]

Aristotelian as well is the (by now) conventional distinction between "well-tempered" (*bene temperatum*) and "diseased" (*viciatum*) regimes.[78] Marsilius calls the general type of well-tempered regime a "polity" (*policia*). He characterizes it as one in which "every citizen participates in some way in the government or in the deliberative function in turn according to his rank and ability or condition, for the common benefit and with the will or consent of the citizens" (*civis quilibet participat aliqualiter principatu vel consiliativo vicissim iuxta gradum et facultatem seu condicionem ipsius, ad commune eciam conferens et civium voluntatem sive consensum*).[79] There are clear echoes of the Aristotelian mixed polity here. "Well-tempered" means governance for the common good, which is only possible through the deliberative involvement of all citizens in public affairs. In the same vein, like Aristotle, Marsilius rejects the idea of democracy as rule of the masses (*vulgus*) or the "multitude of the needy" (*egenorum multitudo*) for their own benefit rather than for the "common benefit according to proportion" (*ad commune conferens secundum proporcionem convenientem*).[80]

In true Aristotelian methodological fashion, "by induction" (*induccione*), Marsilius also provides his own version of what had become the standard argument against assumptions of aristocratic superiority ever since Aristotle refuted Plato's elitist arrogance: "Most of the time," he declares, "all or most [citizens] are of sound mind and reason" (*in pluri tempore...omnes enim aut plurimi sane mentis et racionis sunt*).[81] And therefore, he continues, it is simply not true that "the wise can discern what should be enacted better than can the whole multitude, in which the wise are included together with the less learned" (*quod sapienties sciant statuenda discernere magis tota multitudine, in qua comprehenduntur ipsi cum reliquis minus doctis*).[82]

Marsilius, we can safely assume, very much understood his task as one of adapting the political thought of Aristotle to the issues of his own time. Yet, adaptation does not mean mere regurgitation. Just as Thomas had used the Christian code of faith as an irrefutable conceptual background for a discussion of something else, the placement of worldly affairs within that Christian order, so does Marsilius use the Aristotelian code of a natural political order as the conceptual background for something else again, the discussion of governance the function of which is "to regulate matters of justice for the common benefit" (*iusta et conferencia communia regulare*).[83]

Aristotle had thought of justice in terms of a mixed constitutional order in which citizens were to govern and be governed. For the sake of stability, he held, in reference to the Greek tradition all the way back to Solon, that it was wise to "assign [to the many] some deliberative and judicial functions."[84] This was a matter of practical wisdom in order to achieve the final goal, the good life. Because of that goal, a mixed polity was preferable to other regimes. The reasonable end was to determine the political means. There was no consideration given to the constitutional question of who had primary authority over the determination of those political means. Aristotle in fact carefully separated the constitutional or "supreme" act of legislation from the ordinary business of deliberation and adjudication. This is where Marsilius would depart from the Greek master. In what doubtlessly is the central passage of the entire *Defensor Pacis*, he refers to the above quote about the assignment of deliberative and judicial functions, but then uses it as a point of departure for a radically transformed and extended political theory that centres entirely on the question of the "primary and proper efficient cause of law" (*causam legis effectivam primam et propriam*).[85] Perhaps for the first time in the history of political thought, the constitutional question of who possesses primary legislative authority will be separated from the old question of regime types.[86]

While the classical view associates different regimes of government with different sources of authority (one, few, or many), the regime question is nearly irrelevant for Marsilius. The primary cause of law, he continues, is none other than "the people or the whole body of citizens" (*populum seu civium universitatem*).[87] This seemingly radical statement does not amount to anything like a modern idea of democracy based on individual and universal citizenship. But what it does provide is a radical change of perspective from government to governance: Marsilius no longer asks the old question about the best—ideal or possible—government. Instead, he wants to determine the constitutional foundation of lawful governance under any form of well-tempered government. And well-tempered means nothing other than adherence to the law as established by the primary human legislator.

Just who exactly that human legislator is has been the most controversial question in the interpretation of Marsilius's rank as a political thinker. The main reason for this controversy is a qualification that is thrown into the definition of the human legislator almost as an aside. Marsilius does not just say that the primary cause of law is the people or whole body of citizens. The entire passage reads more fully:

> The legislator, or the primary and proper efficient cause of law, is the people or the whole body of citizens, or the weightier part thereof, through its election or will expressed by words in the general assembly of the citizens (*legislatorem seu causam legis effectivam primam et propriam esse populum seu civium universitatem aut eius valenciorem partem, per suam eleccionem seu voluntatem in generali civium congregacione per sermonem expressam*).[88]

This obviously begs two questions: Who are the citizens and what constitutes the weightier part? The answers to both are in fact quite easy and straightforward. The reason why there has been so much controversy has much to do with the aforementioned attempts at portraying Marsilius as a radical democrat espousing no less than a full-fledged theory of popular sovereignty.[89] In refuting such overdrawn and modernizing claims, however, the baby need not be thrown out with the bath water.

Once again with direct reference to Aristotle, Marsilius defines a citizen as one who participates in public affairs, "according to his rank" (*secundum gradum suum*). Children, slaves, aliens, and women are explicitly excluded.[90] What Marsilius means by "according to rank" becomes clear from his earlier discussion of the "parts of the state" (*partibus civitatis*) or composition of society.[91] He lists the various "parts or offices" (*partes seu officia*) of the state in classical fashion, but then groups them into two classes or categories of citizens: the "honourable class" (*honorabilitas*), comprising those with priestly, military, and judicial or deliberative functions; and the "common mass" (*multitudo vulgaris*), comprising all others with necessary functions in the state including peasants, artisans, and those involved in matters of money.

We have already heard that for Marsilius a well-tempered polity is one in which all citizens participate "in some way" in public affairs. Such a polity is therefore different from both an aristocracy in which the "honourable class" (*honorabilitas*) would rule alone, and from a democracy in which the common multitude (*vulgus*) would rule alone.[92] In other words, all members of the necessary parts of the state have citizenship status and hence the right to participate in public affairs. This is a significant departure from Aristotle, who had excluded from citizenship the common masses who would not have the leisure to develop political skills.

Two reasons account for this departure. One is a changed political reality. In the upper Italian city republics such as Marsilius's own native Padua, craft guilds and professional colleges played an active role in politics. This is not to say that Marsilius necessarily used Padua as a blueprint for his political theory. But it must have been patently obvious to this commoner and physician-turned-university-professor that the same urbanization trends that had provided the environment for the new universities had also led to the rise of newly organized political forces. A general theory of politics of the kind he had in mind surely could not ignore this.

We are only some 50 years away from the 1378 *Ciompi*-riot of Florentine wool workers during the course of which, according to Machiavelli's account in his *Istorie Fiorentine*, one of the civic leaders or *Gonfaloniere*, Luigi Guiccardini, warns the rebellious guild leaders that the disunity between guilds and nobles will only make the city vulnerable to foreign domination. And then one of the *Ciompi* leaders calls for armed action with the truly Aristotelian observation that while "good men are always poor," all those "who attain great riches and great power have attained them by means of either fraud or force."[93] Obviously, it was possible for the vulgar masses to develop considerable political insight and skills once they had learned how to organize.

The second and more important reason for Marsilius's departure from Aristotle by including the *vulgus* in the process of governance has to do with the fact that this changed political reality also required a different and more differentiated analysis and conceptualization of the system and operation of politics. Marsilius not only distinguishes between legislator and ruler, he also introduces a detailed and differentiated procedure for the legislative process.

The ruling part (*pars principans*) is established, together with all other parts of the state, by the human legislator (*legislator has partes statuit*).[94] Whoever ends up being this ruling part should govern on the basis of the law (*dominari principantes secundum* [*leges*]).[95] And, as Marsilius explains in his lengthy discussion of the pros and cons of hereditary v. elective monarchy, "the elected kind of government is superior to the non-elected" (*genus electum principatus prestancius esse non electo*).[96] Marsilius further insists on and devotes an entire chapter to the idea that the ruling part or government in the city or state needs to be unitary in number and action (*de numerali unitate principatus civitatis seu regni*).[97] Under no circumstances, in other words, must the plurality of legitimate interests and functions spill into a situation where governing authority speaks with competing voices. This insistence, of course, lies at the root of his attack upon the papacy as such a competing voice and source of disunity.

By separating legislative and executive (ruling) functions, and by tying the latter to the primary authority of the former, Marsilius brings on its way the idea that social plurality can result in responsible unity of action without stifling that plurality into uniformity. Because of this separation also, it is more easily possible for Marsilius to admit the common multitude to citizenship and governance because the wool worker may have a say in legislation but will not automatically become a ruler as well. In the Aristotelian formula of to govern and to be governed, as in Athenian political practice more generally, such a distinction was not made. The result was a more restrictive view of citizenship. Its purpose was to make reasonable governance possible by limiting the plurality of access.

The legislative process is broken down into three distinct phases. The first phase pertains to the "investigation, discovery, and examination" of the law (*leges ... querendas seu inveniendas et examinandas*). Marsilius suggests that these initial deliberations are best left to an elected committee of the prudent. During the second phase, a proposed law must then be put before the general assembly of citizens for adoption or rejection (*leges ... approbande vel reprobande*). If the law is adopted, the third phase then consists of its final passage and promulgation, either by the general assembly itself, or again by an elected and representative committee of experts.[98]

Elsewhere, Marsilius affirms that in principle the initial discovery of law "can pertain to any citizen" (*invenire potest ad quemlibet civem pertenire*), but that it is simply more convenient and efficient to leave this task to those more prudent (*prudentes*) because of their leisure, seniority, and expertise (*potencium vacare, seniorum et expertorum*).[99] Again, this distinction between the discovery and the adoption or authorization of the law makes it more plausible to grant common citizens a role in public affairs because the wool worker or mechanic, while perfectly capable of judging the merits of a law, will not have to bear the burden of legislative expertise.

A more inclusive definition of citizenship, final authorization of the law by the general assembly or an elected representative committee, and the separation of a lawful and accountable executive from this legislative function: One can easily see why some interpreters of Marsilius would celebrate the *Defensor* as a medieval theory of popular sovereignty and representative government. However, there is this peculiar qualification in the definition of the human legislator whereby the cause of law is the people ... "or the weightier part thereof" (*aut eius valenciorem partem*).[100]

It is this qualification which has caused most of the interpretive headache. For some, "weightier" refers to the majority of citizens if not the entire community. For others, it denotes a reduction of active citizenship to a small minority elite. For others again, it constitutes a deliberately ambiguous cop-out: Marsilius did not want to be pinned down to an endorsement of any particular form of governance.[101]

In reality, however, there is little if any ambiguity.[102] Marsilius seemed to know exactly what he was doing. In particular, he was fully aware that his concept of the "weightier part" (*valencior pars*) required further explanation in order to be understood correctly. In fact, the *Defensor* provides not just one but three such explanations. First, Marsilius specifies that the "weightier part" should be determined in "consideration of the quantity and the quality of the persons in that community over which the law is made" (*considerata quantitate personarum et qualitate in communitate illa super quam lex fertur*).[103] He then adds, secondly, that "the weightier part of the citizens should be viewed in accordance with the honourable custom of polities; or else, thirdly, it should be determined in accordance with the doctrine of Aristotle in the Politics, Book VI, Chapter 2" (*Valenciorem vero civium partem oportet attendere secundum policiarum consuetudinem honestam, vel hanc determinare secundum sentenciam Aristotelis 6° Politicae, capitulo 2°*).[104]

The first explanation, about the "quantity and quality of persons," can be easily understood as a direct recourse to Marsilius's distinction of *vulgus* and *honorabilitas* as the two categories of citizens. The common class is quantitatively larger but less qualified in terms of expertise and prudence. The reverse is true for the honourable class. Both are included "in some way" in the legislative process. The second explanation, about the "honourable custom of polities," only confirms the first: Marsilius has defined in principle the well-tempered polity as a mixed regime composed of *honorabilitas* and *vulgus*. This obviously corresponds closely to the political practice in city republics like Padua. In its affirmation of ordinary citizens as part of the legislative process, this second explanation also reflects the growing importance of large and free cities as a third estate in the empire, next to nobility and clergy.

The third explanation, then, can be found in the usual recourse to Aristotle. In the chapter referred to, Aristotle discusses political equality as a balancing principle that "implies that the poor should have no more share in the government than the rich, and should not be the only rulers, but that they should rule equally according to their numbers." And, "since there are two classes out of which a state is composed—the poor and the rich—that is to be deemed law, on which both or the greater part of both agree; and if they disagree, that which is approved by the greater number, and by those who have the higher qualification."[105]

The weightier part, either as a body representing the entire community on behalf of the general assembly or as a committee for the discovery of the law, can be understood and clearly appreciated as a composite entity of corporate governance in which the two categories of citizens, the few and the many, the rich and the poor, or the honourable and the common, must come to an agreement. Marsilius may not be entirely precise as to how exactly such agreement is supposed to come about in the end. But the principle is very clear: In a society divided by different interests or politically organized group identities, majority rule is not an option. Legitimacy of governance instead requires a high level of consent which can only be operationalized by some form of weighted decision-making.

"Corporate" in this context of a medieval city means that society is structured into organized segments with highly regulated conditions for access and membership. This is "democratic" only for those who are "incorporated" into this structure. Marsilius does not raise the issue as to what constitutes a right to be part of it. The notion of individual citizenship is alien to him.

When he wrote *Defensor*, the inclusion of guilds and colleges, especially from the minor ranks of society, in some inclusive form of governance was by no means uncontested. Corporate governance in many upper Italian cities had already been replaced by authoritarian princely rule. The tension between the complex idea of plural governance in a mixed regime on the one hand, and the simpler and more efficient resort to the unity of princely rule during a volatile time of competing territorial power claims remained. It would resurface and find reflection much more bluntly two centuries later in the political thought of Niccolo Machiavelli.

Critical Evaluation

According to one fairly representative kind of conventional wisdom, it was the "Christian encounter with politics" that "revitalized" the tradition of political thought during the later Middle Ages. Thus, it was the reception and adaptation of Aristotle in Thomas Aquinas's *Summa* which made it possible to think about a just society within a Christian order. And when that order came apart in the wake of the Renaissance and Reformation (Machiavelli's *Prince* was written four years before Luther's 95 Theses appeared), the grounds were prepared for a discussion of politics outside the hierarchical confines of the Christian framework.

According to the same kind of conventional wisdom, by comparison, Marsilius of Padua does not quite cut it because he "retained strong traces of the medieval outlook." Hence, the author of *Defensor* does not deserve more than a brief reference because, at best, he "foreshadows" something that only the sixteenth century will accomplish: the reassertion of the "radical autonomy of the political order."[106]

At first glance, this seems outright strange. Why would so much credit be given to an author who became an undisputed authority only in the nineteenth century; whose political thought remained so subordinated to a Christian "hierarchy of ends";[107] and who insisted on a definition of political rule as *dominium* which flies in the face of everything that modern enlightened political thought would later stand for?

By the same token, why would so little credit be given to an author who can be traced to many political thinkers that followed him, including Machiavelli and Hobbes; whose deconstruction of papal supremacy served as justification for the separation of the Church of England from Rome; who separated legislative and executive functions of governance and therefore preformulated one of the central tenets of modern governance; and who radically broke not only with hierocratic Christian unity but also with medieval dualism by declaring the human legislator as the sole cause of the law?

At second glance, this is not so strange at all. As I claimed at the outset of this book, one of the main purposes of constructing a classical canon in the history of political thought was to provide retroactive justification for the modern, centralized, and unitary territorial nation-state with its juxtaposition of individual citizenship and state sovereignty. From that perspective, and with that objective in mind, Thomas's hierarchical universalism naturally appears as a far more convenient tool of historical ideology construction than the plural fickleness of the Paduan physician.

One can still appreciate Thomas's political thought for what it is, a monumental and momentous effort at reconciling what in reality remains irreconcilable, reason and faith as conflicting sources of political order and authority. One can also appreciate that it was indeed this uneasy truce between faith and Aristotelian natural philosophy that first admitted politics to the list of legitimate subjects of human inquiry in a Christian world. And maybe one can even say that it was Thomas's half-hearted endorsement of the philosopher's intellectual legacy that allowed Marsilius to go all the way shortly thereafter. But it requires a certain preconceived blindness not to recognize the primary importance of Marsilius's political thought as a gateway to a secular and humanistic understanding of politics.

In that respect, the obvious enthusiasm that the builders of the Church of England had for Marsilius's antipapist polemics was essentially disingenuous. By fusing the powers of church and state in the person of the British monarch, the old dualism between spiritual and secular authority was eliminated. But the source of religious conflict in political affairs that Marsilius had sought to eliminate, remained. Religion would continue to dominate politics. This would lead to civil war and the Puritan Revolution in the seventeenth century.[108] The fusion of religion and politics would eventually be exported to the New World as well, when the civic New England mind became imbued with theocratic sentiments of order.[109] The resilience and resurgence of politicized religious fundamentalism at the beginning of the twenty-first century strongly suggest that the teachings of Marsilius (and Averroes) have not lost much of their relevance and urgency.

But Marsilius not only provides us with a secular political theory, the first such theory perhaps since the days of classical Athens. He also provides us with a remarkably "modern" analysis of the political process: by separating legislative and executive functions; by bridging the old dichotomy between the common sense of the many and the superior wisdom of the few in a mixed regime of divided governance; and by suggesting that the result of governance among an organized plurality of collective (corporate) political actors can nevertheless result in the unity of political action.

It is this latter corporate quality of Marsilian political thought, however, that separates the *Defensor* from the modern view of politics as the juxtaposition of sovereign state and individualized society.[110] Perhaps, then, the final recognition of Marsilius's contribution to the history of political thought had to wait until that modern view became contested itself. In practice, we are observing the resilience of all kinds of functional and identity groups and communities within and across nation-state boundaries.

In what has been heralded as a new age and dawning of a global society, it seems more than clear that governance will not come about by any kind of social contract among individual global citizens, nor resort to majority rule in the name of democracy. Instead, if it is going to come about at all in a manner of reasonable and peaceful accommodation among conflicting and competing interests, governance will have to rely on carefully negotiated agreements among a plurality of collective actors. Global law, in other words, will lastingly require a human legislator composed of different parts that are weighted in accordance with the quantity and quality of the people involved.

In theory, the modern idea of the unencumbered individual self has been challenged for some time, and for some time it has been tempered by notions of communitarian group identity. Acknowledging the collective legitimacy of such identities in public affairs certainly makes governance more complex and complicated. One can see this as the resurgence of neomedieval anarchy,[111] but one can also see it as a tradition of organized civic culture that had its roots all the way back in those upper Italian city republics and their corporate ways of governing.[112] From a macrohistorical perspective, such a claim may be methodologically and empirically questionable. From a perspective of common sense, however, it appears entirely convincing.

CHAPTER 5

Class Politics

Machiavelli's Prince *v.* The Discourses

To some, Machiavelli is "Old Nick," the devil and teacher of evil. To others, he is the first theorist of modernity and champion of *realpolitik*. This is an enormous gulf of opinion that the great Florentine realist has been posthumously burdened with. There are probably two main reasons why opinions differ so much and so fanatically when it comes to Machiavelli. One is that he is closer to us than, say, Plato or Thomas, and perhaps even Locke or Rousseau. His opinions and judgments get under the (thin) skin of modern civilization more quickly. The other reason is that he is also more modern in the blunt directness of what he has to say, and the way he says it. Quoting him out of context, therefore, the kind of "selective textualism" that haunts all great thinkers of the past, also leads to more extreme evaluations of his thought.[1]

We depart in this chapter from the usual set-up of comparing two authors with differing approaches to the politics and political theory of their time. Instead, we focus on a comparison of Machiavelli's two main works, *The Prince (Il Principe)*,[2] and *The Discourses (Discorsi)*.[3]

Machiavelli's notorious reputation almost entirely stems from the *Prince*, a short book much more often quoted than read. In it, Machiavelli appears to give a blunt account of what princely rulers need to do to be successful: deceive, cheat, punish, and kill if necessary. Not surprisingly, the loudest protests against this account came from the rulers themselves. In particular, during the age of absolutism, these rulers obviously did not wish to have their mantle of divine authority besmirched with revelations about what rulers really do when they rule. At the present time, however, as a quick search at amazon.com will reveal, Machiavelli's admonitions of ruthlessness seem to have found a more affectionate reception among corporate elites who have no qualms about admitting that ruthlessness is the name of the game in the world of profit.

In the other and much more voluminous work, the *Discourses*, even less read and hardly ever quoted, Machiavelli's focus is on republican governance as a mixed regime among conflicting classes rather than on princely rule. In it he advances a much more complex picture of what he sees as the socioeconomic roots and historical foundations of power and conflict, and the kind of politics resulting from different times and circumstances. The conventional explanation for the difference between the two works is that Machiavelli interrupted his work on the *Discourses* (1513-20) and wrote the *Prince* (1513) when he realized that, with the Medici returning to Florence as princely rulers, the republican cause was lost for his native city. Hence, the *Prince* sets out to outline the nature of princely rule when republican governance is not possible.

It has been pointed out that there is in fact little in the *Prince* that cannot also be found in the *Discourses*. Therefore, while the *Prince* "is for the busy executive," the *Discourses* are "for the potential prince with time on his hands."[4] The *Prince*, in other words, remains the principal perspective for which the *Discourses* only provide a somewhat more elaborate backdrop. The argument advanced in this chapter will be different. The *Discourses* will be taken seriously as providing Machiavelli's core ideas on politics and political theory. This will not only put the *Prince* in its proper place as an elongated footnote to one particular problem raised in the *Discourses* (the problem of civic corruption beyond repair), it will also make it possible to detect in the *Prince* itself the conditionality of Machiavelli's endorsement of ruthless princely rule.

Context

When Niccolo Machiavelli (1469-1527) was born, Renaissance Florence was at the peak of its splendour and glory. After the 30-year reign of Cosimo de' Medici (1434-64), the city's political and financial pre-eminence seemed secure. The Medici could prevent rivalling cities from waging war by simply withdrawing their money from circulation there.[5] Florence was then the centre of what would later be called the Italian Renaissance of an enormous outburst of human creativity in architecture, painting, and literature, as well as in the sciences. Gone were the medieval impositions of collective frugality and religious subordination. Individual ingenuity and pagan exuberance reigned supreme.

Completed in 1436 as a revolutionary feat of engineering, Filippo Brunelleschi's dome towered over the cathedral and the city of Florence. With a span of 143 feet, it remains to this day the largest dome ever built entirely by bricks and mortar. Revolutionary change also became visible in painting. Medieval church iconography had required artists to paint Madonnas and saints with impersonalized heavenly faces. They now took on the features and expressions of real people, Tuscan peasants and city folk. Speaking for the time like no other, Pico della Mirandola (1463-94), one of the brightest stars at the court of Lorenzo de' Medici,[6] a young man in his early twenties proficient in many languages including Hebrew and Arabic, and a student of philosophy, mathematics, music, physics, and theology, put into God's own words what he saw as man's destiny: "Thou, constrained by no limits, in accordance with thine own free will, in whose hand We have placed thee, shalt ordain for thyself the limits of thy nature" (*Tu, nullis angustiis coherci-tus, pro tuo arbitrio, in cuius mano te posui, tibi illam prefinies*).[7]

When Cosimo died in 1464, he was given the honourary title of "father of the fatherland" (*padre della patria*).[8] But, as Machiavelli would point out, fortune is fickle, and the times, they were a-changin' quickly. In 1494, two years after the death of Cosimo's grandson Lorenzo, who was called "The Magnificent" (*Il Magnifico*), the Medici were ousted from Florence and city was turned back into the kind of republic it had been before the Medici came to power. It only lasted until 1512, when the Medici returned to the city. They would continue to rule, with another republican interruption (1527-30), until 1737.

It was during the earlier republican period, 1494-1512, that Machiavelli began a promising career as a public servant. Born into a well-educated Florentine family, he had studied humanities and law.[9] In 1498 he was appointed secretary of the republic's Second Chancery. In that position he was responsible for administrative as well as military matters, but he also spent a good deal of his time on diplomatic missions that would take him all over Italy as well as into France and Germany.

In 1512, however, when the Medici returned to Florence, he lost his appointment. He was even briefly incarcerated and tortured on accusation of conspiracy. He then retreated, with his wife and six children, to a small coun-try estate, Sant'Andrea in Percussina, just on the southern outskirts of Florence. There, he would grow the wine that one can still drink as Chianti Classico Niccolò Machiavelli,[10] and write the books that would make him famous.

Apart from the *Prince* and the *Discourses*, Machiavelli's other main works were *Seven Books on the Art of War* (*Sette libri dell'arte della guerra*, 1521), in which he elaborated on his idea of the superiority of a militia army over the Florentine practice of relying on a hired army of mercenaries; sev-eral plays among which *Mandragola* (1518, published 1524), a comedy on the art of seduction, enjoyed some success; and *Florentine Histories* (*Istorie fiorentine*, usually translated as *History of Florence*, 1525). That the latter work was commissioned by the Medici was a signal that Machiavelli was finally back in princely favour, but, after a brief and not very meaningful return to public life, he died in 1527.

The political history of Renaissance Florence, then, is one of a see-saw, of princely rule interrupted by brief periods of restored republicanism. These, of course, are the two forms of government that are the subject matter of Machiavelli's two main political works, the *Prince* and the *Discourses*. His own career was linked to the republic, and he lost a position that he had obviously cared about when Florence was returned to princely rule in 1512. A lot has been made of the fact, therefore, that he dedicated the *Prince* to the returning Medici. Was he just a political careerist who did not care what form of government prevailed as long as he could have a part in it?

One can doubt whether Machiavelli seriously intended or hoped to write himself back into the services of the Medici. At least he was not willing to sacrifice his opinions for the sake of a job. In a letter dated April 9, 1513, to Francesco Vettori, he writes about his recent predicaments. He mentions his imprisonment and torture by "rope" (*funa*) and then continues to remark how things "frequently turn out differently from the opinions and ideas we have" (*molte volte succedere e casi fuora de' discorsi et concetti che si fanno*). But, he adds, fate and fortune have condemned him to "reason about politics" (*ragionare dello stato*) regardless of the consequences. The only alternative for him would be to "shut up" (*stare cheto*) and remain silent altogether.[11]

Silent he did not remain, and the picture of princely rule painted in the *Prince* is not exactly flattering and was also not so received by the Medici. The higher classes (*grandi*) are always out to "dominate and oppress the people" (*comandare et opprimere el populo*), Machiavelli tells them.[12] The main purpose of the *Prince* is then to call for "a new prince" (*uno nuovo principe*)[13] who will rely on support from the people rather than the nobles because "a prince must always live with the same people, but he can well do without the nobles" (*è necessitato ancora el principe vivere sempre con quello medesimo populo; ma può ben fare sanza quelli medesimi grandi*).[14] In other words, what Machiavelli is telling the returning Medici is that they will be successful only if they change their ways and adopt a new (his!) approach.

Machiavelli's stubborn commitment to what he thinks is the "real truth" of all political matter (*verità effettuale dell cosa*)[15] also permeates his *Florentine Histories*. Since this work was commissioned by the Medici, he duly lavishes praise on the reigns of Cosimo and Lorenzo.[16] But then he cannot abstain from sneaking in what he really thinks about all the Medici glory and splendour. Thus, he writes that during the reign of Lorenzo, whom he describes as "hot with youth and prowess" (*caldo di gioventù e di potenza*),[17] civic attention would be diverted from public affairs to "gaming and women" (*in giuochi e in feminine*).[18] And, due to financial mismanagement, the great Florentine benefactor of the arts would in the end have to be bailed out "by his country with large sums of money" (*che la sua patria di gan somma di danari lo suvvenisse*).[19]

But it is for Cosimo that Machiavelli reserves his most devastating assessment, and he sneaks it in with relish and in a semiclandestine fashion. Just before proceeding to sing Cosimo's praise as the father of the fatherland and as "so extraordinary an individual I was compelled to speak with unusual praise" (*uomo raro ... io sono stato necessitato con modo estraordinario lodarlo*),[20] he embarks upon a seemingly innocent theoretical digression. The "founder of a republic" (*fondatore di una republica*) — meaning Cosimo ascending to power in 1434 — may establish his reputation and influence in two ways, he writes. He can either acquire political leadership the "public way" (*vie publiche*) through battle, conquest, diplomacy, and counsel; or he can rely on private means (*modi privati*) by "conferring benefits to this, that and the other citizen, defending them against the magistrates, supporting them with money, bestowing on them undeserved honours, and by endearing himself to the general population with games and public donations" (*beneficando questo e quell'altro cittadino, defendendolo da' magistrati, suvvenendolo di danari, tirandolo immeritamente agli onori, e con giochi e doni publici gratificandosi la plebe*). And, as Machiavelli continues, while this latter and private method of governing is pernicious because it produces "factions and partisanship" (*sette e i partigiani*), the former and public method is beneficial and avoids such factiousness because "it is founded upon the public good, and not upon private advantage" (*è fondata sopra un bene comune, non sopra un bene privato*).[21]

A page or so later, Machiavelli finally comes to the intended point: Cosimo "chose the latter; for he well knew that, under this form of government, and with the bags filled with the names of his friends, he incurred no risk, and could control his state whenever it suited him" (*... ultimo elesse; perché sapeva bene che in tale modo di governo, per essere le borse piene di suoi amici, egli non correva alcuno pericolo, e come a sua posto poteva il suo stato ripigliare*).[22]

In order to understand what Machiavelli is saying here, we need to take a look at the form of government he was referring to.[23] Florentine republicanism had evolved over the course of several centuries. Essentially, it consisted of the Signoria, an executive group of senior public administrators, and two legislative assemblies: the Council of the People, composed of 300 representatives of the colleges and guilds including the members of the Signoria; and the Council of the Commune, whose members were 40 aristocrats and 160 members of the common classes. New laws, which the councils could not initiate themselves, had to be approved by a two-thirds majority in both legislative assemblies.

This relatively conventional set-up of republican governance was complemented by two rather more distinctive features. One was the so-called scrutiny (*squittino*), the periodic selection of citizens eligible for public office. The names of citizens in good (financial) standing were placed into special "bags" (*borse*) from which office-holders were drawn for usually brief periods of tenure. By means of massive bribery, the Medici interfered with this process and made sure that they had a secure number of loyal friends "in the bag." They also paid off the debts of loyal families who then became eligible for public office.

The other distinctive feature was the special governing councils (*balie*). In essence, these were emergency governments for limited periods of time with powers that could override the two legislative councils. They were frequently established for special purposes and crisis situations such as tax matters or wars. Again, through bribery and political pressure, the Medici made sure, first, that loyal majorities in the legislative councils voted in favour of a requested *balia*; second, that the composition of the *balia* was the one the Medici wanted (through manipulation of the *squittino* and *borse*); and third, that the duration of such established and controlled *balie* was more and more extended, from only a few months to several years.[24]

We can now appreciate the gist of Machiavelli's critique of Medici rule. They never took on political leadership "the public way" but preferred to manipulate the system from behind the scenes with money. Thus, the Medici controlled the government of Florence without ever standing for public office or openly overthrowing its republican form. When they were driven out of Florence in 1494, there were some institutional changes made, such as the creation of an even larger legislative council, the Greater Council of 3,000, but in essence the city reverted to the kind of multifactious style of republican government that had existed before the ascendance of the Medici in 1434.

One of the key questions that preoccupied the former secretary of the republic was precisely this factiousness and instability of the 1494-1512 republic, which ended with the triumphant return of the Medici and Machiavelli's painful expulsion from public life. The usual explanations for the city's see-sawing political fortunes were external. As a major metropolis of trade and finance, Florence always got caught up in European power politics and, ever since the beginning of the battle between pope and emperor back in the Middle Ages, Italy had remained a main focus for territorial rivalry and conquest. Thus, the Medici were driven out of Florence in 1494 because they had made unpopular concessions to the invading army of King Charles VIII of France, and they returned in 1512 in the baggage train of a Spanish army.

Machiavelli himself, at the end of the *Prince*, deplores these "foreign inundations" (*illuvioni esterne*) and expresses hope that it would be up to "a new prince" (*uno principe nuovo*) to liberate Italy from this "barbarous tyranny [that] stinks in everyone's nostrils" (*a ognuno puzza questo barbaro dominio*).[25] However, his analysis of the republic's instability and downfall is a different and domestic one nevertheless: "A corrupted people, having acquired liberty, can maintain it only with the greatest difficulty" (*uno popolo corrotto, venuto in libertà, si può con difficultà grandissima mantenere libero*).[26]

Machavelli, in other words, squarely puts the blame for the instability of the republic on the Medici's preceding regime of disguised power and blatant corruption. And this is the context in which both the *Prince* and the *Discourses* have to be read.

The Prince *(1513)*

The most notoriously infamous book of political theory ever written begins rather innocuously. All states are either republics or principalities, Machiavelli informs the reader, and since he will deal with republics elsewhere, presumably in the *Discourses*, this is his treatise on principalities. What follows are a few chapters on different types of principalities, hereditary or composite (by which he means put together from pre-existing territories). There is also a discussion of the different ways in which principalities can be created or acquired: by conquest, crime, or constitution. Only in the latter case does he speak of a civil regime (by which he means, in obvious reference to Florence, that a prince governs with limited authority either on the basis of popular support or at the helm of an aristocratic regime of nobles).

Machiavelli, in other words, by distinguishing different forms of government, follows a tradition that goes all the way back to Plato and Aristotle. To be sure, there are some blunt observations along the way. For instance, he tells the prince that, once in office, "you cannot keep the friendship of those who have put you there" (*non ti puoi mantenere amici quelli vi ti hanno messo*),[27] but that is hardly an outrageous piece of advice, and certainly not from a modern perspective of government ethics. More controversial perhaps is a statement in conjunction with his advice to rely on popular support rather than support from fellow nobles. This a prince should do not only because he needs the former more than the latter but also because the intentions "of the people are more honest than those of the nobles because the latter want to oppress the people, whereas they only want not to be oppressed" (*perchè quello del populo è più onesto fine che quello de' grandi, volendo questi opprimere, e quello non essere oppresso*).[28] But, then again, Aristotle

79

had already observed similarly that "the encroachments of the rich are more destructive to the constitution than those of the people."[29]

  It is almost halfway through the *Prince* that Machiavelli begins to strike a more drastic note. There is no point, he declares, in giving advice to a prince that is based on "imagination" (*immaginazione*) rather than the "real truth of the matter" (*verità effettuale della cosa*). Many have already written about states, republics, or principalities, "which have never in truth been known to exist" (*che non si sono mai visti né conosciuti essere in vero*). Instead, "because the gulf between how one should live and how one does live is so wide that a man who neglects what is actually done for what should be done learns the way to self-destruction rather than self-preservation" (*perché elli è tanto discosto da come si vive a come si doverrebbe vivere, che colui che lascia quello che si fa per quello che si doverrebbe fare, impara più tosto la ruina che la preservazine sua*), Machiavelli's prince will be instructed to "learn how not to be good, and to make use of this or not according to necessity" (*imparare a potere essere non buono, et usarlo e non usare secondo la necessità*).[30]

  Here it is then, Machiavelli's revolutionary renunciation of the classical focus of political theory on the "ideal" or "best" state, and his turning to what Jürgen Habermas grandly termed a brave new "world demystified by real politics."[31] Was it really so revolutionary, though? Had not Thucydides already reported how the Athenians told the Melians that they didn't give a damn about ethics as long as their actions furthered their own power?[32] And had not Marsilius described even the popes' political conduct as "stealthy double-dealing" (*horum subintrans prevaricacio*)?[33]

  There is a difference, though, and it is this difference that so alarmed contemporaneous as well as later readers of the *Prince*. While historians had always chronicled the abusive behaviour of rulers, political theorists had tried to hold them to ethical standards, and especially so in the so-called princely mirrors of the Christian Middle Ages, to which Machiavelli refers when he writes about princely advice based on imagination rather than reality. The radical break with that tradition in the *Prince* is that political theory is no longer constructed upon a set of metaphysical ethical standards outside the realm of real politics. Instead, what rulers really do when they rule becomes itself the subject matter of political theory. That Machiavelli theorizes about the amorality of successful political behaviour, however, does not necessarily imply that he endorses or likes it.

  In fact, Machiavelli emphasizes again and again that a prince should not only "appear to be compassionate, faithful to his word, kind, guileless, and devout," but that "indeed he should be so" (*parere pietoso, fedele, umano, intero, relligioso, et essere*). But then he also adds that the prince must be prepared and know how to be the opposite because, in order to "maintain his state, he is often forced to act in defiance of good faith, of charity, of kindness, of religion" (*sendo spesso necessitato, per mantenere lo stato, operare contro alla fede, contro alla carità, contro all umanità, contro alla relligione*).[34]

All this comes in the context not of a state of affairs in which the city finds itself at peace, internally and externally, but one that finds it in crisis and therefore requires a prince who is ready to do battle (*combattere*). In principle, Machiavelli explains, there are two ways of fighting: by law, which is natural to men; and by force, which is natural to beasts. The embattled prince, however, must learn to make use of both. And in order to do so, he must learn from the fox and the lion. He must be "a fox in order to recognize traps, and a lion to frighten off wolves" (*golpe a conoscere e' lacci, e lione a sbigottire e' lupi*).[35]

A fox and a lion, perhaps, but not a rabid animal out of control: The conduct of a prince should be "tempered with prudence and humanity" (*temperato con prudenzia e umanità*); it is "safer to be feared than to be loved" only if it is "impossible to be both" (*più securo essere temuto che amato, quando si abbia a mancare dell'uno de' dua*).[36] As far as this fear is concerned, it should always come without hatred, which a prince can easily avoid "if he abstains from the property of his citizens as well as subordinates, and from their women" (*quando si astenga dalla roba de' sua cittadini e de' sua sudditi, e dalle donne loro*).[37] And finally, there is no license to kill: If it "proves necessary to execute someone, this is to be done only when there is proper justification and manifest reason for it" (*bisognassi procedere contro al sangue di alcuno, farlo quando vi sia iustificazione conveniente e causa manifesta*).[38]

A key term to the proper understanding of all this obviously is "necessity" (*necessità*).[39] Since the term crops up in all kinds of contexts and connotations, one might indeed suspect Machiavelli of endorsing some kind of unrestrained political decisionism or *realpolitik* of the worst kind: anything goes as long as the end justifies the means. In fact, however, Machiavelli's understanding of *necessità* can be read more convincingly as achieving the opposite. "I believe," Machiavelli declares towards the end of the *Prince*, "that the one who adapts his policy to the times prospers, and likewise that the one whose policy clashes with the demands of the times does not" (*Credo … che sia felice quello che riscontra el modo del procedere suo con le qualità de' tempi; e similmente sia infelice quello che con il procedere suo si discordano de' tempi*).[40]

This means that, yes, indeed a prince must act decisively and ruthlessly in a crisis situation, and especially so since he will be confronted in such a situation with others who are as deceitful as he must be himself.[41] By the same token, however, this also means that a prince must play by the rules of the book when this is in turn what the "demands of the times" require. From the pages of the *Prince* this may not be readily apparent. It is important to bear in mind, therefore, that the *Prince* must be placed in the context of the *Discourses*, which lay out the causes and conditions calling for princely rule in the first place.

It is in the *Discourses* that Machiavelli not only reiterates that "men should take account of the times, and act accordingly" (*debbono considerare i tempi, e accommodarsi a quegli*),[42] but then goes on to declare that "a republic has a fuller life and enjoys good fortune for a longer time than a principality, since it is better able to adapt itself to diverse circumstances" (*una republica ha maggiore vita, ed ha più lungamente buona fortuna, che uno principato, perché la può meglio acommodarsi alla diversità de' temporali*).[43] Such conditions of republican good fortune can also exist in what Machiavelli calls a constitutional or "civil principality" (*principato civile*).[44] They "come to grief when the transition is being made from limited power to absolutism" (*sogliono questi principati periclitare quando sono per salire dall'ordine civile allo assoluto*).[45]

Act accordingly: This finally brings the discussion of Machiavelli's *Prince* to those two terms which doubtlessly have been the subject matter of the most acrimonious debates and interpretations. At the outset, Machiavelli writes that a prince may succeed in his endeavours "either by fortune or by virtue" (*o per fortuna o per virtù*).[46] The reason for all the fuss is that Machiavelli comments elsewhere that "fortune is a woman and if she is to be submissive it is necessary to beat and coerce her" (*fortuna è donna, et è necessario, volendola tenere sotta, batterla et utarla*),[47] and that he declares that practising what is conventionally called "virtue" may in fact "ruin" a prince (*seguendola sarebbe la ruina sua*).[48] While the first quote not only outs Machiavelli as a sexist,[49] but moreover seems to associate — and condone — princely political conduct with violence and rape, the second quote even more generally appears to repudiate conventional moral virtue altogether as a useful tool in public affairs.

It is possible to arrive at a rather more simple, more accurate, and less contentious explanation of how fortune and virtue interact and complement one another in the context of necessity. "Fortune," Machiavelli explains in a more sober passage, "is the arbiter of half the things we do, leaving the other half or so controlled by ourselves" (*la fortuna sia arbitra della metà delle azioni nostre, ma che etiam lei ne lasci governare l'altra metà, o presso, a noi*).[50] To control that other half is precisely what Machiavelli calls "virtue" (*virtù*) in a political sense. What Machiavelli means by *virtù*, then, is neither just "prowess" nor a generally amoral disposition but instead inspired political leadership recognizing that part of human affairs that can be controlled.

The figure of the "prince" stands for someone who is both "prudent" and a "virtuoso" of politics (*uno prudente e virtuoso*),[51] someone who knows how to take the political initiative for what is necessary in consideration of time and circumstance.

Even the most careful and sympathetic reading of the *Prince* cannot take away the bluntness with which Machiavelli advises a ruler to take charge. Instead of taking on the old moral question of the good life, Machiavelli's *Prince* almost entirely focusses on the technical question of political survival. What such a careful reading can bring to the fore, though, is the conditionality of princely power. The *Prince* is not a "recipe book for the technically correct calculation of power"[52] in an abstract or general sense. Not all states need to be principalities, Machiavelli has told us at the outset, and not always does a principality require a prince to act like a fox and a lion. Nowhere does Machiavelli suggest that politics inevitably and forever comes down to this one general question of survival and therefore requires one and only one political solution. Only Hobbes will make such a radically reductionist suggestion more than a century later.

For the great Florentine realist, the most general problem in politics is something else. "Two different dispositions one can find in every city" (*in ogni città si truovano questi dua umori diversi*), he writes.[53] We already know what they are: that of the people who do not want to be dominated or oppressed, and that of the nobles who are out to dominate and oppress. From these "two appetites" (*dua appetiti*) arise different possibilities for how the affairs of a city may be conducted: by "princely rule, liberty, or anarchy" (*o principato o libertà o licenzia*).[54] The question as to which will prevail and, more importantly, why, is the subject matter of the *Discourses*.

The Discourses (1513-20)

The full title of Machiavelli's main work of political theory is *The Discourses on the First Ten Books of Titus Livius (Discorsi sopra la prima deca di Tito Livio)*. Titus Livius (59 BCE-CE 17), for whatever reason called Livy in English, was a historian at the time of Rome's first emperor, Augustus. Of the 142 books on the history of the "city since its foundation" (*Ab urbe condita libri*), only some 35 have survived. The first 10 chronicle the rise of Rome from its beginning to the height of republican power.

That Machiavelli wrote his main political work as a series of discourses on Livius is not of particular significance in and of itself. The *re-naissance* was so called (much later) because it was a *re-birth* of interest in the classical heritage of antiquity. Comparative references to the classical past abounded in fashion, arts, and science. Before Brunelleschi built his famed dome on top of the cathedral in Florence, he had spent considerable time studying whatever had remained of antique buildings in Rome. Sandro Botticelli's most famous painting was not a Madonna and child but *The Birth of Venus* (1482-86). Michelangelo's *David* (1501) more resembled a naked pagan hero than a symbol of Christian faith.

Machiavelli turned to Livius because he thought that by "comparing ancient with modern events" he could "more easily draw those practical lessons which one should seek to obtain from the study of history" (*secondo le cognizione delle antique e moderne cose...possino più facilmente trarne quella utilità per la quale si debbe cercare la cognizone delle istorie*).[55] He wanted to use the example of the Roman republic as a backdrop for what his *Discourses* really were all about: to prove the superiority of the republican form of government over princely rule, and to explain why the Florentine republic fell and had to revert to princely rule in 1512.

But what exactly does Machiavelli mean by "republican"? When he set out to write the *Discourses*, some significant additional pages to the work of another classical historian of Roman history had just been rediscovered. This historian was Polybios (200-120 BCE), a Greek who had originally been brought to Rome as a hostage of war. Like his compatriot Aristotle before him, Polybios thought that the best possible state was a mixed polity, and he explained the success of republican Rome accordingly, as a system of checks and balances between the consulate (monarchy), senate (aristocracy), and people's assembly (democracy). And that is exactly how Machiavelli would see it, too.

After reiterating the old and venerable assumptions about the different forms and cycles of (good and bad) government,[56] Machiavelli goes on to describe a well-designed city as a mixture of "principality, aristocracy and democracy," each of which "would keep watch over the other" (*perché l'uno guarda l'altro, sendo in una medesima città il Principato, gli Ottimati, e il Governo Popolare*).[57] Thus, he obviously learned from Polybios, and it is this threefold regime of checks and balances that lies at the heart of his republicanism. One can already see quite clearly where his prince fits into this scheme. In a well-functioning republic, this prince is but one part in a balanced system of political institutions. Only when the other two parts fail to play their part will the prince have to come to the rescue all on his own — and that is what that other book, *Il Principe*, is all about.

Polybios did not reflect on how the different parts of a polity or city would represent the interests of different social classes.[58] In this way he departed from the socially embedded political theory of Aristotle.[59] Machiavelli, on the other hand, made social analysis the centrepiece of his political theory: "In every republic," he declares, "there is an upper and a lower class" (*in ogni republica sono uomini grandi e popolari*).[60]

84

Aristotle, we remember, had advanced the idea that political stability depended on a solid middle class which would arbitrate between the opposed interests of rich and poor. His mixed polity was synonymous with a middle-class regime in which the extreme opposites of rich and poor would be neutralized. The best constitution would be a mix of oligarchy and democracy. He never explained with sufficient precision what that mix would look like or how it would come about.

Machiavelli disagrees with the idea of stability in the middle, and, by doing so, adds a new and dynamic dimension to the theory of mixed government. "To find a middle way between the two extremes," he writes, "I do not think possible" (*trovare un modo, mezzo infra l'uno e l'altro, non credo si possa*).[61] And when he comes to this conclusion, he has already put on paper what amounts to his most significant political idea. After reiterating what we already know from the *Prince*, namely that "in every republic there are two different dispositions, that of the populace and that of the upper class" (*sono in ogni republica due umori diversi, quello del popolo, e quello de' grandi*),[62] he declares that "all legislation favourable to liberty is brought about by the clash between them" (*tutte le leggi che si fanno in favore della libertà, nascano dalla disunione loro*).[63] If you come to think of it, this is far more modern and revolutionary than anything Machiavelli has put down in the *Prince*. Liberty is the result of class struggle.[64] Almost in anticipation of Marx's historical dialectics, Machiavelli writes that since "human affairs are ever in a state of flux, they either move upwards or downwards" (*essendo le cose umane sempre in moto, o le salgano, o le scendano*).[65] "All that is solid melts into air" is how the *Communist Manifesto* will put it 300 years later.[66]

In order to understand the enormity of the transformation that Machiavelli assigns to the history of political thought, we need to recapitulate. The idea that the stability and success of a polity depends on a mixed form of government as the expression of class compromise was not new. For Aristotle, it had simply been an observation that a polity would be served best if the antagonism between the rich and poor was bridged by a reflection of democratic and oligarchic interests in the ordinary process of legislation, and that this was most likely to happen in a polity with a large middle class. In the political thought of Marsilius, then, this kind of class compromise had gained constitutional status: The legitimate source of the law was to be a human legislator that included both upper class (*honorabilitas*) and lower class (*vulgus*).

In both instances, the prescriptive purpose inherent in these social ideas of political stability was to quell or avoid altogether the kind of class-based conflict that routinely spelled political ruin. This was a theme well known in Florence as well. It is echoed in Machiavelli's rendering of the famous

Ciompi-riot of cloth workers in 1378 when he has one of the city patricians and *gonfaloniere* (elected government advisers), Luigi Guicciardini, admonish the guild leaders at the beginning of the riot: "Then why would you, by your discords, reduce to slavery in a time of peace, that city, which so many powerful enemies have left free, even in war?" (*Perché volete voi adunque che le vostre discordie quella città, nella pace, faccino serva, la quale tanti nimici potenti hanno, nella guerra, lasciata libera?*).[67]

In the *Discourses*, however, Machiavelli completely disagrees with this view: "I say that those who condemn the tumults between nobles and plebs are in my view blaming the very things that were the primary cause of retaining Rome's liberty" (*Io dico che coloro che dannono i tumulti intra i Nobili e la Plebe, mi pare che biasimino quelle cose che furono prima causa del tenere Roma libera*).[68] And then, after the already quoted assertion that liberty has its foundation in the clash between the two dispositions (*due umori*) that exist in every city,[69] and after describing the way in which republican Rome dealt with these tumults as "striking examples of virtue" (*tanti esempli di virtù*), Machiavelli proceeds to enunciate a political theory of human development and progress that is both profound and startling: "these good examples proceed from good education, good education from good laws, and good laws from those very tumults which so many inconsiderately condemn" (*li buoni esempli nascono dalla buona educazione, la buona educazione dalle buone leggi; e le buone leggi, da quelli tumulti che molti inconsideratamente dannano*).[70]

The theory is profound in its commitment to a dynamic modernity. The human condition is no longer a given. It is instead constructed (or "made" as Vico would have put it) by competing societal forces. This is the essence of republican civic virtue. The theory is startling, however, because if Machiavelli really believes that civic liberty springs from the kind of class-based strife and disorder that so often haunted his native city, then why would order ever have to be restored by the ruthless means of his prince?

The answer to this question once again reveals the dialectical nature of Machiavelli's political thought. Just as the prince must know how to be good and bad, and human history unfolds as a clash between two different dispositions, so can this clash itself lead upward into liberty or downward towards crisis and the loss of liberty. The reason for the latter is political corruption. As Machiavelli explains:

> It is possible, then, to arrive at this conclusion: when the material is not corrupt, tumults and other troubles do no harm, but, when it is corrupt, good legislation is of no avail unless it is initiated by someone in so extremely strong a position that he can enforce obedience until such time as the material has become good. (*E si può fare questa conclusione, che, dove la materia non è corrotta, i tumulti ed altri*

scandoli non nuocono: dove la è corrotta, le leggi bene ordinate non giovano, se già le non sono mosso da uno che con una estrema forza le faccia osservare, tanto che la materia diventi buona.)[71]

It requires only a little imagination to see that this may have been the very moment when Machiavelli put aside the *Discourses* and, by quickly penning the *Prince*, explored the conditions and possibilities, almost as an aside, of how someone in such an "extremely strong position" might succeed in eliminating corruption from the city, and perhaps even from Italy.

We also already know what Machiavelli has in mind when he speaks of corrupt material: the Medicean regime of bribery that seeks to have the entire city "in the bag" but instead only produces "factions and partisanship" (*sette e i partigiani*).[72] And this is not just a problem of a particular city or a particular ruling clan. "Just look at the conduct of human beings," Machiavelli lets one of the ring leaders exclaim in his account of the 1378 Ciompi-riot, "and you will realize that all those who achieve great wealth or great power have done so either through force or fraud" (*noterete il modo del procedere degli uomini, vedrete tutti quelli che a ricchezze grandi e a grande potenza pervengono o con frode o con forza esservi pervenuti*).[73]

There is, in other words, a general and crucial difference between the tumults (*tumulti*) that give timeless and constructive civic expression to the differences of class-based interests, and the factions (*sette*) which the power struggles for personal gain and advantage produce, mostly within the ranks of the higher classes themselves. Moreover, even the tumults that arise over the distribution of material wealth between the "haves" and "have-nots" are "more often than not caused by the 'haves,' since ... men are inclined to think that they cannot hold securely what they possess unless they get more at others' expense" (*più delle volte sono causati da chi possiede, perché ... no pare agli uomini possedere sicuramente quello che l'uomo ha, se non si acquista di nuovo dell'altro*).[74]

Those corporate managers who are told to fancy Machiavelli as a soulmate should take particular note of this passage in the text. It is true, of course, that the great Florentine realist does not really cast moral judgment on the fact that there will always be rich and poor, although he despises those who live in idleness and from the revenues of their estates.[75] But in praising the ancient example of Sparta where the law prescribed "more equality of property and less equality of rank" (*più equalità di sostanze, e meno equalità di grado*),[76] he leaves no doubt that it is excessive social inequality he has in mind when he finally explains how a general state of corruption takes hold of a city and destroys its civic culture: "For corruption of this kind and ineptitude for a free mode of life is due to the inequality one finds in a city"

(*Perché tale corruzione e poca attitudine alla vita libera, nasce da una inequalità che è in quella città*).[77] In the end, only the powerful are in a position to make law, and they do so solely to advance their own cause further.[78] It is a devastating verdict on much more than just the public splendour of the Medici court. Make no mistake, Machiavelli remarks later, "those who talk about the peoples of our day being given up to robbery and similar vices, will find that they are all due to the fact that those who ruled them behaved in like manner" (*chi discorrerà i popoli che ne' nostri tempi sono stati tenuti pieni di ruberie e di simili peccati, vedrà che sarà al tutto nato da quegli che gli governavano, che erano di simile natura*).[79]

When the corruption initiated for personal gain by those with power and money becomes endemic in a city, then, and only then is it time to take steps which are "by no means normal" (*grandissimi straordinari*)[80] — enter the prince. In analogy to ancient Roman practice,[81] however, and quite similar to the Florentine practice of establishing emergency governments (*balie*),[82] such a prince is to take over the reins of government for a limited period of time only: "until such time as the material has become good" (*tanto che la materia diventi buona*).[83]

It would appear, then, from the pages of the *Discourses*, that the whole idea of the *Prince* is but a brief and illusionary digression from Machiavelli's republican theory of politics. He will never come back to it in later works.[84] More than that: From the *Discourses* themselves one can hardly avoid the impression that Machiavelli just barely stops short of renouncing the entire idea of a prince coming to the rescue as not much more than a desperate flight of fancy with little hope for success. He even explicitly puts himself at odds with his venerated source, Titus Livius, when he sums up what the comparative analysis of republican Rome and contemporary Florence ultimately yields: "government by the people is better than government by princes" (*sono migliori governi quegli de' popoli, che quegli de' principi*).[85] And the reason given is the same that he might have already found in Aristotle and Marsilius:

> A republic has a fuller life and enjoys good fortune for a longer time than a principality, since it is better able to adapt itself to diverse circumstances owing to the diversity found among its citizens than a prince can do. (*Una republica ha maggiore vita, ed ha più lungamente buona fortuna, che uno principato, perché la può meglio accomodarsi alla diversità de' temporali, per la diversità de' cittadini che sono in quella, che non può uno principe.*)[86]

There is no doubt in Machiavelli's mind that the healthy plurality of a republican civic culture is preferable to the solitary machinations of even the most cunning fox and lion.

Critical Evaluation

How do we evaluate Machiavelli against himself? Most latter-day inter-preters do not even bother. On the one hand, there are nicely balanced accounts such as Quentin Skinner's, who puts the "adviser to princes" side by side with the "theorist of liberty," and who also pays due respect to the military thinker.[87] The princely turn in Machiavelli's thought in these accounts is usually explained, in Machiavelli's own terms, by the necessity of time and circumstance: the return of the Medici in 1512, and his need for a job. Little if any effort is made at trying to see the *Prince* and the *Discourses* as two sides of one and the same coin.

On the other hand, there are those interpretations that largely focus on only one side of the coin to begin with. Machiavelli then becomes the theo-rist of an "economy of violence" at the hands of a prince committed to the "'pure' use of power, undefiled by pride, ambition, or motives of petty revenge."[88] From these interpretations Machiavelli emerges as the technician of survival, and his political theory as one of pure politics (or *realpolitik*) detached from socioeconomic conditions and moral impositions alike.

Finally, there are the very few who look only at the other side of the coin. Bernard Crick, in an introduction to the *Discourses* that is of unparalleled elegance and insight, goes as far as to suggest that at the core of Machiavelli's political thought lies the idea of civic virtue or "active citizenship." Such citi-zenship, Crick continues, may be "one of the factors shaping the modern world as are bureaucracy, land and the peasantry, and industrialism."[89] From that perspective, the *Prince* almost appears as a tragic renunciation of Machiavelli's republican idealism, a pessimistic turn comparable to Plato's descent from the lofty heights of his philosopher-king idealism in his *Politeia* to the lowlands of pedantic law enforcement in the *Nomoi*.

Yet, Crick also opens up a possible path to synthesis. Machiavelli "chal-lenges the whole traditional view that morality must be of one piece," he writes, and then comes to the conclusion that the "many different and fervid interpretations of Machiavelli's 'real meaning' [are] all designed to evade this awkward duality, this ultimate incoherence, not in Machiavelli, but in our whole culture — perhaps in the nature of things."[90]

The "real" Machiavelli, in other words, is the one who gives expression to the dialectics of human nature, history, and politics. In the *Discourses*, he explores the conditions that maintain or destroy republican liberty. There can be no doubt that he believed that a regime of republican liberty was a possibility. If anything else, his turn to the *Prince* was meant to demonstrate the fragility of such liberty. The checks and balances only work when the sys-tem is not corrupted by those with power and money. Excessive inequality destroys the republican balance of powers.

When that happens, only a princely regime can rescue the state. This uncomfortable truth is not at all an endorsement of political action in the name of some abstract reason of state. It can in fact be read as the exact opposite, a blunt reminder that political liberty and social justice are inextricably linked. The question of democracy or dictatorship primarily becomes one of material equality or excessive inequality. The question of the presence or absence of institutional formalities such as elections, while important, takes second place.

Machiavelli was not a democrat, of course. His ideal of a republican mixed constitution was one in which the cards were stacked in favour of the higher classes even though the lower classes were not entirely powerless. "If the blueprint for the mixed constitution is captured in the formula 'one-few-many,'" Alois Riklin writes about republican Rome, then the reality was "a mixture of few and many with superiority of the few."[91] So it was in Machiavelli's model of good governance in republican Florence.

This opens the door to a more disturbing interpretation of how the *Prince* and the *Discourses* might fit together: The mixed constitution is an attempt to preserve existing class relations by stabilizing social conflict with the illusion of broad political participation, however limited.[92] The adherence to a mixed regime of governance in this sense serves as an ideological tool for the exercise of hegemonic control. When the ruling classes become too divided by their own corruption and greed, however, and inequality becomes excessive, the masses begin to question the legitimacy of the system. They then become corrupted themselves by ideas of greed and revolutionary action, like that leader of the Ciompi-riot whom Machiavelli also reports as calling for plunder and pillage because only "small crimes are punished but the big and serious ones are rewarded" (*i falli piccoli si puniscono, i grandi e gravi si premiano*).[93] The only way to stabilize the system then, when the higher and more powerful classes (*grandi e potenti*) have lost hegemonic control, is by dictatorship. This, incidentally, is also how another great Italian thinker and student of Machiavelli, Antonio Gramsci, explained the rise of Italian fascism in the twentieth century.[94]

Machiavelli provided the history of political thought with a merciless analysis of corruption and inequality as the conditions from which arises the necessity of princely rule. This analysis goes a long way in explaining the inevitability of dictatorship in many parts of the modern world that have yet to see the rise of a solid middle class. Machiavelli's equation of skewed republican class relations with civic virtue and liberty, on the other hand, disturbingly raises the question as to what extent modern democracy is in fact grounded in more than just temporary success on the part of those with power and money. For Machiavelli, this would be success in manufacturing consent and compliance, not via media control as Noam Chomsky's most notoriously famous treatise suggests,[95] but through the institutions of republican checks and balances themselves, as the American Federalists understood full well when they defended their new constitution.[96] Indeed, Machiavelli may come closest to his reputation as a merciless analyst of *realpolitik* when he suggests that republican checks and balances, then and now, more likely invoke an "imagination" *(immaginazione)* of democracy than a democracy that is real *(effettuale)*.

Machiavelli's dialectical views of human nature and politics allowed him to remain an optimist at heart. There is in the *Discourses* enough of the old faith in the practical reasonableness of the people that precludes it from seeing its author as only a cynical advocate of autocratic leadership. Like Gramsci, who was a communist but opposed to the bureaucratic centralism of official Marxism-Leninism, Machiavelli remained committed to the traditional and Aristotelian view according to which a plurality of ideas and social forces serves people better than the uniformity of one idea and one universal solution. Only Hobbes, confronted with a much more calamitous world than Machiavelli could ever have imagined, would give political theory its decisive pessimistic turn by renouncing this Aristotelian heritage as naive and erroneous.

CHAPTER 6

Sovereignty
Hobbes v. Althusius

It should have been an exciting time of optimism and progress. Humanism and the Renaissance had opened up enormous new resources in arts and science, and in individual human ingenuity more generally. It led Columbus to discover the New World of the Americas. The Reformation added a new faith in individual conscience and responsibility. Aspiring to make a good living on earth no longer meant forfeiting a better life to come.

Yet this age of transition, from the old scholasticism to the new science, and from Christian universalism to a diversity of states and faiths, turned out to be a traumatic experience of instability, cruelty, and war. Unspeakable crimes were committed against the Native peoples of the Americas out of greed for their treasures. Even so, all the Mexican silver was not enough to prevent belligerent statecraft from running into bankruptcy. And on the home front, while the Inquisition raged in the Catholic countries, religious wars devastated most others in which Protestantism had spread. The crimes against humanity that had once been reserved for crusades against the infidel were now committed against fellow Christians as well.

Even though he lived a long life of relative comfort and privilege among the educated, rich, and powerful of his age, Thomas Hobbes wrote, when he was 63, that life was "solitary, poore, nasty, brutish, and short."[1] And in 1672, when he was 84, he rhymed, in a curious autobiographic poem written in Latin, about being born prematurely when his mother received the shocking news of the Spanish Armada sailing up the English Channel:

> And hereupon it was my Mother Dear
> Did bring forth Twins at once, both Me, and Fear.
> (*Atq; metum tantum concepit tunc mea mater,*
> *Ut pareret geminos, méque metúmque simul.*)[2]

93

Context

Fortune is fickle. In 1519 Charles V was elected to become ruler of the Holy Roman Empire, the largest realm in existence since the days of ancient Rome. Only a couple of years later, however, at the Imperial Diet at Worms in 1521,[3] he had to deal with a rebellious monk who would in due course smash the Empire to pieces. That monk was Martin Luther (1483-1546), who had intended nothing more than to invite a scholarly disputation about church corruption, but who now, summoned to appear before the emperor, stubbornly refused to recant. With his life in danger by the resulting imperial ban, Luther took his famous refuge at the Wartburg castle where he used his time to translate the New Testament into German. That was probably his most revolutionary deed, as it wrested from the clergy the (Latin) monopoly of biblical interpretation and opened the door to an individual (vernacular) Christian conscience.

Charles was obsessed with the preservation of both the idea and the reality of a universal Christian empire. Yet, he would be the last emperor to be crowned by the pope. For years preoccupied with warfare against his main rival, Francis I, the king of France, he only found time to take on the German Protestants in 1547, soundly defeating them in the battle of Mühlberg. But it was too late. Luther's initial action had caused a chain reaction that could no longer be stopped.

In Germany, the territorial princes quickly learned to exploit the issue of religious faith as an ideological boost in their quest for sovereignty. As sanctioned by the *cuius regio eius religio* (whose land, his religion) formula of the 1555 Augsburg Religious Peace Treaty, they gained the right to determine the officially sanctioned religion in the lands they owned and ruled. Caught in the maelstrom of continuing dynastic rivalries, however, the Protestant and Catholic German territories eventually became the main theatre for one of the longest and bloodiest wars of all time, the Thirty Years War, 1618-48. This was the first war of a truly European dimension, with losses of up to 40 per cent of some of the involved populations. Its outcome, as recorded in the Westphalian Peace Treaties of Münster and Osnabrück, only confirmed what had already been written on the wall at the beginning of the war: the disaggregation of the Empire into a new system of territorial states defined by sovereign physical, as well as religious, boundaries. In that vein, the Westphalian Peace Treaties also sanctioned the successful revolt of the Reformed Netherlands against Catholic Spain.

In France, it was Calvin's Reformed brand of Protestantism that began to divide what had already become a much more consolidated nation than existed in Germany or Italy. As elsewhere, however, the domestic conflict over faith quickly became intertwined with foreign policy schemes. The

Catholics received financial support from Spain, the Reformed Huguenots from England. Nearly 40 years of intermittent religious warfare ensued after a first attack on Huguenot worshippers in 1562. But nothing would compare to the infamous St. Bartholomew Day Massacre of 1572 when as many as 20,000 Huguenots perished in a frenzy of killing that lasted several days and lingered on for weeks. This was the first modern mass murder with broad public support. It not only divided the nation, it also divided the thinking.

"On the morrow of Saint Bartholomew," wrote Harold Laski, "Europe awoke to a new epoch in the history of its political doctrines."[4] On the one hand, it produced the radical literature of the so-called monarchomachs, who openly called for, and theoretically tried to justify, tyrannicide as a form of self-defence against religious suppression.[5] On the other hand, it brought forth the first political theory of absolutism, by Jean Bodin, who defined sovereignty as "absolute and perpetual power" (*puissance absolue & perpetuelle*), or, in the Latin version, as the "ultimate power over citizens and not bound by its own laws" (*summa in cives legibusque soluta potestas*).[6]

Across the Channel in England, the Reformation would result in the most profound transformation yet. Henry VIII had broken with Rome (1534) and created the Church of England with himself as its head because the pope would not grant him a divorce. Protestantism was not foremost on his mind: self-aggrandizement was. The eventual consolidation of the Church of England as a hierarchical state church under the reign of Elizabeth I (1558-1603) did not satisfy the more radical Protestant aspirations of the Puritans, who either wanted to rid the church of its top-heavy structure (the Presbyterians), or even rejected any kind of church constitution in favour of radical congregationalist autonomy (the Independents).

By the time the English Civil War broke out in 1642, however, religious dissent had long since become intertwined with economic interest. The Puritans in Parliament not only wanted church reform, they also represented a new class of commercial interests opposed to traditional royal privilege. The country was even divided geographically: While the king's support mainly came from rural and economically backward areas in the north and west, Parliament drew its strength from the economically advanced south and east, with London already acting as the commercial and trading centre of it all.[7]

Parliament won. Oliver Cromwell's army of Independents first defeated the king's army of Cavaliers in 1644. Other successful battles followed with Cromwell now leading the New Model Army. In 1648 Cromwell expelled the Presbyterians from Parliament and continued to govern with what was now called the Rump Parliament. It was under this Parliament that Charles I was executed a year later, in 1649, and the monarchy was replaced with the Commonwealth of England. This was also when the revolution turned conservative. Cromwell became Lord Protector with quasi-monarchical powers at the helm of what was not much more than a military dictatorship. He began to suppress the Levellers, a more radical faction among the Independents seeking not only religious freedom but economic and political equality as well.

In the end, the monarchy was restored in 1660. Eventually, after the (mostly but not entirely bloodless) Glorious Revolution of 1688, it became a constitutional monarchy in which the king could no longer govern arbitrarily and without the consent of Parliament in most matters. Yet, the Glorious Revolution was also a victory of traditional class interests.[8] The propertied classes, who had fought each other for the better part of a century over who should get the larger piece of the pie, now made a deal with the monarchy in order to avoid more socially radical consequences. Radical dissenters, religious or otherwise, remained sidelined if not outright suppressed.

It was at the height of revolutionary and military action at the time of Charles's execution and Cromwell's final victory over the royalist Scots at Dunbar (1651) that Thomas Hobbes would give to the world a book of political theory with the most awesome title of them all: *Leviathan*.

Thomas Hobbes (1588-1679)

The Spanish Armada was soundly defeated, by bad weather as much as by the English fleet. More traumatic for the life of young Thomas Hobbes was probably the fact that his father was a drunk who abandoned his family. Hobbes's education was secured by an uncle. He studied at Oxford and, after graduation in 1608, became first tutor and then secretary of William Cavendish, Earl of Devonshire. For someone of rather humble origin this was a considerable piece of luck. He and the earl went hunting together. But as it had become customary for young gentlemen to include extended travels in their education, Hobbes was also to spend years touring the continent where his aristocratic companion helped open the doors to an extraordinary intellectual awakening. In Paris, Hobbes met Descartes and other leading philosophers; in Florence, he visited Galileo; in Venice and Rome, he dined and conversed with statesmen and bishops.[9] Back home, he also served briefly as a secretary to Francis Bacon. With few interruptions Hobbes would remain in the service of the Cavendishes for all of his long life.[10]

In 1640, with the parliamentary forces in ascendance and open hostilities only a matter of time, Hobbes, who was known for his royalist position, fled to Paris. There, amidst Europe's leading philosophers, he led a scholarly life. He briefly (1646-48) became the math tutor of the exiled Prince of Wales, the future King Charles II, and he wrote his main political works, *On the Citizen* (*De Cive*) and *Leviathan*. The composition of the latter work coincided with the final phase of the civil war and Cromwell's victory, and there was a perception that Hobbes had switched sides by accepting parliamentary sovereignty as an alternative to monarchy. Since the *Leviathan* also contained open and harsh condemnation of the papal church, his position both at Charles's court and in Catholic Paris more generally became untenable, and so in 1651 he returned to what had by now become Cromwell's English commonwealth.

This in turn would get him into trouble with the royalists after the restoration of 1660. But it seems that the restored monarch himself, Charles II, continued to value Hobbes's intellectual qualities and even bestowed upon him a small annuity. He lived on the Cavendish estates, in London and Derbyshire, which provided him with a sheltered environment for his remaining years, allowing him a comfortable lifestyle that apart from studying and writing also included playing tennis and smoking his pipe. He died in his ninety-second year at Hardwick, on the premises of his lifelong benefactors who did all they could to ease his last weeks and days, and who buried him almost as if he was one of their own.

Thomas Hobbes was not a turncoat at all. In fact, while engaging in a great variety of intellectual endeavours that included translations of Thucydides and Homer, as well as mathematics, geometry, and the rest of the sciences, his political doctrine, rewritten three times, first in *Elements of Law* (1640), then in *Citizen* (1642), and finally in *Leviathan* (1651), was essentially to remain the same. This doctrine was grounded in a fierce renunciation of everything Aristotelian, and especially so of anything that smacked of power-sharing, leave alone a mixed republican regime. "A Kingdome divided in it selfe cannot stand," he exclaims in *Leviathan*,[11] obviously reflecting on the power struggle between the king and Parliament in wartorn England, and, after providing a definition of sovereignty much like Bodin's ("incommunicable and inseparable"),[12] he qualifies it even further by asserting that "all Governments, which men are bound to obey, are Simple, and Absolute."[13]

What is interesting and makes the political thought of Hobbes so remarkable is not his unwavering turn to absolutism but the way in which he deduced both its necessity and foundation. This will briefly return our discussion to methodology. Hobbes's studies at Oxford had still been steeped in Aristotelian metaphysics. During his continental sojourns, however, he had become exposed to the new science of Galileo and Descartes. We remember how the Neapolitan philosopher Giordano Bruno had already challenged the old cosmological understanding of the universe by claiming that man was but a microcosm of that universe, and how Galileo had replaced the old Aristotelian cosmology with a world view based on mathematical calculation of its parts.[14]

Hobbes was particularly impressed by Galileo, and in his first major scientific-political treatise, *Elements of Law*, begun shortly after his visit to Florence in 1636, he writes that "the original and summ of Knowledge stands thus: there is nothing that truly exists in the world but single and individuall Bodyes producing single and individuall acts or effects."[15] One can almost hear a sigh of relief through these lines, alongside the arrogant confidence of the newly converted: No longer was it necessary to come to a judgment about the vagaries of warring parties and changing coalitions through moral reasoning of right and wrong, leave alone through a qualitative assessment of their shifting collective passions and desires. Instead, the situation could simply be assessed as a clash of individual interests in social orbit. If it was possible to tame and control these individual human particles, peace and order could be restored.

It has often been asked where Hobbes got his pessimistic view of human nature from, a view in which "man is man's wolf" (*Homo homini Lupus*),[16] and, accordingly, the state of nature is characterized as "that condition which is called Warre; and as such a warre, as is of every man, against every man."[17] The most provocative explanation has been that of C.B. Macpherson. He claimed, with considerable textual evidence, that Hobbes was in fact describing not a fictitious state of nature but a vicious early-modern capitalist society in England, with the civil war primarily a war fought over economic advantage. In particular, this interpretation points to Hobbes's later work on the civil war, *Behemoth*, in which he characterizes the war as one among "mortal enemies": between "merchants, whose profession is their private gain," and the government of the king, whose profession is to raise taxes for the common good.[18]

But while this interpretation seems entirely plausible, one can also and far less controversially point to Hobbes's scientific conversion as a main source for his understanding of human nature. Man functions much like a machine put together from different parts, he writes in the introduction to *Leviathan*, and the state is only an aggregation of such men, an "Artificiall Man," as it were. In the state of nature, however, before being put together like a clock, society moves by random movements of its parts, "by chance," as he says in *On the Citizen*,[19] and therefore needs to be forcefully put in order if chaos is to be avoided. A body only comes to rest, Hobbes notes, when "somewhat els stay it."[20]

At that, Hobbes's ideas of human nature are not even particularly pessimistic. He simply transposed the new physical science onto human affairs. Action equals reaction (*actio est reactio*), as his countryman Isaac Newton would define one of the fundamental axioms of physics a few years later. To adopt such an axiom as the basis for the understanding of human affairs was indeed a renunciation of Aristotle, who had carefully distinguished between *episteme*, exact knowledge in the sciences, and *phronesis*, the only kind of practical wisdom available in the arts and, therefore, politics. One can find such an understanding of human affairs catastrophically reductionist, but it certainly appears well in line with the new selfish individualism of the age, capitalist or otherwise. In different reincarnations, it reverberates throughout the entire modern age, from assumptions about the iron law of supply and demand down to the view of the world as a zero-sum game of rational choice.[21]

Everything else in Hobbes is a perfectly logical deduction from these first assumptions. In a clock, all motion is controlled by whoever has the key to wind the central spring. No other part, or combination of other parts, can be allowed to move autonomously. "Factions are the source of sedition and civil war" (*ex factionibus seditio & bellum*), Hobbes comments on parliamentary proceedings: "When a faction is short of votes but superior or not much inferior in strength, then they try to get by arms what they could not get by eloquence and intrigue" (*Quando autem factio sufragiis minor, viribus maior vel non multo minor est, tunc quod eloquentiâ & arte obtiunere non potuere, id armis tentant*).[22]

For the same reason, the idea of a mixed republic with shared powers among the king, the magnates, and the people is rejected out of hand: "If this condition could actually exist, it would not advance the liberty of the people at all. For as long as they are all in agreement with each other, the subjection of individual citizens is as great as it could possibly be; but if they disagree, civil war returns" (*Quod si fieri posset, vt huiusmodi status existeret, nihilo magis ciuium libertati consultum esset. Quamdiu enim omnes consentiunt inter se, subiectio singulorum ciuium tanta est, vt maior esse no possit; sed si dissentiant, bellum ciuile reducitur*).[23]

Hobbes, in other words, has no sense whatsoever for deliberation and compromise in politics, and he certainly resents even the possibility of open social conflict. At one point in *Leviathan*, he even seems to lash out explicitly against Machiavelli in this regard. We remember that Machiavelli had surmised, from his studies of republican Rome, that liberty can spring from social tumults (*tumulti*) in a society—as long as that society is not tainted by corruption and excessive inequality. "Writers [who] have grounded their Civill doctrine, on the opinion of the Romans," Hobbes appears to retort, "have gotten a habit (under a falseshew of Liberty), of favouring tumults, and of licentious controlling the actions of their Soveraigns; and again of controlling those controllers, with the effusion of so much blood."[24]

What becomes quite clear from this passage is, firstly, that despite the Magna Charta, the old continental tradition of mixed regimes and republican institutions had remained quite alien to politics and political minds in

England, and that, secondly, the bloody events of the civil war were interpreted by Hobbes as the consequence of political developments that at least seemed to emulate conditions of republican power-sharing. His views may have also been reinforced by his witnessing, in France, the so-called *Fronde* (1648-53), a period of political and social unrest that began as an attempt on the part of the nobility and parliaments to curb royal powers but ended in mob riots, factionism, and the resolve, on the part of the monarchy, to strengthen absolute rule even further.

Machiavelli, of course, had linked the destructive force of social conflict to corruption and inequality. Strangely, even though he castigated the new merchant class in Puritan England as interested only in the "glory" of growing "excessively rich,"[25] Hobbes never gave serious thought to the social underpinnings of political power and conflict. Thus, if Machiavelli had argued that civic virtue came from the kind of good education that in turn was the result of class conflict and legislative compromise, Hobbes obviously had to ground his quest for civic stability in a different kind of theory.

Since human beings have no natural instinct for forming communities, with their interactions in the state of nature happening by chance rather than natural inclination, Hobbes insists that "man is made fit for Society not by nature, but by training" (*Ad Societatem ergo homo aptus, non naturâ sed disciplinâ factus est*).[26] The purpose of such training or discipline is to find a way as certain as geometry by which "ambition and greed, whose power rests on the false opinions of the common people about right and wrong, would be disarmed" (*ambitio & auaritio quarum potentia falsis vulgi circa ius & iniuriam opinionibus innititur, inermes essent*).[27]

And now it comes, the great fictitious leap of faith that marks the beginning of the so-called social contract tradition: Somehow all citizens must be brought to enter into a contract or covenant whereby they all volunteer to renounce their own vulgar understandings of right and wrong in order to "conferre all their power and strength upon one Man, or Assembly of men, that may reduce all their Wills, by plurality of voices, unto one Will."[28] The loaded meaning of this one sentence, by which Hobbes sums up the foundational act of the commonwealth = leviathan, is extraordinary indeed. First of all, even though Hobbes later talks about "the consent of the People assembled,"[29] and further qualifies consent as that of the "major part,"[30] there is no indication as to how, on the basis of their vulgar opinions, the common people would ever do such a thing. There is, in other words, no indication of how exactly that transition from state of nature to civil society might come about. Deliberation and compromise, as we already know, are certainly out of the question. The conferral of power is simply assumed as a rational act by human beings who are anything but rational.[31]

Secondly, what Hobbes is talking about is not a social contract at all. It is a contract of state, or a governmental contract. Its purpose is not a pledge to live together in mutual harmony but a commitment to establish a common power, which then becomes the guarantor of a society that is held to behave in a civil manner. Hobbes is quite adamant about emphasizing that a mere covenanted pledge of joining together is quite useless unless it includes the creation of a "Common Power, to keep them in awe, and to direct their actions to the Common Benefit."[32] In one way, this is quite commonsensical: a pledge to stop at red traffic lights only works when there are sanctions against violations. In another way, however, as a grand theory of civil society, it is also quite reductionist: Hobbes's prior assumptions about human nature do not allow for the possibility that human beings might simply get together and agree on something.

Thirdly, this one formulation, "reduce all their Wills ... unto one Will," also reveals what it is that the power of the leviathan is ultimately to achieve. In his rejection of traditional Aristotelian moral philosophy and the quest for scientific certitude, Hobbes wants to establish a public ideology and political language of what is officially sanctioned as right and wrong, good and bad. This is what got him into trouble with the royalist and church establishments because what it amounts to is an endorsement of some sort of civic religion. One can even read it as a plea for religious toleration, because once it is clear that there is only one official truth about right and wrong in the state, it no longer matters what people believe or worship privately.

The problem with this core idea in Hobbes's political theory is not that it recommends the creation of a binding and universal set of norms for public discourse and, consequently, behaviour. This part of his recommendation is in fact entirely consistent with modern lawful statehood under which citizens have a common understanding of liberties and sanctions. It is also in line with England's tradition of habeas corpus, which had become a matter of dispute during the seventeenth century when the Stuart kings arbitrarily pressed monies from citizens and threw them into prison without trial if they refused to pay. The Habeas Corpus Amendment Act of 1679 restored legal limits on royal action and laid the groundwork for the modern understanding of the rule of law.

The problem lies elsewhere, in the creation of "unlimited ideological authority"[33] unrestrained by any kind of public discourse or control. Not only does the "great Leviathan" thus created have "so much Power and Strength conferred on him, that by terror thereof, he is inabled [read: enabled] to (con)forme the wills of them all."[34] As the simple and absolute sovereign, he is also beyond reproach: The covenant/contract, once established, cannot be altered without his permission.[35] He cannot be accused of injustice; he is the judge of all public opinion and action and makes all the rules pertaining to public life. He is both legislator and judge, and he appoints all ministers and public servants.[36] And, because sovereignty has been established, however fictitiously by the consenting voices of the majority, the minority of dissenters must now consent as well, or be "destroyed by the rest."[37]

The absolute power of the "great Leviathan," in other words, requires absolute unity and conformity on the part of the civil society it commands. At the same time, as has been noted, Hobbes is "surprisingly liberal."[38] Because it is impossible to regulate everything, it follows that "in all kinds of actions, by the laws praetermitted, men have the Liberty, of doing what their own reasons shall suggest, for the most profitable to themselves."[39] But this is an authoritarian brand of liberalism. The sovereign alone determines the extent to which something is praetermitted by the laws — or not.

It is the end of Aristotelianism indeed. In his concluding polemical attack on the "Darknesse from Vain Philosophy, and Fabulous Traditions," Hobbes bluntly rejects all historical experience and practical prudence as an exercise in useless frustration. Only the kind of reasoning that is based on exact measurement like geometry is true philosophy and produces "generall, eternall, and immutable Truth."[40] It is at that a grandly deductivist truth. Everything is seen and judged from the vantage point of that one first principle that power must never be divided. Therefore, there is no real difference between monarchy and tyranny. Tyranny is just another word for the same thing, used by those who are "discontented under Monarchy."[41]

Therefore also, Hobbes can make peace with the idea of government by assembly — as long as that assembly is as absolutely sovereign as a monarch. This despite some lingering doubts as to whether such a sovereign assembly can provide unity of action when its members might put private before public interest. Monarchy therefore remains preferable as a matter of "Convenience, or Aptitude to produce the Peace," because only in a monarchy "the private interest is the same with the publique."[42]

Hobbes may have made his peace with England's first experiment in government by assembly, but he most certainly disagreed with the arguments made in its defence. In a most revealing passage, he attacks one of the key principles forwarded against monarchical absolutism according to which kings are superior to any individual part of their realm (*"singulis majores"*) but remain subordinate to the collective will of the realm as a whole (*"Universis minores"*).[43] This was an old principle.[44] It had already been the key argument against papal supremacy in the church council movement of the fifteenth century.[45] A century later, it had prominently resurfaced as an argument against religious suppression in Protestant political thought.[46] This is how it came to England. The Presbyterian radical and Scottish commissioner to the

Westminster assembly, Samuel Rutherford (1600-61), used it in his famous *The Law and the Prince* (*Lex, Rex*, 1644) in order to argue that kings had their sovereignty from the people rather than holding it by divine right.[47]

It was a principle and argument widely used by parliamentarian writers during the English revolution,[48] and it was the one Hobbes took on with relish and considerable sophistry. "There is little ground for the opinion of them, that say of Soveraign Kings, though they be *singulis majores*, of greater Power than everyone of their Subjects, yet they be *Universis minores*, of lesse power than them all together," he scoffs. It is outright "absurd" to argue, he continues, that the sovereign should be subordinate to "them all together" when that is exactly what the sovereign is: "them all together" in a "collective body as one person." And he adds, not without some undertone of snickering, that "they" can obviously see this absurdity in the case of a sovereign assembly, because "they" will obviously want to see themselves, in assembly, as being "all together," but "in a Monarch they see it not; and yet the power of Sovereignty is the same in whomsoever it be placed."[49]

Maybe this is why the Stuarts made their peace with Hobbes when the monarchy was restored in 1660, and Rutherford's *Lex, Rex* was ordered to be burnt. Rutherford knew well that monarchy and tyranny were not just different names for the same thing. "Every tyrant is a furious man, and is morally distracted," he had exclaimed in *Lex, Rex*.[50] As evidence, he cited the political theory of a fellow Protestant who had argued 30 years earlier, in a book of politics that was among the most widely read in Reformed circles, *Politica Methodice Digesta*,[51] that the "people only has a conditional obligation to obey" (*populus vero conditionaliter est obligatus ad obtemperandum*), and that this conditionality had its foundation "in the nature of the contract between people and ruler" (*ex natura pacti inter magistratum & populum*).[52] This fellow Protestant was the German Johannes Althusius who, according to the programmatic title of his book, was ever so intent as Hobbes to provide his readers with a political theory "set forth methodically" (*methodice digesta*). But his was a method very different from that of the Englishman. And so was the result.

Johannes Althusius (1557-1638)

Born of peasant stock in a small village in the Reformed part of Germany, Johannes Althusius nevertheless received the kind of education normally unavailable to someone of such modest background. Sponsored by his territorial lord, the Count of Sayn-Wittgenstein, he studied in various places including the University of Cologne, and in Calvinist Geneva, which had become a gathering place for prominent Huguenots who had fled France after the St. Bartholomew Day Massacre. In 1586 Althusius became a doctor of both laws (canon and civil) at the University of Basel, and in the same year he was appointed, first as instructor and then as professor of law, at the *Hohe Schule* (academic school) of Herborn.[53]

At the time, Herborn was one of the most remarkable places of learning in all of Europe. The school had been founded in 1584 by Johan the Elder, Count of Nassau-Dillenburg, a brother of William of Orange, the slain hero of the Dutch Revolt against Spain. The student body was international, including Germans, English, Scots, French, Dutch, and Poles. The curriculum included jurisprudence, philosophy, classical languages, and medicine. Everyone had to attend church sermons several times a week, a particular chore for the medical students who also had to go out collecting medicinal herbs in the vicinity of the city twice a week.

The main purpose of the school, however, was to provide a European centre of learning and scholarship for political Calvinism, or, as it was specifically termed at Herborn, "federal theology." At the heart of this doctrine was a radical reinterpretation of the biblical story of the Exodus and the pact or covenant (Latin: *fedus*) between God, Moses, and the tribes of Israel. Reformed theologians at Herborn (and elsewhere) argued that God had entered into this covenant not only with the kings of Israel but also and directly with the people themselves.[54] Therefore, there existed a second covenant with mutual obligations between the rulers and the people. From this, they deduced a right of resistance against rulers who did not uphold their part of the mutual obligation, and this obligation obviously included respect for, and toleration of, the people's particular version of the Christian faith.

It was during his tenure at Herborn that Althusius published the first edition of his political theory in 1603. The lengthy title, *Politica, methodice digesta et exemplis sacris et profanis illustrata* (*Politics, methodically set forth and illustrated with religious and secular examples*),[55] is important and programmatic because it was indeed Althusius's ambition to separate, in method and content, politics and political science from other disciplines, such as theology and jurisprudence in particular. The numerous examples drawn from the Bible and secular juridical texts were in this sense really meant as illustrations that would not affect the construction of political theory proper. This insistence on political science as an independent discipline got Althusius into particular trouble with the theological university establishment because it constituted a direct attack on "federal theology" as a doctrine that would derive justification for political action from theological argument and interpretation.

Theologians and jurists routinely use arguments "improper and alien to political doctrine" (*impertinentia & aliena ad ... doctrinam politicam*), Althusius thunders in the preface to the 1603 edition.[56] Political science, he continues, is about "how consociation, human society, and social life may be established and conserved for our good by useful, appropriate, and necessary means" (*ut consociatio, humanave societas & vita socialis bono nostro instituatur & conservetur mediis ad hoc ipsum aptis, utilibus & necessariis*). And he adds: "The political scientist properly teaches what are the sources of sovereignty, and inquires and determines what may be essential for the constituting of a commonwealth" (*Politicus enim recte quid & quae sint capita majestatis docet, atque quid ad Rempublicam constituendam essentiale sit, inquirit & judicat*).[57] While the theologian's lectures on Christian piety and charity are "useless and alien to this art" (*supervacua in hac arte & aliena*), the jurist would "overstep his professional boundaries" (*a sua professione aliena tradidit*) if he did more than "treat accurately of the law that arises from the sources of sovereignty and the contract entered into between the people and the prince" (*ex hisce majestatis capitibus initoque contractu inter populum & principem jus oriatur, accurate disserit*).

Once this alien material has been eliminated, Althusius insists, it becomes clear what the proper study of politics reveals: that the rights of sovereignty neither are to be derived from divine prescription, nor belong to whoever is in charge of administering the law in a commonwealth. They belong to "the realm or commonwealth and people" (*regno seu Reipublicae & populo*) and not, as "Bodin clamours" (*clamat Bodinus*), to the "person of the supreme magistrate or prince" (*personae ... summi magistratus & principis*).[58]

This is strong stuff. In essence, Althusius adds to the double covenant a third one that is concluded among the people themselves for the purpose of establishing a commonwealth of organized social life. And it is this third and social covenant that enables the organized body of the people to enter into a government contract with the ruler, prince, or, as Althusius prefers to say, supreme magistrate of the commonwealth thus created. We can already see the fundamental difference between this and the Hobbesian commonwealth construction. While Hobbes collapses social contract and government contract into one act of power alienation, Althusius carefully separates the two contracts. First, the people constitute themselves as an organized collectivity and constituent political power, and then, secondly, a government contract is established between this organized body of the people and a ruler who has a limited mandate as chief executive.

In 1604, a year after the publication of his book, Althusius left Herborn and followed an invitation to become the syndic (chief administrative officer and legal adviser) of the city of Emden in the Empire's northernmost province of East Frisia. He remained in this position until his death in 1638. In Emden, Althusius revised and expanded his *Politica* into two further editions (1610 and 1614), in particular adding chapters on provincial administration and the right of resistance.[59] He also served as a church elder and wrote a major work on law and justice (*Dicaeologica libri tres*, 1617).

Mainly, however, his task in Emden was to defend the rights of the Calvinist city against the Lutheran ruler of the province. His book had obviously not gone unnoticed in a city generally referred to as the *Geneva of the North*.[60] And defend these rights, he did. In 1609 Emden used a Dutch garrison stationed in the city to raid the government chancery in the neighbouring provincial capital of Aurich; in 1618 the ruling provincial lord, Count Enno III, was briefly put under arrest in his own city residence in Emden; and in 1625 Count Enno's successor, Count Rudolf Christian, was denied the customary oath of allegiance until he agreed to change the oath's formula from a unilateral promise to a contract with mutual rights and obligations.

In all these actions, Althusius played a leading or at least supportive part. The issue was always the same. While Emden was a wealthy Calvinist seaport, the province of East Frisia was mostly rural and poor. The Lutheran ruler not only wanted to enforce his faith upon the city, as was his formal right under the Augsburg Religious Peace, he also and more importantly wanted to squeeze increasing amounts of tax money from Emden's wealthy burghers, money that he needed if he was ever to transform his province from a peripheral backwater into a modern military and administrative state. The city, in turn, claimed that it enjoyed de facto autonomy,[61] that it was therefore free to determine its own religion, and that all provincial tax impositions required its agreement.

The city won, at least for the time being. The Dutch garrison, already established before Althusius's arrival, and for the same purposes of defending city rights against what was perceived as continuous attempts at provincial usurpation, also provided protection from the worst excesses of the Thirty Years War. But to the extent that Althusius's stubborn city politics prevented East Frisia's transition to modern statehood, it may have been a contributing factor to the eventual annexation of the province by Prussia in 1744.[62]

At first glance, Althusius's definition of sovereignty as belonging to "the realm or commonwealth and people" does not appear very different from the Hobbesian definition. Hobbes, we recall, had come close to an institutional definition of sovereignty in that he did not care who held it, monarch or assembly, as long as it was held absolutely and undivided. For once agreeing with the jurists, Althusius likewise states that the rights of sovereignty must be "indivisible, incommunicable, and interconnected" (*individua, & incommunicabilia, atque connexa*) because "a superior entity can have no equal or greater superior" (*superioritas parem aut superiorem majoremque habere nequeat*).[63]

But then and almost immediately everything becomes very different. "The people, or the consociated members of the realm, have the power of establishing this right of the realm and of binding themselves to it" (*Juris hujus regni statuendi & se obligandi ad id, potestatem populus, seu membra regni consociata habent*), Althusius begins, still almost in line with what Hobbes would say about the foundational act of the commonwealth. But then he continues that "these rights can, however, be lawfully delegated" (*committi vero haec jure possunt*),[64] and that there is therefore a fundamental difference between the "right of sovereignty" (*jus majestatis*), which belongs to the people, and its exercise, the "universal power of governance" (*potestas imperandi universalis*), which is in the hands of a ruler, prince, king, or supreme magistrate.[65]

It all comes down to Althusius's distinction between the original social covenant and the government contract. It is the (already) organized and "united body of the people" (*populus in corpus unum*),[66] a formula repeated many times throughout the book, that owns the rights of sovereignty:

> By their common consent, they are able to establish and set in order matters pertaining to it. And what they have once set in order is to be maintained and followed, unless something else pleases the common will. (*communi consenso de illo disponere & constituere possunt, & quod semel disposuerunt, id servare & praestare tenentur, nisi communi voluntate aliud placeat.*)[67]

"Unless something else pleases the common will": Just by itself, this formulation, written 150 years before Rousseau's *Contrat social*, is extraordinary if not sensational, and there is some circumstantial and textual evidence that Rousseau read Althusius. Rousseau, after all, had grown up as a citizen of Calvinist Geneva, and therefore had been exposed to a very similar set of ideas and values.[68]

Althusius, of course, was neither a democrat nor a populist, and his understanding of the common will as expressed by the organized body of the people is very different from Rousseau's *volonté générale*. But for sure there is also none of the Hobbesian absolutism. Again, the difference does not lie in the definition of sovereignty itself. On its own, the Hobbesian provision, according to which the covenant once established cannot be altered without permission of the sovereign, is not much different from the Althusian formulation: Here as there, it can be altered if that pleases whoever is the sovereign. Yet, the Hobbesian sovereign has absolute and unchecked control over the scope and dimension of his own government power. In sharp contrast, the Althusian sovereign is the organized body of the people, which establishes, maintains, and changes the "universal power of governance" as it sees fit.

It can no longer come as a surprise, then, that Althusius also fully subscribes to the old adage of Aristotelian, republican, or council governance so mockingly rejected by Hobbes, according to which the ruler is superior to all parts of the realm individually (*major singulis*) but remains under the control of the collective power of all parts together (*minor universis*):

> The opinion of the combined orders and estates prevails over the opinion of the presiding officer or the supreme magistrate. For greater is the authority and power in the many than in the one who has been constituted by the many and is less than they are. (*Sententia igitur universorum statuum & ordinum praevalet praesidis seu summi magistratus sententiae. Nam major autoritas & potestas in multis, quam in uno, qui a multis illis est constitutus, iisque minor.*)[69]

In fact, this is a fairly accurate description of the decision-making rules that were in place at the Imperial Assemblies (Diets) of the Holy Roman Empire. The orders and estates were the nobility, clergy, and (with lesser rights in imperial practice) the free cities. We already know, of course, that the Empire was about to falter and disintegrate into a plurality of sovereign absolutist statehood. Quick and superficial judgment on Althusius, therefore, has been that he only systematized the "accidental relations" of a bygone era, whereas it was the achievement of Hobbes to provide a "scientific" theory of modern state politics.[70]

It is true, of course, that the organizational success of unitary and centralized statehood relegated the political theory of Althusius to the dustbin of modern political history, but this does not necessarily mean that it is bad theory. On the contrary, it is quite possible to argue that while the democratically mitigating achievements of modern statehood, accountability, and representative inclusiveness had to be won against Hobbes's postulates of power rationalization, they can draw considerable support from Althusius's old-fashioned theory of politically organized plurality.

Once again, the difference lies in the method. Both Althusius and Hobbes begin with human nature. While Hobbes subscribes to a view according to which "man is man's wolf," Althusius reproduces the Aristotelian notion of *zoon politikon*: Man is by nature a political being with a natural inclination to live in community.[71] Hobbes proceeds from his assumption directly to the postulation of absolute sovereignty as the most general principle of political organization and deduces from this principle the requirements of social organization in order to guarantee such sovereignty. Althusius begins by analyzing and describing all specific forms and purposes of social organization, such as families, professional colleges, villages, cities, provinces, and finally, the universal commonwealth. Only after that does he determine, by means of induction rather than deduction, what general kind of sovereignty construction befits this social plurality.

Obviously, this methodological approach is similar to the Aristotelian *Topics* with its insistence on examining a subject matter from all possible and plausible angles before making final adjudicating decisions. Strangely, though, Althusius's main methodological inspiration was that of French logician Pierre de la Ramée, a Calvinist who had perished in the St. Bartholomew Day Massacre, and who had once claimed that everything that Aristotle had taught was false.[72] Ramist logic, however, was in reality a fairly close adaptation of the topical method. One of its central rules was that every argument "should be placed with the nearest class of things to which it belongs rather than with matters on a higher or lower level of generality."[73]

And this is precisely what led Althusius to reject the idea that sovereignty could be some universal rule of one-fits-all. As a simple reality check would reveal, families, cities, and provinces were all clearly governed by special sets of rules specific to them, and not by a general rule of sovereignty. From a historical perspective, they also and just as clearly preceded realms and had existed prior to them "just as the simple or primary precedes in order what has been composed or derived from it" (*eoque notior est & simplex, seu primum id quid compositum seu ortum a primo est, antecedit ordine*).[74] Hence, the rights of sovereignty as the ultimate end could not be located exclusively in the highest order of governance. Instead, it followed logically that their source must be located in the organized body of the people.

The most general principle of politics that Althusius employs, then, is not sovereignty but organized social life in all its plural manifestations. "Politics," he begins in the first chapter of the *Politica*,

> is the art of consociating men for the purpose of establishing, cultivating, and conserving social life among them. Whence it is called symbiotics. The subject matter of politics is therefore consociation, in which the symbiotes pledge themselves each to the other, by explicit or tacit agreement, to mutual communication of whatever is useful and necessary for the harmonious exercise of social life. (*Politica est ars homines ad vitam socialem inter se constituendam, colendam & conservandam consociandi. Unde* συμβιωτικὴ *vocatur. Proposita igitur Politicae est consociatio, qua pacto expresso, vel tacito, symbiotici inter se invicem ad communicationem mutuam eorum, quae ad vitae socialis usum & consortium sunt utilia & necessaria, se obligant.*)[75]

Just about everything is already said in this one opening paragraph. In Aristotelian fashion, politics is about living together in a community. The social pact or contract is a horizontal agreement among fellow human beings. Nothing at this point is said about authority and hierarchy. Mutual communication, as Althusius explains a little later, pertains to "things, services and common rights" (*rebus, operis, juribus communibus*).[76] While

109

"things" include public goods held in common, such as forests, pastures, and waters, alongside granaries, mines, schools, and breweries,[77] and "services" comprise the labour and other activities of the professions and crafts,[78] it is the communication of rights that is of particular interest because it is here that Althusius locates the source of government authority.

"Called the law of consociation and symbiosis," (*lex consociationis & symbiosis*), this "communion of right" (*juris communio*) has a twofold character. On the one hand, it prescribes a "plan and manner for the communication of things and services" (*rationem atq; modum res & operas communicandi*).[79] According to the needs and desires of each consociation, the extent to which the resulting social order is regulated can vary, from "more extensive" (*major & amplior*) to "more restricted" (*minor restrictiorque*).[80]

On the other hand, the communication of rights provides the law for the "direction and governance of social life" (*socialis vitae directioni & gubernationi*). This law in turn is either "common" (*lex communis*) or "specific" (*lex propria*).[81] While "common and unchanging law" (*communis & perpetua lex*) establishes as a matter of principle that in every consociation or community there are those who rule and are superior (*praefecti seu superiores*), and those who obey and are inferior (*obsequentes, seu inferiores*),[82] specific or "proper laws" (*propriae leges*) are those by which particular consociations are governed in practice, and which "differ in each species of consociation" (*in singulis speciebus consociationis ... diversae sunt*).[83]

What Althusius has "set forth methodically" (if not pedantically) thus far may not immediately strike us as terribly earth-shaking. He simply seems to describe and systematize the plurality of the European political order as it had continued to exist beyond the Middle Ages. Had he stopped there, Habermas would not have been far off the mark with his criticism that only Hobbes provided a scientific answer to the turmoils of a time when the disintegration of the old order was already written on the wall.[84]

Even the Althusian postulation of sovereignty as rightfully belonging to the organized body of the people only might appear to give expression to the obvious: In the Empire there was an overlapping plurality of rule. The emperor could not make decisions without the approval of the major estates and political forces of the land. And sovereignty, if it could not be located exclusively in the person or office of the emperor, by default had to exist elsewhere, somewhere in the collective political process of all participants—if it existed at all. This insecurity and chronic instability of "somewhere" is exactly what Thomas Hobbes wanted to eliminate by concentrating all public authority in one exclusive hand or institution of power. Althusius begged to differ, obviously not in response to Hobbes, who wrote a generation later, but in direct response to Bodin who had already provided a similar theoretical solution to the disorders of the time a generation earlier.[85] But did he have a convincing alternative and answer?

In order to provide an alternative solution to the plurality/stability conundrum, Althusius had to go well beyond the scope of Aristotelian, Marsilian, and even Machiavellian politics, by placing the old political theory of the *polis*, community, or city into the new and larger context of rapidly expanding territorial states and economies. And in doing so, he had to provide a set of political principles that would demonstrate convincingly how the old plurality of rule could be preserved rather than destroyed without, however, giving way to the kind of factionism and civil war that had compelled Bodin and Hobbes to formulate their radically reductionist solutions.

More specifically, Althusius was confronted with two challenges. He had to show, firstly, how organized plurality could produce unity of action so that there was indeed a final and supreme authority of decision-making and political arbitration; and, secondly, he had to find a rule or principle by which it was possible to distinguish, in lawful fashion, who was allowed to do what under a regime of governance that was to retain its plurality of governing powers. Althusius's answer to the first challenge was his construction of a federal (or confederal) political system as an ascending chain of representational relationships. And he provided an answer to the second challenge by preformulating what would much later become known as the principle of subsidiarity.

In ascending order, Althusius treats families and clans; guilds and professional colleges; cities and rural areas; and provinces.[86] In principle, governance in each of these particular consociations is organized in the same way, by a council, senate, or assembly of representatives from the next lower level of consociation (e.g., the representatives of guilds and colleges in the city council; the representatives of cities and the land in provincial assemblies), and an elected prefect or magistrate who is superior to individual council members but cannot overrule a council decision reached by agreement or majority rule. In practice, there are some exceptions and anomalies:

- Within families and clans, the male head of the family obviously governs without council or election. Althusius was not a feminist. He nevertheless, and contrary to the Aristotelian distinction of polity (*polis*) and household (*oikos*), insists that the treatment of families (as well as of guilds and colleges) properly belongs to political science because they are to be organized according to universal political principles of mutual communication and governance.[87]
- In the case of provinces, Althusius makes a concession to political reality in the Empire by admitting that provincial lords or prefects are not

111

elected but receive their position and authority from imperial privilege. Nevertheless, he insists, the same rules of governance apply: The provincial ruler is bound by the collective decisions of the assembled provincial orders.[88]

- Finally, at the level of the universal commonwealth, Althusius makes one of his most peculiar institutional suggestions. In addition to his accountability to the general assembly of the commonwealth,[89] the supreme magistrate is guided in his acts of governance by a college of so-called ephors (*Ephori*), who, as a general rule, should be elected from among those with "great power and wealth" (*magnam habent potentiam & opes*) and serve as "custodians of the public welfare" (*custodes publicae salutis*).[90] There are also special ephors who represent particular provinces or regions.[91] These ephors elect the supreme magistrate and, as a college that "represents the universal consociation or polity" (*repraesentat universalem consociationem, seu politiam*), they have "greater power and authority than the supreme magistrate" (*majorem potestatem & autoritatem, quam summus magistratus*).[92]

Althusius very much intended to write systematic political theory and not just provide a detailed description of contemporary political reality. In imperial practice, access to political power and decision-making was based on a mix of tradition and privilege. For Althusius it is a matter of principle and universal inclusion. Contrary to imperial practice, for example, he insists that rural areas, alongside cities and towns, be rightful members of provincial consociations, and contrary to political practice almost everywhere else in Europe (but not in East Frisia), he also includes the peasants' estate in the political system. And, finally, the ephors, while to some extent emulating the position the electoral princes held in the Empire, nevertheless take on a much more fundamental role as an inner cabinet providing supervision and collective control over the actions of the supreme magistrate.[93]

Althusius does not use the term "federalism."[94] But his construction of a composite commonwealth does appear as a system of consecutive federalization. However, this system unfolds more like a multilevel chain of second-chamber governance than a modern federal state with two legislative chambers. There is no directly elected parliament. Instead, there are legislative bodies like upper-chamber senates, which do not represent individual citizens but rather corporate entities, such as, in the case of the Althusian system, colleges, cities, and provinces.

Althusius also does not explicitly employ the term "subsidiarity," which only surfaced prominently much later in the encyclical *Quadragesimo Anno* of Pope Pius XI in 1931, which contained the admonition that the modern state must not destroy or absorb the intermediary powers of organized social life.[95] The term has resurfaced even more recently in the construction of the post-Maastricht European Union as a principle of political guidance according to which decisions should be left to be taken at the lowest level possible.[96] In substance, however, the principle of subsidiarity originated much earlier. In 1571 the church synod of Emden passed a resolution declaring that "no parish should predominate over another"; that provincial or general synods "must not deliberate on matters already decided" (at the local level) but should instead deal with those matters only upon which previous agreement "could not be reached," or "with matters pertaining to all parishes of the province."[97]

It is this stipulation that Althusius incorporated almost literally into his political theory. First, he reiterates that old Roman law principle according to which "what touches all ought also to be approved by all" (*quod omnes tangit, ab omnibus quoque approbari debet*).[98] Then, he specifies how this principle of consent is to be operationalized:

> When, however, there are differing votes ... the decision may be made according to the judgments of the more numerous or larger part in the things that concern all order together, but not in those that concern them separately. (*Conclusio autem, quando sunt disparia suffragia ... fit secundum plurium sententias, seu numerum & partem majorem suffragiorum in iis, quae simul universos ordines concernunt, no quae seorsim singulos.*)[99]

What this means is that majority decisions can only be made on issues that are the same for all members of a commonwealth, and in such a way as to ensure that they apply to all members equally. Individual members retain a veto over decisions that affect them in a particular or exclusive way. Issues that cannot be resolved by means of a general rule, or, in modern parlance, framework legislation, therefore remain in the domain of particular legislation at the next lower level of consociation.

This is precisely what Althusius means when he attributes the rights of sovereignty to the organized body of the people. Sovereignty is indivisible in principle, but it a co-sovereignty shared by all members of the commonwealth. Consequently, there is also no unitary code of law, or a constitution with a clearly enumerated catalogue of divided powers. The "highest law of the land" (*lex fundamentalis regni*), Althusius declares, is

> nothing other than those covenants by which many cities and provinces come together and agree to establish and defend one and the same commonwealth by common work, counsel and aid. (*nihil aliud, quam pacta quaedam, sub quibus*

plures civitates & provinciae coïerunt & consenserunt in unam eandemque Rempubl. habendam & defendam communi opera, consilio & auxilio.)[100]

Althusius's political theory of federalism, in other words, differs significantly from the theory and practices of modern constitutional federalism. It is a kind of "treaty federalism" that compels all participants in a federation to engage in a permanent process of multilevel deliberation and negotiation over fundamental questions of unity and diversity.[101]

Critical Evaluation

One can easily see why Hobbes became famous and Althusius did not. With bold strokes, Hobbes paints a picture of politics in a world consumed by conflict, war, and the need for stability no matter what. Obviously this is a picture that his contemporary and future readers found compelling even though perhaps frightening and, from an idealistic perspective, disillusioning.

By comparison, Althusius provides an account of politics that is often more pedantic than compelling. It frequently gets lost in detail, and is written in a Latin prose that at times borders on the incomprehensible. Moreover, in his attempt to squeeze into a coherent and universal theory of politics the enormous variety and plurality of contemporaneous political reality, Althusius gets caught in contradictions and has to make concessions (such as in the case of the provincial rulers who are not elected as they should be) that are at odds with his theoretical claims.

It is, however, always easier to construct a grand theory as a metanarrative that conveniently brushes over the annoying details of reality. Hobbes's picture of a state where all political power is concentrated in one hand or one institution did not exist in England before, during, or after the English Civil War. As Montesquieu observed half a century later in what had become Lockean rather than Hobbesian England, it was a republican division of powers that characterized the constitutional monarchy after all.[102]

And, even though exclusive state sovereignty did become the dominant ideology as Hobbes had wanted, it has never really existed in the modern world either: not during the age of absolutism in France when, as Tocqueville observed, "eccentric solutions" to the problem of good government spread despite political centralization and censorship;[103] nor in the modern democratic capitalist state where, as Charles Lindblom noted, political power, democratic or otherwise, always remains contested by corporate power.[104]

In his disavowal of all notions of plurality, community, and partisanship, Hobbes provided a strangely neutered model of politics. It is a model of political power in which "the power to act required only the elimination of hindrances rather than the active enlistment of the private power and support of the citizens."[105] In this sense, Hobbes's political theory marks the complete renunciation of Aristotelian politics, indeed of the very idea that the well-being of a polity requires the active involvement of its citizens. The political (in its classical sense) is eliminated from politics.

This can very well be seen as the beginning of modern liberalism, not as a justification of modern capitalist market society, as Macpherson suggested,[106] but in its separation of political state and privatized society that made such a justification possible, by insulating market capitalism from the rules of political accountability. The citizen, under such a set of assumptions, was to become the unpolitical bourgeois, standing aside from power and leaving the dirty work of politics to others. This is a dangerous proposition, as Thomas Mann found out, who had brought it to literary fame in his *Betrachtungen eines Unpolitischen* (*Reflections of an Unpolitical Man*, 1918), but who was compelled to reconsider when the omnipotent Nazi state attacked his bourgeois existence, in 1936, by declaring that his citizenship and academic honours would no longer be "praetermitted" by the law.[107]

It is as easy to register disapproval for Thomas Hobbes's political theory of absolutist sovereignty as it appears futile to muster recognition — leave alone enthusiasm — for Johannes Althusius's *Politica*. In 1880 the German professor of "fellowship law" (*Genossenschaftsrecht*), Otto von Gierke, published a book in which he celebrated Althusius as a central figure in the development of modern political theory.[108] It contributed to Gierke's fame, not to that of Althusius. In 1932 Carl Joachim Friedrich published an abridged version of *Politica* in the Harvard Political Classics series.[109] It became a cornerstone of Friedrich's scholarly reputation but hardly furthered any interest in Althusius. And then there was the dean of American studies in federalism, Daniel J. Elazar, who always remained committed to the Althusian origins of covenanted federalism. Perhaps exactly for this reason, he always remained an outsider in American political science.[110]

The paradox is that Althusius gets mentioned in just about every major treatment of the history of political thought but at the same time is on nobody's primary list of classics.[111] Althusius, so much should be clear by now, does not fit well into the reconstruction of the classical canon from a modern liberal statist perspective. He conceptualizes politics not as a universal blueprint based on immutable truth but instead as a plurality of diverse and interconnected social relationships. He has no patience for abstract notions of sovereignty. Instead, he understands it as a form of power-sharing that can only manifest itself and exist as ultimate authority when all those involved and affected agree on its use. And he rejects the distinction of public state and private society as a preordained fact of natural or scientific rationality.

While Althusius does distinguish between the private interests of families, guilds and colleges, and the public interest of cities, provinces, and realms, he maintains that they are nevertheless all part of politics. Nobody can claim to be exempt from the basic rules of political conduct, the mutual sharing of things, services, and rights. What needs regulation as a public good, however, and what can be left to the disposition of private interest, is the quintessential matter of organized political discourse.

Plurality and diversity of social organization; confederal organization of multilevel governance; framework legislation with the intent to regulate only what is common to all: It is small wonder that the star of Althusius has been shining at least a little more brightly in the European Union more recently. When the European Commission under the leadership of Commission President Jacques Delors came up with the principle of subsidiarity, it did take notice of its Althusian origins.[112] And when the ill-fated European Constitution was drafted more recently as a treaty document establishing political union as a confederal system with shared sovereignty, the vice-president of the European Constitutional Convention, Giuliano Amato, a former Italian prime minister, gave prominent credit to Althusius as the source of inspiration for what was to be a new model of federalism different from the conventional federal state.[113]

Obviously, the conceptualization of Europe as such a conventional federal state (with unquestioned national supremacy as in the American model) is not even a matter of discussion. The idea of a European Union built on Hobbesian principles of absolute sovereignty, however, would be an outright Orwellian nightmare. And it would even be more so on a global level where it seems that, if at all, the rapidly increasing needs of policy coordination and governance can be addressed only by some sort of Althusian solution.

The usual counter-argument is that Althusian principles may be nice but that they are also highly impractical when nobody is willing to agree (and civil war returns, as Hobbes would predict). Yet, this is an argument that not only overlooks the extent to which the Hobbesian principle of absolute sovereignty has been a catastrophic failure in the construction of lasting peace over the past 350 years. It is also an argument that remains in denial about a world in which lingering superpower dreams of unitary will formation increasingly turn out to be destructively delusional.

Nay, the construction of a political system at least as conducive as possible to mutual agreement is the only option, however difficult and cumbersome, in a complex world entirely lacking any predisposition for social, cultural, and ideological hegemony. The point is not that the construction of such a world must inevitably fail and lead to war, but that the threat of war may yet compel its peoples and communities to commit themselves, not to a grand scheme of global democracy, but to small and varied steps of mutual communication, of things, services, and rights, as the next best option in practice.

At the beginning of what we now call the modern age of states and societies, the political theories of Thomas Hobbes and Johannes Althusius offered two grand designs for the organization of political power. Each was a response to what Hobbes called "the disorders of the present time,"[114] religious, socioeconomic, and territorial conflict occasioned by the confluence, in Max Weber's terms, of religious affiliation and social stratification,[115] or, in the words of Sheldon Wolin, by the Protestant rediscovery of political complexity.[116]

One of these grand designs demanded the elimination of political complexity by the creation of one unitary and absolute source of sovereignty that would render competitive power claims impossible. The other design aimed at the stabilization of political complexity in structures of plural governance and shared sovereignty that would facilitate peaceful cooperation. To a considerable extent, the history of political thought ever after can be seen as the further exploration of these two alternatives.

CHAPTER 7

State and Society

Locke v. Montesquieu

In its search for stability and peace, political thought after the Reformation had mainly focussed on sovereignty, the organization of reliable political authority. This focus changed when the eventual consolidation of political power and authority in a new system of sovereign territorial states set free enormous societal energies.

Trade and commerce flourished; specialized goods production marking the beginning of the age of industrialization did away with the traditional patchwork of local market economies; and a new bourgeois class of monied men began to rival the old landed aristocracies. "The wealth of the nation," wrote Jonathan Swift (1667-1745), "that used to be reckoned by the value of land, is now computed by the rise and fall of stocks."[1] The newly consolidated states required increasing amounts of the new (and old) money for modernization purposes, internal administration and policing, as well as external protection and defence. What had people all worked up, therefore, and became the new hot topic in politics, was the protection of property from excessive and arbitrary taxation.

This was particularly so in England, where the bourgeois classes had won a decisive victory over the old feudal order a century ahead of the rest of Europe. And it was also in England that political theory first and decisively shifted its focus from the formation of government power to the organization of government constraint.

Context

The chain of events surrounding the English Civil War was extraordinary. In 1640 Parliament defied the king's prerogative by declaring that it could be dissolved only with the agreement of its members. It became known as the Long Parliament and it was formally dissolved only in 1660. After the execution of King Charles I in 1649, the monarchy was transformed into the

Commonwealth of England during the so-called Interregnum (1649-60). Parliamentary rule was all but suspended under the Protectorate of Oliver Cromwell (1653-59), which for all practical purposes was a military dictatorship. The monarchy was restored in 1600 and Charles II became king. But his successor, James II, was again overthrown in the Glorious Revolution of 1688 and replaced a year later by the joint reign of William and Mary. In the end, and contrary to Thomas Hobbes's fears, the ultimate outcome of the English Revolution was not brutish disorder but the emergence of modern statecraft under a constitutional monarchy.

Cromwell's New Model Army was so called not only because it was reorganized under the unified command of professionals. It was also new in that it was better paid and, therefore, more disciplined. Better payment required increased levels of taxation. As it turns out, the major contribution of the interregnum years and its Long Parliament may not have been so much the contestation (and temporary suspension) of monarchical rule but its innovative approach to the problem of taxation and public finance.[2]

The Long Parliament regularized the use of direct taxes such as the Monthly Assessment, levied on a regional or district basis and resulting in very uneven tax rates. Its main fiscal weapon, however, was the so-called Excise, a series of indirect consumption taxes levied on various luxury goods as well as "necessaries." Although the regressive character of such taxes was recognized, the official argument was that the poor should have to share the burden of taxation. At the same time, the Excise was also a means to get money from the royalists who otherwise continued to enjoy a variety of tax privileges.

Some of these tax measures became undone after the restoration of the monarchy in 1660, when the standing army was decommissioned as well. But when exclusive parliamentary control over tax matters resumed after the Glorious Revolution, it became clear that a new regime of public finance had been lastingly established, culminating with the creation of the Bank of England in 1694. With Parliament in the grip of the new party of Whigs, led by noblemen but essentially representing the interests of money, the new regime of taxation and public finance was biased in favour of merchants and industrialists. Landowners and the poor bore the brunt of it.[3]

The Glorious Revolution was a bourgeois revolution by and for the rich men who now dominated the parliamentary system. In Christopher Hill's concluding assessment: "Anyone rich enough can buy himself into Parliament, and once there he has good chances of winning returns on his investment."[4] The Glorious Revolution, in other words, was as much a rebellion against the last monarch with absolutist ambitions on England's throne as it was "directed against the lower classes" and their ambitions of social inclusion if not equality.[5] The political reforms that the Glorious Revolution achieved were a means to an end, and that end was what Parliament would become obsessed with from now on, the protection of property. As Cromwell's son-in-law Henry Ireton had already put it during the English Civil War: "Liberty cannot be provided for in a general sense if property be preserved."[6]

Throughout the following eighteenth century, continuously tightened property requirements made sure that the legislative power of Parliament remained in the hands of a privileged upper class that even excluded small landowners. Between 1660 and 1819, according to one count, that power was used to enact no less than 187 statutes of capital punishment, mostly for property offenses ("poaching a rabbit"), and rarely for the protection of human life (attempted murder remained a misdemeanour until 1803).[7]

Thus, it cannot really come as a surprise that the first and foremost political thinker at the beginning of the epoch, John Locke, set out to define "political power" as the "Right of making Laws with Penalties of Death, and consequently all less Penalties, for the Regulating and Preserving of Property."[8] For some, even that was not enough. In a pamphlet submitted "to the Consideration of the Two Houses of Parliament" in 1701 and titled, *Hanging, Not Punishment Enough*, the anonymous author referred to a "late Statute" that imposed the death penalty for the theft of five shillings. He then demanded that the offenders of more serious crimes should be punished by measures such as breaking on the wheel or whipping to death, so that "the Pains of Death would be so often repeated before they would expire."[9]

To be sure, crime and punishment were not the primary focus of Locke's political theory. But, as the Whig historian Basil Williams wrote some time ago, it was Locke's emphasis on a "merely protective duty of the state" that "encouraged a Whig oligarchy to regard one of the chief objects of government to be the protection of their own rights of property and to adopt an attitude of neglect or indifference to social evils affecting the lower classes of society."[10] As Leon Radzinowicz observed, it was not until the mid-1700s that the political theory of Montesquieu first changed the emphasis of contemporary penal doctrine from the kind of "retaliation in full rigour," that Montesquieu thought typical for despotic countries, to resocialization by "a just temperature of punishments and rewards."[11]

So it certainly was what C.B. Macpherson aptly coined as the spirit and practice of "possessive individualism"[12] that dominated the development of state and society in eighteenth-century England. The groundwork for its ideological justification, however, was laid well before that time, during England's preceding century of revolution. "The poor are the hands and feet of the body politic...who hew the wood and draw the water of the rich," exclaimed the dean of Worcester, George Hickes, in 1684, and he added that this was "necessary for the establishment of superiority and subjection in human society."[13]

These were commonplace assumptions at the time. Empiricist thinkers like John Locke, who believed that all human understanding could be derived from simple experience and observation, even gave them the halo of natural law: "By the natural and unalterable state of things in this world," he wrote in his main philosophical work, it was not to be expected that "the greatest part of mankind, who are given up to labour, and enslaved to the necessity of their mean condition ... should be more knowing in the variety of things done in the world than a packhorse."[14] And, in an essay opposing the idea of state-regulated interest rates, he offered the insight that for the wheels of trade and commerce to run, it was not necessary to place "any great Sum of Money" in the hands of labourers, whereas he affirmed with much eloquence that it was the "Landholder, who is the person, that bearing the greatest part of the burthens of the Kingdom, ought, I think, to have the greatest care taken of him, and enjoy as many Privileges, and as much Wealth, as the favour of the Law can with regard to the Publick-weal confer upon him."[15]

Wealth and law, property and government, had indeed become the inseparable two sides of the same coin in postrevolutionary England. In Machiavelli's Florence, corruption and fraud had been necessary in order to secure excessive inequality. In the Whigs' England 200 years later, such inequality could simply be legislated. Such is progress.

John Locke (1632-1704)

Born the son of a Calvinist attorney and small landowner, John Locke began his education at Westminster School in London and then spent his undergraduate years at Oxford.[16] Apparently bored with classical education, he attended lectures but otherwise mainly read romance novels. Still at Oxford, he was appointed as a teacher of classics, Greek, and moral philosophy. It was during these years, 1658-66, that he became interested in medicine as well as empiricism, the latter eventually leading to the publication of his main philosophical work, *An Essay Concerning Human Understanding* (1689).

In 1667 Locke left Oxford and joined the household, as secretary and physician, of Anthony Ashley Cooper, later the first Earl of Shaftesbury and founder of the Whig Party. Under the tutelage of Shaftesbury, Lord Chancellor since 1672, Locke also became involved in politics, as secretary of the Council on Trade and Plantations (1673-75). This appointment overlapped with his personal interests as he had at that point already invested money in both the colonies and the slave trade.

The next three and a half years Locke spent in France, while on the home front, his mentor Shaftesbury increasingly got himself into trouble. For his advocacy of, among other things, annual parliamentary elections, Shaftesbury even spent some time imprisoned in the infamous Tower of London. But it was after Locke's return that the plot really began to thicken. In 1680 Locke penned the first of the *Two Treatises of Government* in response to the posthumous publication of Robert Filmer's *Patriarcha*.[17] As Locke summed it up himself, the purpose of this response was to demonstrate, against Filmer's advocacy of absolute monarchy, that "Rulers now on Earth" could "derive any the least shadow of Authority" from biblical references to "Adam's Private Dominion and Paternal Jurisdiction."[18] In the same year, the House of Commons passed a bill meant to exclude Charles II's Catholic brother James from royal succession. Charles responded, in 1681, by dissolving Parliament. Shaftesbury, the parliamentary ring leader, was arrested and charged with high treason. Acquitted by a pro-Whig jury, he immediately began, in 1682, to plot a rebellion against James's succession. When it failed to gain support, he fled to Holland where he died a year later.

In the meantime, during those same tumultuous years, Locke had also drafted his Second Treatise. It contained the observation that "Revolutions happen" when kings notoriously govern according to their "Arbitrary Will" rather than the "Law of the Society."[19] Even unpublished, this was a dangerous thing to put on paper at a time when the restored monarch, Charles II, had a habit of having opponents executed. Consequently, Locke chose to go into Dutch exile himself for the next six years (1683-89).

When he returned, the revolution had taken place. James II, who had indeed succeeded Charles, had fled, and Parliament was about to reign supreme again under the new joint monarchs, William and Mary. The threats of Catholicism and absolutism were finally gone for good. Locke could now publish the two works already existing in draft, the *Two Treatises of Government* (anonymously in 1689), and *An Essay Concerning Human Understanding* (dated 1690). With his reputation as a philosopher established by the latter work, he spent his remaining years as a scholar increasingly drawn to questions of religious interpretation, and also again in public service, appointed to a new Board of Trade and Plantations in 1696.

Scholars have made a great deal of the fact that John Locke indeed wrote the Second Treatise before the Glorious Revolution and not afterwards, as justification in hindsight.[20] Yet while this fact may put Locke the man more squarely into the radical camp at the time, it does not really shed much additional light on Locke the political theorist. Given his Calvinist background and his association with Shaftesbury in particular, it cannot come as a great surprise that the *Two Treatises* would speak out against monarchical absolutism and in favour of parliamentary legislative control. Even the advocacy of a right of resistance or revolution was old hat in radical Reformed circles. What was different, however, was the way in which Locke blended traditional elements of Reformed political theory with a new Whiggish individualism.

The state of nature, he begins the Second Treatise, is a state of reciprocal equality wherein "no one ought to harm another in his Life, Health, Liberty, or Possessions."[21] If such harm happens, "every Man hath a Right to punish the Offender, and be the Executioner of the Law of Nature."[22] Echoing prevalent sentiments of the time, that right had two parts: punishment "for restraint," and "reparation."[23] The difference between this state of nature and civil society as characterized by "Freedom of Men under Government," Locke then points out, is the rule of law, "a standing Rule to live by."[24]

Thus far, the argument is not much different from the Hobbesian liberty as "praetermitted" by the laws. However, and in sharp contrast to Hobbes, the pursuit of life, health, liberty, and possessions is an act of self-preservation that requires "Freedom from Absolute, Arbitary Power." To surrender to any such power would be concomitant with slavery, which is only legitimate as a result of conquest in a legitimate state of war.[25] Obviously, Locke does not see the state of nature as synonymous with such a state of war.

The transition from this state of nature to "Political, or Civil Society" is achieved when "any number of men are so united into one Society, as to quit every one his Executive Power of the Law of Nature, and to resign it to the publick."[26] The basis for this achievement is a social contract or "original Compact,"[27] but, in sharp contrast to Hobbes again, what is surrendered to the public is only executive power. Thus, when Locke writes elsewhere that all political societies begin as a "voluntary Union, and the mutual agreement of Men freely acting in the choice of their Governours, and forms of Government,"[28] he does seem to distinguish, at least implicitly, between an original social covenant and a subsequent government contract.[29] Sovereignty, as "one Supream Power," remains with the "Legislative,"[30] which is "put into the hands of divers Persons who duly Assembled, have ... a Power to make Laws, which when they have done, being separated again, they are themselves subject to the Laws, they have made."[31]

At first glance, these passages would appear to identify Locke's political thought as perfectly in line with what we already know from Althusius as the central tenets of seventeenth-century Calvinist political theory. There is no evidence whatsoever that Locke had direct knowledge of Althusius. However, he had met leading Huguenots during his visit to France, and he spent years in the Reformed Netherlands. In fact, his description of the people's options against arbitrary rule or tyranny, "to provide for themselves, by erecting a new Legislative, differing from the other, by the change of Persons, or Form, or both as they shall find it most for their safety and good,"[32] is very similar to how Althusius had justified the Dutch Revolt against Catholic Spain: If the prefect fails to provide protection and support, and thus acts cruelly or tyrannically, the people "can submit themselves to another" (*illi se alii submittere possunt*).[33]

Also similar to Althusius, or to Calvinist political theory more generally, are the contractual or covenanted origins of political society as "mutual agreement"; the separation of superior legislative authority from executive power as the technical solution to limited and accountable power of governance; and the insistence that those who hold legislative power collectively, as a representative body, nevertheless remain subordinate to that power individually, as members of society. All this may have sounded radical in the Stuarts' England, and it had found, in Locke's diction, a more modern form of expression. But in substance, it was rather conventional.

Not conventional at all, however, at least in terms of political Calvinism, were two other elements in Locke's theory, pertaining to majority rule and representation. In his most precise description of the foundational act creating political society, Locke writes: "When any number of Men have so consented to make one Community or Government, they are thereby presently incorporated, and make one Body Politick, wherein the Majority have a Right to act and to conclude the rest."[34] This sounds outright Hobbesian and, indeed, we read shortly thereafter, in Locke's one and only direct reference to Hobbes, that even the "mighty Leviathan" could not endure for long without adherence to the principle of majority rule.[35] What is missing here, is the careful distinction, so prominent in Althusius, between majority rule, which applies only when a matter is of such generality that it can be regarded as affecting all in the same way, and consent, which is required when particular interests are at stake. For Locke, in other words, majority rule becomes the default option for all legislative decision-making, and herein one can see the conceptual beginning of the British parliamentary tradition.

The only rational justification for majority rule as the default option is the underlying assumption that society is made up of individuals ("any number of Men") who are sufficiently similar in their overriding needs and desires (the preservation of life, liberty and property) so that collective particularity (such as religion) no longer plays a decisive role in how "men" see themselves situated in society. Locke had of course already argued earlier in favour of religious toleration, at least among Protestants.[36] But even at that, the formula of "any number of men" consenting to make "one community" was a radical break with the older (e.g., Althusian) view of society as an ordered plurality of different communities.

Locke obviously neither shared the Althusian view of a plural society held together by a series of carefully negotiated agreements, nor the Hobbesian view according to which a society of individuals, in order to remain stable, had to be in general awe of a superpower Leviathan. Instead, he thought that an assembly of "Representatives of the People" as "Law-Makers of the Society" would do the trick.[37] If this was really written in 1680-83 rather than after Parliament had taken over in 1689, it was a remarkable leap of faith indeed.

But this is only where the interpretative controversy begins. According to one camp, Locke is the first great political theorist of liberal individualism, popular sovereignty, and representative government.[38] According to another camp, by no means the only one,[39] but the one containing the most serious attack on the seventeenth-century beginnings of individual liberalism, Locke's theory remains caught in the narrow confines of property and money interests that had gained the upper hand during the English century of revolution, as a "theory which justified a class state from the postulates of equal individual natural rights."[40]

The textual evidence is fairly clear. Locke describes the "Legislative" as "made up of Representatives chosen ... by the People."[41] He goes on to discuss how representative assemblies must be convoked and renewed periodically, and that even when the right of convocation or dissolution remains with the executive power (the monarch), it must be exercised regularly and cannot be misconstrued as executive superiority.[42]

Locke then comes to the crucial point, the representative composition of the legislative assembly itself. In seventeenth-century England, the parliamentary franchise was "a privilege attached to particular types of property."[43] In fact, as "Chief Justice Holt insisted," in the famous *Ashby v. White* case of 1703, "the vote was a species of property of which the owner cannot be deprived."[44] It was, in other words, very difficult to change the electoral system. As Locke observes, this created a discrepancy between, on the one hand, a world "so constant in a Flux" that "People, Riches, Trade, Power, change their Stations," and, on the other hand, the continued reliance on "Customs and Priviledges, when the reasons for them are ceased." As a result, "Representation becomes very unequal and disproportionate to the reasons it was first establish'd upon."[45]

Locke's remedy of reforming the franchise and the electoral districts had been part of Shaftesbury's Whig agenda all along.[46] It was confronted with two problems, however: how to justify franchise adjustment as a matter of principle rather than a violation of established rights; and how to find criteria for its application in practice.

In principle, if franchise reform was to come from "the Executive, who has the power of Convoking the Legislative," the impression had to be avoided that what it amounted to was a coup d'état from above, so to speak, the disenfranchisement of some by the enfranchisement of others. Locke's answer to this problem is couched in grand rhetoric: Surely, he exclaims, the good of the people as the highest law of the land ("*Salus Populi Suprema Lex*") ought to be that the composition of the legislative must be "observing rather the true proportion, than fashion of Representation." And if it does, then franchise reform does not mean "to have set up a new Legislative, but to have restored the old and true one."[47]

Locke's practical advice as how to determine criteria, "not by old custom, but true reason" for the reapportionment of the franchise is straightforward and simple: "the number of Members, in all places, that have a right to be distinctly represented" ought to be determined "in proportion to the assistance, which it affords to the publick."[48] By public assistance, he means taxes.[49] The prerequisite for inclusion into the body politic, therefore, is taxable property.

What Locke describes and takes for granted is a political system in which those who have property and are therefore taxed demand to be represented in Parliament where they then decide, collectively, upon measures and levels of taxation. Taken by itself, this does not necessarily amount to an early-modern capitalist conspiracy theory. After all, it is a line of argument that will lead straight to the American revolution a century later ("no taxation without representation"). Nevertheless, Locke's almost exclusive focus on matters of property and taxation raises the question whether his political theory is meant to be universal and inclusive in the sense that its principles eventually can be applied to all citizens, or whether it is meant to be partial to the interests of the propertied classes and therefore remains fundamentally flawed from a perspective of universal political equality.

To be sure, this is essentially the same critical question that can also be levelled against Aristotle, among others. We remember: The great Greek philosopher of practical prudence had defined politics as a system of to-govern-and-to-be-governed among citizens affluent enough to afford leisure. However, Aristotle also argued that the best polity was one with as large a middle class as possible. At least in principle, therefore, he suggested that the larger the level of inclusion, the better for his political principles to work.

Is this door of inclusion also open in Locke's theory? In the famous (or infamous, depending on one's perspective) fifth chapter of the Second Treatise, "Of Property," he develops a line of argument that is clearly meant to establish lasting inequality as a matter, not just of nature, but of civil agreement as well.[50] He begins by defining private property as the result of one's own labour, which includes wage labour ("the Turfs my Servant has cut").[51] At this point, however, the right to private appropriation is still a "moderate" one, limited to "the Extent of Mens Labour, and the Conveniency of Life."[52]

Then, the invention of money ("a little piece of yellow Metal") is introduced as a means to increase economic activities beyond the point of personal "conveniency" or need. The social justification for this extended conveniency is that it allows the cultivation of land that would otherwise be "lyeing wast in common." Locke at this point even provides what may be the first rendition of the so-called trickle-down theory of economics: "He who appropriates land to himself by his labour, does not lessen but increase the common stock of mankind."[53]

All of a sudden, however, the money argument changes, from convenience, or economic efficiency, to a social argument, justifying inequality. "In the beginning," Locke writes, meaning before the introduction of money, "all the World was America." As he knew from his involvement in colonial affairs, land and resources were mostly held in common and shared "fairly" among American "Indians." But when "the Use and Value of Money" was discovered and agreed upon, it became possible for "Man...to enlarge his Possessions."[54] More than that: It became possible that "Gold and Silver... be hoarded up without injury to any one." And hence "it is plain, that Men have agreed to disproportionate and unequal Possession of the Earth."[55]

Nobody (at least among the major political philosophers) had said that before. To be sure, inequality, the existence of rich and poor, had always been taken for granted. But nobody had gone as far as to suggest that the poor had agreed to be poor, or, at least, that they had agreed that there would always be and should always be poor.

There are essentially three arguments contesting this reading of Locke as a theorist of social inequality. The first is the social mobility argument. While political rights (the franchise) are obviously linked to property, Locke does point out that the world is in a constant flux and that, therefore, adjustments to the political system ought to be made in accordance with the changing distribution of fortunes in civil society. This is not a very convincing argument because, on the one hand, it still leaves political rights linked to money which remains distributed unevenly, and because, on the other hand, there is no doubt in Locke's mind that due to the "natural and unalterable state of things in this world," the vast majority of men will inevitably remain "enslaved to the necessity of their mean condition."[56] Social mobility, in other words, is understood by Locke mainly if not exclusively as a lateral move of fortunes within classes.

The second argument is about limits to property. Locke is careful in pointing out that the overall purpose and end of society is the common good.

And his arguments about private appropriation and property are accompanied by an assurance that while some will obviously be very rich, there will always be enough for everyone else. Further, as James Tully in particular has pointed out,[57] Locke places upon the acquisition of property a limiting obligation to "Charity," which "gives every Man a Title to so much out of another's Plenty, as will keep him from extream want."[58]

This one sentence can be seen as the foundational creed of the new individual liberalism: charity as the continuation of the trickle-down economy with other means, or, put only slightly more polemically, as a means for the suppression of Protestant guilt. Before the age of Locke, greed and avarice had been deadly sins. Now they were being celebrated as the fulfilment of God's plan of nature, but, just in case, charity would assuage lingering doubts about one's worthiness to step past the Pearly Gate.

In one of his last contributions to the debate, Locke gave a pretty clear indication just how far he thought charity should go in practice. During his time as a member on the Board of Trade and Plantations, he submitted a proposal on government policy towards the poor in which he suggested, among other things, that the children of the poor should be placed in work-schools at the age of three, and that they should be fed bread and (in winter) "water-gruel."[59] Charles Dickens could not have described it any better. Charity as understood by Locke, in other words, was not something that would affect the propertied classes in any substantive way. Moreover, it would be something left to their discretion as a moral obligation, and not be part of organized political society and the rule of law.

The third argument, finally, denies that the narrow discussion of property and money in the fifth chapter of the Second Treatise applies directly to the general principles of political organization because Locke, at the beginning of his discourse on the "Ends of Political Society and Government" defines property much more widely as "the mutual Preservation of ... Lives, Liberties and Estates."[60] The purpose of government, and the constraints placed upon it by means of the separation of legislative and executive powers, as well as representation and majority rule, according to this argument, is not just to protect property and money interests but indeed to extend the preservation of individual liberty in a free society more generally.

Coming from the pen of someone who had set out to define political power as the "Right of making Laws with Penalties of Death, and consequently all less Penalties, for the Regulating and Preserving of Property,"[61] however, this emphasis on lives, liberties, and estates may have a much narrower meaning. It may simply be a reflection of extant stipulations of contemporaneous criminal law. In 1691 a capital punishment statute was passed, which distinguished between the breaking and entering of empty properties, and of properties with the owner, his family, or other persons present. While the former could be punished as mere larceny, the latter, by putting lives and liberties "in Fear," demanded capital punishment without benefit of clergy.[62] But even if this is not what Locke actually had in mind, the formula of lives, liberties, and estates did not make much sense for most in a society where pickpocketing was often the only means of survival, and its punishment was death, imprisonment, or deportation.

The point in all of this is not to denounce Locke as merely an ideologue of those propertied and monied interests who had just won their decisive victory against the old powers of monarchical absolutism, and in whose company he spent most of his life. Rather, it is to recognize the dramatic contradiction inherent in this beginning of modern liberal political theory, between its "assertion of the free rational individual as the criterion of the good society,"[63] and its construction of a political system from which, by means of property qualifications, the vast majority of individuals would remain excluded. The question, raised and answered negatively by Henry Ireton, as to whether individual liberty in a general sense could ever be secured in a political system premised on the preservation of property, still remains unanswered today.[64]

The point that political practice did not necessarily live up to the lofty political principles it was supposed to be based on was not lost on the French aristocrat Montesquieu, who visited England a few decades later (1730-31). After praising the English system for its separation of powers, Montesquieu observed that liberty in England "will perish when the legislative power shall be more corrupt than the executive" (*Il périra lorsque la puissance législative sera plus corrompue que l'exécutrice*), and he added: "It is not my business to examine whether the English actually enjoy this liberty, or not. Sufficient it is for my purpose to observe, that it is established by their laws; and I inquire no further" (*Ce n'est point à moi à examiner si les Anglais jouissent actuellement de cette liberté, ou non. Il me suffit de dire qu'elle est établie par leurs lois, et je n'en cherche pas davantage*).[65]

Montesquieu (1689-1755)

Unlike Hobbes, the French aristocrat Charles-Louis de Secondat, Baron de La Brède et de Montesquieu did not require noble accompaniment to have the doors of Europe's rich and powerful opened to him. He also did not have to hang on someone else's coattails, as in the case of Locke and Shaftesbury, in order to secure an upwardly mobile position in life. All the more surprising, then, is that this aristocrat turned out to be a champion not only of republican liberty but of a type of social republicanism mindful of the dangers of excessive inequality.

In his posthumously published collection of "Thoughts" (*Pensées*), Montesquieu notes that it is in a republic, under conditions of equality (*où les conditions sont égales*), that each citizen benefits from the wealth of the nation and also contributes to it (*jouit du fond des biens de la Nation & cherche à le grossir*).[66] He also remarks that the invention of money has above all contributed to the formation of large empires (*l'invention de la monnaye a beaucoup contribué à faire de grands empires*) from whence, as he insinuates at least implicitly, spring inequality and despotism.[67] And in an aside to himself, he admits that wealth is a kind of injustice that needs redress (*les richesses sont un tort que l'on a à réparer*).[68]

Montesquieu was born at the family castle, La Brède, near Bordeaux, where the family owned considerable stretches of valuable vineyards. When he was sent to be educated at the prestigious Collège de Juilly near Paris (1700-05), his allowance was at some point augmented by an additional 50 livres so he and his brother could afford to drink wine.[69] After studying law in Bordeaux and Paris, Montesquieu became a counsellor in the regional *Parlement* in Bordeaux (1714). Two years later, he inherited from his uncle the barony of Montesquieu and with it the parliamentary position of president, a title which he later sold, presumably in order to better afford his lavish lifestyle in Paris. By then, he had published his first important work, the irreverent and satirical *Persian Letters* (*Lettres persanes*, 1721).[70] Although published anonymously, it made him an instant celebrity, as well as getting him elected to the French Academy (1728).

Montesquieu spent the next four years travelling all over Europe, to Germany and Italy in particular, and finally to England, where he stayed for almost two years and became an ardent student of the institutions and workings of the constitutional monarchy, as well as a member of the Royal Society. After his return to France in 1731, he began to divide his time between La Brède and the salons of Paris, writing first *Considerations on the Causes of the Greatness of the Romans and their Decline* (*Considérations sur les causes de la grandeur des Romains et de leur décadence*, 1734),[71] and, finally, as his major work summing up all previous experience and observation, *The Spirit of the Laws* (*De l'esprit des lois*, 1748). After its publication in Geneva, *The Spirit of the Laws* almost instantly became required reading throughout political and intellectual Europe. It would also become a major source of inspiration for the framers of the United States Constitution a few decades later. John Adams, Thomas Jefferson, and James Madison probably read the English translation that had appeared in 1750.[72] During that year, Montesquieu published the first of several responses to various criticisms. A year later, the book was put on the Papal Index. In 1755 Montesquieu died in Paris of a fever.

At first glance, the aristocrat Montesquieu might appear an unlikely candidate for the position of irreverent anti-establishment writer in prerevolutionary France. The *Persian Letters* are a series of fictitious letters written by two Muslims travelling through Europe. That alone was bordering on the outrageous since the publication came at a time when the threat of Turkish expansionism into the heart of Europe was still remembered well. In 1683 the Turks had laid siege to Vienna. And only in 1717, a mere four years before the publication of the *Persian Letters*, had they been beaten back decisively by Prince Eugen of Savoy, whom Montesquieu would later meet in Vienna.

Publication of the *Persian Letters* was all the more outrageous since Montesquieu had the two travelling Muslims, Usbek and Rica, comment freely not only on the despotic nature of the French monarchy as well as that of the papacy, but also on the decadent and self-indulgent nature of the French aristocracy to which he belonged himself. To a certain extent, the popularity of the *Persian Letters* can be explained by the fact that the most absolutist of absolutist French rulers, Louis XIV, had just died in 1715. For the moment, at least, the country seemed to let out a sigh of relief and enlightenment.[73] But there is also evidence that Montesquieu's election to the French Academy was met with some opposition from the quarters of those who thought he had gone too far.

Montesquieu had gone quite far indeed, as in letter 24, for instance:[74] Rica writes to a friend back home in Smyrna that the French king is the most powerful ruler in Europe because he extracts more riches from his subjects' vanity, by the sale of honorific titles, than the neighbouring king of Spain can extract from all his gold mines. And a few lines later, he mocks the pope as someone who uses magic tricks of persuasion against the people as well as the king.

The Baron from La Brède could perhaps afford such satirical outbursts because his social and political well-being did not depend on the goodwill of superiors. But the *Persian Letters* were also written for the sheer thrill of entertainment and contained stories about eunuchs, harems, and all kinds of amorous adventures. Montesquieu was bored as a judge in Bordeaux,[75] and it seems that after the success of the *Persian Letters* had opened the doors to Parisian high society, he sought and enjoyed such adventures himself, leaving to his wife at La Brède most of the domestic chores, as well as the education of their children.

When Montesquieu set out to write the *Considerations* after his return from England in 1731, both his tone and ambition had changed. Even though his approach was essentially the same, commentary on French politics and society through the prism of a different and distant place, ancient Rome in this case, his readers were far less amused. The book had a simple message: As long as Rome had maintained its republican liberties, it had been great, but when it sank into despotism, it was doomed to decline. All empires, one might agree with Montesquieu in hindsight, have tended to neglect this insight.

While it had been in England that Montesquieu found his love for republican liberty and its separation of powers, there was also an Italian sense of time and circumstance in the *Considerations*, reminiscent of both Machiavelli, whom he had obviously read without taking him to be the devil incarnate, and of Vico, whose *New Science* had appeared in 1725.[76] Montesquieu may have even met Vico during his visit to Naples in 1728-29.[77]

Thus, Montesquieu certainly echoes Machiavelli when he comments on "popular tumults" (*tumultes populaires*) as "necessary dissensions" (*divisions nécessaires*) because, "as a general rule, whenever we see everyone tranquil in a state that calls itself a republic, we can be sure that liberty does not exist there" (*pour règle générale, toutes les fois qu'on verra tout le monde tranquille dans un État qui se donne le nom de république, on peut être assuré que la liberté n'y est pas*).[78]

Also in the *Considerations*, Montesquieu first develops a historical and sociological method of inquiry that is entirely at odds with the new scientific reasoning of the age.[79] As he will later repeat in the preface to *The Spirit of the Laws*, he declares that "it is not chance that rules the world" (*ce n'est pas la Fortune qui domine le monde*). Instead, whatever people or rulers do remains confined within the parameters of "general causes" (*causes générales*) and, therefore, "the main trend draws with it all particular accidents" (*l'allure principale entraîne avec elle tous les accidents particuliers*).[80] Thus far, he may still be in line with the new scientism. These general causes, however, do not point to some abstract historical truth or principle. Instead, again they are embedded in what Montesquieu calls a "general spirit," which "exists in each nation," and "on which power itself is based" (*il y a, dans chaque nation, un esprit général sur lequel la puissance même est fondée*). If power "shocks this spirit it strikes against itself" (*quand elle choque cet esprit, elle se choque elle-même*).[81]

These formulations of cultural relativism certainly appear reminiscent of Vico's "common sense" as the collective prudence of a people or nation, and they help to explain Montesquieu's deeply felt resentment of any form of arbitrary or despotic rule. "It is an error to believe," he exclaims, "that any human authority exists in the world which is despotic in all respects" (*c'est une erreur de croire qu'il y ait dans le monde une autorité humaine, à tous les égards despotique*).[82] This exclamation in turn foreshadows not only his opposition to any kind of absolute or unrestrained sovereignty but also provides a conceptual backdrop for what he means by the title of his next and major work: The "spirit of the laws" is fulfilled, not in accordance with some abstract principle of individual right or wrong, but when the laws give expression to the general spirit of a society or nation, when they, in other words, are a true reflection of the "necessary relations derived from the nature of things" (*les rapports nécessaires qui dérivent de la nature des choses*).[83]

When Montesquieu turns to the development of political theory proper, he begins quite conventionally, with a discussion of different forms of government. For him, there are only three: republican, monarchical, and despotic.[84] A republican form of government can be either a democracy, when "the people as a body have sovereign power" (*le peuple en corps a la souveraine puissance*), or an aristocracy, when "sovereign power is in the hands of a part of the people" (*la souveraine puissance est entre les mains d'une partie du peuple*).[85]

Montesquieu then proceeds with a discussion of the kind of laws most appropriate for each form of government. In the case of a democracy, governance has to come from magistrates, a council, or senate, the members of which must be elected because "the people are admirable for choosing those to whom they should entrust some part of their authority" (*le peuple est admirable pour choisir ceux à qui il doit confier quelque partie de son autorité*).[86] For Montequieu, this elective and representative democracy is clearly the principal yardstick for all other forms of government. If there is an aristocracy, he writes, then at least it should be as inclusive as possible and therefore come as close to a democracy as possible.[87]

But it is in the context of his discussion of laws appropriate for a monarchy that Montesquieu makes his first thoroughly original contribution to modern political thought. While the prince is the source of all political and civil power in a monarchy, he declares, such a monarchy nevertheless cannot exist without what he calls "intermediate powers" (*pouvoirs intermédiaires*), without which a monarchy would soon become either a popular or a despotic state.[88] Naturally, Montesquieu sees the nobility as the most likely intermediate power, acting as a buffer and transmitter of the law in between the monarch and the people. Yet, intermediate powers themselves need some restraint, in the form of political bodies such as assemblies or parliaments, which "announce the laws when they are made and recall them when they are forgotten" (*qui annoncent les lois lorsqu'elles sont faites et les rappellent lorsqu'on les oublie*).[89]

These political bodies are necessary as "depositories of laws" (*dépôt de lois*) because "the ignorance natural to the nobility, its laxity, and its scorn for civil government require a body that constantly brings the laws out of the dust in which they would be buried" (*l'ignorance naturelle à la noblesse, son inattention, son mépris pour le gouvernement civil, exigent qu'il y ait un corps qui fasse sans cesse sortir les lois de la poussière où elles seraient ensevelies).*[90]

Montesquieu obviously has no sympathy for despotic government, which he likens to a lawless regime characterized by laziness, ignorance, and the neglect of public affairs.[91] What becomes quite clear from the entire discussion, however, is that what Montesquieu is after is not so much a clear distinction of different models of government according to the old classification scheme of the rule of one, few, or many. Rather, it is to identify those common elements of lawful governance that make a political system stable regardless of whether it is formally a democracy, aristocracy, or monarchy.

Montesquieu rejects any kind of absolute or unrestrained power, be it in the hand of the people, a ruling aristocracy, or a monarch. Underlying this rejection is his sociological analysis — and acceptance — of a stratified society with different and identifiable sets of collective interests: class interests. It is from this opening position that Montesquieu moves on to the discussion of the two cornerstones of his political thought: the separation of powers, and federalism.

"Political liberty is found only in moderate governments" (*La liberté politique ne se trouve que dans les gouvernements modérés*), Montesquieu begins his discussion of the separation of powers. By moderate governments, he means a constitutional framework that precludes any sociological group from having unrestrained power over others. Therefore, he continues, the abuse of power must be prevented by a constitutional arrangement in which "power must check power" (*le pouvoir arrête le pouvoir*).

This principle of checks and balances is Montesquieu's second thoroughly original contribution to modern political thought. It leads directly to his discussion of the separation of powers in the famous sixth chapter of the eleventh book of *The Spirit of the Laws*, which is titled, "On the Constitution of England" (*De la constitution d'Angleterre*). For the first time, Montesquieu not only separates the legislative from the executive power, as Locke had already done, but he also demands that the judicial power in particular be kept separate because it would lead to arbitrariness if the legislator was also the judge, and to outright oppression if the judge was also in charge of executive powers. The fusion of all three powers, finally, would result in the most despicable form of despotism.

Equally important in Montesquieu's thinking is the idea that a combination of these powers in the hands of a particular social class, prince, nobles, or people would be deleterious to the political liberty of the others. Hence, following the English example, Montesquieu suggests that the legislative power should be divided into separate chambers for the nobility and the people, with the nobility allowed to veto but not enact what we would today call money bills. Mutual checks and balances are also to be established between executive and legislative powers, but again the executive monarch can only veto and not enact the law. As a result, Montesquieu writes, these mutual checks and balances will not result in gridlock because these three powers "will be forced to move in concert" by the "necessary motion of things" (*par le mouvement nécessaire des choses...elles seront forcées d'aller de concert*).[92]

A lot of ink has been spilled regarding Montesquieu's alleged inability to fully understand how the English system really worked. In particular, he did not discuss the evolving party and cabinet system, and neither did he dwell on the prime minister's links to the Crown. Therefore, he misjudged the extent to which legislative and executive powers were already fused rather than separated. In hindsight, then, it would appear that what Montesquieu described was something much closer to the American constitutional system of checks and balances: After all, the American Federalists would declare only a few decades later that Montesquieu was their "oracle" of political wisdom.[93]

However, Montesquieu did provide a fairly accurate picture elsewhere of English party politics,[94] and therefore must have had his reasons why he omitted this discussion from the chapter on English constitutional liberty. The purpose of this chapter was, as he put it himself, to describe the constitutional principles that befit a free people,[95] and not their corrupted practice. In this way, Montesquieu "dignified and rationalized the concept [of power separation], linked it to a theory of liberty, and handed it to posterity as a doctrine far more practical than its proponents had known."[96]

In the England chapter, Montesquieu wanted to lay down the principles of power separation as his astute analytical mind had distilled them from English political practice. That is why, at the end of the chapter, he remarked that he would not inquire whether or not the citizens of England actually enjoyed the liberty given to them in principle by their constitution. That may well have been a reference to the already visible fusion of legislative and executive powers in what would gradually emerge as the Westminster system of parliamentary governance.

Montesquieu also observed, still in the same chapter, that England's constitutional liberty would "perish when the legislative power shall be more corrupt than the executive" (*Il périra lorsque la puissance législative sera plus corrompue que l'exécutrice*).[97] A year after the publication of *The Spirit of the Laws*, the Englishman William Domville wrote to Montesquieu asking him what he thought were the main reasons that might lead to a decline of English constitutionalism and liberty. Montesquieu replied that it would be the influence of certain local notables who, because they were corrupt themselves, would have a corrupting influence upon parliamentary elections by, among other things, throwing lavish feasts, providing intoxicating liquor, and spreading hatred and malice (*dans les élections . . . il y a quelques pincipaux qui corrompent, parce qu'ils sont corrompus eux-mêmes . . . [du] genre particulier de corruption . . . sont des repas . . . des liqueurs enivrantes . . . des haines ou des piques*).[98]

Obviously, then, Montesquieu understood quite well what the English ruling class did when it ruled. He also understood that the spirit of republican constitutional liberty would not be fulfilled without significant social adjustment. Republican liberty, he noted, requires considerable equality of social condition among different classes, and, consequently, in the distribution of wealth (*plus d'égalité dans les conditions, &, par consequént, plus d'égalité dans les fortunes*).[99] It seems that Montesquieu wanted to tell his aristocratic readers in prerevolutionary France that simply changing the form of government would not be good enough.

The republican spirit of the laws is only fulfilled when the principle of constitutional checks and balances is supported and made possible by real social balance put into practice. Political institutions, in other words, must be made meaningful by serving more than just the letter of the law. The same idea is also reflected in Montesquieu's observations about representation. The "people as a body should have legislative power" (*il faudrait que le peuple en corps eût la puissance législative*), he writes, but their representatives should not be "drawn from the body of the nation at large" (*tirés en général du corps de la nation*). Instead, it should be up to "the inhabitants in every considerable place to choose a representative from it" (*dans chaque lieu principal, les habitants se choisissent un représentant*). Such representatives will "know much better the needs of one's own town" (*connaît beaucoup mieux les besoins de sa ville*), and, consequently, will be well equipped to discuss "public affairs" (*discuter les affaires*).[100]

Perhaps it is this reflection on the interests and needs of particular places that led Montesquieu to the idea of a "federal republic" (*république fédérative*), which he describes as "a society of societies" (*une société de sociétés*).[101] This was not an idea he could possibly have developed from his analysis of the English constitution. Perhaps it came from his own experiences as a regional wine grower. During one of his visits to Paris, Montesquieu conveyed to the central government regional concerns and opposition to a proposed tax on wine.[102] Most certainly, however, he drew inspiration and observation from those countries that were already organized in a federal manner, and which he knew from both his travels and his studies: "Holland, Germany, and the Swiss leagues," which "are regarded in Europe as eternal republics" (*la Hollande, l'Allemagne, les Ligues suisses, sont regardées en Europe comme des républiques éternelles*).[103]

In what way did Montesquieu think these federal republics were eternal? As he had already explained at the end of Book Eight of *The Spirit of the Laws*, the ultimate political goal, a regime of republican political liberty, is only possible in small states because for the sake of efficient decision-making large empires require a despotic form of government.[104] Only large countries, however, will have the resources to withstand external enemies. Therefore, Montesquieu points out, in the following Book Nine on security and defence, there is a principal dilemma: "If a republic is small, it is destroyed by a foreign force; if it is large, it is destroyed by an internal vice" (*Si une république est petite, elle est détruite par une force étrangère; si elle est grande, elle se détruit par un vice intérieur*).[105] The way out of this dilemma is a federation of small republics. Only such a federation would combine the "goodness of the internal government of each one" (*la bonté du gouvernement intérieur de chacune*) with the defensive strength, "by force of the association," (*par la force de l'association*) of a large monarchy.

From his German, Dutch, and other examples, Montesquieu develops a number of principles that are deemed essential for the success of such a federal arrangement.[106] First of all, the members of a federation must all be republics so that there is a similarity of political culture and predisposition. Secondly, the members of a federation must not be able to enter into new treaties or alliances by themselves. Thirdly, the process of joint decision-making and governance in such a federation must be organized on the basis of weighted votes (three, two, or one, according to size) among the participating member units, and the cost for running the federation distributed accordingly. Fourth and finally, the judges and magistrates of the constituent member units can either be elected by the common council of the federation, or they can be determined by the member units themselves. Montesquieu seems to prefer election by the common council.

Again, Montesquieu's ambition was not to provide an exact or empirical account of the federal republics he drew inspiration from. Instead, he used these examples to point out what struck him as principles of federal organization worthy of consideration. And even though his theory of federalism is confined to a few pages in *The Spirit of the Laws*, it does identify some of the most contentious questions of modern federalism: the question of how to strike a balance between unity and diversity; the question of symmetry or asymmetry in the construction of central governing institutions; and the question of power allocation, especially with regard to foreign policy, between different orders of government.

As mentioned before, all this comes in a chapter that is primarily devoted to external security. Nowhere does Montesquieu suggest that the small republics participating in this larger union should yield to this larger union any other powers than those necessary for common defence. In this sense, Montesquieu's understanding of federalism remained much more confederal than his American interpreters would later have it.[107] This would suggest that Montesquieu belongs to an older European tradition of confederal federalism rather than to the newer and American idea of a strongly centralized federal state that would only begin at the Philadelphia Convention of 1787.

In fact, one of the intriguing but lastly unanswerable questions is whether Montesquieu had known or read Althusius. Obviously, he referred to the same historical examples that Althusius drew from: Germany, Holland, and Switzerland. At one point he mentions the "ephors" as intermediary powers of political accommodation and arbitration in ancient Sparta, an uncommon reference at least outside the orbit of political Calvinism.[108] His description of "the federal republic of Germany" (la république fédérative d'Allemagne) as governed by a "magistrate of the union" (le magistrat de l'union)[109] is on the whole out of line with German politics and general political diction in his own time, but it closely resembles the state of the Holy Roman Empire as described by Althusius. This description also makes use of the Althusian terminology of the "supreme magistrate" (summus magistratus).[110] Finally and most importantly, however, Montesquieu's description of how federal unions are formed almost reads like a synopsis of the Althusian Politica:

> This form of government is an agreement by which many political bodies consent to become citizens of the larger state that they want to form. It is a society of societies that make a new one, which can be enlarged by new associates that unite with it. (Cette forme de gouvernement est une convention par laquelle plusieurs corps politiques consentent à devenir citoyens d'un État plus grand qu'ils veulent former. C'est une société de sociétés, qui en font une nouvelle, qui peut s'agrandir par de nouveaux associés qui se sont unis.)[111]

That Montesquieu did not cite Althusius can hardly be taken as evidence that he did not know or had not read him. He also did not cite Locke even though it would appear certain that he took the French words for legislative and executive power (pouvoir léglislatif and pouvoir exécutif) from a contemporary French translation of Locke's Second Treatise.[112] Indeed, Robert Shackleton's biography of Montesquieu is full of references to the works of others from which Montesquieu may have drawn without identifying his source. For instance, Shackleton's suggestion is that Montesquieu took his ideas on federalism from Algernon Sidney (1623-83), a liberal politician and writer.[113] But as in the case of Althusius, Sidney is not among the authors whose works were included in Montesquieu's large library at La Brède.[114] There is evidence that Montesquieu had made notes from Sidney's work, but, as Shackleton observes, he probably made such notes from many more works, and not all of them have survived.[115]

Lastly, of course, as in the case of Vico referred to earlier, it does not matter whether or not Montesquieu actually took his ideas about federalism from Althusius. What matters is that these ideas must obviously be placed in the context of a political tradition and culture opposed to absolute sovereignty and centralized power but committed to political plurality and social diversity. Althusius still took this plurality for granted as the natural order of things and did not foresee the overwhelming historical success of politically enforced uniformity under the emerging regime of state absolutism. Montesquieu, by comparison, writing almost a century and a half later, could go a step further and ask why, given their love for liberty, people did not rise everywhere against the forces of despotism.

The reason is, he writes in one of the most revealing passages of *The Spirit of the Laws*, that a moderate government requires far more human effort than a despotic one.[116] A despotic government is "uniform throughout" (*uniforme partout*), and "everyone is good enough for that" (*tout le monde est bon pour cela*). A moderate government of civic liberty, on the other hand, requires a "masterpiece of legislation" (*chef-d'œuvre de législation*) in which one must "combine powers, regulate them, temper them, make them act" (*combiner les puissances, les régler, les tempérer, les faire agir*).[117] Such a government, in other words, does not come about by itself. It requires a tremendous and ongoing political will and effort, an effort which cannot be expected from people who are only driven by the need for sheer survival.

In his only explicit reference to Hobbes, at the outset of *The Spirit of the Laws*, Montesquieu eschews the idea of a state of nature among warring individuals and instead suggests that "peace would be the first natural law" (*la paix serait la première loi naturelle*), followed by the natural urge to "seek nourishment" (*chercher à se nourrir*), the "natural inclination [human beings] always have for one another" (*la prière naturelle qu'ils se font toujours l'un à l'autre*), and finally the "desire to live in society" (*le désir de vivre en société*).[118]

Again, these are natural desires that allow almost an infinite variety of practice. Throughout Montesquieu's work, there is an underlying sentiment of cultural relativism, which also leads him to explore whether the differences in political and cultural traditions between different peoples might have something to do with climate, geography, commerce, religion, and the particularities of history.[119] And not least because of this cultural relativism, he is almost entirely dismissive of the concept and practice of slavery, which almost inevitably comes with notions of racial and/or cultural superiority and its corollary, ignorance. Montesquieu scoffs at the idea that conquest can establish servitude as one of its legitimate ends.[120] "The right of slavery," he writes, comes only "from the scorn that one nation conceives for another, founded on the difference in customs" (*le droit de l'esclavage vient du mépris qu'une nation conçoit pour une autre, fondé sur la différence des coutumes*).[121]

In an ironic rant worthy of a major award for political comedy, he identifies as the main justification for slavery, with a straight face, as it were, and among other things such as colour of skin and the price of sugar, that: "the peoples of Europe, having exterminated those of America, had to make slaves of those of Africa in order to use them to clear so much land" (*les peuples d'Europe ayant exterminé ceux de l'Amérique, ils ont dû mettre en esclavage ceux de l'Afrique, pour s'en servir à défricher tant de terres*).[122] Elsewhere, he declares, entirely seriously again, that "as all men are born equal, one must say that slavery is against nature" (*comme tous les hommes naissent égaux, il faut dire que l'esclavage est contre la nature*), and he qualifies this statement only by admitting that certain conditions may be conducive to slavery, such as a lack of political freedom to begin with, or a hot climate in which arduous work will only be done if someone usurps the rights of others.[123] He also points to prejudice as the only cause that can justify this form of inhumanity: "Knowledge makes men gentle, and reason inclines towards humanity; only prejudices cause these to be renounced" (*Les connaissances rendent les hommes doux; la raison porte à l'humanité: il n'y a que les préjugés qui y fassent renoncer*).[124]

There is a truly enlightened level of human universality, or universal humanism, shining through in these lines that is new in the history of political thought. Not surprisingly, then, it is the relationship between political liberty and justice that marks the most innovative step in Montesquieu's exploration of the spirit of the laws.[125]

As we already know, Montesquieu expanded Locke's separation of legislative and executive power by adding the judiciary as an important third power in its own right, which had to be kept separate by all means. In the context of his sociologically inspired doctrine of power separation, this meant not only that those making the law should not also be in charge of punishing its violations. It also meant that there should not be a regime of class justice: "judges must be of the same condition as the accused, or his peers" (*les juges soient de la condition de l'accusé, ou ses pairs*), and jurors should be "drawn from the body of the people" (*par des personnes tirées du corps du peuple*) accordingly, and for the duration of a given trial period only. In this sense, Montesquieu notes, "the power of judging, so terrible among men," (*la puissance de juger, si terrible parmi les hommes*) will become "invisible and null" (*invisible et nulle*). People will fear the law, but not those who administer it.[126]

The reason why Montesquieu puts so much emphasis on the constrained and temporary character of the judiciary is that while the other two powers, legislative and executive, pertain to the "general will of the state" (*la volonté générale de l'État*), the administration of justice pertains to individuals.[127] The political liberty that the spirit of the laws is ultimately meant to establish and uphold is individual liberty, as was already the case in the political thought of Locke. Yet, Montesquieu's emphasis on how the spirit of the laws is to be exercised, in the administration of laws as they afflict individuals, is quite different from the Lockean emphasis on the defence of property rights, however defined.

As a judge in Bordeaux, Montesquieu had been part of a judicial system that still used torture. So he knows what he is talking about when he observes that "severity in punishment suits despotic government, whose principle is terror" (*la sévérité des peines convient mieux au gouvernement despotique, dont le principe est la terreur*).[128] When he comments further that the excessive use of the death penalty is a sign that the purpose of criminal law is not "correcting the guilty" but instead "avenging the prince" (*Il n'est pas question de corriger le coupable, mais de venger le prince*), he uses Japan as his example.[129] As Montesquieu made a literary career of describing one system through the ironic lens of another, it might at least be permissible to point out that the excessive use of the death penalty in Lockean England could not possibly have escaped his attention and notice.

As was already mentioned in the introduction to this chapter, Montesquieu must be counted among the great reformers of criminal law.[130] The textual evidence for this judgment is mainly Book Six of *The Spirit of the Laws* where Montesquieu discusses the nexus between the form of various types of government, their laws, and their judicial as well as penal systems. In moderate states, he insists, the law should "insist less on punishing crimes than on preventing them" (*s'attachera moins à punir les crimes qu'à les prévenir*).[131] It should provide "a just tempering of penalties and rewards" (*un juste tempérament des peines et des récompenses*).[132] Montesquieu then adds as his main comparative sociological observation:

> It would be easy to prove that in all or nearly all the states of Europe penalties have decreased or increased in proportion as one has approached or departed from liberty. (*Il serait aisé de prouver que, dans tous ou presque tous les États d'Europe, les peines ont diminué ou augmenté à mesure qu'on s'est plus approché ou plus éloigné de la liberté.*)[133]

Political liberty is a reflection of a state's spirit and administration of the law. A harsh penal system is also an indication of a lack of liberty. As we already know, such liberty requires considerable equality of condition. In Montesquieu's mind, there is clearly a link between a state's level of social inequality and its regime of punishment.

"Luxury," he continues in the following Book Seven, "is always proportionate to the inequality of fortunes" (*Le luxe est toujours en proportion avec l'inégalité des fortunes*).[134] There is no assumption of a trickle-down economy here. On the contrary, Montesquieu cautiously endorses redistributive policies such as land reform, because without moderation as a general principle of social organization, a republic will be ruined by the vanity of those for whom the law stands in the way of their desire for luxury.[135] The spirit of the laws will deteriorate into one that only promotes acquisitiveness and greed, but even if it succeeded in satisfying an ever-growing number of citizens, it would not only remain a zero-sum game leaving proportionate inequality in its wake, it would also and ultimately bring little if any satisfaction to the newly rich and famous, "as everyone wants to be looked at, no one is noticed" (*comme tout le monde veut se faire regarder, on ne remarque personne*).[136]

Critical Evaluation

In the political thought of John Locke, the focus is on a free society in which the government is reduced to the function of providing compulsion and punishment, foreshadowing the classical liberal notion of the state as a night watchman. Society is thought of as a society of free individuals uninhibited by traditional ties of family or community. Liberty is understood as negative liberty, the absence of harm to life and property. This is what the state has to provide, and if it doesn't, each and every one has a right of resistance or revolution.

How exactly that right of revolution is to be exercised remains unclear. Locke does say that people can respond to violations of their interests by giving themselves a new legislature.[137] Presumably, this will happen by electing a new Parliament, which will govern with a new majority. What comes to the fore here, however, is that for Locke the parliamentary system is not one of alternating government and opposition, as an acknowledgment of a plurality of social or class interests, but one that somehow represents the uniform will of a coherent society driven by homogeneous interests.

It is this abstract reductionism of social plurality that emerges as the only justification for the legitimacy of majority rule, be it in the electoral process of constituting a legislature, or in the exercise of governance by that legislature. And, because of that assumption of homogeneity, majority rule is released from social contingencies or a carefully framed political process: It becomes a Hobbesian authority in its own right.[138] Gone are the Althusian

143

precautions according to which majority rule only applies when a decision affects all in the same way, whereas consensus is required when particular interests are at stake. Locke does not need this distinction because the assumption now is that majority decisions will always affect all in the same way.

What makes Locke's theory "a classic theory of individual popular sovereignty,"[139] is the assumption that any number of men have consented to make *one* government wherein the majority has the right to act and decide. Ultimately, it does not matter whether Locke conceived this theory, as Macpherson argued, as a theory protecting the interests of taxpaying property owners only.[140] The point is that he conceived it as a theory that allowed for the political manifestation and representation of only one universal and homogeneous societal interest expressed by the noble, but ultimately fuzzy, formula of lives, liberties, and estates.

It is easy to see why this theory would prove so appealing to the propertied classes. In its assumption that men had universally consented to an unequal possession of the earth, and that the introduction of money meant that they had further given their blessing to the unrestrained acquisition of wealth, it removed, in one bold stroke, bad conscience and guilt from the acquisitive mind. Avarice was no longer one of the deadly sins as it had been throughout the Middle Ages.

For the real majority in Lockean England, this formula did not amount to a hill of beans. The problem was not that private property in its narrow material sense had been included, for the first time, as a central tenet in the pursuit of life, liberty, and happiness. It was that without such property, the pursuit of life and liberty, leave alone happiness, appeared rather meaningless.

For an aristocrat in prerevolutionary France, of course, property was not an issue. One simply had it. Montesquieu did not yet see, as his fellow aristocrat Tocqueville thought he did a century later, the dawning of a democratic age of equality. But Montesquieu's genuine concern for civic liberty, his perception of distinct social interests, and his exposure to a political system in England, which was by no means democratic but at least had bestowed real political power upon some commoners, made him think about politics as a compromise among different classes and spatial constituencies. And he was keenly aware that to sustain such politics in a stable and peaceful manner required a balanced social system in which the gap between rich and poor would not be excessive.

This clearly puts the French baron into a tradition of political thought that has Aristotle, Marsilius, Machiavelli, and Althusius among its antecedents. There is much that separates these political thinkers, but what Montesquieu has in common with all of them is his understanding of politics as a plural process of societal collaboration and deliberation. This is an understanding that is almost entirely missing in that other tradition of political thought that has Plato at its beginning and finds its modern continuation in the social contract theories that stretch all the way from Hobbes and Locke to John Rawls. What unites this tradition, despite all other and serious differences, is that the unity of an efficient system of administration replaces plural participation as the primary rationale of political organization. Politics, therefore, becomes stripped of its classical participatory core and is reduced instead to a technique of government entirely divorced from an essentially depoliticized society.[141]

In such a society, as Locke hammers home time and again, liberty means protection by the law from "the arbitrary will of another."[142] In Montesquieu's political society, by comparison, liberty takes on an almost Kantian connotation of categorical rights and obligations:[143]

> In a society where there are laws, liberty can consist only in having the power to do what one should want to do and in no way being constrained to do what one should not want to do. (*Dans une société où il y a des lois, la liberté ne peut consister qu'à pouvoir faire ce que l'on doit vouloir, et à n'être point contraint de faire ce que l'on ne doit pas vouloir.*)[144]

Montesquieu rarely gets read as a theorist of civic culture and pluralism. At least in the English-speaking world, his usual place in the history of political thought is that of a footnote to the American Revolution. He provided the American framers with the idea of checks and balances, and of federalism as a means of adding to the horizontal separation of powers among the different branches of government another and vertical separation among different levels of government.

Radical democrats take offense to this system of checks and balances because, as put so eloquently by the American Federalists themselves, "society will be broken into so many parts, interests and classes of citizens, that the rights of individuals, or of the minority, will be in little danger from interested combinations of the majority."[145] The intention, for the Federalists as for Montesquieu, was clearly conservative, to prevent the loss of privilege and status to the majority of ordinary citizens. For the Americans, however, this was more of a problem, in theory and in practice, because they had written individual freedom and equality on their revolutionary banner. For Montesquieu, at the time, well before the Bastille was stormed, the intention was also a liberal one in that it acknowledged and tried to build into a balanced system of politics an active participatory role for different social classes. And his federalism, by securing the autonomy of small republics within a larger union, was meant to strengthen the social communities making up this balanced system of politics, and not to weaken and undercut them, as was the Federalists' intention.[146]

By comparison with Locke's individual liberalism, then, Montesquieu must appear as an old-fashioned theorist who, not unlike Althusius again, meant to design a stable political system from the traditional building blocks of society. But by articulating this design in a political language of plurality and complexity, he left the door open, at least in principle, for the inclusion of collective identities and interests other than those of old nobility and new bourgeoisie, which appeared to him as the predominant social forces at the time.

These are still basic choices in the design and operation of politics and society. From a Lockean perspective, inclusion is only possible if and when each and every one has adopted the same basic predisposition or interest, and agrees in seeing the protection of individual rights as the paramount task of the state. From the perspective of Montesquieu, such a simplification of politics and society is not possible. Instead, the spirit of the laws must aim at the conciliation and not the dissolution of differences.

While for Locke inequality was the inevitable and even natural price to pay for individual liberty, Montesquieu more cautiously argued that liberty could not last without at least a reasonable measure of what he called equality of conditions (*égalité dans les conditions*).[147] Two revolutions and a century later, equality of conditions appeared as the paramount driving force of history to another French aristocrat, Alexis de Tocqueville. But because Tocqueville feared that this condition would inevitably lead to a tyranny of the majority, he never referred to that other French political thinker, Jean-Jacques Rousseau, who had conjured up, only a few years after Montesquieu, the sublimation of majority power in the romantic notion of the general will.

CHAPTER 8

Power of the Majority
Rousseau v. Tocqueville

Up to this point, not a single one among our political theorists and philosophers had ever entertained the thought that all men — leave alone all men and women — should be unqualified citizens, and that a majority of such citizens should have an unconditional right to determine the course of politics. Typically, there had been two constraints placed upon political participation by the many. One was the idea of a mixed constitution by which the powers of majority and minority, quantity and quality, poor and rich, people and nobility, would be tied into a governmental system of mutual cooperation and control, with the scale usually tipped in favour of the few. The other was the idea of limiting legislative majority rule by some form of citizenship qualification, usually based on economic status.

The two great revolutions, in America and in France, changed all that by setting free liberal energies that could no longer be taken back for good. In America, the Virginia Declaration of 1776 unmistakably stated that "all men are by nature free and independent," and that "all power is vested in, and consequently derived from, the people." In France, the *Declaration of the Rights of Man and of the Citizen* (*Déclaration des droits de l'Homme et du Citoyen*) of 1789 pronounced that "law is the expression of the general will" (*la loi est l'expression de la volonté générale*), and that "all citizens, being equal in the eyes of the law, are equally eligible to all dignities and all public positions" (*tous les citoyens, étant égaux à ces yeux, sont également admissibles à toutes dignités, places et emplois publics*).

This was the language of Jean-Jacques Rousseau. With the publication of his famous *Social Contract* (*Du contrat social*) 27 years earlier, Rousseau had provided the history of political thought with the most radical manifesto of political, economic, and social equality yet, and the French Revolution with all its important cues.

147

Context

France during the second half of the eighteenth century was a confusing and dangerous place.[1] Books with critical content routinely had to be printed outside the country, in Geneva or Amsterdam, but then they often could be imported and read nevertheless. It was also advisable to publish such books anonymously, even though in most cases everyone knew who the author was. Strangely, for a feudal system in its last and most decadent convulsions, it seemed more dangerous to attack the church than to preach equality. When Rousseau had to flee Paris in 1762, it was because of the alleged "blasphemous" content of his works and not for his advocacy of popular sovereignty. In the same year, Protestants were still tortured and put to death in Toulouse. In Paris, it was none other than the minister responsible for publications and censorship, Chrétien Guillaume de Lamoignon de Malesherbes, who had first protected and supported Rousseau in his publishing endeavours but who then tried to cover up his personal involvement in these endeavours when it became clear that both the *Social Contract*, and *Émile*, Rousseau's educational treatise, would have to be banned. And it was Malesherbes yet again who warned Rousseau to leave the country when his arrest was imminent, in a coded message sent through intermediaries.

Prerevolutionary France was a rigid class society. By comparison, as Tocqueville observed a generation later, England appeared infinitely more liberal, even though, as the great French sociologist understood full well, this liberalism was ultimately a phony one: The nobility knew "how to mingle on familiar terms with its inferiors when necessary, and to pretend to consider them its equals" (*quand cela lui paraissait nécessaire, se méler familièrement à ses inférieurs et feindre de les considérer comme ses égaux*). It was "ready to do anything in order to lead" (*prête à tout pour commander*). In sharp contrast, class barriers in France were "always fixed and visible" (*toujours fixe et visible*).[2]

Tocqueville also provided succinct insight into the dynamic that would propel French society towards the revolutionary abyss: relentless centralization, usually associated with the postrevolutionary Jacobin regime but in fact put into place well before the revolution. According to Tocqueville, this centralization had two main effects. On the one hand, in its desperate yet futile effort to get under control the deficit-driven public household of the French court and state, the central government drained from much of the rest of the country badly needed resources, and, with it, even more badly needed loyalties. Tocqueville quotes from a letter written by Montesquieu to a friend in 1740 in which the provincial baron and wine grower complained that "in France nothing exists but Paris and the distant provinces, because Paris has not yet had time to devour them" (*Il n'y a en France que Paris et les provinces*

éloignées, parce que Paris n'a pas encore eu le temps de les dévorer).[3]
On the other hand, centralization exacerbated what Tocqueville called
the "division of classes" (*la division des classes*), because the monarchy had
deprived the wealthy and educated of any meaningful way of participating in
public life and, therefore, of any reason to cooperate. Tocqueville cites from
a secret report to the king, according to which the nation had become "a
society made up of different orders badly united" (*une société composée des
différents ordres mal unis*), where "nowhere is any common interest visible"
(*nulle part il n'y a d'intérêt commun visible*), and "no one cares about anything but his own personal interests" (*personne n'est occupée que de son
intérêt particulier*).[4]
The division very much was an intellectual one as well. At one end of the
spectrum were those who used Cartesian principles for the justification of a
state in which each and every one had their place according to a systematic
and rational construction of society. Theirs was a very "learned" approach,
to be sure, but it also happened to mostly coincide with the interests of those
who were satisfied with their station in public and social life. From the other
end of the spectrum, therefore, arose a rebellion against what was seen as an
unholy alliance between the new science and the conservative forces of old,
and a plea for the return to a more natural and spontaneously rebellious
form of sociability as well as politics.
Push came to shove, well before the great revolution itself, and in an
unlikely arena of human endeavour that was symptomatic of imminent dramatic change nevertheless. In 1752 an Italian opera company visited Paris
and performed, with resounding success, Giovanni Battista Pergolesi's *La
Serva Padrona*. This was a short comic opera (*opera buffa*), a "galant"
rather than "learned" piece of music full of simple melodies and with an
irreverent plot according to which the noble master gets to marry his servant
in the end. Pergolesi's music contrasted sharply with the "learned" harmonic
style of serious French opera (*opera seria*), as exemplified in particular by the
court composer Jean-Philippe Rameau. Rameau was a musical Cartesian
who believed that everything in music had to follow one rational and universal harmonic scheme.
The ensuing intellectual battle between the "learned" and "galant" camps
had all of Paris agitated for several years. It easily overshadowed all other
political and social ills, the loss of Canada in 1759 included. When one of the
leading music critics in Paris came out in unconditional support of the galant
style of music championed by the "buffonists," he was burnt in effigy by the
musicians of the Paris opera. That music critic was Jean-Jacques Rousseau.[5]
In the realm of music, the dispute between learned and galant would only
be settled by the genius of Mozart. The child prodigy from Salzburg had

emulated the style of *La Serva Padrona* in his own opera, *Bastien und Bastienne*, early on in 1768, incidentally using a text by Rousseau. Later, however, especially after his second sojourn in Paris (1777-78), Mozart would define the classiçal musical style as a fusion of learned *and* galant in such a way as to never let the full employment of harmonic mastery detract from the simple pleasure of melody.[6] In the realm of politics, such synthetic sophistication was far from Rousseau's yearning ambition.

Jean-Jacques Rousseau (1712-78)

France's most famous political philosopher was born in Calvinist Geneva, hardly ever went to school, and never saw the inside of a university. He left Geneva when, at the age of 16, and returning late from a walk in the country, he found the city gates closed and simply walked away. By the time he became an instant celebrity at the age of 38, with the publication of his *Discourse on the Sciences and Arts* (*Discours sur les sciences et les arts*, 1750),[7] he had converted to Catholicism (he would later revert to Calvinism); served as a "footman in Turin"; enrolled as "a student at a choir school in Annecy"; and had been "the steward and lover of a Swiss baroness in Chambéry, the interpreter to a Levantine mountebank, an itinerant musician, a private tutor in the family of Condillac and Mably in Lyon, secretary to the French Ambassador in Venice and research assistant to the Dupins at Chenonceaux."[8] Along the way, and through incessant self-study, Rousseau also picked up the education and erudition he had missed out on during his earlier years.

In 1749 the regional Academy of Dijon announced an essay competition on the question: Has the restoration of the sciences and arts had a purifying effect upon morals? The *Discourse on the Sciences and Arts* was Rousseau's entry in this competition, and it won the prize even though it flew in the face of what the scholarly establishment might have hoped for. "Necessity raised up thrones; the sciences and arts have made them strong" (*Le besoin éleva les trônes; les sciences et les arts les ont affermis*), Rousseau declares at the outset. They accomplish this by flinging "flower garlands over the chains" (*guirlandes de fleurs sur les chaînes*) of men who thus are made to "love their own slavery" (*aimer leur esclavage*). As a result, he bemoans, "there prevails in modern manners a servile and deceptive conformity" (*il règne dans nos mœurs une vile et trompeuse uniformité*).[9]

Rousseau, in other words, claimed that the sciences and arts were nothing but convenient ideological tools in the hands of the established powers. In the end, even the scientists and artists themselves will have "sacrificed their taste to those who tyrannize over their liberty" (*ont sacrifié leur goût aux tyrans de leur liberté*).[10] The conformity, however, that Rousseau deplores, disseminated by a "herd of text-book authors" (*cette foule d'auteurs élémentaires*),[11] is not necessarily to be replaced by a plurality of opinions and theories. Rousseau's dislike of the sciences and the arts is quite Cartesian in the end: They are perilous because "falsehood is capable of an infinite variety of combinations; but the truth has only one manner of being" (*le faux est susceptible d'une infinité de combinaisons; mais la vérité n'a qu'une manière d'être*).[12] From the truth as only one manner of being to the general will as the only manner of being political will be just another step.

In his second discourse, *On the Origin and Foundations of Inequality Among Men* (*Sur l'origine et les fondements de l'inégalité parmi les hommes*, 1755), again written for the Dijon Academy,[13] but this time rejected, Rousseau took a decidedly anti-Hobbesian as well as anti-Lockean stand. In the first part of the discourse, he essentially preformulated what would later become a standard criticism of Hobbes: that the author of the *Leviathan* looked at an early-modern bourgeois society driven by *amour-propre*, a factitious feeling of self-centred greed and abuse, and mistook it for the state of nature.[14] Instead, Rousseau argues, with reference to the "tenderness of mothers for their offspring" (*la tendresse des mères pour leur petits*), that human beings have a natural predisposition for "compassion" (*pitié*) which is as powerful as the urge of "self-preservation" (*le désir de se conserver*).[15]

In the second part of the discourse he then takes on the Lockean idea of private property as the harbinger of liberty and happiness, denouncing it as the ultimate cause for the exact opposite, the loss of liberty, by establishing social and political inequality under the biased mantle of science:

> From great inequality of fortunes and conditions, from the vast variety of passions and of talents, of useless and pernicious arts, of vain sciences, would arise a multitude of prejudices equally contrary to reason, happiness, and virtue. (*De l'extrême inégalité des conditions et des fortunes, de la diversité des passions et des talents, des arts inutiles, des arts pernicieux, des sciences frivoles sortiraient des foules de préjugés, également contraires à la raison, au bonheur et à la vertu.*)[16]

And since he is already at it, Rousseau also dispenses with the entire tradition of carefully distinguishing between different forms of government according to certain principles, numbers, or virtues. "The different forms of government owe their origin to the differing degrees of inequality which existed between individuals at the time of their institution" (*Les diverses formes de gouvernements tirent leur origine des différences plus ou moins grandes qui se trouvèrent entre les particuliers au moment de l'institution*), he declares. The "progress of inequality" (*progrès de l'inégalité*), on the other hand, always follows the same pattern: first, the "right of property" (*droit de propriété*) is established; then follows the "institution of magistracy" (*l'institution de la magistrature*), the obvious purpose of which is to uphold and protect that right; and finally a "conversion of legitimate into arbitrary power" (*changement du pouvoir légitime en pouvoir arbitraire*) is achieved which completes the process by establishing a relationship of "master and slave" (*de maître et d'esclave*).[17]

Had he stopped right there, Rousseau would still be in the classical canon as the romantic thinker of "back to nature" who contrasted inequality in civil society with the idyllic life of "men content in their rustic huts" (*les hommes contentèrent dans les cabanes rustiques*),[18] or as the first radical thinker who contemplated the nexus between material and ideological power. It was this discourse on inequality that made a particular impression upon Karl Marx.

But Rousseau did not stop there. He went on to write the *Social Contract* and thus provided the world with what may be the most controversial piece of political thought ever put on paper, a piece that has been as much lauded as the most radical statement of popular sovereignty and democracy as it has been vilified as leading straight to modern totalitarianism. And, of course, as Tocqueville would later observe, radical democracy and tyranny might not necessarily be as far apart as one would think.

As he mentions in the brief foreword to the *Social Contract*,[19] Rousseau's plan was to write a much larger and more comprehensive work on political institutions, which he abandoned because he found it "beyond his powers" to finish. Rousseau destroyed most of his preliminary drafts, and, from what he kept, compiled the *Social Contract* as the expression of only one particular aspect of the larger intended work.[20] As Maurice Cranston has pointed out, Rousseau reveals right at the outset, in the opening paragraph to Book One, what aspect he had in mind, and, therefore, also what he had abandoned. No longer was the purpose to provide a practical theory of *how* political institutions ought to be constructed in order to satisfy critical standards of equality, justice, and legitimacy. Instead, the purpose now was to ponder, much more speculatively, *if* such a legitimate form of governance was possible at all:

> I mean to inquire if, in the civil order, there can be any sure and legitimate rule of administration, men being taken as they are and laws as they might be. (*Je veux chercher si, dans l'ordre civil, il peut y avoir quelque règle d'administration légitime et sûre, en prenant les hommes tels qu'ils sont, et les lois telles qu'elles peuvent être.*)[21]

This, of course, puts Rousseau squarely in the same league as Plato and other idealist political philosophers who dream up perfect schemes of political order. These have their legitimate purpose as critical yardsticks cast against an imperfect and often corrupted political reality. In the realm of practical politics, however, they are often read and interpreted with passionate hearts rather than critical minds. Rousseau's big *if* can be said to have inspired both the revolution that declared all men to be free and equal, and the Jacobin terror that followed in its wake.

Thus, the *Social Contract* opens with the famous fiery words: "Man was born free, and he is everywhere in chains" (*L'homme est né libre, et partout il est dans les fers*).[22] It then proceeds to define the social contract as a "form of association" (*une forme d'association*) resulting in a rather Hobbesian sounding "total alienation by each associate of himself and all his rights to the whole community" (*l'aliénation totale de chaque associé avec tous ses droits à toute la communauté*).[23] And shortly thereafter follows what must truly be one of the most contentious sentences in the entire history of political thought:

> Hence, in order that the social pact shall not be an empty formula ... whoever refuses to obey the general will shall be constrained to do so by the whole body, which means nothing other than that he shall be forced to be free. (*Afin donc que ce pacte social ne soit pas un vain formulaire ... quiconque refusera d'obéir à la volonté générale, y sera contraint par tout le corps; ce qui ne signifie autre chose sinon qu'on le forcera à être libre.*)[24]

Forced to be free: Rousseau's interpreters have certainly hemmed and hawed about the meaning of this sentence.[25] However, it is neither particularly difficult to understand, nor is it necessary to make too much of it.

As Rousseau explains quite clearly, the purpose of the social contract is to unite a multitude into a body politic. This body politic is the sovereign. The general will is the expression of the common public interest by this sovereign body of citizens.[26] So far so good: At this level of generality, what Rousseau tells us is not much different from what we already know from Hobbes, or even Althusius. That he has something rather different in mind, however, becomes clearer by the following sentence: "For every individual as a man may have a private will contrary to, or different from, the general will he has as a citizen" (*En effet, chaque individu peut, comme homme, avoir une volonté particulière contraire ou dissemblable à la volonté générale qu'il a comme citoyen*).[27]

Most political theories before Rousseau assumed that the general public interest was the aggregate of, or compromise among, differing particular or private interests. Public policy, however arrived at, was accepted because it granted liberty to pursue private interests within the confines of common agreement about law and order. For Hobbes, this required the total separation of public power from private society, and the contract therefore became a fictitious act of political will alienation. For Althusius, it required a constant process of communication and deliberation, which left political power located within organized civil society itself.

What Rousseau now proposes is that this dichotomy of self-interest (*amour-propre*) and public interest or compassion (*pitié*), as he called it in the discourse on inequality,[28] is located within each individual themself. The contradictions of politics in a society where men are born free but everywhere in chains are the contradictions of men themselves. "Forced to be free" means obeying the general will as the collective expression of one's own better self. The general will is not just the collective expression of sovereign power. It is the collective expression of a superior moral power.

Still, so far so good: If the general will ordains that we shall stop at red traffic lights, it really does not make much difference whether we do so out of self-interest, because we do not want to get hurt, or out of compassion, because we do not want to hurt others. The point is that nobody gets hurt. The crucial question, however, remains: Who or what gives legitimate expression to the general will, and how can we be sure that the general will really is the general will?

Rousseau rejects out of hand the solution advanced by Locke. "It is contrary to the natural order that the greater number should govern and the smaller number be governed" (*Il est contre l'ordre naturel que le grand nombre gouverne et que le petit soit gouverné*), he declares.[29] He also dismisses the idea of representative government as a travesty of popular sovereignty: "Sovereignty cannot be represented ... its essence is the general will ... either it is the general will or it is something else ... The English people believes itself to be free; it is gravely mistaken" (*La souveraineté ne peut être représentée ... elle consiste essentiellement dans la volonté générale ... elle est la même, ou elle est autre ... Le peuple anglais pense être libre, il se trompe fort*).[30]

The general will, in other words, must come from, and be expressed directly by, the people in their entirety. A majority, however representative, will not do. Rousseau's thoughts are interwoven with references to the virtues of small republics and the classical city states of Greece. He obviously harbours the idea that smallness will not only allow direct democracy through the active participation of all citizens in a legislative assembly, but will also, and at the same time, encourage simpler tastes and desires, and more equality of predisposition, as well as condition.

This line of thought was inspired by the admiration Rousseau felt for his native Geneva, which he deemed to be governed by a general council of "plain citizens" (*simples citoyens*).[31] Geneva was a small republic all right, but in reality it was a Calvinist city tyrannically governed by a religious oligarchy. Rousseau would eventually learn the hard way that he had been much more the romantic yearner than the critical observer when republican Geneva burnt his books, just as monarchical Paris had banned them.

Clearly, however, manifestations of the general will are inextricably linked to the desired goal—political, economic, and cultural equality among citizens. In what arguably is his weakest line of thought, Rousseau insists, not that the general will produces such equality, but, almost in a chicken-and-egg sense, that the general will itself can only become manifest under conditions of equality already achieved.[32] And these conditions must be legislated, as he had already pointed out in his earlier *Discourse on Political Economy* (*Économie politique*), by a government whose primary function is to "prevent extreme inequality of fortunes; not by taking away wealth from its possessors, but by depriving all men of means to accumulate it" (*prévenir l'extrême inégalité des fortunes, non en enlevant les trésors à leurs possesseurs, mais en tant à tous les moyens d'en accumuler*).[33] Rousseau's understanding of equality is not of the redistributive or welfare kind. It foreshadows the socialist maxim that each should be given "according to his needs."[34]

Yet, Rousseau obviously cannot resolve his chicken-and-egg problem. Perhaps it is here that he threw up his arms and abandoned the larger project of a comprehensive theory of political institutions. In the *Social Contract*, however, his solution is the rather bizarre introduction of a "lawgiver" (*législateur*), who is "an extraordinary man" (*un homme extraordinaire*) whose office is "neither that of the government nor that of the sovereign" (*ce n'est point magistrature, ce n'est point souveraineté*), whose "sublime reasoning …soars above the heads of the common people" (*raison sublime…s'élève au-dessus de la portée des hommes vulgaires*), and who will not shy away from what the founders of nations have always done: "appeal to divine intervention" (*recourir à l'intervention du ciel*).[35]

Rousseau has in mind an act of ideal and revolutionary nation-building that is reminiscent of both Plato and Calvin. It is an old idea that crops up almost inevitably among revolutionary elites who see themselves as predestined to lead the people to a better world. "The public must be taught to recognize what it desires" (*il faut apprendre à l'autre à connaître ce qu'il veut*), Rousseau writes.[36] The same idea is still echoed in the 2002 constitution of the Chinese Communist Party, which stipulates in its general program that the party is the "vanguard" of the Chinese working class, people, and nation.[37]

Doubtlessly, Rousseau thought of himself as the genius whose sublime reasoning would soar above that of the common people. Rather pedestrian and "mechanical,"[38] however, is his explanation of just how the general will might operate in practice:

There is often a great difference between the will of all and the general will; the general will studies only the common interest while the will of all studies private interest, and it is indeed no more than the sum of individual desires. But if we take away from these same wills, the pluses and minuses which cancel each other out, the balance which remains is the general will. (*Il y a souvent bien de la différence entre la volonté de tous et la volonté générale; celle-ci ne regarde qu'à l'intérêt commun; l'autre regarde à l'intérêt privé, et n'est qu'une somme de volontés particulières: mais ôtez de ces mêmes volontés les plus et les moins qui s'entre-détruisent, reste pour somme des différences la volonté générale.*)[39]

What this amounts to, at first glance, is majority rule. However, as we already know, Rousseau was hostile to the idea of majority rule.[40] As he continues to explain, therefore, the majority will represent the general will only under certain conditions: when the people are "properly informed" (*suffisamment informé*) and "do not have any communication among themselves" (*n'avaient aucune communication entre eux*).[41] By the latter he means that the opinions of individual citizens should not be prejudiced by the factionism of "sectional associations" (*associations partielles*).[42] If such factions become dominant, he argues, the general will that may exist within them constitutes a sectional or private will with regard to the whole or state. Such sectional associations, therefore, should be avoided, but, if that is impossible, the strategy should be "to multiply their number and to prevent inequality among them" (*multiplier le nombre et en prévenir l'inégalité*).[43] Only under such conditions, he assumes, will the will of the majority, among individual citizens who all think and want the same, become the general will.

This is in fact one of Rousseau's more intriguing contributions to the history of political thought, and it is one that often gets overlooked.[44] It clearly anticipates much later theories of plural interest group democracy. It also and ironically advances an argument similar to that of the American Federalists, according to which "society will be broken into so many parts, interests and classes of citizens, that the rights of individuals, or of the minority, will be in little danger from interested combinations of the majority."[45]

The Federalists, of course, wanted to avoid exactly what appeared to Rousseau as the ultimate goal, the submersion of each and every one into a unanimous state of harmony. While the Federalists hoped that the institutional pluralization of society, by means of multiple checks and balances, would make the general unanimity of public opinion an impossibility, Rousseau expected the exact opposite, the triumph of the general will over all private interests:

The greater harmony that reigns in the public assemblies, the more, in other words, that public opinion approaches unanimity, the more the general will is dominant; whereas long debates, dissensions and disturbances bespeak the ascendance of particular interests and the decline of the state. (*Plus le concert règne dans les assemblées, c'est-à-dire plus les avis approchent de l'unanimité, plus aussi la volonté générale est dominante; mais les longs débats, les dissensions, le tumulte, annoncent l'ascendant des intérêts particuliers et le déclin de l'État.*)[46]

Here we have it again, the yearning for harmony and the disdain for those "disturbances" (*tumulte*) which appeared to Machiavelli as the dynamic precondition for republican liberty.[47] According to the French aristocrat Alexis de Tocqueville, all the checks and balances in the world could not prevent democracy from ending up with a Rousseauian outcome, an outcome he called tyranny of the majority.

Alexis de Tocqueville (1805-59)

It is not surprising that Alexis de Tocqueville should have worried about the inevitable rise of modern mass democracy and the fickle powers of public opinion. His great-grandfather had been guillotined by the French Revolution in 1794. His parents barely escaped the same fate only when luck ran out on Robespierre. That great-grandfather, incidentally, had been the same Malesherbes who had issued the warrant for Rousseau's arrest but had then warned him to get out of Paris. Thirty years later, in 1792, Malesherbes volunteered to come back from retirement in Switzerland to defend Louis XVI before the National Convention. The king's inevitable violent death was followed by Malesherbes's own two years later.

Tocqueville's own life still fell into a period that continued to be interrupted by political upheaval and social unrest.[48] When he was born, Napoléon had just ended the revolutionary first republic by crowning himself emperor in December 1804. Tocqueville's date of birth was in fact still recorded under the republican calendar as 11 Thermidor of the year XIII, rather than July 29, 1805. When Tocqueville was nine, Napoléon's reign was over and a liberal constitutional monarchy was restored under Louis XVII. However, Tocqueville had hardly finished his study of law in Paris and become a judicial officer at the Versailles court of law when the July 1830 revolution broke out against new restrictions on suffrage and freedom of the press under Louis XVII's successor, Charles X. By the time Tocqueville and his travel companion Gustave de Beaumont arrived in Newport, Rhode Island, on May 9, 1831, for their nine-month visit to America, Charles X had been replaced by the "citizen-king" Louis-Philippe, and the constitutional monarchy had taken a more liberal turn again.

After his return, Tocqueville wrote the two volumes of *Democracy in America* (*De la démocratie en Amérique*, 1835 and 1840),[49] and was elected to the French Chamber of Deputies and inducted into the Académie française. This happened during a few years of relative political calm. Politics in France appeared firmly in the hands of a new bourgeois upper class whose values and preferences, while couched in a new language of liberalism, were not all that different from those of the old aristocracy — or at least of its more enlightened part.

Tocqueville remained cautious if not uncommitted. In 1837 he wrote to an English friend that, after living "in a country that for forty years had tried a little of everything without settling definitively on anything" (*un pays qui pendant quarante ans avait essayé un peu de tout sans s'arrêter définitivement à rien*), where "aristocracy was already dead" but "democracy did not yet exist" (*l'aristcratie était déjà morte ... la démocratie n'existait point encore*), his inclination had been not to take sides but to observe by casting "calm glances to both sides" (*des regards tranquilles des deux côtés*).[50]

Tocqueville understood very well what united aristocracy and bourgeoisie in their quest for stability. In a parliamentary speech on January 29, 1848, he remarked that the French Revolution had not gone as far as to destroy the right of property. He warned (a month before the *Communist Manifesto* was published in London) that the "governing class" (*la classe qui gouverne*) was sleeping "on a volcano" (*sur un volcan*), and that if necessary further social reforms were not undertaken, the "working classes" (*les classes ouvrières*) would get ideas aimed at "breaking up the very foundations of society" (*la société, à l'ébranler sur les bases*).[51]

He did not have to wait long. In February 1848, after radicals had demanded not only democratic but also socialist reforms, rioting broke out in Paris and elsewhere. Louis-Philippe abdicated, and a new constituent assembly was elected. Violent worker uprisings in July were suppressed by the army, leaving more than 10,000 dead or wounded in the streets. The second republic was ushered in by the newly elected Louis Napoléon, a nephew of Napoléon Bonaparte.

Tocqueville was elected to the new legislative assembly again, in 1849, winning 110,000 out of 120,000 votes in his Normandy riding,[52] and he even briefly became Louis Napoléon's minister of foreign affairs. By 1852, however, Louis Napoléon had replaced the second republic with a second empire and himself as Napoléon III. Tocqueville's public career was over. In a letter to the *Times* in London, he deplored the loss of liberal freedom and denounced the plebiscitary approval for the ascent of Louis Napoléon to imperial power as obtained by "military terrorism."[53] He was arrested and, after a brief period of imprisonment, retreated to his family seat in Normandy where he wrote and published his last major work, *The Old Regime and the Revolution*.[54] Always in fragile health, he died of tuberculosis three years later.

In the last chapter of that last work, Tocqueville summed up what he thought had been wrong with France all along, before, during, and after the revolution. The French, he declared, while fickle in their commitment to liberty, had an unwavering passion for equality. And that passion could be satisfied, always at the expense of liberty, by institutions of centralization, which, established well before the revolution, were in reality the tools of despotism. Thus, "every time that we have since tried to bring down absolute power, we have limited ourselves to placing liberty's head on a servile body" (*toutes les fois qu'on a voulu depuis abattre le pouvoir absolu, on s'est borné à placer la tête de la Liberté sur un corps servile*).[55]

This was the grand theme to which Tocqueville's entire political thinking was dedicated. In sharp contrast to Rousseau, who had argued that liberty for each and every one could only be achieved under conditions of social, economic, and political equality, Tocqueville was convinced that in fact there was a fundamental and irreconcilable tension between personal and individual liberty on the one hand, and social equality on the other. In France, this conviction endeared him to neither the defenders of liberal democracy nor the champions of a renewed empire. Only the English continued to cherish his thoughts, because the ambivalence with which he had described their liberalism was perfectly concomitant with their own pragmatic understanding of it.[56] So great was their admiration that in 1857, when Tocqueville visited London for the last time, still researching material for a planned expansion of his work on the French Revolution, he would return to Cherbourg aboard an English destroyer put at his disposal by the first lord of the admiralty.[57]

When a more youthful and optimistic Tocqueville set out to observe and study American society 25 years earlier, he did so because he wanted to see whether it might in fact provide a new and unique example of how liberty could be preserved under democratic conditions of equality. For nine months, Tocqueville travelled the breadth and the width of the United States, collecting data, conducting interviews, studying primary documents and literature, and observing political and daily life.[58] The results of his investigations, published in the two volumes of *Democracy in America*, arguably made him the first truly modern social scientist: His approach was both empirical and theoretical, and, on the basis of similar studies in France and other European countries, it was also genuinely comparative.

While the first volume of *Democracy in America* had a clear focus on political institutions and processes, the second volume turned to political culture and civil society. Throughout both volumes, however, one finds three interrelated and interwoven themes that are sometimes difficult to disentangle: the factual description of American politics and society; observations about the general nature of modern society under conditions of democratic equality; and democratic theory proper. If there is a flaw in Tocqueville's design and presentation of the work, then it is, as John Stuart Mill already observed in his review of *Democracy in America*, that he did not separate clearly enough what he saw in America as the characteristics of modern mass society on the one hand, and what he thought was the essence of the democratic form of politics and society on the other.[59] To Tocqueville, America was the model case for the inevitable coincidence of both. Contrary to usual assertions, however, he did not seek to construct his model as a case of "American exceptionalism."[60]

While he thought that America had been the first to achieve democratic equality due to unique circumstances and history, he was nevertheless convinced that a universal trend towards equality of the American kind was unstoppable. This makes the reading of *Democracy in America* particularly interesting in an age of globalization in which the American superpower is exporting what it claims to be universal liberal values. When Tocqueville observed the birth of these values more than 150 years earlier, one may well ask, therefore, was he witness to the rise of universal trends and values of equality and democracy, or was he witnessing the birth of an idiosyncratic American way of life and politics?

Tocqueville begins *Democracy in America* by identifying what appears to him as the most general and all-pervasive quality of life in America — the "equality of social conditions" (*l'égalité des conditions*) which permeate everything from private habits to public attitudes, law, and government.[61] What he means by equality of conditions is that, at least from a European perspective, "the classes are muddled; those barriers raised between men are being lowered; estates are being split up and power shared; education is expanding and men's intelligence tends toward equality" (*les rangs qui se confondent; les barrières élevées entre les hommes s'abaissent; on divise les domaines, le pouvoir se partage, les lumières se répandent, les intelligences s'égalisent*).[62]

Logically, such social conditions have political consequences. "One has to understand," Tocqueville argues, "that equality ends up infiltrating the world of politics as it does everywhere else" (*Il est impossible de comprendre que l'égalité ne finisse pas par pénétrer dans le monde politique comme ailleurs*). Political equality, however, can only be established in one of two ways: "rights have to be granted to every citizen or to none" (*il faut donner des droits à chaque citoyen, ou n'en donner à personne*).[63] Democracy or despotism are the stark alternatives, and, if despotism is to be avoided, a democratic system of government granting rights to every citizen must be grounded in the "sovereignty of the people" (*la souveraineté du peuple*).[64]

Tocqueville was keenly aware that he was breaking new ground: "A new political science is needed for a totally new world" (*Il faut une science politique nouvelle à un monde tout nouveau*).[65] By using the term "democracy" for a new way of politics and social life, Tocqueville was indeed referring to something quite novel in the history of political thought. Throughout that history, democracy had been thought of as an ideal form of direct government by all or the majority, as it had not existed since the time of classical Athens. It was usually criticized as impractical and unjust. Even Rousseau avoided the term in the context of his theory of the general will and only later referred to it as a perfect form of government lastly suitable for a "people of gods" (*peuple des Dieux*).[66]

By the time Tocqueville wrote about democracy, however, the term had moved from the lofty pages of scholarly disputation to the pedestrian arena of everyday political debate.[67] The French Revolution had split society into two camps whose partisans were often referred to as aristocrats and democrats. Democracy was no longer understood merely as a form of government by the many but as a much broader goal for the organization of politics, society, and, at least among socialists, the economy. Still contested in many quarters, democracy had become the expression for a new way of life.

What exactly that meant remained rather unclear. The "people" in their entirety neither governed in republican France nor in England, a constitutional monarchy. When Tocqueville returned from America, however, he provided unmistakable clarification: Democracy was to be understood henceforth as an existing and practicable form of representative government by which the majority governs in the name of the people.

"If we wish to discuss the political laws of the United States," he insists, "we must start with the doctrine of the sovereignty of the people" (*Lorsqu'on veut parler des lois politiques des États-Unis, c'est toujours par le dogme de la souveraineté du peuple qu'il faut commencer*).[68]

Like "will of the nation" (*volonté nationale*), however, popular sovereignty is

> one of those phrases most widely abused by schemers and tyrants of all ages. Some have seen it appear in votes bought by agents of power, others in the votes of a frightened or self-seeking minority. Some have even discovered it in the silence of a nation and have supposed that, from this apparent submission, they had a right to control. In America, the sovereignty of the people is not, as with certain nations, a hidden or barren notion; it is acknowledged in custom, celebrated by law. (*un des mots dont les intrigants de tous les temps et les despotes de tous les âges ont le plus largement abusé. Les uns en ont vu l'expression dans les suffrages achetés de quelques agents du pouvoir, d'autres dans les votes d'une minorité intéressée ou craintive; il y en a même qui l'ont découverte toute formulée dans le silence des*

peuples, et qui ont pensé que du fait de l'obéissance naissait pour eux le droit du commandement. En Amérique, le principe de la souveraineté du peuple n'est point caché ou stérile comme chez certaines nations; il est reconnu par les mœurs, proclamé par les lois.)[69]

How does such recognition and proclamation of democracy come about? Tocqueville explains by summing up the American system of government in one concise paragraph:

In America the people appoint the lawmakers and the executive; they form the jury which punishes breaches of the law. Not only are institutions democratic in principle but also in their consequences; thus the people *directly* nominate their representatives and, as a general rule, choose them *annually* so as to hold them more completely dependent. Therefore, in reality it is the people who rule. Although they have a representative government, it is quite clear that the opinions, bias, concerns, and even the passions of the people can encounter no lasting obstacles preventing them from exercising a day-to-day influence upon the conduct of society.

In the United States, as in any country ruled by the people, the majority governs in the name of the people.

(*En Amérique, le peuple nomme celui qui fait la loi et celui qui l'exécute; lui-même forme le jury qui punit les infractions à la loi. Non seulement les institutions sont démocratiques dans leur principe, mais encore dans tous leurs développements; ainsi le peuple nomme directement ses représentants et les choisit en général tous les ans, afin de les tenir plus complètement dans sa dépendance. C'est donc réellement le peuple qui dirige, et, quoique la forme du gouvernement soit représentative, il est évident que les opinions, les préjugés, les intérêts et même les passions du peuple ne peuvent trouver d'obstacles durables qui les empêchent de se produire dans la direction journalière de la société.*

Aux États-Unis, comme dans tous les pays où le peuple règne, c'est la majorité qui gouverne au nom du peuple.)[70]

In hindsight, we can of course quibble over the question as to whether Tocqueville's bold phrases constitute an accurate description, then or now, of the degree to which "the people" is really sovereign under such a form of representative majority government. But in principle, these paragraphs constitute the first wholly modern formulation of electoral and representative democracy, forever distinguished and distanced from all authoritarian and/or populist regimes, then and now, which only pay lip service to popular sovereignty.

Tocqueville's further discussion of democracy remains embedded in his description of political life and organization in America. Interestingly, he approaches his analysis almost in Althusian fashion, with a bottom-up perspective. Small communities such as municipalities are the natural seedbeds of organized society. The "onslaughts of power" (*invasions du pouvoir*) by centralized national governments incessantly threaten their independence and freedom, and especially so in continental Europe. "However, the strength of free nations," he declares, "resides in the township" (*C'est pourtant dans la commune que réside la force des peuples libres*).[71]

In order to prove his point, Tocqueville develops a particularly interesting comparative argument. There are in every nation or society two types of concerns or interests:

> Certain concerns are shared by all national groups such as the formation of general laws and relations with foreign nations.
>
> Other concerns are of special interest to certain national groups such as, for example, business undertaken by the townships.
>
> (*Certains intérêts sont communs à toutes les parties de la nation, tels que la formation des lois générales et les rapports du peuple avec les étrangers.*
>
> *D'autres intérêts sont spéciaux à certaines parties de la nation, tels que, par exemple, les entreprises communales.*)[72]

The argument is still quite Althusian. The assumption of powers by a national government to deal with what is in the general or shared interest of all is what Tocqueville calls "governmental centralization" (*centralisation gouvernementale*). The assumption of central powers over what is particular to specific communities, however, he calls "administrative centralization" (*centralisation administrative*).[73]

Now comes the interesting part. Tocqueville insists that while governmental centralization is an absolute necessity for a great nation, the concurrent practice of administrative centralization not only diminishes freedom but moreover weakens the nation as a whole. The exercise of centralized power over the interests of particular communities "has the constant effect of diminishing their sense of civic pride" (*elle tend sans cesse à diminuer parmi eux l'esprit de cité*).[74]

Thus, you have England, which has achieved greatness without administrative centralization, and you have the decline of postrevolutionary France, where there is more administrative centralization than in prerevolutionary France under Louis XIV. And, particularly instructive, there is the German Empire, all the way back to its medieval origins, doomed to fail not because of its admirable level of administrative decentralization and autonomy, but because of its lack of governmental centralization. Finally, and here Tocqueville returns to the discussion of the American political system proper, there is the model case of the United States, in which both administrative decentralization and governmental centralization have been carried almost to an extreme.[75]

However, what Tocqueville has in mind here are the individual American states or republics. These he wants to examine before the Union as a whole because it is state government "which answers the ordinary daily needs of society without clear limitations" (*habituel et indéfini, qui répond aux besoins journaliers de la société*), whereas the Union government appears to him as only acting in "exceptional circumstances to meet certain general concerns with very clear limitations" (*exceptionnel et circonscrit, qui ne s'applique qu'à certains intérêts généraux*).[76]

This was of course observed and written before the American Civil War, in which the industrialized Northern States eventually defeated the Southern States and their feudal slave economies, and from whence the idea and practice of centralized economic standardization and regulation began to take shape, eventually resulting in a decisive victory of federal supremacy over states' rights.[77] What is important, however, is not whether Tocqueville could not yet see, or perhaps already misjudged, the lopsided balance of power clandestinely written into the American Constitution. What is important instead is his profound conceptual understanding of decentralization as a means of sustaining a democratic or republican spirit in a society and nation.

Tocqueville resumes his investigations: "What I most admire in America are not the administrative results of decentralization but the political effects" (*Ce que j'admire le plus en Amérique, ce ne sont pas les effets administratifs de la décentralisation, ce sont ses effets politiques*). Because they are more directly involved in public affairs, the citizens of the United States "care about each of their country's interests as they would their own" (*s'attache à chacun des intérêts de son pays comme aux siens mêmes*). And, since so much administrative duty is in their own hands, they do not regard obedience to authority as deference to a superior force. "In America," Tocqueville writes, "one man never obeys another man, only justice or the law" (*en Amérique l'homme n'obéit jamais à l'homme, mais à la justice ou à la loi*).[78]

Tocqueville, as it turns out, had studied Montesquieu well. His discussion of the beneficial effects of separating administrative decentralization from governmental centralization closely resembles what his aristocratic predecessor had written about the combination of security (= centralization) in a large monarchical state with the kind of civic virtue (= decentralization) only possible in small republics. "Small nations have ever been...the cradle of political liberty" (*Les petites nations ont... été de tout temps le berceau de la liberté politique*), Tocqueville writes, and in the end it is the "federal system ...which allows the Union to profit from the strength of a large republic and the security of a small one" (*la forme fédérale...qui permet à l'Union de jouir de la puissance d'une grande république et de la sécurité d'une petite).*[79]

In the last chapter of Part I of *Democracy in America*, Tocqueville provides a concise and insightful analysis of the American constitutional system, focussing on the division of powers, the presidential election, the court system, and the supremacy of constitutional law in particular.[80] He identifies the crucial difference between all previous confederal systems and the new form of American federalism: While central governments in older confederations had remained dependent on the component units' fiscal and administrative compliance, the American federal government for the first time has been set up constitutionally with sufficient powers of its own so that it "can do everything it has the right to do" *(peut faire tout ce qu'on lui donne le droit d'exécuter).*[81]

He also makes a remarkable observation about the executive powers of the president, which he sees as generally more constrained than in other systems of government due to the checks and balances among the different branches of government. By circumstance rather than law, however, this can change. Among the main prerogatives of presidential executive power is foreign policy, Tocqueville explains, and if the United States ever found itself engaged in constant power struggles with other nations, "you would see the prestige of the executive increase in public opinion because of what was expected of it and what it did" *(on verrait le pouvoir exécutif grandir dans l'opinion, par ce qu'on attendrait de lui, et par ce qu'il exécuterait).*[82]

This last observation already identifies what lies at the heart of Tocqueville's understanding of democracy in America: the immediate connection between the majority will of the people and the process of governing. This connection is established and maintained in several ways, through political parties, associations, and a free press.[83] But the most important political transmission belt is "universal suffrage" *(le vote universel).*[84]

It has been pointed out that Tocqueville overestimated the degree of democratization in the America he visited. According to various estimates, no more than 5 per cent of the people may have had the right to vote at the time, and even 20 years later electoral participation—measured against the entire population—may not have exceeded 14 per cent.[85] Yet, Tocqueville was obviously aware of the fact that women, as well as Black and Native populations, were excluded, and that some property qualifications were still in place. What he meant by universal suffrage, therefore, was the principle of equal political rights across class boundaries, and the fact that this principle was universally accepted across the entire Union regardless of continuing differences of region, culture, and economic development. And once the principle is generally accepted, there is no turning back. "When a nation starts to tamper with electoral qualifications," Tocqueville writes, "we can anticipate, sooner or later, their complete abolition" (*Lorsqu'un peuple commence à toucher au cens électoral, on peut prévoir qu'il arrivera, dans un délai plus ou moins long, à le faire disparaître complètement*).[86]

Far more important, however, is Tocquville's analysis of the effects that the principle of universal suffrage has on the quality of government and society. There can be no denying that the French aristocrat was somewhat prejudiced about the prospects of popular democracy, but he would not have been the consummate social scientist if he had not provided balanced judgment and thought-provoking insight nevertheless.

He begins by taking on an argument about universal suffrage that in fact goes all the way back to Aristotle. According to this argument, not all people have the capacity to govern, but their political instincts will collectively lead them to select the most competent leaders. Not so, Tocqueville argues. First of all, and this is again an old Aristotelian argument, excellence, political or otherwise, is only available to the few who have the means and the time to devote their lives to it. And because such luxury will never be available to all, or even a majority, it will ultimately be useless attempting "to raise the intelligence of a nation above a certain level" (*d'élever les lumières du peuple au-dessus d'un certain niveau*).[87]

Secondly, as a consequence, the people will always regard true excellence — or wealth — with suspicion and envy. They will not be inclined to elect to public office those distinguished by either. At the same time, the members of such a distinguished elite will themselves abstain from even seeking public office in the first place. They know that they would not be able to act according to their best knowledge — or their own interests — but instead would have to cater to the lowest common denominator prevalent in society, the will of the majority. Since there is thus no glory to be had from serving the public, "it often comes about that only those who feel inadequate in the conduct of their own business undertake to direct the fortunes of the state" (*il arrive souvent qu'on ne se charge de diriger la fortune de l'État que quand on se sent peu capable de conduire ses propres affaires*).[88]

Not much love is lost between the classes in a democracy, then. The members of the wealthy intelligentsia will keep to themselves rather than become involved in politics, which, after all, would require seeking popular support. The people resent this independence or autonomy of the elite because it violates their sense of democratic equality. "Anything which thrives without their support," Tocqueville resumes, "has trouble in winning their favour" (*tout ce qui s'élève sans son appui obtient difficilement sa faveur*).[89]

The result is general mediocrity. "In a country where education is almost universal," Tocqueville notes, "it is claimed that the representatives of the people cannot always write correctly" (*Dans un pays où l'instruction est presque universellement répandue, on dit que les représentants du peuple ne savent pas toujours correctement écrire).* But that is not the worst of it. Because the people "have always to come to hasty judgments and to latch on to the most obvious of features" (*toujours juger à la hâte et s'attacher au plus saillant des objets*), the conduct of politics easily falls into the hands of "charlatans of all kinds" (*charlatans de tous genres*) who "know full well the secret of pleasing the people" (*savent si bien le secret de lui plaire*).[90]

If this is a devastating verdict on democracy, it is not exactly a new one. That the people were likely to fall for the cheap arguments of sophists had been a standard argument against democracy in ancient Greece.[91] What is new, however, is that Tocqueville no longer rejects democracy as intrinsically bad but instead accepts it as inevitable. And by doing so, he finds praise along with criticism. While involvement in politics through universal suffrage makes for the selection of mediocre leaders, it does have the advantage of creating good citizenship.

"In the United States," Tocqueville writes, "I discovered with amazement to what extent merit was common among the governed but rare among the rulers" (*aux États-Unis, je fus frappé de surprise en découvrant à quel point le mérite était commun parmi les gouvernés, et combien il l'était peu chez les gouvernants*). And no less important, statecraft will be economical because it will essentially be in the hands of the "middle classes" (*les classes moyennes*), for whom "nothing is more disastrous than a heavy tax on a slight fortune" (*qu'il n'y a rien de si désastreux qu'une grosse taxe venant à frapper une petite fortune*).[92]

Democracy, Tocqueville suggests, may generally amount to mediocre middle-class rule, but by granting equal rights of education and political participation to everyone, it also brings forth the conditions for its own existence and stability: "the existence of a very civilized and educated society" (*l'existence d'une société très civilisée et très savante*). As such, it is not the first and most natural form of government, as one might assume, but the one "which had to come about last" (*qu'il n'a dû venir que le dernier*).[93]

It is here that Tocqueville breaks with the entire tradition of previous assessments of the democratic form of government. "I realize that I am treading on live cinders" (*Je sais que je marche ici sur un terrain brûlant*), he writes at the outset of the crucial chapter in question.[94] Because democracy is not tied to the perceived or real wisdom of an elite, leave alone a self-declared philosopher-king, it can only learn by the experience of trial and error. In the end, it turns out, this is democracy's most valuable asset:

> Democracy cannot lay hold upon the truth except by experience and many nations might perish while they are waiting to discover their mistakes.

The great privilege enjoyed by Americans is, therefore, not only to be more enlightened than other peoples but also to have the capacity to repair their mistakes. (*la démocratie ne peut obtenir la vérité que de l'expérience, et beaucoup de peuples ne sauraient attendre, sans périr, les résultats de leurs erreurs.*

Le grand privilège des Américains n'est donc pas seulement d'être plus éclairés que d'autres, mais d'avoir la faculté de faire des fautes réparables.)[95]

Of course, Rousseau had endorsed popular sovereignty before Tocqueville. Yet, his endorsement had been speculative, idealistic, and fraught with immense problems of theoretical consistency as well as practicability. Tocqueville in turn, obviously impressed and inspired by the American example, could treat popular sovereignty as a given. The question was no longer whether democracy was a normative goal or moral obligation. It had become a question of critical assessment.

Tocqueville's assessment is critical indeed and could not be in sharper contrast to Rousseau's idealistic celebration of the general will. He does not waste any time or effort with some convoluted arithmetic about how the general will might be expressed legitimately by the majority. The majority, as we already know, governs in the name of the people.[96] It is the majority, which, in the name of equality, supplies "to the individual a mass of ready-made opinions" (*aux individus une foule d'opinions toutes faites*).[97] The general will, therefore, is a "general will of the majority" (*volonté* [...] *générale* [...] *du grand nombre*).[98]

Under such a despotism of majoritarian conformity, grand declarations of individual rights become meaningless: "You will retain your civic privileges but they will be useless" (*Vous garderez vos privilèges à la cité, mais ils vous deviendront inutiles*).[99] The "tyranny of the majority" (*tyrannie de la majorité*) permeates the entire system of governance:

> When a man or a party suffers from an injustice in the United States, to whom can he turn? To public opinion? That is what forms the majority. To the legislative assembly? That represents the majority and obeys it blindly. To the executive power? That is appointed by the majority and serves as its passive instrument. (*Lorsqu'un homme ou un parti souffre d'une injustice aux États-Unis, à qui voulez-vous qu'il s'adresse? À l'opinion publique? c'est elle qui forme la majorité; au corps législatif? il représente la majorité et lui obéit aveuglément; au pouvoir exécutif? il est nommé par la majorité et lui sert d'instrument passif.*)[100]

It is here that Tocqueville's thinking also breaks with the entire tradition of power balance in a mixed form of government, so admirably upheld and defended by his French compatriot Montesquieu, and almost takes a

Hobbesian turn. Hobbes had rejected the idea of mixed government because it would lead to the return of civil war, but he also argued that it was useless as an advancement of liberty as well: "For as long as they are all in agreement with each other, the subjection of individual citizens is as great as it could possibly be."[101] Tocqueville is blunt:

> A so-called mixed government is an illusion. There is no truly mixed government (in the sense given to this word) because, in every society, one discovers in the end one principle of action which dominates all the others. (*Le gouvernement qu'on appelle mixte m'a toujours semblé une chimère. Il n'y a pas, à vrai dire, de gouvernement mixte [dans le sens qu'on donne à ce mot], parce que, dans chaque société, on finit par découvrir un principe d'action qui domine tous les autres.*)[102]

To some extent, Tocqueville is contradicting himself here because he does in fact praise the checks and balances of American federalism as an important antidote to the dangers of democratic despotism. However, far more important are his insights as to why absolute majority rule is seemingly without opposition or rejection in a democratic republic such as the United States.

The first of his insights has to do with the new culture of equality according to which "more enlightenment and wisdom are found in a group of men than in one man alone" (*plus de lumières et de sagesse dans beaucoup d'hommes réunis que dans un seul*).[103] Tocqueville does not say so, but this is of course again the resurrection of an old Aristotelian idea: "For the many, of whom each individual is not a good man, when they meet together may be better than the few good, if regarded not individually but collectively."[104] Elsewhere, Tocqueville also concedes, this time more in a Machiavellian fashion, that the "bulk of the population very sincerely supports the welfare of the country" (*la masse des citoyens veut très sincèrement le bien du pays*) because "in general the lower social classes seem to be less likely to confuse their personal interests with this support than the upper classes" (*les classes inférieures de la société me semblent mêler, en général, à ce désir moins de combinaisons d'intérêt personnel que les classes élevées*).[105]

But for the French aristocrat, majority rule constitutes an attack on intelligence because it has become an unquestioned moral category. "The moral authority of the majority is also founded upon the principle that the interests of the greatest number must take precedence over those of the smallest" (*L'empire moral de la majorité se fonde encore sur ce principe, que les intérêts du plus grand nombre doivent être préférés à ceux du petit*).[106]

The importance of this insight cannot be emphasized enough. Tocqueville may have outed himself as an unreformed elitist here, but he nevertheless points his finger right at the most categorical justification for democratic majority rule. It is not that majority rule is best because it is utilitarian, serving the interests or happiness of the largest number. It is not because it is, as a famous saying goes, the worst form of government except all others. No, the majority rules because it is declared and understood as morally right. The quantitative argument about the collective insight of the many is turned into a qualitative argument against which political recourse is no longer possible.

Tocqueville's second important insight about why democratic majority rule appears to be unassailable has to do with his analysis of American mass society. America, he explains, was at least originally settled by a very homogeneous class of people, "neither lords nor common people, neither poor nor wealthy, so to speak" (*ni grands seigneurs, ni peuple, et, pour ainsi dire, ni pauvres, ni riches*).[107] As a consequence, he argues, "there is still no natural or permanent antagonism between the interests of the different inhabitants" (*il ne se trouve pas encore de dissidence naturelle et permanente entre les intérêts de leurs divers habitants*).[108] And, without the presence of permanent minorities, "all parties are ready to acknowledge the rights of the majority because they are all hoping to be able one day to exercise them to their own advantage" (*tous les partis sont prêts à reconnaître les droits de la majorité, parce que tous ils espèrent pouvoir un jour les exercer à leur profit*).[109] In other words, and to put it into modern colloquial parlance, the operational principle of democracy in America is you win some, you lose some.

Again, the principle of this insight is more important than the extent to which Tocqueville may have overstated his case. He was well aware that American society was not as egalitarian and homogeneous as it liked to profess that it was. Tocqueville not only mentions slavery as a corrupting influence upon a democratic society,[110] he also comments with remarkable sensitivity on the plight of "Indians and Negroes" (*Indiens et ... Nègres*),[111] and he more generally suggests that American society may in fact be "overlaid with a democratic patina beneath which we see from time to time the former colours of the aristocracy shining through" (*couvert d'une couche démocratique, sous laquelle on voit de temps en temps percer les anciennes couleurs de l'aristocratie*).[112]

The principle to which Tocqueville gives powerful and timeless expression, however, is this: Majority rule can only command unquestioned moral authority in a society that is not deeply divided by opposing and permanent classes or minorities. To the extent that such divisions exist, his analysis provides a powerful antidote to the universal validity claims of social contract theory, which, in its most classical formulation, had suggested that the diverse social and economic interests in a society could be accommodated by "one Body Politick, wherein the Majority have a Right to act and to conclude the rest."[113]

Looking at the novelty of American society, Tocqueville was overwhelmed by what he thought was an inevitable and universal future of democratic equality. "I cast my eye over the countless crowd of similar beings among whom no one stands above or below the rest" (*Je promène mes regards sur cette foule innombrable composée d'êtres pareils, où rien ne s'élève ni ne s'abaisse*), he sums it all up at the end of *Democracy in America*, and he adds: "The sight of this universal uniformity saddens and chills me" (*Le spectacle de cette uniformité universelle m'attriste et me glace*).[114]

Yet, Tocqueville would not be Tocqueville if he just rejected what he saw. In a remarkable passage of self-criticism, immediately following his expression of sadness over a world lost forever, he admits that his predilection for the old world is based on personal bias:

> When the world was filled with men of great importance and extreme insignificance, of great wealth and extreme poverty, of great learning and extreme ignorance, I would turn away from the latter so as to concentrate solely upon the former who delighted my gaze. (*Lorsque le monde était rempli d'hommes très grands et très petits, très riches et très pauvres, très savants et très ignorants, je détournais mes regards des seconds pour ne les attacher que sur les premiers, et ceux-ci réjouissaient ma vue.*)[115]

Tocqueville continues to point out that in the eyes of the creator, ultimate satisfaction is not derived "from the unusual prosperity of the few but the widespread wellbeing of all"(*ce n'est point la prospérité singulière de quelques-uns, mais le plus grand bien-être de tous*).[116] Therefore, democratic equality, as the last and most developed form of the human condition,[117] must be appreciated not for what it tosses out but for what it is capable of achieving: "Equality persists at a lower level perhaps but it is fairer and this fairness constitutes its greatness and its beauty" (*L'égalité est moins élevée peut-être; mais elle est plus juste, et sa justice fait sa grandeur et sa beauté*).[118]

Critical Evaluation

In comparison to the universally acclaimed democratic radicalism of Rousseau, the much more cautious democratic liberalism of Tocqueville has almost remained at the margins. That Tocqueville's *Democracy in America* is "at once the best book ever written on democracy and the best book ever written on America" is an atypical assessment,[119] at least within the mainstream of the history of political thought. That "every president since Dwight D. Eisenhower" has cited *Democracy in America*, not even to speak of Newt Gingrich, who claimed it for his Contract with America, or Hillary Clinton, who linked it to her own book, *It Takes A Village*,[120] is not without some irony.

Tocqueville does provide insightful and timeless commentary on the American political system. Apart from his praise for the federal system itself, he lists, as remedies against renewed despotism, the entire institutional and cultural arsenal which has remained a mainstay in American democratic thinking: freedom of association, freedom of the press, judicial protection of individual rights, and constitutionally defined boundaries of governmental power.[121] He also and genuinely appreciates what constitutes the core of American liberalism, the breakdown of social barriers based on status, which allows easy and direct social interaction across classes and equal respect for all occupations and professions.

But Tocqueville also paints a darker picture of American democracy. The desire for equality results in a crass kind of commercialism that tends to dominate politics.[122] As a direct consequence of this materialistic predisposition in society, Americans will seek relief in extreme forms of spirituality.[123] They may even lose the ability to distinguish between religion and politics.[124] And finally, a society driven by its obsession with conformity will tend to indulge in national vanity,[125] and ignorance about other societies and countries.[126]

Tocqueville also tends to ignore or misjudge the already very unequal and exploitative nature of nineteenth-century American capitalism.[127] While he notes that a new aristocracy is emerging from industrialization,[128] and that America will ultimately remain divided between two classes,[129] with the working class at the mercy of their masters,[130] he does not seem to see this as a serious obstacle on the road to triumphant democratic equality. Thus, at least inadvertently, he lends his support to one of the most ineradicable conservative myths: that meaningful democratic equality can be divorced from the question of social inequality and economic dependency. And he has no sense as yet that the press can perform its role as a safeguard of liberty only as long as it is not monopolized and manipulated by powerful and concentrated corporate interests.

We stated earlier that insofar as Tocqueville believed that American conditions of equality would become universal, he did not subscribe to a theory of American exceptionalism.[131] We may now entertain the idea that at least in part, on the basis of the more peculiar characteristics summarized in the preceding paragraphs, *Democracy in America* has become a theory of American exceptionalism in hindsight because some of these characteristics indeed have remained peculiarly American. This in turn would imply that insofar as the United States, as the world's only remaining superpower, embraces "more openly the idea of empire,"[132] it plays this role on the basis of parochial rather than universal values.

But Tocqueville's place in the history of political thought is not determined by his uncanny gift to spot, at a very early moment in its history, some of the peculiar characteristics of American politics and society, even though it is precisely this gift which makes the reading of *Democracy in America* more entertaining than many other books on politics and political theory. Rather, Tocqueville's timeless contribution to the history of political thought lies in his theory of democracy and majority rule, and it is here that he differs most sharply from Rousseau.

Nobody can take away from Rousseau his epochal cry for equality and indivisible popular sovereignty, and his celebration of the general will as a political force that is morally superior to all other forms of rule, be it by the one, the few, or the many. Without this cry, the French Revolution would doubtlessly have occurred nevertheless, but it would have had to do without one of its most passionate prerevolutionary voices.

In terms of democratic theory, however, Rousseau's doctrine of the general will is next to useless. There is no explanation of how this general will might ever manifest itself as a credible political force, leave alone a legitimate one. Rousseau's flirtation with the idea that a genuine expression of an all-inclusive general will might be achieved under idealized conditions of homogeneity in small communities is based on a romantic misunderstanding of the one small community, Geneva, which he knew and may have had in mind. It is — to return to the musicians' quarrel of "galant" v. "learned" at the outset of this chapter — all seductive melody without much structural or harmonic underpinning.

Particularly problematic in this context is Rousseau's rejection of majority rule as a second-best or at least auxiliary option of democratic decision-making. Perhaps ironically, it is the identification of the democratic will with the rather crude vehicle of majority rule that makes it possible to identify and protect minority interests. American society is described by Tocqueville as one in which legitimacy is derived from the possibility of alternating majorities, and, therefore, as one which has the capacity to repair itself. Rousseau's unstructured general-will society gives expression to a tyranny of generality that is much more frightening than a tyranny of the majority, because it seems no longer possible to identify in whose name a particular political action is undertaken or sanctioned. Repair, then, as conscious civic action of trial and error, is no longer possible.

The merit of Rousseau's social contract theory lies in its unabashed generality. More boldly than any other theorist before him, Rousseau postulates that the people can and must rule. Every political thinker after Rousseau will be judged by this normative yardstick. But Rousseau has no idea, really, how popular sovereignty might become possible in practice. In a way, he simply replaces the absolute right of kings with the absolute right of the people. In terms of theoretical insight, as well as practical guidance, Rousseau's theory falls way below the level of sophistication already achieved before him.[133]

In particular, Rousseau does not give any thought to a differentiation between what is general and what is particular in a society, and he does not provide any suggestions as to how the participatory spirit, on which democracy must rely, might be organized. These are questions that had been discussed at length by thinkers such as Althusius and, more recently, Montesquieu, who were concerned about the rights and freedoms of traditional, smaller, and social communities — or classes — within a larger political context.

These thinkers had assumed, as in the case of Althusius, or perhaps hoped, as in the case of Montesquieu, that societies would continue to be characterized by a plurality of larger and smaller group identities and their interests. Indeed, political theory for them had been the search for a just, or at least fair, balance among these interests. But at least in principle, they had understood the difference between general and particular, and they had also understood politics as a process of perpetual motion and accommodation, rather than a finished product according to some universal normative yardstick or perfect model.

The singular importance of Tocqueville's contribution to political theory lies in the fact that he asks these same questions within the context of modern mass society. As he suggests, the release from the shackles of traditional society does not automatically lead to the kind of participatory spirit that the defence of democratic rights requires. The reason for this, as he suggests further, is that most citizens will not readily identify with issues that are the most general or common to all. They will get agitated instead over issues that are particular to them and their particular communities. The participatory spirit, therefore, lives in the local institutions of politics, the townships, and the main task of institutionalized democratic politics is precisely this: the differentiation between what is particular and requires the approval of those affected, and what is general or universal and can be left to the approval of all. Only in the latter case, as Althusius had already taught, does it seem appropriate to measure approval by means of majority rule.

In what is perhaps the ultimate irony, the cautious aristocrat Tocqueville embraces a much more dynamic understanding of democratic politics than the revolutionary Rousseau, and, in doing so, places himself within a tradition that is Aristotelian and even Machiavellian rather than Platonic or Rousseauist. Machiavelli, we remember, had argued that liberty requires struggle between competing interests and views, and that "good laws" in the end come "from those very tumults which so many inconsiderately condemn" (*le buone leggi, da quelli tumulti che molti inconsideratamente dannano*).[134]

Rousseau, as we saw earlier, is among those who do indeed condemn all forms of disharmony, because "dissensions and disturbances bespeak the ascendance of particular interests and the decline of the state" (*les dissensions, le tumulte, annoncent l'ascendant des intérêts particuliers et le déclin de l'État*).[135] Tocqueville, in sharp contrast and probably not without pain — considering the turmoils he had to live through almost all his life — admits that "there are some honorable types of opposition and some rebellions which are legitimate" (*il y a des résistances honnêtes et des rébellions légitimes*).[136]

It is Tocqueville's and not Rousseau's vision of democracy that provides guidance for an uncertain future. If, as one may almost safely assume by now, that future is dominated by globalizing forces of socioeconomic standardization, leading to new and unprecedented pressures of societal conformity within and across territorial boundaries, we should welcome "dissensions and disturbances." As Sheldon Wolin writes at the end of his account of the history of political thought and its lessons for the future: "The central challenge at the moment is not about reconciliation but about dissonance, not about democracy's supplying legitimacy to totality but about nurturing a discordant democracy."[137] While Rousseau would be horrified, Tocqueville would sadly agree.

CHAPTER 9

Human Rights

Burke (and Rousseau) v. Wollstonecraft

In order to appreciate just how far Tocqueville had gone by acknowledging the greatness and beauty he saw in democratic fairness, we only need to consider how long it would take before this fairness became an undisputed normative category in political theory and practice. Already at the 1815 Congress of Vienna, after Napoleon's final defeat, Europe's leading conservative powers, under the leadership of the Austrian mastermind, the Prince von Metternich, had forged a Holy Alliance against progress. The Christian god was to be sovereign, not the people, and by divine right, Europe's monarchs were to exercise a coordinated patriarchal regime over their subjects: "counter-revolution in the name of Christianity."[1]

One of the books the leaders at the Vienna congress drew particular inspiration from was Edmund Burke's *Reflections on the Revolution in France*.[2] Its publication in 1790 had initially been met with little approval, even from the members of Burke's own Whig Party. But it had propelled into creative overdrive the radical instincts of Mary Wollstonecraft, who would only much later find recognition as the first important feminist — and at that, the first female author — in the classical canon of political thought.

That Burke belongs in that canon can be disputed. He was a brilliantly polemical speaker and writer, but there is little in his political thought that would add significantly to what had already been said and thought. However, the reason why he is included here is twofold: He brought on its way modern conservatism as an ideology that mistrusts all innovation and, therefore, quite literally, wants to conserve the status quo as tried and true; and he provides the backdrop for the discussion of Wollstonecraft's feminist radicalism, which first saw social and gender inequality as the two sides of one and the same coin. It is for this reason alone that this "hyena in petticoats" fully deserves her belated status as a classic in political thought.[3]

Wollstonecraft's "unwomanly" intrusion into the male domain of political thought also invites us to address two questions that have been glossed over thus far: What did the political thinkers discussed previously think about the role of women in politics and society? And: Why is it that no other woman prior to Wollstonecraft has been found worthy of being included in the classical canon? To these questions we turn first.

Context

If, after more than 2,000 years, the first woman author appears in the history of political thought, the context is not just defined by the immediate circumstances of her life and times. The fact that her appearance as a significant female — and feminist — voice cannot be traced back to a like-minded tradition in the history of political thought invites, or even necessitates, a review of that canon, however briefly, from a different and gendered perspective.

For the Greeks, women could be seducers, oracles, or goddesses. Like slaves, children, and the foreign-born, however, they had no civic status in democratic Athens. Plato, on the other hand, in his ideal polity, had not ruled out that women might become educated as guardians and hence qualify, at least in principle, as philosopher-kings, although he probably did not seriously entertain this possibility. As Diana Coole points out, Plato remarks at one point that he will proceed with the discussion of the proper training for rulers after having "disposed of the women and children."[4] We already know what Plato meant by that: In order to make sure that future guardians were not distracted from their education, they would be deprived of traditional family life. Instead, they would live in communes where women and children would be held in common and sexual relations would be determined by the rulers, who would "select women" and "hand them over to the men" for the procreation of healthy offspring.[5]

Because he granted women intelligence and guardian qualities in principle, Plato is usually regarded as less misogynist or sexist than Aristotle, who categorically excluded them from the public sphere (*polis*), entirely assigning their existence to the private realm of the household (*oikos*). Aristotle also states more categorically than Plato that even in the household, where the political maxim of to-govern-and-to-be-governed does not apply, the relationship between a man and a woman is that of ruler and ruled.[6] However, as Coole argues, Aristotle at least accepted that women have some identity of their own in the private sphere of the house, thus leaving them "a space in society," whereas Plato treated them as "a sexually neutral category of servicers of the state."[7]

While Plato thus constructed a totally alienating role for women in his ideal *polis* (wherein, one must not forget, the role assigned to male guardians is not exactly engrossing either), Aristotle only pragmatically reproduced the views and rules prevalent in the societies he observed. These also became the views and rules of the Christian church and thus dominated throughout the Christian Middle Ages. They remained the prevalent views and rules all the way into the twentieth century, not just in Christian cultures, and they certainly have not been eradicated altogether even now.

From whatever origins it sprang, the idea that women are inferior to men resulted in their exclusion from participation in politics. This was as clear for Marsilius as it was for Montesquieu, Rousseau, or Tocqueville. It was not even a question. The *Declaration of the Rights of Man and of the Citizen* (*Déclaration des droits de l'Homme et du Citoyen*) of 1789 was just that: a declaration for *men* as citizens.

There were variations and nuances, though. While Althusius left no doubt that it was the husband who is the ruler of the family, he granted that the relationship between husband and wife was nevertheless founded on mutual rights and obligations.[8] He also had no objection to female succession and admired Elizabeth I of England. There was a strange discrepancy at work in the political thinking of men: Women had no political rights but could be accepted as supreme rulers. Rank proved more important than gender.

A particularly notorious case is that of Machiavelli, who had declared that "fortune is a woman and if she is to be submissive it is necessary to beat and coerce her" (*fortuna è donna, et è necessario, volendola tenere sotta, batterla et utarla*).[9] For Machiavelli, as Hanna Pitkin showed impressively in her seminal study, woman is the "other," that part of human nature that men find hard to understand or control, even the other side in themselves, both weaker and, therefore, dangerous.[10] We shall not explore the question here as to how and to what extent this amounts to misogyny in the literal sense of hatred or contempt for women. But it is clear, in terms of political theory, that Machiavelli's understanding of the female is located entirely outside of what he thinks is political. It is even opposed to it.

As long as the assumption persisted that the differences between the two genders were either part of intended divine creation or simply a fact of natural order, political theory could be constructed coherently by neglecting the woman question altogether. Whatever Machiavelli might have thought about women was simply irrelevant to his understanding of republican liberty or princely rule. He used the woman-as-fortune metaphor to give expression to what appeared to him as the vagaries of political life that the prince-as-virtuoso had to confront. That he did make use of such a metaphor may well reflect that he had little or no respect for women as creatures who are as intelligent and rational as men in general. But whatever his attitude was, it did not really compromise his political thinking, except that it was, of course, as all political thinking up to that date, discriminatory in an exclusionary and gendered way.

Such exclusion became theoretically much more problematic when natural law and social contract theories began to postulate that society is a civil creation among consenting rational individuals. If it was up to men to decide what kind of society they wished to live in, then it was they who also determined the role and status of women.[11] Thus, Hobbes, for whom all authority was constructed and not natural, logically asserts that in the case of family life, those who attribute "the Dominion to the Man onely, as being of the more excellent sex" are mistaken.[12] But then he continues, with a shrug so to speak, that the matter will ultimately be decided by civil law, which will usually favour the husband or father because it is more likely men than women or mothers who make the law.[13]

And that is the end of it, a rather unsatisfactory and contradictory end. That men have a natural right to rule and rule absolutely can no longer be upheld. Instead, it is simply assumed that this will be the normalcy of private and political life. Apart from a "known Right to Soveraign Power," Hobbes writes, all that a ruler needs in order to be accepted by the people is "that they see him able absolutely to govern his own family."[14] The stability of statecraft becomes the excuse for the continuation of business as usual in the domestic sphere.

Unsurprisingly, it is the question of property that keeps women at bay in the end.[15] The logic is rather simple. If the purpose of "Mens uniting into Commonwealths" is "the Preservation of their Property," as Locke writes,[16] and if it is the power of men to "bestow their Estates on those, who please them best,"[17] little if any room is left for women to play a role of their own in politics or civil society, even when it is granted that they are not inferior human beings by nature.

To be sure: Neither Hobbes nor Locke show any particular interest in employing their contractual thinking for the benefit of women's emancipation from traditional assumptions about their natural station in social life. But at the same time, their contractual thinking appears to compel them to waffle around the issue. That women should stay home and shut up remains unsaid. But when it comes to the discussion of power and property, their use of language does not suggest that they would think otherwise.

It is not any different with Rousseau. While his formulations about the general will appear to be gender-neutral, this is so only because of the generality of the language chosen. From the lofty heights of emancipation for all humanity, the petty question of whether that humanity in fact includes women simply does not come up. Elsewhere, however, Rousseau was much less coy about his opinions concerning women. In his discourse on inequality,[18] he carelessly observes that all that a man needs in the state of nature is "food, a female, and sleep" (*la nourriture, une femelle et le repos*).[19] Perhaps one ought not to overinterpret this, but he certainly does not seem to entertain the idea of partnership. Then, in his discourse on political economy,[20] he comes to the point more bluntly. It lies in the nature of the family that "the father ought to command" (le père doit commander).[21] More specifically, "the husband ought to be able to superintend his wife's conduct, because it is of importance for him to be assured that the children, whom he is obliged to acknowledge and maintain, belong to no one but himself" (le mari doit avoir inspection sur la conduite de sa femme: parce qu'il lui importe de s'assurer que les enfants, qu'il est forcé de reconnaître et de nourrir, n'appartiennent pas à d'autres qu'à lui).[22]

The reason for this is not so much sexual control as it is, in Lockean terms, property control. "The goods of the father, of which he really is the master," Rousseau explains, will be bestowed on his own offspring only if "they merit it by constant deference to his will" (Les biens du père, dont il est véritablement le maître ... qu'ils auront bien mérité de lui par une continuelle déférence à ses volontés).[23]

Nowhere did Rousseau come out and say explicitly that women are to be denied citizenship rights in principle. But it is not far-fetched to conclude that he never even entertained the idea. As we remember from the discussion of the social contract in the previous chapter, Rousseau failed to give a succinct explanation of just how the will of all (volonté de tous) is supposed to turn into a general will (volonté générale) that is more than mere majority rule. In his educational treatise Émile, however, he most clearly forwards the idea that it is an appropriate scheme of education that turns men into citizens.[24] And it becomes just as clear that this education is reserved for men only. Men and women "ought not to have the same education" (ils ne doivent pas avoir la même éducation).[25] In fact, "woman is especially constituted to please man" (la femme est faite spécialement pour plaire à l'homme) and should be educated accordingly.[26]

While women should not be kept in ignorance — after all it is they who first turn to the education of young boys and future citizens — their education ought to remain at a practical level and be "directed to the study of men and to that pleasure-giving knowledge" (doivent tendre à l'étude des hommes ou aux connaissances agréables).[27] Anything else would be futile in any case because: "The search for abstract and speculative truths, principles, and scientific axioms, whatever tends to generalize ideas, does not fall within the compass of women" (La recherche des vérités abstraites et spéculatives, des principes, des axiomes dans les sciences, tout ce qui tend à généraliser les idées n'est point du ressort des femmes).[28]

This was written in 1762, when Mary Wollstonecraft was three years old, and more generally at a time when it was by no means universally denied any longer that women had as much capacity to reason as men. The question of political rights for women had already been raised as well.[29] Rousseau's agenda for women, therefore, can no longer be excused as merely traditional. It is in fact deliberately reactionary. But before turning to Wollstonecraft's passionate and reasoned response, we need to address the second contextual question: Why was she the first important female thinker in the history of political thought?

Maybe she was not. Some modern feminists would argue that important female thinkers did exist throughout the history of political thought. They were just ignored.[30] And indeed, impressive lists of female thinkers and writers can be compiled that entirely belie Rousseau's assertion that only men can think in a systematic and principled way.[31] For the most part, however, these women thinkers appear on the scene at a rather late point in time, around the turn from the seventeenth to the eighteenth century. This is the time when socioeconomic modernization and urbanization first began to create something like a middle class, and with it a new class of women, neither confined in the courteous cages of nobility, nor condemned to the drudgery of miserable working lives.

Of course, such women had existed throughout the ages. But for the most part, they had lacked a critical mass of like-minded women with whom they could exchange their ideas and views, and in the company of whom they could free themselves from their dependency on principles and theories provided by the male establishment. One such woman, arguably the first English feminist, was Mary Astell (1668-1731), the daughter of a Newcastle merchant. She chose to live in London by herself, and she was surrounded by a supportive circle of like-minded other women. Thus supported, she could become one of the first advocates of female liberation through education.[32]

Three hundred years earlier, such support had not been available to Christine de Pizan (1364-1430).[33] Here was an extraordinary woman who, Italian by birth, raised at the French court, and widowed at the age of 25, had decided to support her family of six by becoming a professional writer. She wrote about everything from warfare and chivalry to politics and religion. Yet, her views on politics and society were mostly conventional, a mirror of the society she lived in, routinely following the lead of male authors of works with which she was familiar, and inevitably geared towards acceptance by the noble patrons she was dependent on.

Dependent on men, defined by men, and for the most part deprived by men of the kind of educational experience that brought forth the great achievements in the arts and sciences, philosophy, and politics: It is no wonder that few women made it into the illustrious pages of the history of political thought. One does not do the cause of gender equality a favour by first

pretending that intellectual history can be rewritten by rediscovering the neglected women thinkers of the past, and by then finding that their intellectual
achievements were rarely permitted by circumstance to reach beyond the
conventional.

The cause of gender equality is served much better by acknowledging that
these women, despite the extraordinary lives they led, and the extraordinary
efforts they made, simply had little chance of rivalling men in intellectual
achievement. The doors of universities were closed to them, and they were not at
liberty to leave their families behind for the sake of extended educational travel.
Before the invention and availability of modern birth control, a woman's
autonomy and mobility were also restricted by the five to seven pregnancies
she had, "at two and a half year intervals if she lived a normal life span."[34]

It is not coincidental, then, that those few women who did succeed in
making inroads into a world normally reserved for men, oftentimes had to
do, or chose to do, without husbands. Christine de Pizan had to rediscover
herself as a widow. Mary Astell never married to begin with. Shortly before
her, the great artist and botanist Sibylla Merian (1647-1717) left her husband
in order to have the freedom of study. In 1699 she travelled with her youngest
daughter to Dutch Guiana (Surinam) in South America, an unprecedented
undertaking for two unaccompanied women, where she compiled the material for her famous illustrated work on the metamorphosis of insects.[35]

Mary Wollstonecraft (1759-97) did get married in the end, but her husband William Godwin kept a separate place of study up the street which
suited them both. Almost all her important works had been written by then,
because she died from complications in childbirth five months after their
marriage vows had been taken.[36] Richard Polwhele, a minor divine and pro-
lific author of mostly forgotten works, wrote about her death: "she died a
death that strongly marked the distinction of the sexes, by pointing out the
destiny of women, and the diseases to which they are liable."[37]

This particularly "revolting"[38] remark takes us right into a narrower and
more immediate context. The French Revolution had unleashed forces of
change and dreams of liberty. Even though women were for the most part
ignored by the revolution, its general goals were cast in such universal terms
that progress for everyone seemed within reach. The *Declaration of the
Rights of Man and of the Citizen* had promised to sweep away "ignorance,
neglect, or contempt of human rights" (*l'ignorance, l'oubli ou le mépris des
droits de l'homme*), and it had postulated that henceforth "civil distinctions"
(*distinctions sociales*) would be determined solely on the basis of "public
utility" (*l'utilité commune*).[39]

Thus, when "The Right Honourable Edmund Burke"[40] attacked these prom-
ises and postulations as "metaphysically true" but "morally and politically

false,"[41] he attacked the very fundament of enlightened reason on the basis of which women—or any other disadvantaged group—could launch their more specific demands and agendas. In other words, if she wanted to take on Rousseau's educational sexism, Wollstonecraft first had to refute Burke. It is to Edmund Burke, therefore, that we have to turn first.

Edmund Burke (1729-97)

The son of a prominent Irish attorney,[42] Edmund Burke did not find the study of law interesting enough. Hence, he abandoned it and turned to writing. Early publications included *A Philosophical Enquiry into the Origin of Our Ideas of the Sublime and Beautiful* (1757). The somewhat pompous title would later serve Wollstonecraft for her opening salvo against Burke.[43]

Soon enough, Burke turned to politics, his real passion. After various positions as secretary to other politicians of the day, he first became elected as a Member of Parliament in 1765 and served for three different districts until his retirement in 1794. The main bulk of his enormous output as a writer consists of speeches and letters. Only the French Revolution provoked him, in 1790, to pen a larger work, *Reflections on the Revolution in France*.[44] Still, it was composed in the form of a—very long—letter to "a gentleman in Paris." After his retirement, Burke followed suit with some other lengthy epistles which continued the argument first forwarded in the *Reflections*.

Burke started out as a liberal, a member of the Whig Party, sympathetic to the American grievances concerning taxation without representation, critical of the English treatment of Ireland, even more critical of how India was treated by the East India Company, and in favour of—modest—government reform in order to curb corruption and waste at home. It thus came as a complete shock to his friends and colleagues when he reacted quickly and sharply against what he saw as the evil of the French Revolution and its proclamation of universal human rights. Thomas Jefferson, who had received a copy of the *Reflections* within days of its publication, remarked that "the Revolution in France does not astonish me so much as the revolution of Mr. Burke."[45]

If one reads Burke's famous speeches on "American Taxation"[46] and "Conciliation with America,"[47] however, the overall impression is not one of a firm commitment to principles of self-determination or representative fairness. Very much in line with his thinking throughout, Burke seems to advocate repealing the duty on tea in particular, and conciliation more generally, for purely pragmatic reasons of political expediency. One gets the impression that he did not mind accommodating American demands, because that would not change how things were done back home in England. Endorsing the ideals of the French Revolution, on the other hand, would spell disaster, the eventual abrogation of all that was dear to him on the home front. Jefferson and others might simply have misunderstood the motivations of the earlier Burke.

Burke was not a political opportunist. He stood by his opinions and convictions even when this meant putting his own career in jeopardy. In 1765 he provoked the loss of his first political appointment—and most of his income—during a quarrel over the terms of employment with his patron, William Gerard Hamilton, a minor political figure of the day. In 1780 he lost his parliamentary seat in Bristol because he offended the Bristol merchants with his lectures on the commercial rights of Ireland. And the publication of the *Reflections* resulted in a break with almost all his friends, particularly his supporters in the Whig Party. Burke became an isolated and even ridiculed outsider. He did not live to see the belated success that his book would have during the European conservative restoration after 1815.

Until recently, it has been Wollstonecraft who was routinely belittled for lacking scholarship.[48] Yet, while she rather ought to be congratulated for the degree of erudition she acquired despite being a woman, despite growing up in poverty, and despite living in perpetual financial insecurity, it is Burke, for whom all doors were open, whose scholarly approach can be questioned. Apparently, he took his ideas about the French Revolution mainly from anti-revolutionary French men and women, most of whom had left France during the earliest stages of the revolution, and from English newspaper articles. If so, this would not only demonstrate poor scholarship on his part but also put him at odds with his own Whig Party, which "prided itself on the scale and variety of its French connections."[49]

Burke rejects what he calls the "abstract perfection" of universal human rights because civil society is the "offspring of convention," and political reason is therefore "a computing principle," rather than a manifestation of abstract and inflexible truth.[50] And when such truth is declared to be the "right of the people," right becomes confounded with power: "The body of the community, whenever it can come to act, can meet with no effectual resistance; but till power and right are the same, the whole body of them has no right inconsistent with virtue, and the first of all virtues, prudence."[51]

Prudence was one of Burke's favourite concepts. It is the very opposite of abstract theory and denotes the kind of practical wisdom that comes from experience and tradition. It is England Burke has in mind when he exclaims that "in this enlightened age ... instead of casting away all our old prejudices, we cherish them ... and the longer they have lasted ... the more we cherish them."[52] By prejudices, then, Burke does not mean false beliefs that arise from ignorance or conceit. What he means is tradition, the kind of security of thought and action that stems from a familiar path of history: "the accumulated prescription of a thousand years."[53]

At first glance, this sounds like a plea for practical politics, reminiscent of the Aristotelian prudence (*phronesis*) as the art of the possible rather than the Platonic search for the wisdom of absolute truth (*episteme*). It moreover appears to evoke Vico's anti-Cartesian appeal to common sense as a method of historical learning.[54] But a closer look reveals significant differences.

Vico, we remember, had also held that "it is impossible to assess human affairs by the inflexible standards of abstract right" (*non ex ista recta mentis regula, quae rigida est, hominum facta aestimari possunt*).[55] He had then suggested that progress is nevertheless possible by a kind of collective historical learning which allows choices "made certain and determined by the common sense of men with respect to human needs or utilities" (*si accerta e determina col senso commune degli uomini d'intorno alle umane necessità o utilità*).[56] And he had concluded, with reference to ancient Rome's early progression from aristocracy to republicanism, that the historical learning process would result in an age of men as an age of "civil sovereignty" (*i popoli ad esser sovrani*).[57]

Historical learning is not the same as clinging to historical precedent. It is not coincidental that Burke equates historical tradition with prescription. Historical learning also requires a process of deliberation, trial and error, and ultimately, discussion, with history as much as within civil society. This is precisely what Burke abhors. "It has been the misfortune ... of this age," he declares, "that every thing is to be discussed."[58] Such discussion challenges Burke's view of civil society as a "fixed compact" in which each and every one is to be held "in their appointed place."[59]

To be sure, Burke was not altogether opposed to reform.[60] In the case of India, he went on a crusade against what he saw as corruption, injustice, and plunder on the part of the East India Company and the Governor General of India, Warren Hastings. Tenaciously, but ultimately unsuccessfully, he even pursued the impeachment of the latter.[61] Yet, while he asserted that Indians had a right to be treated justly according to principles of natural law, his more sustained and somewhat contradictory concern was the natural flow of trade. "The laws of commerce," he wrote towards the end of his life, in 1795, echoing the new political economy thinking advanced by his friend Adam Smith, "are the laws of God."[62]

Fundamentally, however, reforms could not and should not go beyond what remained for Burke the inviolable boundaries prescribed by tradition. What he meant by that becomes very clear when he turns to his favourite subject, the preservation of property, which is the real objective under the "prescription of a thousand years." What irked him most about the French Revolution was the "seizure of property," the revolutionary belief "that certain men had no right to the possessions they held under the law, usage, the decisions of the courts, and the accumulated prescription of a thousand years."[63]

Burke is talking about the confiscation of church property here, but his argument quickly becomes one about social order more generally:

> The body of the people must not find the principles of natural subordination by art rooted out of their minds. They must respect that property of which they cannot partake. They must labour to obtain what by labour can be obtained; and when they find, as they commonly do, the success disproportioned to the endeavour, they must be taught their consolation in the final proportions of eternal justice.[64]

Such eternal justice must not only compensate for the lack of property because, with it, come social contempt and political discrimination. Attacking one of the early pronouncements of the revolution according to which "all occupations were honourable," Burke retorts that "the occupation of an hair-dresser ...cannot be a matter of honour," and that, while men in such and even lower stations of life "ought not to suffer oppression from the state," it would be the state that suffered oppression if such men, "either individually or collectively, are permitted to rule."[65]

By now, Burke's convictions about the nature of legitimate government can hardly come as a surprise. They only reiterate what had long since become the standard of theory and practice in Lockean England. "The characteristic essence of property," he writes, "is to be unequal." And because this is so, "nothing is a due and adequate representation of a state, that does not represent its ability, as well as its property."[66] In fact, Burke's justification of unequal representation on the basis of property falls way short of Locke's doctrine 100 years earlier.[67]

Locke's theory of property and representation had been constructed upon two pillars. One was the assumption of consent in the accumulation of unequal possessions.[68] The other was the assertion that a fair system of representation had to reflect different levels of property-based taxpaying contributions to the public good.[69] On that basis, however, Locke had at least recommended electoral and franchise reform so that the nexus between taxpaying capacity and representation would be "true" rather than distorted by old "Customs and Priviledges."[70]

By comparison, Burke seems perfectly happy with the prescriptions of custom and privilege. "I shall only say here," he exclaims, "in justice to that old-fashioned constitution, under which we have long prospered, that our representation has been found perfectly adequate to all the purposes for which a representation of the people can be desired or devised."[71] And the justification given is not true proportion or the capacity of contributing to the public good but "hereditary property and hereditary distinction."[72] Indeed, it is a closed class system of property and power he defends, "for, if popular representation, or choice, is necessary to the legitimacy of all government, the house of lords is, at one stroke, bastardized and corrupted in blood."[73]

Bastardized and corrupted in blood: What remains unsaid here is that the House of Lords would lose its status as a guardian of privilege if commoners were to meddle with its legislative prerogatives. The male proprietor of name and estate would lose the power over his property if a political system based on popular representation deprived him of his powers to determine who his children are allowed to marry, and to select his sole inheritor. It is here that Burke's conservatism meets with Rousseau's patriarchy, and it is here that Wollstonecraft finds the angle to take them both on. "Who can recount all the unnatural crimes which the laudable, interesting desire of perpetuating a name has produced," she writes in direct response to Burke's defence of family property, when "the younger children have been sacrificed to the eldest son," when a young man cannot marry without considering "his rank in society," and when "girls are sacrificed to family convenience" to the effect that "if some widows did not now and then *fall* in love, Love and Hymen would seldom meet, unless at a village church."[74]

Burke claimed that he never read Wollstonecraft's reply to his *Reflections*. If so, his ignorance of her argument did not prevent him from describing her as one of those "desperate, Wicked, and mischievously ingenious women, who have brought, or are likely to bring Ruin and shame upon all those that listen to them."[75] It is time to take a closer look at what this ingenious "hyena in petticoats" really had to say.

Mary Wollstonecraft (1759-97)

The one and decisive advantage that Mary Wollstonecraft had over all her male predecessors and contemporaries was that, when writing about women, she knew what she was talking about. She had grown up in a poor farming household with many children, an abusive father and husband, and a docile mother.[76] Looking after her younger siblings was interspersed with limited access to education at local day schools. In 1778, at the age of 19, she left home to pursue what eventually became an independent writing career.

Her first publications, an educational treatise and a semiautobiographical novel, did not yield what was necessary to support herself, as well as her younger siblings and the irascible father, the care of all of whom she had taken on after her mother's death. Consequently, she had to enter into the kind of employment available to women at the time, as a companion and governess in the more affluent households of other women. In between, she tried to gain financial independence by opening a school of her own at Newington Green, a progressive community near London mainly inhabited by liberal intellectuals and ministers. The project failed, but it was at Newington that she first made the acquaintance of Richard Price who became her friend and mentor. Price, a liberal dissenter, had famously defended the American Revolution and had become a close friend of Benjamin Franklin. It was Price's glowing endorsement of the French Revolution that Burke attacked in the *Reflections*, and it was the defence of Price's arguments that triggered Wollstonecraft's reply to Burke.

Encouraged by her publisher, Joseph Johnson, she moved back to London in 1787. It was in the liberal atmosphere of Johnson's bookshop that Wollstonecraft's intellectual self-education became complete. It was there that she first met the radical political philosopher William Godwin, alongside the poet William Blake, the American radical democrat Thomas Paine, and the painter Henry Fuseli, with whom she had an affair. And it was there that she fully honed her literary skills by translating manuscripts and writing reviews for Johnson's journal, *The Analytical Review*.

Burke published his *Reflections* on November 1, 1790. "Infuriated," Wollstonecraft wrote her reply, *A Vindication of the Rights of Men*, within a few weeks. After a first and anonymous edition in early December 1790, the second and corrected edition appeared on December 14, this time with her name on the cover.[77] She was on a roll. A year later, when a French government report on education suggested, very much in line with Rousseau's ideas, that men's public education should be complemented by a different and more domestic kind of education for women, she wrote to the author, a former bishop-turned-finance-minister of the revolutionary government, Charles-Maurice Talleyrand-Périgord, that he should "reconsider the subject" and include women in civic education because, precisely in their assigned role as the domestic educators of children and future citizens, their lack of education would "stop the progress of knowledge."[78]

Sent along with that letter was her magnum opus, *A Vindication of the Rights of Woman*, published a year later in 1792. Contrary to the vicious reaction that the revelation of the circumstances of Wollstonecraft's unconventional life and — rather more conventional — death provoked when they became public in Godwin's *Memoirs*,[79] her second *Vindication* found a fairly benign reception for the time being. Conservatives were vitriolic, to be sure, but there was during those early years following the French Revolution a liberal climate, in England as elsewhere, that allowed the questioning of the prescriptions of tradition in the name of human progress. In fact, Wollstonecraft was not the only writer, male or female, who made the point that the rights of men should be extended to women.[80]

At that point, in 1792, Wollstonecraft had another five years to live. She travelled to France where the reception of the *Vindication* had been enthusiastic. There, she met an American businessman, Gilbert Imlay, with whom she fell in love and had a daughter, Fanny, born in 1794. When Imlay left her and left her alone back in London, she attempted suicide twice in 1795. Circumstances surrounding the first attempt appear unclear. The second time she put on her heaviest clothes and jumped from a bridge into the river Thames. She was already unconscious when she was pulled out of the water at the last moment. Then in 1796 she met Godwin again, and her life moved precipitously from a satisfying intellectual, as well as romantic, relationship to pregnancy, marriage, the birth of her second daughter, and death. All the while, she never stopped writing.[81]

That second daughter was Mary Wollstonecraft Godwin (1797-1851), who would elope to continental Europe with the poet Percy Byssche Shelley at the age of 15 (1812), marry him (1816), and stake her own claim to immortal fame as the author of the classic horror novel *Frankenstein* (1818). But it was Shelley who would put into immortal romantic verse the radical spirit that had united Wollstonecraft and Godwin:

> Rise like Lions after slumber
> In unvanquishable number —
> Shake your chains to earth like dew
> Which in sleep had fallen on you —
> Ye are many — they are few.[82]

Up to this point in this review of the history of political thought not nearly as much attention has been given to any other author's personal life circumstances and crises. The suspicion might arise, therefore, that this is happening now because Wollstonecraft is a woman and the account of her tragic life is a matter of misplaced chivalry. But nothing could be further from the truth. The life of Mary Wollstonecraft *was* different because she *was* a woman. She would have been the first to admit, nay, insist, that her particular experiences as a daughter, mother, lover, wife, as well as governess, teacher, journalist, and single professional woman writer profoundly influenced her political thinking. Some of these experiences, such as her dependence on employment in other and more well-to-do households, were class-specific and were shared with other political thinkers of nonnoble birth such as Hobbes, Locke, or Rousseau. But in combination with her gender-specific predicaments, they amounted to a unique life experience. The way it translated into her political thought foreshadowed the feminist slogan of a much later time: the personal is the political.

Like Burke, Wollstonecraft was not a trained philosopher. Like Burke also, she was gifted with acerbic wit and an uncanny knack for memorable formulations. She accused Burke of having a "mortal antipathy to reason"[83] and chided Rousseau for his "flight back to the night of sensual ignorance."[84] She called the ruling classes, nobility and clergy, the "pestiferous purple which renders the progress of civilization a curse,"[85] yet reserved her most profound contempt for the "vice and misery that arise in society from the middle class apeing the manners of the great."[86] And with unrestrained scorn she described the social position of middle- and upper-class women as "confined ... in cages like the feathered race" with "nothing to do but to plume themselves, and stalk with mock majesty from perch to perch."[87] Wollstonecraft does not calmly state her case. She does not say, remark, or observe. Instead, she exclaims, cries out, and scoffs. Behind this polemical facade of journalistic fire, however, Wollstonecraft advances serious arguments about the methods of social inquiry, about history and its prescriptions, about the politics of inequality, and about the role of religion in traditional society.

In his early *A Philosophical Enquiry into the Origin of Our Ideas of the Sublime and Beautiful* (1757), Burke had associated the sublime with "pain and danger,"[88] and always "some modification of power."[89] Beauty, on the other hand, he connected to a "sense of joy and pleasure,"[90] and generally to something "light and delicate" rather than great or strong.[91] For Wollstonecraft, who rebelled against a society that defined men as strong and women as weak, this became the more than welcome opener for a refutation of all that Burke stood for.

"Truth, in morals, has ever appeared to me the essence of the sublime; and, in taste, simplicity the only criterion of the beautiful," she begins her reply to Burke.[92] But what she has in mind is not a redefining of aesthetic categories. She aims at nothing less than a wholesale attack on Burke's entire way of thinking. The superficial plausibility of his reasoning, she insists, is derived from what he declares to be the "known truths" of an artificial and arbitrary tradition he venerates. This kind of plausibility, she exclaims, "can only be unmasked by shewing [*sic*] the absurdity it glosses over, and the simple truths it involves with specious errors."[93] As in the society she detests, with its artificial dichotomy of strong and weak, male and female, this kind of reasoning entirely misses the point: "complicated rules to adjust behaviour are a weak substitute for simple principles."[94]

The simple truths and principles Wollstonecraft has in mind, however, are not to be gained from abstract reasoning or a yearning for absolute truth and certainty. They are lessons to be learned from a sober look at history. The venerable civic institutions that Burke wants to preserve against the rising tide of liberalism were the result of "customs ... established by the lawless power of an ambitious individual ... or a weak prince ... obliged to comply with every demand of ... licentious barbarous insurgents ... or the more specious requests of the Parliament, who only allowed him conditional support."[95]

In one sweeping paragraph, Wollstonecraft tosses out as a Platonic lie or founding myth the entire tradition of a social contract or other form of broad societal agreement as the legitimating basis of state and society. Almost 200 years later, historical research into the genesis of modern state formation will confirm: "We discover a world in which small groups of power-hungry men fought off numerous rivals and great popular resistance in the pursuit of their own ends."[96]

In direct reference to that passage in Burke's *Reflections*, where we read that the English cherish their prejudices because it "renders a man's virtue his habit,"[97] Wollstonecraft counters that("all power built on prejudices, however hoary," is nothing but "the boasted prerogative of man—the prerogative that may emphatically be called the sceptre of tyranny."[98] At this particular moment, she is talking about the power relationship between men and women, but her point applies just as much to the political power relationships among different social classes. Burke's preference for the prescriptions and prejudices of tradition, Wollstonecraft thunders elsewhere, this "reverence to the rust of antiquity" that keeps humanity "for ever in frozen inactivity," is sound reasoning only "in the mouth of the rich and short-sighted."[99]

A few pages later, Wollstonecraft comes to the point more generally. What this insistence on the prescriptions of prejudice and tradition is ultimately meant to protect is social status and property: "Security of property! Behold, in a few words, the definition of English liberty," she exclaims.[100] And later, in the more elaborate second *Vindication*, she writes that "the whole system of British politics" is constructed in such a way as to "grind the poor and pamper the rich," and that it constitutes "a lucky turn-up of patronage for the minister, whose chief merit is the art of keeping himself in place."[101]

Up to that point, not even Rousseau had put it that bluntly. And again, Wollstonecraft's insights into what really drove British politics would be corroborated much later by historical research coming to the—albeit more moderately balanced—conclusion that in Burke's England, the prevailing doctrine had long since become that "the poor should share the burden of taxation," and that this doctrine, as a break with Elizabethan and Stuart traditions, had been "fortified" by the political theories of Thomas Hobbes and John Locke.[102]

Locke had defined property to include "the Grass my Horse has bit" and "the Turfs my Servant has cut."[103] It is for precisely this predisposition that Wollstonecraft criticizes Burke because it appears to her as tantamount to considering "the poor as only the livestock of an estate."[104] This critique of accepting and justifying systemic social inequality is important because it foreshadows her analysis of gender inequality, which she deems not only unjust but immoral and dangerous. "Private virtue," she insists, is the "cement of public happiness."[105] Whether with regard to the poor, or to women, there "must be more equality established in society, or morality will never gain ground." Otherwise, "ignorance and pride" of those deprived of "virtuous equality" will always undermine the civic stability of society in its entirety.[106]

With merciless bluntness, Wollstonecraft also unmasks how conservatives like Burke make use of religion as an ideological tool of enforcing morality without equality. The English system, Burke had written, had no need for the kind of factitious "cabals" that rocked revolutionary France, because it had been kept together "by the sanctions of religion and piety." Religion, "we know, and what is better, we feel inwardly," is the "basis of civil society."[107] Wollstonecraft replies that Burke must know very well that the English system owes whatever are its more acceptable traits to "bold rebellion," and that factions have been "the leaven" for the production of public good.[108] Religion is only brought into play to prevent the prevailing regime of state, church, and property from being questioned. "Of all hypocrites," she writes, "my soul most indignantly spurns a religious one."[109]

Hypocrisy is also what Wollstonecraft accuses Burke of in his few references to women. We have already seen earlier in this chapter how men tended to overlook what they generally thought of as the natural inferiority of women when rank (of a queen) trumped gender. It is no different with Burke who, without ever having been there, describes the spectators in the galleries of the French National Assembly as "a mixed mob of ferocious men, and of women lost to shame,"[110] while pouring out his heart over the cruel fate of the doomed queen, Marie Antoinette, whom he celebrates as an apparition "of life, and splendor, and joy."[111]

But it is when Burke describes the first convulsions of the revolutionary outburst and contrasts the dignity of the royal captives, dragged from Versailles, this "most splendid palace in the world," with the "shrilling screams" of the "vilest of women" accompanying the spectacle[112] that Wollstonecraft pinpoints his double standard: "Probably you mean women who gained a livelihood by selling vegetables or fish," she retorts, women "who never had had any advantages of education; or their vices might have lost part of their abominable deformity."[113]

The point is not to belittle the cruel indignities the queen of France had to endure before her life was ended by the guillotine. It is that injustice and indignity are the same for everyone regardless of social status or gender. "The great and small vulgar, claim our pity," Wollstonecraft writes.[114] That social and political inequality are demeaning Rousseau had already pointed out. Here, Wollstonecraft concurs wholeheartedly. But she now turns to the plight of that half of the human race he forgot to mention. Yet again, to her mind this is not primarily a matter of political or social rights but one of simple principle. Status is ultimately measured by the ability to exercise one's own reason in whatever realm of human endeavour one may choose: "This was Rousseau's opinion respecting men. I extend it to women."[115]

Wollstonecraft's investigation into the rights of women begins with a fundamental question that anthropologists, historians, political theorists, philosophers, and feminists have raised time and again ever since: Is the inequality that exists between man and man as well as between man and woman a fact of nature, or is it the result of socialization? Wollstonecraft's answer is unequivocal. After much study and observation, she arrives at "a profound conviction that the neglected education of my fellow-creatures is the grand source of the misery I deplore."[116]

A Vindication of the Rights of Woman mainly constitutes a series of arguments about women's right to education, and in particular argues against Rousseau's suggestion in *Émile* that boys and girls should be educated separately. It also contains critical reviews of other contemporary authors who have written on the subject. In Wollstonecraft's mind, however, the question of education metaphorically stands for emancipation and equality much more fundamentally. Education, in that age of revolutionary hope, appeared to her as the great gate through which, and through which alone, it seemed possible that all human beings can be put into a condition enabling them to exercise their own reason. And only this exercise of reason will allow them to gain control of their own destiny.

Rousseau's educational treatise or novel is considered to be a milestone in that it takes education, and children, seriously. But in its last chapter, *Émile* embarks upon a romantic rant about the education of women, which according to Rousseau had only one purpose: preparing women to serve and please their masters. In order to understand Wollstonecraft's counter-argument, it is not actually necessary to give any detailed account of Rousseau's thoughts on female education in all their triviality.

Wollstonecraft's counter-argument is quite simple. Human and social progress cannot be had from a turn back to nature, Rousseau's "flight back to the night of sensual ignorance."[117] It can only come from the advancement and the interrelated exercise of "reason, knowledge and virtue."[118] If then, as everybody appears to agree, it is women who are in charge of first educating children, boys and girls, they must for reasons of simple logic receive the same kind of education as men or else they will fail in this their assigned duty:

> Do the women who, by the attainment of a few superficial accomplishments, have strengthened the prevailing prejudice, merely contribute to the happiness of their husbands? Do they display their charms merely to amuse them? And have women, who have early imbibed notions of passive obedience, sufficient character to manage a family or educate children?[119]

Wollstonecraft advances the idea that women actually have enormous power in the societies of her time, not unlike despots. Not trained by reason, they manipulate society by the licentious lure of "temporary gratifications," which, given their pivotal role as wives and mothers, corrupts "the whole aggregate of society." Therefore, Wollstonecraft argues, "till women are more rationally educated, the progress of human virtue and improvement in knowledge must receive continual checks."[120]

This is an important argument, and an important invitation to think further. In its simplest form, it is a weakest-link-in-the-chain argument. If society is supposed to think and act rationally, it must be supplied with reason in all its parts. To make that argument, of course, requires thinking of society as a whole that is both functional and interdependent. Women and their function in the household cannot simply be separated from a more heroically sublime public sphere.

In *Symposium*, Plato had suggested that this was possible. "The only kind of boys who grow up to be real men in politics," he has Aristophanes declare, are the ones whose education stems from their sexual relationship with other and older men who have already proven to be "bold and brave and masculine."[121] How these boys might spend time with their mothers in the kitchen, in other words, is irrelevant. Plato, as we remember, had also recommended that the education of future guardians be altogether extricated from conventional domesticity. During the communal upbringing of children, no mother would be allowed to know the identity of her own children.[122] Obviously for Wollstonecraft and the society she lives in, neither is an option.

But Wollstonecraft's argument is not just that the civic virtue of a society is in danger unless all societal parts are included in the educational process of establishing such virtue. She claims that women, despite the seemingly unpolitical and domestic role they are assigned to play in society, in fact command a key role in the production and maintenance of a society's civic reason. Although women do not have access to the reins of political power, they are in a key position to determine just how that power will be used: like the triage nurse on whose diagnostic skills the life of patients depends before they are ever seen by the surgeon; like the school teacher, whose pedagogical skills have a lot to do with what the university professor will have to work with; or like public water resource operators on whose technical skills and diligence the health of entire communities depends.

Wollstonecraft, in other words, urges her readers to disregard whatever may be the differences of rank, status, or prestige in society and to focus instead on equality of function. If asked, she surely would have also argued that such societal gatekeepers should receive the broadest education and training possible, that such equality ought to be reflected in respective levels of financial compensation, and that the lack of such compensation was indeed hazardous to civic functionality and health. "Women, I allow, may have different duties to fulfil; but they are *human* duties, and the principles that should regulate the discharge of them, I sturdily maintain, must be the same."[123]

Mary Wollstonecraft was not a radical feminist in a modern sense. She did not argue that women should or could play the same role in society as men, and neither did she advance the thought that women should withdraw their traditional services from society. She only wanted these services to be accepted as equal in importance to those that men traditionally performed. And she convincingly showed that the different duties that women would perform as equals required full access to reason, virtue, and knowledge. Ultimately, in order to be able to perform their human duties, women needed to gain independence both from men and their demeaning station in life: "The being who discharges the duties of its station is independent; and, speaking of women at large, their first duty is to themselves as rational creatures, and the next, in point of importance, as citizens, is that, which includes so many, of a mother."[124]

In order to achieve such independence, Wollstonecraft argued, women must have equal access to education. This gave her the opportunity to call for thorough reform of the school system as it existed at the time. Wollstonecraft was critical of both private education at home, which turns pupils into self-important tyrants, and education in the alienating environment of boarding schools, which are breeding grounds of mischief and vice. Instead, she recommended the establishment of a national system of day schools for boys and girls.[125] This would not deprive children of regular domestic affection while exposing them to a learning environment among their peers. Government-funded, the teachers of such schools would not be dependent on parents' whims for their subsistence. And, receiving the same education, boys and girls would learn to regard each other as companions rather than merely distant objects of sexual desire.

Thus equipped with basic education, women could begin to chart a more autonomous path for their own lives. Choices would become possible. There would be options other than merely to "loiter with easy grace." Women could become "physicians as well as nurses." They might even "study politics," so they could understand "the character of the times." And they could turn to "business of various kinds," allowing them to earn a decent living rather than being obliged to marry for support or be forced into prostitution. They would become respectable in their own right rather than merely existing as men's pleasure providers.[126]

However, all this must become possible as a matter of basic human right rather than convention or mere toleration. "In order to render their private virtue a public benefit," Wollstonecraft insists, women "must have a civil existence in the State, married or single; else we shall continually see some worthy woman, whose sensibility has been rendered painfully acute by unde-served contempt."[127] Wollstonecraft knew what she was talking about. It was her most contentious demand and as such the one to which the male estab-lishment of society would object most violently. After all, it challenged the exclusivity of male property control. "During the marriage," the distin-guished Oxford law professor William Blackstone had written in 1758, "the legal existence of the woman is suspended."[128]

Ultimately, civic status will eventually have to include political rights. Wollstonecraft is well aware that she is moving, for the time being at least, from possible reform to wishful thinking. "I may excite laughter," she admits, "by dropping an hint, which I mean to pursue, some future time, for I really think that women ought to have representatives, instead of being arbitrarily governed without having any direct share allowed them in the deliberation of government."[129]

It would take another 126 years before women, in 1918, gained the right to vote in the United Kingdom, and to stand for election as a Member of Parliament. They were still not equal before the law because voting rights were restricted to women over 30 years of age as compared to 21 years of age for men. This was changed only 10 years later, in 1928. Ironically, the first women to be elected to the British Parliament were not exactly the ones Wollstonecraft had in mind as carriers of emancipation. The first was Countess Constance Markievicz, an Irish nationalist and member of Sinn Fein who was in an English prison when she was elected to Parliament in 1918. She did not take her seat as she refused to swear allegiance to the King. The second was Lady Nancy Astor, who did take her seat when she succeeded her husband as a conservative representative for Plymouth in 1919.[130]

Wollstonecraft's manifesto of women's rights does not amount to a fully developed political theory. The seminal importance of her contribution to the history of political thought lies elsewhere, in the linkages she draws between the private and the public. "Why then do philosophers look for public spirit?" she asks, when "public spirit must be nurtured by private virtue, or it will resemble the factitious sentiment which makes women care-ful to preserve their reputation, and men their honour."[131] And a few pages later, she adds that "a truly benevolent legislator always endeavours to make it the interest of each individual to be virtuous; and thus private virtue becoming the cement of public happiness, an orderly whole is consolidated by the tendency of all parts towards a common centre."[132]

These passages are reminiscent of Althusius again. Althusius, we remember, had separated the private from the public sphere according to his distinguishing particular from general interests. He had nevertheless insisted, however, that all forms of social community or consociation, from the family to the city, province, and universal commonwealth, were in essence political and governed by the same set of basic principles, the mutual communication of "things, services and common rights" (*rebus, operis, juribus communibus*).[133] In this, he had dissociated himself from the Aristotelian separation of public and private, *polis* and *oikos*, as operating under distinct principles of governance.

Later on, of course, Hobbes had also rejected the distinction between private and public when he wrote that all a ruler needs in order to be accepted by the people is "that they see him able absolutely to govern his own family."[134] But it was obviously a different kind of common governance he had in mind. This is where Wollstonecraft can use the parallelism of this argument in her attack on patriarchy: "The *divine right* of husbands," she writes, "like the divine right of kings, may, it is to be hoped, in this enlightened age, be contested without danger."[135]

The most important point about Wollstonecraft's *Vindications* is that they are not just about women's rights to do something useful with their lives rather than just providing their husbands with after-hours entertainment — although they are about that too. Rather, Wollstonecraft's point throughout is that women's rights to personal autonomy are an important precondition for the stability and productivity of a free society as a whole. And this is not just a strategic argument so that men might grant the freedom she craves.

Women's emancipation from men's prejudices and the emancipation of society are two sides of the same coin. When Wollstonecraft cites one of the most abominable stupidities from *Émile*, the one where Rousseau declares that "women have, or ought to have, but little liberty" because "they are apt to indulge themselves excessively in what is allowed them,"[136] she does so precisely because her purpose is to point out the dangers of this confinement for society as a whole: "The bent bow recoils with violence, when the hand is suddenly relaxed that forcibly held it."[137] This goes for women as much as for slaves or other groups of people suffering from oppression. Yet, Wollstonecraft does not turn this into a discourse on class struggle wherein one group seeks to and ultimately wins over another. "The very point I am at," she affirms, is that "I do not wish [women] to have power over men; but over themselves."[138] Personal autonomy, as a simple yet universal principle, Wollstonecraft is telling us, is the moral, as well as practical, precondition of organized politics. The personal is the political indeed.

Critical Evaluation

Few would argue in this day and age that the contribution of Edmund Burke to the history of political thought is anything more than an "exemplary statement of the modern conservative cast of mind" that is "unrelentingly hostile" to the "rationalist Enlightenment and the French Revolution which it spawned."[139] Fewer still would deny that Mary Wollstonecraft rightly and fully belongs to that history, not only for her contribution to feminism but also for her redrawing of the lines of the political, away from the "sublime" heroics of power and towards the "simple beauty" of personal autonomy and social equality. At least to this extent the tide has turned, finally.

To be sure, conservatism is a legitimate political ideology. Against the radicalism of all kinds of iconoclasts, conservatism points to the importance — and beauty — of what is "tried, tested and true." To the extent that the conservative mind is open enough "to preserve and to reform," as Burke wrote,[140] the disagreement between conservatism, liberalism, and radicalism may often be no more than a matter of degree and urgency. Burke can rightly point out that the evolutionary constitutionalism of England spared its citizens the terror of revolutionary upheaval in France.

It is a mistake, however, to think that Burke's arguments are theoretically sound just because he predicted the Jacobin terror that would follow in the wake of the revolution. In fact, this is the general fallacy of the conservative mind: By always predicting the worst possible outcome for each and every step taken away from the status quo, conservatives can boast to having been right on occasion, but they will conveniently gloss over all those instances when they have been wrong. After all, the sky did not fall when hairdressers were finally granted the same honourable civic status as the propertied elites, and politics did not sink to a level of hysterical indulgence when women finally got the vote.

Yet, Wollstonecraft's critique of Burke does not primarily aim at his rejection of new ideas. It is his ideologically skewed presentation of historical fact and contemporary circumstance that she condemns most vigorously. It is simply not true that the English state evolved from broad societal agreement, and it is misleading to pretend that the British system of political representation at the outgoing eighteenth century was "perfectly adequate to all the purposes for which a representation of the people can be desired or devised."[141] Wollstonecraft's most urgent point is that the formula of "to preserve and to reform" becomes entirely meaningless when the dominant ideology of the ruling classes covers up all that is in dire need of reform. A process of prudent historical learning becomes impossible. In fact, it is precisely this kind of conservative stonewalling that may trigger a more disruptive and revolutionary path to democratic progress.

Burke surely would have argued that he was right in the end. Britain eventually moved towards democracy through an evolutionary — if reluctant — sequence of reforms. And in France, where the revolution collapsed and the regime reverted to autocratic rule, even empire, democracy ultimately arrived in the very same piecemeal way. Wollstonecraft's reply would have been that both could only happen precisely because of the abstract and inflexible declaration of universal human rights that Burke so abhorred, and which the French Revolution put out as a critical yardstick for all time to come.

Wollstonecraft's reaction to Rousseau is both simpler and more complicated. It is simpler because it can be summed up by her demand that universal human rights of choice and reason be extended to women as well as men. It is more complicated, however, because she criticizes Rousseau not only for having forgotten the other half of humanity in his quest but also for the path he prescribes and which she characterizes as a "flight back to the night of sensual ignorance."[142]

Although she may have polemically overstated her case, Wollstonecraft identifies the crucial problem in Rousseau's political thinking very well. Rousseau, we remember, had rejected the complex and confusing advances of modernity, in the sciences and arts, because they appeared to him as the ideological glue that kept the ruling classes in power.[143] Hence, he had demanded the return to a simpler form of life in which all men could become brothers as in German poet Friedrich Schiller's romantic "Ode of Joy." Rousseau's political theory of the general will could only make sense in such a simplified societal context.

Wollstonecraft forcefully advances the argument that modernity can be put to better use, by turning its intellectual achievements against the forces of old. Like her later feminist colleague, Charlotte Perkins Gilman, she believed in the promise of modernity. As Gilman would put it in 1898: "the duty of human life is progress, development...we are here, not merely to live, but to grow."[144] Maybe Wollstonecraft's optimistic faith in the liberating powers of progress was driven by a kind of naïveté opposite to that of Rousseau. But she was not naive about the difficulties and complexities of the task ahead. When she suggested, for instance, that women would eventually have to gain the right of political representation, she meant representation of women and women's issues, and not of women as part of an undifferentiated body of citizen-brothers.

Because Wollstonecraft understood women's issues mainly in rather traditional terms, as mothers and educators, or as members of a new urban professional class, latter-day feminists have on occasion chided her for advancing only the cause of married middle-class women.[145] Such criticism is as much historically unfair as it shortchanges the broader radical context in which Wollstonecraft placed her feminist demands. It is historically unfair because at the outgoing eighteenth century, middle-class women were the only women on whom Wollstonecraft could pin her emancipative demands and hopes. As in the case of their male bourgeois colleagues who staged the

French Revolution, middle-class women were the only possible carriers of the revolutionary torch at the time. The criticism of promoting only a kind of liberal middle-class feminism, however, shortchanges Wollstonecraft's radical ambitions because she was equally adamant about ending social inequality more generally. The women who sold fish or vegetables, whom Burke found so vile, were not to be left without education or dignity in the end.

The astonishing fact is that the issues over which Burke, Wollstonecraft, and Rousseau disagreed so profoundly are very much defining issues of the twenty-first century. A large segment of humanity is still living in poverty and ignorance, and the gap has been widening rather than narrowing in many places. Among the poor and disenfranchised, women as a rule still suffer more than men. In the rich countries of the industrialized West and North, conservatives still — or again — use religious arguments to justify what they proclaim as traditional inequalities of gender, and to withhold civic dignity from what they consider deviant sexual orientations.

Wollstonecraft's vindications of the rights of men and women provide a powerful antidote to the self-righteousness of prescribed prejudice. If reason leads to the proclamation of universal principles and human rights, then these must be extended to each and every one. Wollstonecraft deduces this insight from the prudence and logic of historical learning. Humanity has never stood still in frozen inactivity. Against Burke, Wollstonecraft argues that whoever wants to bring the wheels of progress to a grinding halt does so by obfuscating history and spreading false consciousness. Against Rousseau, she holds that the wheels of progress cannot be turned back to a simpler world. Instead, the energies unleashed by the new advances in arts and sciences must be wrested from those who will only abuse them for their own advantage and put to use for the common good of all.

The nineteenth century would push the world into a frenzy of hyperactivism never known or experienced before. Whether the future of that world would be characterized by a culture of equality, and a herd mentality suffocating all sublime or singular heroics, as Friedrich Nietzsche saw it, or whether that culture of equality would be the new ideological smokescreen behind which the politics of inequality and exploitation continued with unrestrained brutality, as Karl Marx insisted: This is the debate in the next and last chapter.

CHAPTER 10

Modernity and Beyond
Nietzsche v. Marx

The nineteenth century threw Western civilization into an accelerating vortex of industrial modernization. By mid-century, exponential growth had decisively replaced what essentially had been a steady-state economy for most if not all of the preceding 2,000 years of human history.

It was the century of the bourgeois classes defending the victory they had won in the French Revolution. A victory it had been, despite revolutionary failure and conservative restoration: The liberal achievements of political participation and influence on the basis of property and wealth could no longer be undone. That wealth now demanded support and protection from the state it had erstwhile combated. National markets had to be built and maintained by standardized means of communication and transportation. Language and culture for the first time became tools and weapons of territorial consolidation. The flow of raw materials from colonial territories had to be secured.

Most importantly, the state was called upon to make sure that the liberal principles of political and social equality did not spread into the large armies of labourers who were the main source of the new wealth, in the factories, mines, and sweatshops. Late, almost too late, did the new captains of industry realize that the "great transformation" that had made them rich amounted to a "satanic mill"[1] headed for social revolution. To stem the tide, they endorsed the first measures of what would eventually become the modern welfare state. The first stirrings of social conscience and legislation were, as Karl Polanyi put it, the work of "enlightened reactionaries."[2]

With unprecedented social transformation came a new level of intellectual polarization. While bourgeois philosophers like Georg Wilhelm Friedrich Hegel (1770-1831) sought to tame the radical ideals of the French Revolution by celebrating law and order of the state as the crowning achievement of human rationality, radicals like Karl Marx (1818-83) saw this state as the very embodiment of oppression and exploitation, designed to prevent any further dynamic of social emancipation. At the end of the century, however, when the French syndicalist Edouard Berth declared, polemically, or as an act of wishful thinking, that "the state is dead" (*L'État est mort*),[3] his point of reference was not Marx but Friedrich Nietzsche (1844-1900), who had declared in 1882 that "God is dead" (*Gott ist todt*).[4]

Context

Just as Tocqueville had prophesied that America's crass commercialism would lead to it craving extreme spirituality,[5] so did the naked materialism of the new bourgeois society in the Old World lead it to develop a yearning for philosophy. The world, it dawned upon the members of this new society, was an entirely human construction and could not be explained any longer by the assumption of a divine plan or by the forces of natural law. This is precisely what Nietzsche had in mind when he declared that God was dead. He meant to say that the traditional recourse to God as a redemptive way out had become "unbelievable" (*unglaubwürdig*).[6] At that, his assessment of the situation was not all that different from that of Marx, who had proclaimed in the *Communist Manifesto* that "all that is holy is profaned, and man is at last compelled to face with sober senses, his real conditions of life, and his relations with his kind" (*alles Heilige wird entweiht, und die Menschen sind endlich gezwungen, ihre Lebensstellung, ihre gegenseitigen Beziehungen mit nüchternen Augen anzusehen*).[7]

Those were the "wild years of philosophy."[8] They were wild because the radical transformations of social life caused by the Industrial Revolution, in combination with the radical hopes raised by the French Revolution, provoked a wholesale rethinking of what it meant to be human, to be alive, and to live in society. At a moment of unprecedented materialism, philosophy took centre stage, and for the first time (perhaps also the last time?) the subject matter of so much philosophical inquiry, the new bourgeois civil society, was keenly interested in the outcome. At stake was nothing less than to find new explanations and a new moral code of conduct for a new world made by human beings themselves.

In the Berlin of the 1820s, Hegel's public lectures were routinely attended by an audience of more than 200, with "veterinarians, insurance brokers, civil servants, opera tenors and company clerks" among them.[9] These members of the new bourgeois middle class obviously liked what they heard. The state, Hegel declared, is the entirely rational "actualization of freedom."[10] What he meant by that was that the state was an objective force or spirit of the world and of history, and not the result of civic efforts or political accountability. Those who argued that "the discharge of all public business would come from below, from the people itself," Hegel polemicized in the opening pages of his *Philosophy of Right*, would only dissolve the objectivity of that state into a subjective "broth of heart, friendship, and inspiration."[11]

For the time being, Hegel's message of "all is well because the state is good and makes us better" was immensely popular. It gave that state, the Prussian state, what it wanted, and it absolved the adoring bourgeois audience of its civic responsibilities. They could go after their business without a bad conscience. The state would take care of the rest. In particular, it would defend itself, and the bourgeois society it protected, against what the Prussian minister of education called "the arbitrary postulation of empty ideals."[12] By that the minister meant the ideals of the French Revolution, universal liberty and equality. And against those who took these ideals seriously, the state took action. Learning about his imminent arrest, the dramatist Georg Büchner had to flee, first to France and then to Switzerland, after he had written, in 1834, that the sweat of the peasant was "the salt on the nobleman's table."[13] The poet Heinrich Heine had his works forbidden by the authorities after he had rhymed, in 1844, about a "better world" in which the lazy bellies of the rich would no longer be filled by the toiling hands of the poor.[14]

Heine chose to live most of his life in French exile, and it was in Paris where he met and befriended another exiled German radical, Karl Marx, who had moved there in 1843. In the case of Marx, the arms of German state authority were even longer. He had to leave Paris in 1845 when Prussian government officials were successful in convincing their French colleagues that he should be expelled. Marx moved on to Brussels. Threatened with deportation yet again three years later, this time by the Belgian authorities, Marx had to move again, and eventually settled in London.

Hegel's rational authorities knew what they were afraid of. In 1832 a huge gathering of some 30,000 mostly young people at the *Hambacher Fest* (an outdoor festival near Hambach Castle in southern Germany) demanded mild democratic reforms, including the recognition of women as equal members of human society.[15] Nothing dramatic or outright law-defying really happened during the three days of the event, but the ringleaders, among them many students and professors, were persecuted, imprisoned, and, in some instances, executed. And where the "arbitrary postulation of empty ideals" spread into the ranks of real working people, those whose toiling hands did fill the lazy bellies of the rich, the authorities came down with full military force. Such was the case with the uprising of the Silesian weavers in 1844. The weavers would weave a "threefold curse" into the shroud of Germany, the poet Heine rhymed afterwards: against God, who would not listen to their prayers; against the king, who would not stop their exploitation by the rich, having them "shot like dogs" instead; and finally against a false fatherland doomed by rot and disgrace.[16]

In Paris, Marx also renewed his earlier acquaintance with Friedrich Engels, the son of a German textile industrialist. Engels had just completed a sojourn of some 20 months in England, ostensibly to complete his business training at his father's Manchester firm but in reality to gather material for his study on *The Condition of the Working Class in England* that he published in 1845. In this book, Engels first conjured up the image and vision of a mercilessly exploited industrial proletariat on the verge of inevitable revolution. To this end, he probably overgeneralized from the reports he studied and the personal impressions he collected.

But nobody could be left untouched by what Engels reported, most vividly from the coal mines, and especially from those in which the passages were kept so narrow that "the women and children, who haul the coal, have to crawl on their hands and knees fastened to the tub by a harness and chain which is generally passed between their legs." Because children start working at such an early age (most are over eight years old, but some are as young as four), Engels's report continues, they receive next to no education. And because they are all so overworked (the working day normally lasts 11 or 12 hours, but double shifts are common), it is not surprising that miners "should take to drink." Ever the outraged and dismayed moralist, Engels concludes: "In the dark loneliness of the mines men, women and children work in great heat and the majority of them take off most (if not all) of their clothes. You can imagine the consequences for yourself."[17]

This was the cue for Marx. The relentlessness and intensity of labour exploitation and alienation could only have one possible outcome: a revolution of the oppressed against their oppressors. Betterment in the form of social progress would never come from lofty philosophical ideas and moral principles. It could only come through a radical change of the material conditions themselves. In order to prepare for such radical change, philosophy had to be turned into political economy.

In sharp contrast, Nietzsche remained entirely oblivious to social and economic realities. For him, there should not even have been a "labour question" (*Arbeiter-Frage*). Workers were already doing "far too well" (*viel zu gut*), and, having on their side "the great number" (*die grosse Zahl*), would obviously demand ever more. The opportunity "for developing a group of modest and self-sufficient types" (*dass hier sich eine bescheidene und selbstgenügsame Art Mensch ... herausbilde*) had been lost. The protagonists of modernity and its irresponsible politics of social conscience had only to blame themselves: "If you want slaves, then it is stupid to train them to be masters" (*will man Sklaven, so ist man ein Narr, wenn man sie zu Herrn erzieht*).[18]

Friedrich Nietzsche (1844-1900)
His aphorisms, nay, his aphoristic understanding of the world, would influence just about everything and everybody, from literature and philosophy to architecture and painting. His work had little direct political impact but later and falsely became associated with the Nazi movement. Later still, the postmoderns would detect in him a kindred spirit who preferred a deconstructed world of chaos to a world of systemic order.

Yet, Friedrich Nietzsche was an unlikely candidate for so much influence.[19] Born as the son of a Lutheran minister in a small German town, he received a classical school education and went on to study classical languages and literature at the University of Bonn. Even before finishing his Ph.D. in 1869, he was appointed as professor of classical philology at the University of Basel in Switzerland. His only major publication in the classics field, *The Birth of Tragedy*,[20] was met with derision by his colleagues. His relationship with the composer Richard Wagner began as a friendship of kindred spirits but ended in discord and contempt.

In 1879 he resigned his professorship for health reasons and began a restless life of wandering. In Switzerland, he had his major philosophical inspiration in the alpine surroundings of a mountain village. In various Mediterranean cities, his unstable mind oscillated between depression and euphoria.

He met the one woman, Lou Salomé, whom he may have loved, in St. Peter's Basilica in Rome, April 1882. He proposed marriage almost immediately but was rejected. The relationship lingered on for a few months and ended badly. There was a moment, on a Swiss hilltop, *Monte Sacro*, when "something" might have happened but Lou Salomé, who was only 21 when she met the 38-year-old Nietzsche and would outlive him by 47 years, later remarked: "Whether I kissed Nietzsche on the Monte Sacro—I don't know any more."[21]

Throughout the next seven years, he wrote incessantly, resigned to living alone in various cheap boarding houses where he produced his major works: *Human, All Too Human;*[22] *The Gay Science;*[23] *Thus Spoke Zarathustra;*[24] *Beyond Good and Evil;*[25] and *Genealogy of Morals.*[26] Then there is the string of last works all dating from 1888: *The Anti-Christ; Ecce Homo; Twilight of the Idols; The Case of Wagner;* and *Nietzsche contra Wagner.*[27] There are also seven volumes of his notes, some of which have been compiled as *The Will to Power* after his death.[28] And all this neither includes five volumes of early works nor seven volumes of letters.

This enormous output within such a short period of time is all the more astonishing because Nietzsche was afflicted almost all his life with a variety of ailments, including debilitating nerve pains and migraines. The Austro-Jewish writer and biographer Stefan Zweig (1881-1942) later composed a depressingly realistic image of Nietzsche's living conditions and work habits:

the small, narrow, modest, coldly furnished *chambre garnie*, where innumerable notes, pages, writings, and proofs are piled up on the table... Back in a corner, a heavy and graceless wooden trunk, his only possession, with the two shirts and the other worn suit... on a tray innumerable bottles and jars and potions: against the migraines, which often render him all but senseless for hours, against his stomach cramps, against spasmodic vomiting, against the slothful intestines, and above all the dreadful sedatives against his insomnia, chloral hydrate and Veronal. A frightful arsenal of poisons and drugs, yet the only helpers in the empty silence of this strange room in which he never rests except in brief and artificially conquered sleep. Wrapped in his overcoat and a woolen scarf (for the wretched stove smokes only and does not give warmth), his fingers freezing, his double glasses pressed close to the paper, his hurried hand writes for hours — words the dim eyes can hardly decipher. For hours he sits like this and writes until his eyes burn.[29]

At the beginning of 1889, Nietzsche was in the Italian city of Torino.[30] He had enjoyed a few months of feeling relatively healthy, he had reread his own books and found them to be "made very well" (*sehr gut gemacht*). He attended operettas, visited the cafés and outdoor markets. His landlady saw him dancing naked in his room. "A certain fatality" leads "to cheerfulness" (*eine gewisse Fatalität... zur Heiterkeit*), he wrote to a friend. At some point during the first days of January, he observed how a coach driver mistreated his horse. Breaking into tears, Nietzsche threw his arms around the animal and then collapsed. He would never think another lucid thought again. He would live another 11 years, mentally, and, also increasingly, physically incapacitated. First his mother and then his sister would look after him. During his last years, his sister would have him propped up on a little platform so as to better show off the deranged philosopher to an array of bewildered visitors. His sister would also administer and manipulate the mountain of unpublished manuscripts and notes so that they began to conform to her own Nazi ideology. Only after World War II would critical scholarship begin to set the record straight.

Nietzsche was a philosopher's philosopher. His main concern was to situate the life of human beings within a world they cannot understand. As a self-declared "nihilist" (*Nihilist*),[31] he believed that the philosophical search for truth as a rational set of explanations and moral values was in vain. What human beings had to cope with instead were the valuelessness and aimlessness of all existence. Such a philosophy has no primary interest in political order. Nietzsche's political thought is more antipolitical than political.

The philosophy begins and comes right to the point with the first sentence in his first major work, *The Birth of Tragedy*. Art as the imitation of life, Nietzsche declares, is "bound up with the Apollinian and Dionysian duality" (*an die Duplicität des Apollinischen und des Dionysischen gebunden*).[32]

While the Apollinian principle stands for the quest—or illusion—of measured perfection and wisdom, the Dionysian is anchored in life's spontaneous and often barbarous intoxications, the unbridled greed for life as a joyous if incomprehensible party.

Nietzsche argues that these two opposing sides of human existence had found a balanced—or dialectical—expression in the synthesis of Greek tragedy. He then accuses Socrates of destroying that balance by bringing into the world "the unshakable faith that thought, using the thread of causality, can penetrate the deepest abysses of being, and that thought is capable not only of knowing being but even of correcting it" (*jener unerschütterliche Glaube, dass das Denken, an dem Leitfaden der Causalität, bis in die tiefsten Abgründe des Seins reiche, und dass das Denken nicht nur zu erkennen, sondern sogar zu corrigieren im Stande sei*).[33] Socrates ruined the party, so to speak. "The fanatics of logic are as unbearable as wasps" (*Die Fanatiker der Logik sind unerträglich wie Wespen*), Nietzsche had already noted earlier, in a lecture on "Socrates and Tragedy" ("Socrates und die Tragödie").[34]

According to Nietzsche, the victory of Socrates's unshakable faith in rational thought over the Dionysian celebration of ecstasy has devastating consequences for the quality of life. Because truth and perfection are never attainable and lastly incomprehensible, human beings lose the capacity to enjoy life. Because their actions always fall short of the ideal, they begin to feel guilty. With guilt comes the fear of damnation, and with this, the fear of death.

This is the situation which the Christian religion inherits and begins to exploit by offering a convenient way out: Redemption in the afterlife both makes the misery of life on earth more bearable and mutes the fear of death. While traditional Western philosophy[35] and science have only helped to reinforce this depressing picture of human existence and its futile search for "ideality," Nietzsche wants to recreate philosophy as a "gay science" (*fröhliche Wissenschaft*)[36] that liberates the Dionysian joy of life from the overwhelming and stifling embrace of Apollinian rationality. Philosophy, he argues, must be constructed directly from life as lived and not as a recourse to some abstract moral code or ideal state.

In order to accomplish this, God, understood as the myth of otherness, must be declared dead. Human beings must become nihilists in that they believe that there is nothing other than what is before them. The famous *Übermensch* ("overman" rather than superman), whom Nietzsche celebrates in his *Zarathustra*, is the one who has accomplished all that, who has mastered the fear of death without having to take refuge in religion. "I teach you the overman," Nietzsche has Zarathustra say. "Man is something that shall be overcome" (*Ich lehre euch den Übermenschen. Der Mensch ist Etwas, das überwunden werden soll*).[37]

The "overman" (*Übermensch*), in other words, is the one who has "overcome" the fear of life and death and can live without the false bottom of Christian morality, which in turn is only a security blanket for the misunderstood and misinterpreted impositions of rationality. He who can live without that false bottom will have unlocked what is "the secret for harvesting from existence the greatest fruitfulness and the greatest enjoyment... to live dangerously!" (*das Geheimnis, um die grösste Fruchtbarkeit und den grössten Genuss vom Dasein einzuernten, heist... gefährlich leben!*).[38]

However, even the *Übermensch* cannot do without some recourse to metaphysical consolation. The major inspiration Nietzsche has near Sils Maria, the Swiss Alpine village where he spent several summers after his resignation from the University of Basel, is that of "the eternal recurrence of sameness" (*die ewige Wiederkunft des Gleichen*).[39] The promise of another life to come is replaced by the idea of the same life repeating itself for all eternity. The world is aimless and repetitive "chaos" (*Chaos*),[40] nothing better than "the eternal recurrence of war and peace" (*die ewige Wiederkunft von Krieg und Frieden*).[41]

Surprisingly, it is joy that comes from this realization. As Nietzsche explains in his notes, "we should imprint the image of eternity onto our life" (*Drücken wir das Abbild der Ewigkeit auf unser Leben*). He adds that this idea offers more than all those religions "which despise this life as fleeting and yearn for another uncertain life" (*welche dies Leben als ein flüchtiges verachten und nach einem unbestimmten anderen Leben hinblicken*).[42] And he points out that this is also a doctrine that treats unbelievers "mildly" (*milde*), rather than threatening them with hell and damnation. The only self-inflicted consequence for the unbeliever will be "a fleeting life in his own consciousness" (*ein flüchtiges Leben in seinem Bewußtsein*).[43]

Finally, the idea of eternal recurrence offers a categorical imperative of a different kind: Instead of "looking out for faraway unknown beatifications and blessings and reprievings" (*nach fernen unbekannten Seligkeiten, und Segnungen und Begnadigungen ausschauen*), we should "live so as we would want to live again and would want to live for all eternity" (*so leben, daß wir nochmals leben wollen und in Ewigkeit so leben wollen*).[44] And precisely from this imprinting of eternity onto our own consciousness comes joy: "For all joy wants—eternity" (*denn alle Lust will—Ewigkeit*).[45]

So far so good: Even if one may not want to follow Nietzsche's radical and irreverent critique of Western civilization and Christian morality all the way, it still invites us to critically rethink some of the traditional and no longer questioned assumptions about the good life. The implications that all of this has for the nature of the political, however, at least in Nietzsche's own mind, are rather more problematical.

Ordinary human beings need order. So, they make for themselves a world they can understand, with boundaries and rules, a make-believe world of error and fiction, because "without these articles of faith nobody could endure life" (*ohne diese Glaubensartikel hielte es jetzt Keiner aus zu leben*).[46] What Nietzsche means by error is essentially the construction of a rational world based on universal principles and rights. Once caught in this self-made web of faith and fiction, however, human beings lose their natural instincts. Instead of cultivating freedom as something "that you will, that you win" (*das man will, das man erobert*),[47] they begin to understand it as a given set of universal rights. Hence, they begin to think that they are "in danger of a new sort of slavery when the word 'authority' is so much as spoken out loud" (*in der Gefahr einer neuen Sklaverei, wo das Wort 'Autorität' auch nur laut wird*).[48] The underlying idea again is that of the erroneousness of universality. Conquest is not something that can be done universally because it implies winners and losers.

This is Nietzsche's "critique of modernity" (*Kritik der Modernität*).[49] It is a critique of cultural decline resulting from universal equality as a rational principle of social order. For him, social order should serve greatness and leadership. It should revolve "around growth and expansion, around power — in accordance with the will to power which is the will to life" (*um Wachsthum und Ausbreitung, um Macht, gemäss dem Willen zur Macht, der eben der Wille des Lebens ist*). Modern rationality subordinates this quest for greatness to "the smell of the distress and overcrowding of small people" (*Kleiner-Leute-Geruch von Noth und Enge*).[50]

Nietzsche comes to the point of politics quite bluntly. Politics, he asserts, is actually quite natural, in line with human nature, insofar as we see it as a struggle "of one quantum of power against another" (*eines Quantums Macht gegen ein anderes Quantum*).[51] This definition of politics already indicates that its nature and goal are not some kind of common good. Politics is seen as operating beyond good and evil in a traditional moral sense. In fact, Nietzsche is convinced that humanity has been advanced so far by "the strongest and most evil spirits" (*die stärksten und bösesten Geister*).[52] The point is that human action cannot be divided neatly into good and evil according to some abstract and absolute moral standard. Such moral certainty only impedes true progress.[53]

Such moral certainty is the morality for the fearful and meek because it makes life easier. At that, it is a "slave morality" (*Sklaven-Moral*), which "is essentially a morality of utility" (*ist wesentlich Nützlichkeits-Moral*). Nietzsche contrasts it with a "master morality" (*Herren-Moral*) that has only "contempt for the cowardly ... [for] those intent on narrow utility" (*verachtet wird der Feige ... der an die enge Nützlichkeit denkende*).[54] While considerations of utility may satisfy the vast majority, they will be rejected by the genius of those "higher human beings" (*die höheren Menschen*) who are able to overcome "the desire for certainty" (*das Verlangen nach Gewissheit*),[55] and who are therefore capable of propelling humanity forward.

Machiavelli had already said it more clearly and more simply three centuries earlier: While only a few seek freedom in order to "obtain authority over others" (*per comandare*), most people just want freedom "to live in security" (*per vivere securi*).[56] But he also had said it without contempt for the ordinary and common interests and desires of people. And he had argued that these common interests and desires were only unfit for political participation under conditions of corruption and excessive inequality.[57] Nietzsche's critique of modernity entirely leaves out the social and economic dimensions of that modernity. His contempt takes aim at modern mass culture, which he consistently characterizes as driven by a "herd instinct" (*Heerden-Instinct*).[58] Nietzsche has a deliberately primitive understanding of human society:

> Where someone rules, there are masses; and where we find masses we also find a need to be enslaved. Where men are enslaved, there are few individuals, and these are opposed by herd instincts and conscience. (*Wo geherrscht wird, da giebt es Massen: wo Massen sind, da giebt es ein Bedürfnis nach Sclaverei. Wo es Sclaverei giebt, da sind der Individuen nur wenige, und diese haben die Heerdeninstincte und das Gewissen gegen sich.*)[59]

Somewhat cruder than Tocqueville or Mill, Nietzsche pays tribute to the liberal fear that excellence, in the arts as in the quest for knowledge more generally, will be drowned out by a mass culture that jealously guards against anything and anyone threatening its mediocre conformity with unfamiliar challenges. Democracy is the political form of that mass culture. But unlike either Tocqueville or Mill, Nietzsche is unwilling to make peace with the inevitability of democratic equality.

Modern democracy, Nietzsche declares, is "the form in which the organizing force manifests its decline" (*die Niedergangs-Form der organisierenden Kraft*).[60] It is, in other words, that form of political organization which can no longer organize greatness because the natural master-slave relationship declines into a mushy brew of equalized mediocrity. In a particularly appalling passage, Nietzsche likens this deplorable decline to what he describes as an equally deplorable decline of traditional marriage. What used to be "the smallest unit of domination" (*das kleinste Gebilde der Herrschaft*), in which "the husband had sole juridical responsibility" (*juristische Alleinverantwortlichkeit des Mannes*), appears to be degenerating into some sort of legal partnership. This, however, makes it impossible to pursue what are the sole purposes of marriage: "sex drive" (*Geschlechtstrieb*); the "drive for property" (*Eigenthumstrieb*); and the "drive to dominate" (*Herrschafts-Trieb*). Marriage becomes useless.[61] So does democracy.

No wonder, then, that Lou Salomé politely declined. Or had second thoughts: One never quite knows with Nietzsche. There is always an undertone of irony, of sarcasm, and of deliberate provocation. At least in part he may castigate traditional marriage because of an equally strong contempt for the domestic certainty of home and hearth that it stands for. But there can be no doubt about his general condemnation of all forms of social order that are not based on a clear and undisputed hierarchy of the strong over the weak, master mentality over slave mentality.

From this vantage point of sweeping generality, there is also no difference between opposing ideological forces. Liberal institutions "undermine the will to power" (*unterminiren den Willen zur Macht*) by promoting a "herd animalization" (*Heerden-Verthierung*) of levelled moral values.[62] Socialism similarly leads to the "annihilation of the individual" (*Vernichtung des Individuums*), this time by its desire for an "abundance of state power" (*Fülle der Staatsgewalt*), and by the use of this state power, not for greatness and leadership, but in a pedestrian way as a "useful organ of the community" (*zweckmässiges Organ des Gemeinwesens*).[63]

Logically, then, Nietzsche also dismisses the parliamentary form of modern democracy (or what at the time goes by that name) as a meaningless organization. "Parliamentarism" (*Parlamentarismus*), he sneers, only "flatters" (*schmeichelt*) those who would "like to seem independent and individual" (*gerne selbständig und individuell scheinen*). In reality, however, it does not make any difference whatsoever "whether the herd is commanded to have one opinion or permitted to have five" (*ob der Heerde Eine Meinung befohlen oder fünf Meinungen gestattet sind*).[64]

Nietzsche's sarcastic dismissal of parliamentary plurality is logical because for him it is a plurality of opinions among "lesser natures" (*geringere Naturen*).[65] They ultimately all want the same, a "miserable type of well-being that grocers, Christians, cows, females, Englishmen, and other democrats dream about" (*verächtliche Art von Wohlbefinden , von dem Krämer, Christen, Kühe, Weiber, Engländer und andere Demokraten träumen*).[66] Parliamentarism is the organized form of "herd animalization." It aims at the opposite of what Nietzsche considers to be the ultimate human goal, a state of individual self-responsibility that can only be achieved by "becoming indifferent to hardship, cruelty, deprivation, even to life" (*dass man gegen Mühsal, Härte, Entbehrung, selbst gegen das Leben gleichgültiger wird*).[67] It seems as if Nietzsche's own tormented body and mind have dictated these lines.

Parliamentarism is not the only form of organized collectivity Nietzsche rejects. Another one is nationalism, which appears to him as a particularly misguided repository of well-being. Nationalism is something that is artificially imposed by "cunning, force and falsehood" (*List, Lüge und Gewalt*) in the interest "of certain princely dynasties and of certain classes of business and society" (*bestimmter Fürstendynastien [und] bestimmter Classen des Handels und der Gesellschaft*).[68] At the height of nineteenth-century European nationalism, with the great clashes of the twentieth century already written on the wall, Nietzsche understands very well that nationalism is a fabrication meant to serve, not national societies, but national capitalism.[69] But unlike Marx, Nietzsche is not concerned about inequality, exploitation, and imperialism. To him, nationalism is just another form of herd culture. As a mentality of "grocers," it stands in the way of true greatness yet again, as another attempt at constructing a false sense of certainty.

In the same vein, Nietzsche also takes on another and closely related issue of the time: racism, and anti-Semitism in particular. The itinerant philosopher commented often and freely on the different nationalities and races he saw in Europe, and he freely reproduced all the prejudices and clichés fomenting under the umbrella of nationalism — only to mock them as yet another deplorable manifestation of what happens when cultural judgment is left to the narrow-mindedness of "small people." And the Germans certainly do not fare any better than the Jews in the scathing snippets of comparative cultural critique strewn throughout his work.

The Germans, Nietzsche declares, are a contradictory mixture of "profundity" (*tief*) and a four-square preference for "beer" (*Bier*). It was this mixture that he accused his former friend Richard Wagner of having "finally set to music" (*die... Richard Wagner zuletzt noch in Musik gesetzt hat*). Germans marvel at everything that is shrouded in mystery. Thinking that this is what makes for profundity, they look at the world with "faithful, blue, empty, German eyes" (*treuen blauen leeren deutschen Augen*).[70]

The Jew, on the other hand, may have a crooked nose, and, "keeping with his business circles and the past of his people" (*gemäss dem Geschäftskreis und der Vergangenheit seines Volks*), rarely will be credited with philosophical profundity. Yet, the Germans in particular should be most grateful to the Jews because it was Jewish influence that taught them to make "finer distinctions, more rigorous inferences, and to write in a more luminous and cleanly fashion" (*ferner zu scheiden, schärfer zu folgern, heller und sauberer zu schreiben*). Logic, Nietzsche resumes, "is no respecter of persons and makes no distinction between crooked and straight noses" (*kennt kein Ansehn der Person und nimmt auch die krummen Nases für gerade*).[71]

Nietzsche was not a multiculturalist in the modern sense. His concern was not the autonomy and equality of different nationalities, or, in the mis-

guided terminology of the time, races. Nietzsche's message is that true superiority, the superiority of the *Übermensch*, must pick and choose from all
cultural sources. Like Marx, Nietzsche believes that it is trade and industry
that will eventually overcome the artificial production of "national hostilities" (*nationale Feindseligkeiten*). The end product will be a "mixed race...
of European man" (*Mischrasse... des europäischen Menschen*).[72] "Incidentally" (*Beiläufig*), this would also take care of the "Jewish problem" (*Problem
der Juden*). It is "cruel" (*grausam*) to single out Jews as the only ones with
dangerous or despicable characteristics. And only within a nationalist context can they be made to serve as "scapegoats" (*Sündenböcke*) for whatever
ails particular nations and their societies.[73]

While these powerful lines should put to rest the lingering myth, mainly
put into the world by his sister, that Nietzsche was an anti-Semite and proto-
Nazi philosopher, they do not take back his unabashed elitism. In the end, it
is a club of warrior-philosophers that is to rule the world. In one of his most
bizarre suggestions for an ideal form of politics, Nietzsche suggests that a
law-giving body should be composed of trustworthy men who are at the
same time masters and experts, and who "select one another through a
process of mutual scenting out and recognition" (*sich auszuscheiden, durch
gegenseitige Auswitterung und Anerkennung*). And on each matter before
them, the decision should be left only to the respective experts among them,
as a matter of "honour and simple decency" (*Ehrenhaftigkeit... und einfach
zur Sache des Anstands*).[74]

Nietzsche's contemporary Karl Marx was not an anti-Semite either,
although he, too, reproduced standard anti-Semite clichés of the time according to which Jews were given to "Huckstering" (*Schacher*) and "Money"
(*Geld*).[75] For Marx, however, the Jews had only mastered what was the essence
of bourgeois society, and their final emancipation would require not only
incorporation into a secularized and no longer Christian state but also first
and foremost the emancipation of bourgeois society from its haggling self.

Like Nietzsche, Marx did not like the kind of modernity that was being
formed before his eyes. Unlike Nietzsche and his *Zarathustra*, however,
Marx did not yearn for the recurrence of a bygone world of masters and
slaves propelled forward anew by the intellectual heroics of the *Übermensch*.
The "honour and simple decency" of a few experts was not going to be good
enough to fix what was wrong with modernity. Marx instead saw in this
flawed modernity the revolutionary seeds for a better world to come.

Nietzsche had remained a disciple of Hegel's idealism at least insofar as
he maintained that it was willed consciousness, in the form of either a master
or a slave morality, that determined the reality of state and society. Marx
would posit the exact opposite by "standing Hegel on his feet," so to speak:[76]

"It is not the consciousness of men that determines their being, but, on the contrary, their social being that determines their consciousness" (*Es ist nicht das Bewußtsein der Menschen, das ihr Sein, sondern umgekehrt ihr gesellschaftliches Sein, das ihr Bewußtsein bestimmt*).[77]

Karl Marx (1818-83)

For someone idolized as the greatest revolutionary thinker of all time, his biography is surprisingly bourgeois.[78] Karl Marx was born into a German-Jewish family. As so many Jews at the time, his father, a lawyer by profession, had converted to Christianity in order to be able to pursue a bourgeois career. Marx studied Greek philosophy and initially intended to pursue an academic career before turning to publishing and writing. He married the aristocratic Jenny von Westphalen with whom he raised three daughters (another daughter and two sons were lost at an early age).

After some turbulent years in France and Belgium, often only a step ahead of the Prussian authorities demanding his arrest and extradition, Marx eventually settled in London. There, he spent much of the rest of his life studying in the Reading Room of the British Museum, and writing nearly undecipherable tracts on political economy, most of which nobody wanted to read or publish at the time.[79]

Initially living in abject poverty, the family survived with the help of financial contributions from Marx's lifelong friend and collaborator, Friedrich Engels, who, ironically, derived income from his father's textile mills. All the while, Marx appears to have enjoyed tobacco, alcohol, Victorian novels, and, occasionally, the housekeeper, Helene Demuth. The result of his liaison with the latter was a son, Freddy, who was given up for adoption and never acknowledged by his father. Demuth, on the other hand, remained with the family, and, after Marx's death, was taken in by the Engels household until her own death in 1890. The whole affair was hushed up so thoroughly that it came to full light only a century later, from bits of evidence in various letters and documents.

A few minor inheritances and a pension from the ever-generous Engels eventually stabilized the situation. The Marx household increasingly took on the characteristics of bourgeois respectability: a newer and larger house was rented and refurbished, balls and dinner dances were organized for the daughters, and vacations were taken. Bourgeois also was a tendency to always spend more than the family could really afford. Letters to Engels begging for money and debt relief remained an embarrassing periodical necessity. According to his own testimony, Marx also tried speculating on the stock market. In later years, he would also make occasional visits to the spa in Carlsbad.

After the death of his wife in 1881, Marx went on a last trip, as much in desperate search of consolation for his loss as in search of sunshine for his chronic bronchitis. He travelled to Algiers, where he had his famous beard shaved off; to Monte Carlo; to Argenteuil near Paris, where his oldest daughter Jenny was married; to Vevey in Switzerland; and to Ventnor on the Isle of Wight. It was in Ventnor that Marx learned, in January 1883, that his beloved daughter Jenny had died as well. Two months later, on March 7, 1883, Engels found him dead at home, in his favourite armchair next to the fire.

As a revolutionary, then, Marx was clearly a desk-bound mastermind. Contrary to Engels, he did not take an active part in any of the revolutionary outbursts that accompanied the rise of modern industrial capitalism during the nineteenth century. Yet, the authorities understood full well the revolutionary danger coming from his mind and pen. As his friend Heinrich Heine had mockingly rhymed about the Prussian customs officers searching him for forbidden contraband:

Ye fools, who turn my boxes out,
There's nothing there forbidden;
The contraband I travel with,
In my head is safely hidden!
...
Oh, many a book I have stowed away;
I am speaking in moderation
When I tell you my brain is a warbling nest
Of books for confiscation.[80]

Strangely enough, in hindsight it was not the *Communist Manifesto* that first earned Marx the reputation as a dangerous revolutionary. That reputation mainly came from his journalistic activities as an editor and writer of various radical newspapers and yearbooks in Germany and France. For 11 years, from 1851 to 1862, he was also a regular contributor to the *New York Daily Tribune*.

But it was the *Manifesto* that would turn out to be Marx's masterpiece after all. In dramatic fashion and with forceful clarity, he put on paper what can be read as a synthesis of his entire train of thought. In doing so, he bridged his earlier philosophical writings with his later works on political economy by providing a brilliant analysis of capitalism, and, as he assumed, its inevitable demise. As Karl Korsch, one of Marx's first important twentieth-century interpreters, pointed out, Marx's train of thought can best be appreciated as a sequence of interrelated critiques: a critique of bourgeois philosophy and history; a critique of bourgeois society and ideology; and a critique of capitalism, the material basis upon which bourgeois society and ideology operate.[81]

While the *Communist Manifesto* opens with the famous exclamation: "A spectre is haunting Europe — the spectre of Communism" (*Ein Gespenst geht um in Europa — das Gespenst des Kommunismus*), Marx almost immediately turns to an interpretation of the past: "The history of all hitherto existing society is the history of class struggles" (*Die Geschichte aller bisherigen Gesellschaft ist die Geschichte von Klassenkämpfen*).[82] In this one sentence, Marx sums up what had mainly haunted him up to that point, "standing Hegel on his feet" indeed, a radical reinterpretation of how ideas and realities connect and interact throughout the course of history.

From Hegel Marx learned to understand the course of human history as a sequence of dialectical steps. The conceptualization of an idea (or thesis) in the human mind would lead to the construction of a certain world reality. This reality would then be challenged or questioned by a critical counter-idea (or antithesis). The problem would be resolved by a new idea (synthesis), which would in turn lead to a new stage in world reality. For Hegel, the modern state was the end product and last stage of this process, and at that the incarnation of idea-turned-reality.

What Marx wanted to turn upside down, or, rather, right side up, was not the sequence or direction of dialectical steps as such. He wanted to locate the origin of the dynamic driving the dialectical process of history. For Hegel, Marx reminisced later, it is the "idea" (*Idee*) that is the subject and driving force of the "real world" (*des wirklichen*) as its object. For him, Marx, the relation of subject and object is exactly the opposite: "With me, on the contrary, the ideal is nothing else than the material world reflected by the human mind, and translated into forms of thought" (*Bei mir ist umgekehrt das Ideelle nichts andres als das im Menschenkopf umgesetzte und übersetzte Materielle*).[83]

This is what Marx meant in the earlier quote about consciousness being determined by social existence.[84] The process of history is not driven by lofty ideas that change the world and propel humanity forward to an ever nobler end. Instead, history is driven and changed by the periodicity of social revolutions of the oppressed and exploited against their oppressors and exploiters. The most obvious recent stage in this process has been the bourgeois (French) revolution against the old aristocratic regime. The next (and last?) stage, at least for Marx, will be the revolution of workers against bourgeois capitalists.

The driving forces in each case are the material conditions of class inequality. Ideas cannot bring forth revolutionary change because in every epoch "the ruling ideas" (*die herrschenden Gedanken*) which dominate society as a whole are nothing but "the ideas of the ruling class" (*die Gedanken der herrschenden Klasse*).[85] Elsewhere, Marx points out in almost Nietzschean terms that oppression and exploitation are "willed" forms of domination: "The presupposition of the master-servant relation is the appropriation of an alien will" (*Die Aneignung fremden Willens ist Voraussetzung des Herrschaftsverhältnisses*).[86] Precisely for this reason, social and political changes cannot come from ideas but must be initiated by the material conditions of life itself.

Back in the *Manifesto* again, Marx describes these conditions as "class antagonisms" (*Klassengegensätze*): Society in its entirety "is more and more splitting up into two great hostile camps, into two great classes directly facing each other: Bourgeoisie and Proletariat" (*spaltet sich mehr und mehr in zwei große feindliche Lager, in zwei große, einander direkt gegenüberstehende Klassen: Bourgeoisie und Proletariat*).[87] Of course, the argument is far from Nietzschean here. The members of the proletariat are not the ones already doing "far too well."[88] They are instead the carriers of revolutionary hope, and as such hold the key to communism as "the riddle of history solved" (*das aufgelöste Rätsel der Geschichte*).[89]

One would expect, therefore, that Marx will now delve into a grand tirade against the bourgeoisie as the carrier of oppression and exploitation, holding back the ultimate progress of humanity. But far from it: What follows is an almost unabashed celebration of bourgeois achievements. The bourgeoisie "has accomplished wonders far surpassing Egyptian pyramids, Roman aqueducts, and Gothic cathedrals; it has conducted expeditions that put in the shade all former Exoduses of nations and crusades" (*Sie hat ganz andere Wunderwerke vollbracht als ägyptische Pyramiden, römische Wasserleitungen und gotische Kathedralen, sie hat ganz andere Züge ausgeführt als Völkerwanderungen und Kreuzzüge*).[90] And it has done so by means of "subjection of Nature's forces to man, machinery, application of chemistry to industry and agriculture, steam-navigation, railways, electric telegraphs, clearing of whole continents for cultivation, canalisation of rivers, whole populations conjured out of the ground" (*Unterjochung der Naturkräfte, Maschinerie, Anwendung der Chemie auf Industrie und Ackerbau, Dampfschiffahrt, Eisenbahnen, elektrische Telegraphen, Urbarmachung ganzer Weltteile, Schiffbarmachung der Flüsse, ganze aus dem Boden hervorgestampfte Bevölkerungen*).[91]

With these passages, we are finally and unmistakably thrown right into modernity.[92] In its course, Marx foresees that "national one-sidedness and narrow-mindedness become more and more impossible" (*nationale Einseitigkeit und Beschränktheit wird mehr und mehr unmöglich*). Production and consumption will take on a "cosmopolitan" (*kosmopolitisch[en]*) character.

National "seclusion" (*Abgeschlossenheit*) will give way to a "universal inter-dependence of nations" (*allseitige Abhängigkeit der Nationen*). Even national and local literature will be replaced in the end by a new "world literature" (*Weltliteratur*).[93]

In one of the most brilliant and beautiful passages that surely belongs to that world literature, Marx analyzes how and why all this must and will happen:

The bourgeoisie cannot exist without constantly revolutionising the instruments of production, and thereby the relations of production, and with them the whole relations of society. Conservation of the old modes of production in unaltered form, was, on the contrary, the first condition of existence for all earlier industrial classes. Constant revolutionising of production, uninterrupted disturbance of all social conditions, everlasting uncertainty and agitation distinguish the bourgeois epoch from all earlier ones. All fixed, fast-frozen relations, with their train of ancient and venerable prejudices and opinions, are swept away, all new-formed ones become antiquated before they can ossify. All that is solid melts into air, all that is holy is profaned, and man is at last compelled to face with sober senses, his real condition of life, and his relations with his kind. (*Die Bourgeoisie kann nicht existieren, ohne die Produktionsinstrumente, also die Produktionsverhältnisse, also sämtliche gesellschaftlichen Verhältnisse fortwährend zu revolutionieren. Unveränderte Beibehaltung der alten Produktionsweise war dagegen die erste Existenzbedingung aller früheren industriellen Klassen. Die fortwährende Umwäl-zung der Produktion, die ununterbrochene Erschütterung aller gesellschaftlichen Zustände, die ewige Unsicherheit und Bewegung zeichnet die Bourgeoisepoche vor allen anderen aus. Alle festen eingerosteten Verhältnisse mit ihrem Gefolge von altehrwürdigen Vorstellungen und Anschauungen werden aufgelöst, alle neugebildeten veralten, ehe sie verknöchern können. Alles Ständische und Stehende verdampft, alles Heilige wird entweiht, und die Menschen sind endlich gezwungen, ihre Lebensstellung, ihre gegenseitigen Beziehungen mit nüchternen Augen anzusehen.*)[94]

The critical critic does not quite leave it at that, of course. With an almost Shakespearean sense of rhetorical drama, however reversed ("I come to bury Caesar, not to praise him"),[95] Marx in the same breath tears apart the pro-gressive facade of the bourgeois revolution. It has swept away the kind of "religious fervour" (*fromme Schwärmerei*) and "philistine sentimentalism" (*spießbürgerliche Wehmut*) that had kept the old feudal society in check, but by doing so it has "resolved personal worth into exchange value" (*die per-sönliche Würde in den Tauschwert aufgelöst*), and it has substituted "the numerous indefeasible chartered freedoms" (*[die] zahllosen verbrieften und wohlerworbenen Freiheiten*) of the old order with "naked, shameless, direct, brutal exploitation" (*offene, unverschämte, direkte, dürre Ausbeutung*) in the name of "Free Trade" (*Handelsfreiheit*).[96]

Exchange vålue and exploitation: These two terms already foreshadow what will be the core of Marx's critique of the modern capitalist political economy. Since history is a history of class struggle, exploitation has always existed. But under precapitalist or feudal conditions this exploitation had a different character. The serfs working on the land or in the workshops were not a commodity that could be freely bought and sold at the market. They were a vital resource for the well-being of the noble landowner. If that landowner wanted a larger castle or a more luxurious lifestyle, he could not trade in his castle or exchange his labourers for more efficient or more exploitable ones. He had to go back to the same resource, the labour of the serfs or tenants he owned or controlled.

In conjunction with the Industrial Revolution, modern capitalism changed all that. Factory work and the mechanization of agriculture created a huge "industrial reserve army" (*industrielle Reservearmee*)[97] of wage labourers who could be hired and fired according to capitalist need. Labour, which had been a vital human resource, could now be treated like any other commodity, raw material, or machine. Still, in 1906, a surprisingly "enlightened" doctoral dissertation in economics described the new relations of production quite adequately:

> The worker was treated before the law in the same way as the entrepreneur; labour was considered a commodity, and the worker was the seller of this commodity. The worker was distinct from the entrepreneur, however, by the fact that he could not manipulate the price of his commodity like other sellers who could withdraw theirs from the market. The worker ... had to sell at any price if he did not want to starve.... The reasons for this were ... on the one hand, surplus labour ... and on the other hand, the worker's lack of a capital reserve.[98]

Marx, of course, wanted to dig much deeper and find a scientific explanation for the role that the exploitation of labour played in the process of capitalist accumulation. To this end, he developed in *Capital*, his major work on political economy, a general and rather complicated theory of capital accumulation, which, however, contains a simple core idea, the famous "M-C-M" formula.[99] Under the M-C-M formula, the industrial capitalist converts money capital (M) into commodity capital (C), or, more specifically, means of production. By then selling whatever is produced, the commodity form of capital is "re-converted" (*rückverwandelt*) into money, or, as Marx says, "more accurately" (*vollständiger*) into more money (M). More money means profit. As more money is then reconverted or reinvested into more productive commodity capital, which yields more profit yet again, the process of capital accumulation appears as an endless, and, because of competitive pressure, relentless circuit of commodification and monetarization (M-C-M-C-M, and so on).

The question is: Where is this profit coming from? Marx had already approached this question in *The Grundrisse*, his notebook(s) on a critique of political economy from 1857-58.[100] His starting point is quite Newtonian.[101] Whatever goes into the production process must be "equivalent" (*äquivalent*) to what comes out of it. Profit, in other words, cannot be created out of the blue. Like the rabbit in the magician's hat, it must already be there. What goes into the production process is the value of raw material, machinery, and labour. Since Marx is sure that the value of raw material and machinery does not undergo any change on its own, he concludes that the "surplus value" (*Mehrwert*) leading to profit can only be added by labour.

Workers, he concludes, are not being paid the full equivalent of what they have put into the process but only a fraction of it — whatever is necessary to keep them alive and/or as little as any worker is willing to do the work for. The rest is retained by the capitalist and constitutes profit: "What appears as surplus value on capital's side appears identically on the worker's side as surplus labour in excess of his requirements as worker, hence in excess of his immediate requirements of keeping himself alive" (*was auf seiten des Kapitals als Mehrwert erscheint, erscheint exakt auf seite des Arbeiters als Mehrarbeit über sein Bedürfnis als Arbeiter hinaus. also über sein unmittelbares Bedürfnis zur Erhaltung seiner Lebendigkeit hinaus*).[102] This is what Marx means by capitalist exploitation.

Exploitation in this sense is not used as a moral category or judgment. Marx simply seeks to analyze and describe the production process during which labour gets "exploited" like any other resource or commodity. But it becomes a moral category when Marx turns to the effects that industrial labour has on the life and consciousness of workers. Through the division of labour that accompanies the extensive use of machinery in industrial production, the worker becomes a mere "appendage of the machine" (*bloßes Zubehör der Maschine*).[103] As the importance and sophistication of machines increases, the value of labour decreases and is reduced to the "most simple, most monotonous, and most easily acquired knack" (*der einfachste, eintönigste, am leichtesten erlernbare Handgriff*).[104] On the one hand, this facilitates exploitation because labour becomes nearly worthless and easily replaceable. On the other hand, by turning workers into tools or robots, it robs them of their creative capacity and autonomy.

This is what Marx calls "alienation" or "estrangement" (*Entfremdung*), a concept which he developed and elaborated on especially in his early notebooks of 1844, known as the *Economic and Philosophic Manuscripts*. The estrangement that workers suffer under conditions of capitalist production is threefold: They are estranged from the product of their work, from themselves, and from their fellow workers:[105] contrary to medieval workers, who accompanied and controlled the production process from beginning to end, modern industrial workers neither know where the raw materials are coming from, nor what the finished product will look like, or to whom it is going to be sold. In this way they are estranged from the product of their work. As mere cogs in the machinery of industrial production, workers are also estranged from themselves. Marx is convinced that they can fulfil their human nature only through free conscious activity in control of the entire production process. And finally, this estrangement of workers from their work and from themselves also results in the further estrangement from their fellow workers to whom they can no longer relate directly, as workers.

In the *Communist Manifesto*, Marx gives another reason for this last form of estrangement: "the competition among the workers themselves" (*die Konkurrenz unter den Arbeitern selbst*).[106] These workers or "labourers," Marx writes, "who must sell themselves piece-meal, are a commodity, like every other article of commerce, and are consequently exposed to all the vicissitudes of competition, to all the fluctuations of the market" (*Arbeiter, die sich stückweis verkaufen müssen, sind eine Ware wie jeder andere Handelsartikel und daher gleichmäßig allen Wechselfällen der Konkurrenz, allen Schwankungen des Marktes ausgesetzt*).[107] It is this competition that pits workers against one another and prevents them from developing a sense of solidarity and class consciousness.

It is nevertheless here that Marx begins to talk about the inevitable and revolutionary demise of the capitalist system. Eventually, according to Marx, the relentless process of labour commodification would foment the revolutionary class of a proletariat no longer willing to endure exploitation and estrangement.[108] Marx was unable to foresee both the proactive resolve of "enlightened reactionaries," who would stem the revolutionary tide with the introduction of social legislation, and capitalism's own productive breadth, which would stabilize modern middle-class society.

Marx was also convinced that the capitalist system of production bore its own seeds of destruction, "like the sorcerer, who is no longer able to control the powers of the nether world whom he has called up by his spells" (*gleich dem Hexenmeister, der die unterirdischen Gewalten nicht mehr zu beherrschen vermag, die er heraufbeschwor*).[109] In the *Communist Manifesto*, he speaks of the "epidemic of overproduction" (*Epidemie der Überproduktion*).[110] This is the core idea of his theory of capitalist crisis.[111]

We already know that the capitalist production process, apart from raw materials, depends on two resources or factors of production: machines and labour. Marx believed that in order to minimize the production cost per unit of output, and to maximize profit, capitalists will intensify the use of machinery. At some point, however, the productive capacity achieved by the intensive use of machinery, automation, etc., will produce more output than can be sold. The M-C-M circuit breaks down. To put it differently: Capital gets stuck or fixed in its current commodity form (machines, factories). It can no longer be reconverted into its money form, leave alone into more money, and, subsequently into a more profitable form of production. This is the essence of what Marx means by an epidemic or crisis of overproduction.

Its corollary is underconsumption, hinted at in the *Manifesto* when Marx states that "the conditions of bourgeois society are too narrow to comprise the wealth created by them" (*Die bürgerlichen Verhältnisse sind zu eng geworden, um den von ihnen erzeugten Reichtum zu fassen*).[112] Under-consumption is also a logical consequence of labour exploitation: If the working part of the population is paid for only a fraction of its contribution to the production process, the gap between the productive and consumptive capacities of a society must inevitably widen.

This permanently looming overproduction/underconsumption crisis is the ultimate reason for the relentless dynamic of capitalist reproduction. But what had been described with such literary eloquence as "all that is solid melts into air" at the outset, is now identified in rather more brutal terms. Capitalism deals with this crisis "on the one hand by enforced destruction of a mass of productive forces; on the other, by the conquest of new markets, and by the more thorough exploitation of the old ones" (*einerseits durch die erzwungene Vernichtung einer Masse von Produktivkräften; anderseits durch die Eroberung neuer Märkte und die gründlichere Ausbeutung alter Märkte*).[113]

Marx foresaw both the rise of globally expanding market economies, and the manipulation of domestic consumer markets by ever more refined marketing techniques. And as far as the enforced destruction of productive forces is concerned, one does not have to follow Marx's unveiled suggestion that this might be the role assigned by capitalism to a "universal war of devastation" (*allgemeiner Vernichtungskrieg*).[114] All one has to do, in North America at least, is to take a bus tour around the Great Lakes, where one can still see pockets of the old heartland of industrial capitalism now turned into a rust belt by the creative destruction of abandonment, both of the industrial landscape and its former working populations.

As such a crisis of overproduction/underconsumption, the Great Depression of the 1930s would almost prove Marx's predictions right. Yet again, he misjudged the resilience of capitalism to rebuild itself, and, by doing so, to contain the revolutionary potential of the proletariat.

On the one hand, capitalism learned to "regulate" the relationship between mass production and mass consumption by "the continual adjustment of mass consumption to rises in productivity."[115] This new "mode of regulation" came to be called "Fordism" because Henry Ford was thought to have been the first to introduce higher wages for his workers when he realized that otherwise there would not be any consumers for his mass-produced automobiles. As a corollary, in the words of critical Marxists like Alain Lipietz, the introduction of higher wages also "led to huge changes in the life-style of wage-earners," which in turn led workers to accept the capitalist system or even become its willing accomplices.[116]

On the other hand, there was the eventual rise of the Keynesian welfare state. In his *General Theory of Employment, Interest and Money* of 1936, the British economist John Maynard Keynes suggested that the volatility of capitalist boom and bust cycles could be managed by public fiscal intervention (macroeconomic steering). In times of economic crisis, consumption levels should be sustained by public assistance policies financed by budget deficits, which could then be paid down by fiscal surpluses once the economy had recovered. Keynesianism has fallen into discredit in recent years because political expediency led politicians to embrace deficit spending more readily than subsequent deficit reduction. But there can be no doubt that the avoidance of another economic crisis like the Great Depression in the advanced capitalist world is largely owed to a sustained commitment to state intervention, be it in the general form of unemployment insurance, or in the specific form of targeted sectoral relief.

For the Marx of the *Communist Manifesto*, the state is indeed nothing but a convenient tool of control and regulation in the hands of the ruling class. The government as "the executive of the modern State is but a committee for managing the common affairs of the whole bourgeoisie" (*Die moderne Staatsgewalt ist nur ein Ausschuß, der die gemeinschaftlichen Geschäfte der ganzen Bourgeoisklasse verwaltet*).[117] The rest of the *Manifesto*, however, is strangely void of a more detailed analysis and critique of the modern state. Or perhaps it is not so strange: Just as Nietzsche had wanted to explain the totality of social phenomena through the lens of a critique of mass culture (e.g., herd instinct), so too does Marx want to explain it through the lens of a materialist critique of political economy. In either case, politics in the conventional sense remains underexposed.

The state in fact is as uninteresting to Marx as is the Christian promise of heavenly bliss. Like religion, he notes in his earlier essay *On the Jewish Question*, the state proclaims that "every member of society is an equal partner in popular sovereignty" (*jedes Glied des Volkes zum gleichmäßigen Teilnehmer der Volkssouveränität*). However, the state does not abolish the distinctions of birth, social rank, education, or occupation when it makes this proclamation. Rather, it makes them "non-political distinctions" (*unpolitische Unterschiede*). Thus, man leads a "double existence—celestial and terrestrial. He lives in the political community, where he regards himself as a communal being, and in civil society where he acts simply as a private individual" (*ein doppeltes, ein himmlisches und ein irdisches Leben, das Leben im politischen Gemeinwesen, worin er sich als Gemeinwesen gilt, und das Leben in der bürgerlichen Gesellschaft, worin er als Privatmensch tätig ist*). In this sense, "the political state, in relation to civil society, is just as spiritual as is heaven in relation to earth" (*Der politische Staat verhält sich ebenso spiritualistisch zur bürgerlichen Gesellschaft wie der Himmel zur Erde*). In this political state, man "is the imaginary member of an imaginary sovereignty, divested of his real, individual life, and infused with an unreal universality" (*ist er das imaginäre Glied einer eingebildeten Souveränität, ist er seines wirklichen individuellen Lebens beraubt und mit einer unwirklichen Allgemeinheit erfüllt*).[118]

This is powerful stuff even when it must be acknowledged that Marx once more underestimated the degree to which the modern democratic representative state would guarantee civic equality as a universal code of individual rights and freedoms. But then again, as already in the case of Locke, such guarantees would not amount to a hill of beans if they did not come with an equally secure level of social existence.

The *Communist Manifesto*, of course, is mainly known and vilified as an appeal to the proletariat to unite and overthrow the capitalist system, and the modern state with it. In hindsight, it is almost touching to read the list of first general measures Marx wanted the communists to put into practice after the revolution. Apart from some more drastic measures, such as the abolition of private property in land and the right of inheritance, they include a progressive income tax; the creation of a national bank administering the credit system; a centralized public system of communication and transportation; the extension of public enterprise; and free education for all children in public schools.[119]

From such measures, Marx imagined, would result the disappearance of class distinctions, and with it the disappearance, not of the state, but of political power understood as "the organised power of one class for oppressing another" (*organisierte Gewalt einer Klasse zur Unterdrückung einer andern*).[120] In the end, the great revolutionary dreamed about a utopia of social harmony and freedom more Althusian than Hobbesian, and most certainly one that could not be confused with Leninism and Stalinism:

In place of the old bourgeois society, with its classes and class antagonisms, we shall have an association, in which the free development of each is the condition for the free development of all. (*An die Stelle der alten bürgerlichen Gesellschaft mit ihren Klassen und Klassengegensätzen tritt eine Assoziation, worin die freie Entwicklung eines jeden die freie Entwicklung aller ist.*)[121]

Critical Evaluation

At first glance, the verdict seems clear: Nietzsche's attack on mass culture, his invitation to think outside the rational box and to "live dangerously" by rejecting the conventional, obviously strikes a powerful note with all those who are tired of a modernity that is essentialized as universal-rationality-turned-conformity. Nietzsche not only proclaimed that God is dead but moreover, and more importantly, that the world is nothing but uncontrollable chaos. "Some people are born posthumously" (*Einige werden posthu[m] geboren*), he had declared about himself.[122] And as he had predicted, when conventional modernity was challenged more thoroughly, he gained iconic status, posthumously, as the "most important nineteenth-century thinker in relation to postmodernism."[123] Thus, Nietzsche became the champion for all those who sought to deconstruct "the entire enterprise of Western culture," and, with it, "the puffery of the 'sovereign theorist' who presumes to have discovered an encompassing system of truth."[124]

By comparison, the economic determinism of Marx appears as a reductionist attempt at pressing social life's multi-faceted plurality to one imperative causal agent, the driving force of capitalist accumulation. The champions of postmodern deconstruction are rightly and righteously offended by such reductionism.[125] "At best," Marx offers "valuable insights into the nature of human alienation" as caused by the systemic inequality resulting from, and perpetuated by, the capitalist process of reproduction. "At worst," however, he "plays into the hands of those who, under the guise of pursuing equality, would destroy freedom, shackle individuality, and stifle difference" — as evidenced by the "totalitarian communist regimes" that sprang up in his name during the twentieth century.[126]

Conveniently coinciding with the collapse of these regimes, and the collapse of the Soviet Union in particular, a new "post-Marxism without apologies" appeared on the scene, arguing that Marx's political economy thought was at best of limited historical value.[127] Because a new "radical democracy" had to address "an increasing number of social relations," so went the argument, political identity (i.e., the way modern society is structured into different segments of interest and belonging) "can no longer be conceived in terms of class."[128]

First things first: As Marx himself once remarked: "If anything is certain, then it is that I am not a Marxist" (*Wenn etwas feststeht, dann, daß ich kein Marxist bin*).[129] While critical research has done away with Nietzsche's reputation as a proto-Nazi philosopher, it will probably take many more years before Marx's contribution to the history of political thought will be appreciated in its own right rather than for what Marxism-Leninism and Stalinism made of it. This does not mean that we should not hold Marx responsible for the impact of his political thought upon political practice in the same way we hold Hobbes responsible for his absolutism; Rousseau for his totalitarian illusion of an undifferentiated general will; or Machiavelli for his endorsement, however framed by the imperatives of time and circumstance, of a *realpolitik* according to which the end justifies the means. But it means that, like all other philosophers and thinkers, he deserves to be taken seriously in his own right, for the timeless substance of his political and economic thought.

The same goes for Nietzsche as well, of course. He freely talked about race, but he was not a racist. His idea of a "mixed European race" is the very antithesis of racism — the core of which is racial purity. The Nazis could take from Nietzsche his contempt for democracy and parliamentary procedure, his arrogant endorsement of cruel mastery over the ordinary, and his primitive understanding of civil society as a combination of rulers and masses more generally. But in no way can Nietzsche's philosophy of uncertainty and chaos be misunderstood as an ideological brew of totalitarianism. As even one of the most influential Nazi philosophers, Ernst Krieck, remarked with mocking irony: "All things told: Nietzsche was opposed to socialism, he was opposed to nationalism, and he was opposed to the idea of race. Other than that, he might have made for an excellent Nazi."[130]

What, then, is it about the postmodern fascination with Nietzsche? It can be explained quite simply. The core of Nietzsche's philosophy is encapsulated in his beyond-good-and-evil formula. By that he meant that life could not be comprehended by a dichotomy of right and wrong, good and evil. For Nietzsche, these were fictitious distinctions born out of the same craving for simple certainty that had led human beings to believe in a Christian god. In order to free oneself from the depressing cage of bad conscience and guilt, and to enjoy life as something that could be celebrated by a "gay science," one had to learn to live with the uncertainty of a moral relativism that did not attempt to judge everything from a yardstick of absolute truth and rationality. And this is how he caught on, posthumously, so to speak, with a postmodern mindset seeking to deconstruct life's totality into a plurality and diversity of social phenomena in their own right, and insisting that each had to tell its own story rather than live up to some grand narrative of all-encompassing truth.

What the postmodern reading of Nietzsche ignores or even "suppresses,"[131] however, is that his deconstruction of modernity does not give way to suggestions for a better world but ends in the reactionary vision of an archaic society of hierarchy and leadership, a society without compassion or respect for the "other." Nowhere does this become so clear as in Nietzsche's ideas about women. We already heard how Nietzsche waxed about the sole purpose of marriage being a male drive for sex, property, and domination.[132] In one of his best-known aphorisms, still cited with a cosy shudder by all kinds of male chauvinists, Nietzsche has Zarathustra receive the following instruction: "You are going to women? Do not forget the whip!" (*Du gehst zu Frauen? Vergiss die Peitsche nicht!*).[133]

Never mind that in the one photo that exists of Nietzsche with Lou Salomé, together with Paul Rée, the third person in this peculiar ménage, it is Lou holding the whip. Never mind whether or not Nietzsche was in fact one of the few thinkers in the history of political thought to whom the misogynist label applies. What counts is that his philosophy, in its obsessive search for the salvation of singularity, completely and utterly rejects, nay, destroys any notion of cooperation, companionship, or sociability. This is the deeper and darker meaning of the "eternal recurrence": reproduction and salvation only through the self.

All this goes way beyond the postmodern deconstruction of universality. The ultimate purpose of such deconstruction is, after all, in the famous formulation of the late Iris Marion Young, the rediscovery of a kind of "eroticism" that sparks from encounters with, and respect for, the "other" as the "novel, strange, and surprising."[134] By comparison, Nietzsche's deconstructivist efforts amount to what Sheldon Wolin calls a "politics of critical totalitarianism," which "takes the form of relentless destruction, of emptying the world of established forms of value, religion, morality, politics, and popular culture,"[135] without, however, replacing it with anything else. It is, in Nietzsche's own terms, a "nihilism" (*Nihilism*) that "aims at nothing and achieves nothing" (*dass ... nichts erzielt, nichts erreicht wird*).[136]

By comparison, then, Marx is the old-fashioned philosopher who believes in progress and wants to make the world a better place. By comparison also, he explains rather than merely rejects modernity. While Nietzsche had only contempt for the distress of ordinary people thrown into the maelstrom of modernity, Marx saw the merciless commodification of labour and explained it as the inevitable consequence of capitalist competition. And while Nietzsche would only scoff at the cultural defects of modern mass society, Marx identified their root cause in the alienating conditions of the modern division of labour.

Marx exaggerated and simplified, and he made predictions that were proven wrong. Yet, his critique of capitalism has remained eerily up to date. As he recognized first, capitalism *is* a form of labour exploitation and surplus extraction. "So long as sufficient numbers of people, having no alternative means of subsistence, are compelled by circumstances to sell their labour-power; and so long as those who purchase it are able to employ it profitably, meaning that the product (which they own) embodies surplus (realised through its sale) over and above the costs which they have invested in its production,"[137] Marx's critical analysis of the capitalist system remains the most cogent explanation of that system.

One can put it even more simply: So long as the life chances of the vast majority of women and men in this world remain dependent on the decisions made by a very few who find themselves in an infinitely more powerful and secure position, Marx's critique of capitalism, as one particular historical form of exploitation, remains as relevant as when it was first conceived more than 100 years ago. And, judging by the applause Marx has been receiving after the collapse of those corrupted regimes associated with his name, even billing him as "the next big thinker,"[138] the question no longer seems to be whether *he* was right or wrong.

The dividing line is now lastingly marked by the moral assessment of the system of surplus appropriation and the question of whether *it* is right or wrong. When Locke had written, at the dawn of the (first) great bourgeois revolution, that "he who appropriates ... does not lessen but increase the common stock of mankind," he had effectively absolved surplus appropriation from the deadly sin of avarice.[139] The propertied classes could now feel good about their accomplishments, and the labouring classes could be told to put up with their lot. The Lockean defence of inequality through appropriation is still echoed in John Rawls's theory of justice: It is justified as long as it can be "reasonably expected to be to everyone's advantage."[140]

Forgotten or ignored is the Machiavellian verdict that great power and wealth are inevitably acquired "either through force or fraud" (*o con frode o con forza*)—which means, of course, at the expense of others.[141] As Locke before him, Rawls entirely "resists attributing the origins of inequality to class structures"[142]—this would reopen the door to making inequality a moral issue about power exercised by human beings over other human beings, instead of conveniently leaving it located in the domain of rational and efficient administration.

In sharp contrast, Marx redefines the unequal power relationship among different classes as the source and origin of social inequality for the capitalist epoch. Perhaps even more importantly, he points out the dramatic ideological impact of the liberal state as a provider of formal equality. Against the backdrop of existing material inequality and exploitation, the recipient of rational and efficient administration in this state is "the imaginary member of an imaginary sovereignty, divested of his real, individual life, and infused with an unreal universality" (*das imaginäre Glied einer eingebildeten Souveränität, ist er seines wirklichen individuellen Lebens beraubt und mit einer unwirklichen Allgemeinheit erfüllt*).[143]

The domination and alienation of human existence by illusion and deception are moral issues. Contrary to Nietzsche, Marx did not take the escapist route into moral relativism. After it had swept away "all fixed, fast-frozen relations,"[144] the modern world had to deal with the question of right and wrong, or it would fail. As Marx saw it, this new modernity contained tremendous potential and promise. It could be squandered by the continued self-interest of ruling classes, or it could be harnessed and salvaged for the common good of all. This is an existential issue. Contrary to Nietzsche, who counted on the arrogance of singularity, Marx was convinced that salvation could only come from a collective effort.

Notes

Chapter 1: Time to Rethink

1. *Two Treatises of Government*, Treatise II, para. 95.

2. David Held and Anthony McGrew, "The Great Globalization Debate," in *The Global Transformation Reader*, ed. David Held and Anthony McGrew (Cambridge: Polity Press, 2004), 11.

3. See Stephen K. White, *Political Theory and Postmodernism* (Cambridge: Cambridge University Press, 1994).

4. "Sokrates und die griechische Tragoedie," in *Kritische Studienausgabe*, vol. 1 (München: DTV, 1999), 541; own translation.

5. *Social Contract*, Book II, Chapter 3.

6. George Sabine, *A History of Political Theory*, 4th ed., rev. Thomas L. Thorson (Hinsdale, IL: Dryden Press, 1973).

7. *Rules for the Direction of the Mind*, in *Philosophical Writings*, vol. 1 (Cambridge: Cambridge University Press, 1985), III.

8. *On the Study Methods of Our Time* (Ithaca: Cornell University Press, 1990), VII.

9. See David Boucher, *Texts in Context* (Dordrecht: Nijhoff, 1985).

10. J.G.A. Pocock, *Politics, Language & Time* (Chicago: University of Chicago Press, 1989), 7.

11. Ibid., 4-5.

12. *The Spirit of the Laws*, Preface.

13. *The Old Régime and the French Revolution* (Garden City: Double Day, 1955), Part II, Chapter 10; French edition: *L'Ancien Régime et la Révolution* (1856; reprint, Paris: Gallimard, 1952).

14. *The Old Regime and the Revolution* (Chicago: The University of Chicago Press, 1998).

15. *Politica Methodice Digesta*, Praefatio, 1614.

16. *Two Treatises*, II, 95.

17. Ibid., II, 158.

18. *Politics*, 1277a20-b15.

19. James Tully, "Locke," in *The Cambridge History of Political Thought 1450-1700*, ed. J.H. Burns (Cambridge: Cambridge University Press, 1991), 618.

20. C.B. Macpherson, *The Political Theory of Possessive Individualism: Hobbes to Locke* (London: Oxford University Press, 1962), 221.

21. See Pocock, *Politics, Language & Time*, 36.

22. See R.B.J. Walker, *Inside/Outside: International Relations as Political Theory* (Cambridge: Cambridge University Press, 1993).

23. Jürgen Habermas, *Theorie und Praxis* (Frankfurt: Suhrkamp, 1974). Admittedly,

Theorie und Praxis is a collection of essays. But since they are all his own, there is a sustained argument throughout the collection.

24. Macpherson, *Possessive Individualism*.

25. Ibid., 269.

26. See White, *Political Theory*, op. cit., 4-5.

27. Charles Tilly, ed., *The Formation of National States in Western Europe* (Princeton: Princeton University Press, 1975).

28. Veit Valentin, *Knaurs Weltgeschichte* (München: Droemersche Verlagsanstalt, 1959).

29. See J.L. Granatstein, *Who Killed Canadian History?* (Toronto: HarperCollins, 1998), and the response by A.B. McKillop, "Who Killed Canadian History? A View From the Trenches," *Canadian Historical Review* 80, no. 2 (June 1999): 269-300.

30. Marshall Berman, *All That Is Solid Melts Into Air* (New York: Penguin, 1988), 6.

31. Robert Nisbet, *The Social Philosophers: Community & Conflict in Western Thought* (New York: Washington Square Press, 1983).

32. See the remarks at the end of this chapter.

33. Sheldon S. Wolin, *Politics and Vision: Continuity and Innovation in Western Political Thought* (Princeton: Princeton University Press, 2004).

34. Ibid., 46.

35. Ibid., 39.

36. Ibid., 550.

37. Ibid., 605-06.

38. Edmund Burke, *Reflections on the Revolution in France* (London: Penguin, 1986), 153.

39. *Economic and Philosophic Manuscripts of 1844*, "Private Property and Communism," in *The Marx-Engels Reader*, ed. Robert C. Tucker (New York: Norton, 1978), 84.

40. *The Will to Power*, Book I, para.12(A); *Kritische Studienausgabe*, vol. 13, 46-47.

41. Pierre E. Trudeau, *Federalism and the French Canadians* (Toronto: Macmillan of Canada, 1968), 147.

Chapter 2: Method of Inquiry

1. Karl Marx, *Manifesto of the Communist Party*, 1848, "I. Bourgeois and Proletarians."

2. See Jürgen Habermas, *Technik und Wissenschaft als 'Ideologie'* (Frankfurt: Suhrkamp, 1969), 146-68; also Melissa Williams, "Toleration, Canadian-Style: Reflections of a Yankee-Canadian," in *Canadian Political Philosophy*, ed. Ronald Beiner and Wayne Norman (Don Mills: Oxford University Press, 2001), 216-31.

3. See Kenneth D. McRae, "Ramist Tendencies in the Thought of Jean Bodin," *Journal of the History of Ideas* XVI (1955): 306-23.

4. *Leviathan*, Chapter 44, (original pagination 334).

5. *Nicomachean Ethics*, 1094b10-25.

6. *Topics*, 100a20-105a35.

7. *Discourse on the Method*, Part II.

8. See editorial footnote in John Cottingham, Robert Stoothoff, and Dugald Murdoch, eds., *The Philosophiocal Writings of Descartes*, vol. 1 (Cambridge: Cambridge University Press, 1985), 116.

9. René Descartes, *Rules for the Direction of the Mind*, Rule Three; the Latin text is available at <http://pedagogie.ac-toulouse.fr/philosophie/descregulae.htm>.

10. See John Cottingham, "General Introduction" to *Meditations on First Philosophy*, by René Descartes (Cambridge: Cambridge University Press, 2005), xxi, xxv-xxvi.

11. The French text is available at <http://www.mala.bc.ca/~johnstoi/descartes/Discours.htm>.

12. See *Discourse*, Part IV for the following observations, and as a solid basis of introductory interpretation more generally, see Cottingham, "General Introduction," xxviii-xxx.

13. *Discourse*, Part IV.

14. René Descartes, *Meditations on First Philosophy*; the Latin text is available at <http://www.wright.edu/cola/descartes/medl.html>.

15. Among those who also commented was Thomas Hobbes.

16. See Bernard Williams, "Introductory Essay" to *Meditations on First Philosophy*, by René Descartes (Cambridge: Cambridge University Press, 2005), vii-xvii.

17. In English: *Principles of Philosophy*.

18. See John Cottingham, "Translator's Preface," in *The Philosophical Writings of Descartes*, vol. 1, by René Descartes (Cambridge: Cambridge University Press, 1985), 177-78.

19. René Descartes, *The Passions of the Soul*, Part One, para. 1.

20. Ibid., Part Three, para. 212; the French text is available at <http://pedagogie.actoulouse.fr/philosophie/phpes/descartes.htm>.

21. On these and the following biographical details see Robert Stoothoff, "Translator's Preface" in *The Philosophical Writings of Descartes*, vol. 1, by René Descartes (Cambridge: Cambridge University Press, 1985), 325.

22. W.W. Rouse Ball, *A Short Account of the History of Mathematics* (New York: Dover, 1960), 269.

23. Quoted in Elio Gianturco, "Translator's Introduction" to *On the Study Methods of Our Time*, by Giambattista Vico (Ithaca: Cornell University Press, 1990), xxxii.

24. Descartes, *Rules*, Rule Three.

25. Ibid.

26. Ibid.

27. Descartes, *Discourse*, Part I.

28. Ibid.

29. Ibid., Part II.

30. Marshall Berman, *All That Is Solid Melts Into Air* (New York: Penguin, 1988), 150.

31. See Jancis Robinson, *The Oxford Companion to Wine* (Oxford: Oxford University Press, 1999).

32. Descartes, *Discourse*, Part II.

33. Ibid.

34. Ibid.

35. Author's Letter, *Principles of Philosophy*; the French text is available at <http://visualiseur.bnf.fr/Visualiseur?Destination=Gallica&O=NUMM-94260>.

36. Ibid.

37. On this and the following see Peter Burke, *Vico* (Oxford: Oxford University Press, 1985), 10-31.

38. *Theorie und Praxis* (Frankfurt: Suhrkamp, 1974), 49; own translation.

39. As cited in Burke, *Vico*, 2.

40. Biographical details are based on Burke, *Vico*, 10-31.

41. Giambattista Vico, *On the Study Methods of Our Time*; the original Latin text can

be found in Giambattista Vico, *Opere di Giambattista Vico*, vol. 1 (Naples: Fulvio Rossi, 1972).

42. *Study Methods*, VII.

43. *Study Methods*, IV.

44. *Study Methods*, VII.

45. Ibid.

46. *Study Methods*, III.

47. *Study Methods*, VII. Here, as elsewhere, there seems to be an evident discrepancy between the original Latin text and the English translation. Since it pertains to wording rather than meaning, I have left the English translation untouched.

48. See Habermas, *Theorie und Praxis*, 52.

49. *On the Most Ancient Wisdom of the Italians;* the original Latin text can be found in Vico, *Opere*, vol. 1.

50. *Ancient Wisdom*, Chapter I, Section 1.

51. The *New Science* is published as *The New Science of Giambattista Vico*, trans. Thomas Bergin and Max Fisch (Ithaca: Cornell University Press, 1984); the original Italian text can be found in Vico, *Opere*, vol. 2. This was in fact Vico's second *New Science*; a first version had been published in 1725. There are significant differences between the two, but these are of limited relevance for the methodological discussion advanced here.

52. See Gianturco, "Translator's Introduction," xlii.

53. Compare Habermas, *Theorie und Praxis*, 49-50.

54. Vittorio Hösle, "Einleitung" to *Prinzipien einer neuen Wissenschaft über die gemeinsame Natur der Völker*, vol. 1, by Giovanni Battista Vico (Hamburg: Felix Meiner, 1990), xxxiii. Hösle's *Einleitung* (Introduction) to the German critical edition of *New Science* is nearly 300 pages long and hence about half as long as the text to be introduced.

55. Quoted in Burke, *Vico*, 7.

56. Like Descartes's *Philosophical Principles*, and with the same textbook ambition in mind, Vico's *New Science*, while organized in books and chapters, is presented as a continuous chain of numbered paragraphs; only the paragraphs will be cited henceforth.

57. Vico, *New Science*, para. 141.

58. See endnote 47.

59. *New Science*, 142.

60. *New Science*, 314. I am deviating from the translation in *The New Science* (Cornell University Press, 1984), here, because it is entirely unhelpful.

61. *New Science*, 349.

62. *New Science*, 330.

63. Ibid.

64. *New Science*, 331.

65. See Vico's own summary in *New Science*, 31.

66. *New Science*, 1101.

67. Vico does continue that corruption led to civil war and that stability had to come from the establishment of a monarchy, which would keep people content. *New Science*, 1102-05.

68. Burke, *Vico*, 78.

69. Ibid.

70. To write "his or her" in the context of Descartes's philosophical endeavour is warranted because he obviously had no hesitation in counting women among his disciples. On

the other hand, when it came to the political construction of a social contract, the "his or her" still had to wait for quite some time.

  71. *Schenck v. U.S.*, 249 U.S. 47 (1919).

  72. *Capital*, Volume II, Part IV, Chapter XV (London: Allen and Unwin, 1949), 367.

Chapter 3: Nature of the Political

  1. According to most estimates, Athens in the fifth century had about 300,000 inhabitants of which only some 30,000 were citizens because women, children, slaves, and the foreign-born were excluded. The public assemblies were held 40 times per year and regularly attended by 6,000 or more citizens.

  2. Thucycides, *The Peloponnesian War*, Book II, Chapter VI (para. 37) (New York: Modern Library, 1934).

  3. Ibid., V, XVII (105).

  4. Kant made the suggestion in the first Definitive Article of his *To Eternal Peace*, 1795.

  5. Thucydides, *The Peloponnesian War*, VIII, XXV (67).

  6. Quoted in Mark Munn, *The School of History* (Berkeley: University of California Press, 2000), 137.

  7. Ibid., 295-96.

  8. Ibid., 290.

  9. *Seventh Letter*, 326a. It is not entirely clear whether Plato actually wrote the *Seventh Letter* himself. If not, then it was someone who captured Plato's sentiments and convictions very well.

  10. Plato's authorship of the *Letters* is not clear in all instances because his works have come down to us only from compilations undertaken long after his death. For a complete edition and critical discussion of authorship and chronology, see Plato, *Complete Works*, ed. John M. Cooper (Indianapolis: Hackett, 1997), especially the introduction, vii-xxviii.

  11. *Politeia* is usually translated as "Republic" because this is the English word that most closely corresponds to Cicero's Latin translation of *res publica* (public matter). I find the term "republic" far too loaded with modern meaning ("the American republic") and prefer the more neutral—if equally imprecise—"state." A state can be a republic, monarchy, dicatorship, federation, etc. However, I see no reason why students of Plato should not use the original title. Compare Allan Bloom, *The Republic of Plato* (New York: Basic Books, 1991), 439-40.

  12. *Protagoras*, 322e-323a.

  13. *Protagoras*, 333a-c.

  14. *Gorgias*, 356d-e.

  15. *Gorgias*, 452e.

  16. *Gorgias*, 481e.

  17. Socrates, of course, only speaks to us through Plato and may be as much a victim of Plato's own sophistry as Plato claims the Athenians are to the sophists. Later in the dialogue Plato even has Socrates anticipate his own fate (*Gorgias*, 522b-c): "I'll get whatever comes my way."

  18. *Gorgias*, 513a.

  19. *Gorgias*, 515e.

  20. *Politeia*, 372d-373e.

21. *Politeia*, 374b.
22. *Politeia*, 414b-415c.
23. Plato first distinguishes only two classes, guardians and ordinary citizens, but he then further divides the guardians into rulers and warriors, calling the latter auxiliaries because their role is to enforce the will of the rulers and stability in general.
24. Munn, *The School of History*, 222-28.
25. Ibid., 272.
26. *Politeia*, 331e.
27. *Politeia*, 338d-339a.
28. In other translations: minding one's own business.
29. *Politeia*, 433a-b.
30. *Politeia*, 434a-b.
31. Mainly in *Politeia*, Books IV and VI-VIII.
32. Apparently, this was not as outlandish an idea in ancient Greece as one might think.
33. *Politikos*, 293e.
34. *Politikos*, 297b-d.
35. *Politeia*, Book IX.
36. *Politikos*, 302d-303b.
37. *Laws*, 739a.
38. *Laws*, 739d.
39. *Laws*, 797a-c.
40. Sheldon S. Wolin, *Politics and Vision: Continuity and Innovation in Western Political Thought* (Princeton: Princeton University Press, 2004), 31.
41. Bloom, "Interpretive Essay," in *The Republic of Plato*, 2nd ed., trans. Allan Bloom (New York: Basic Books, 1991), 410.
42. *Laws*, 746b.
43. See Martin Ostwald, "Introduction" to *Nicomachean Ethics*, by Aristotle (Indianapolis: Bobbs-Merrill, 1962), xi-xiii.
44. *Nicomachean Ethics*, 1294a25. Here, I have used the older Ostwald translation cited above in endnote 43 because the more literal translation in Barnes (see next endnote) is nearly incomprehensible. The readability of Ostwald probably already constitutes a significant step in text interpretation that the Barnes translation seeks to avoid.
45. See Jonathan Barnes, ed., *The Complete Works of Aristotle*, 2 vols. (Princeton: Princeton University Press, 1984).
46. *Nicomachean Ethics*, 1181a10.
47. *Ethics*, 1181a15.
48. *Ethics*, 1095a1.
49. Aristotle, *Politics*, Book VII, Chapter 17 is very similar to Plato, *Laws*, Book VII; see the introductory commentary by Trevor J. Saunders in Aristotle, *The Politics* (London: Penguin, 1981), 444.
50. Since the translation of *Ethics* and *Politics* is not problematic, references to these works will be made in English.
51. This is a pun: "Peripatetic" not only means "itinerant" or "footloose," it is also a reference to *peripatos*, the name usually given to the school of Aristotle's successors, which literally means "place of walking about"—lectures were typically delivered while walking; see Ostwald, "Introduction," xii.

52. Both adjectives were added by later editors. While *eudaimon* means "happy, usually in the sense of happiness attained by a man through his own efforts," *Nicomachean* is a reference to Aristotle's son Nichomachos, who is said to have edited the later work; see again Ostwald, "Introduction," and the glossary in Aristotle, *Nicomachean Ethics* (Indianapolis: Bobbs-Merrill, 1962), xviii-xix, 307.

53. *Politics*, 1253a1.

54. *Politics*, 1094b10.

55. *Politics*, 1096a20-25.

56. *Politics*, 1140b20.

57. *Politics*, 1140a30. In the following passage, 1140b5, Aristotle cannot suppress another little stab at Plato by explicitly referring to Pericles as one of those who have practical wisdom.

58. *Politics*, 1141b20-30.

59. In *Politics*, Book V, constitutional change is treated as revolutionary regime change. Munn reports that the statutory distinction between constitutional laws and political decrees originated from the experience with the tyranny of the Thirty which had overthrown the democratic constitution by means of decrees; *The School of History*, 264-72.

60. *Politics*, 1132b30.

61. *Politics*, 1134a20-25.

62. *Politics*, 1134b10-15.

63. *Ethics*, 1181b10-15.

64. Similarly in Plato, *Laws*, 756e.

65. *Politics*, 1288b20-1289a10.

66. *Politics*, 1261a20.

67. *Politics*, 1261a30.

68. *Politics*, 1295a35. Aristotle then goes on to identify the many as those who bear arms—an obvious reference to Athens where the democratic extension of citizenship was linked to the military contributions of ordinary people.

69. *Politics*, 1277a20-b15.

70. *Politics*, 1279a35.

71. *Politics*, 1279b35.

72. *Politics*, 1279b5-10.

73. Which he mentions, however, in passing: *Politics*, 1279b1-10.

74. *Politics*, 1279b5.

75. *Politics*, 1293b30.

76. *Politics*, 1294a1-5.

77. *Politics*, 1294215-20; the noble are explained as being a mixture of excellence and wealth.

78. *Politics*, 1294b15.

79. *Politics*, 1295b20.

80. *Politics*, 1295b25.

81. *Politics*, 1295a25.

82. *Politics*, 1295b1.

83. *Politics*, 1295b35.

84. *Politics*, 1297a1-5.

85. *Politics*, 1297a5-10.

86. *Politics*, 1318a10-35.
87. *Politics*, 1320a30-35.
88. *Politics*, 1278a5 and 1328b35.
89. *Politics*, 1332a35-40.
90. John Locke, *An Essay Concerning Human Understanding*, volume II, xx.2.
91. Ibid.
92. *Politics*, 1281a40-b1.
93. *Politeia*, 525b-c.
94. *Nicomachean Ethics*, 1294b25.
95. Wolin, *Politics and Vision*, 55-59.
96. See Diana H. Coole, *Women in Political Theory* (Boulder: Lynne Rienner, 1988), 29-48.
97. Charles Tilly, *Durable Inequality* (Berkeley: University of California Press, 1998).
98. Wolin, *Politics and Vision*, 59.
99. Ewart Lewis, *Medieval Political Ideas* (New York: Cooper Square, 1976), 433; the emperor Justinian who finally closed the Athenian Academy is also the one to whom we owe the systematic collection of what has become the body of Roman law.
100. Anthony Black, *Political Thought in Europe 1250-1450* (Cambridge: Cambridge University Press, 2000), 4.
101. Ibid.
102. Hedley Bull, *The Anarchical Society: A Study of Order in World Politics* (New York: Columbia University Press, 1977).

Chapter 4: Governance
1. *The City of God*, Chapter 13.
2. The formula most notably applied to the king of France after the partition of the empire among Charlemagne's grandchildren.
3. Helmut Quaritsch, *Staat und Souveränität* (Frankfurt: Athenäum, 1970), 162. The original invitation can be found at the digital site of *Monumenta Germaniae Historica*, <http://www.dmgh.de> (under "Leges," and there under "Constitutiones," 2:1198-1272, page 333). The emperor complains about his excommunication, the pope's military aggressions in upper Italy, and advertises his own plans for reconciliation and reform.
4. See John H. Hallowell and Jene M. Porter, *Political Philosophy: The Search for Humanity and Order* (Scarborough: Prentice Hall, 1997), 180.
5. See Anthony Black, *Political Thought in Europe 1250-1450* (Cambridge: Cambridge University Press, 2000), 20-22.
6. He presumably wrote all his work during the 20-odd years after he had begun teaching in Paris. Reportedly, he routinely worked on several projects at a time, availing himself of a number of scribes to whom he dictated his thoughts simultaneously.
7. Sometimes: *Theologica*.
8. Aquinas, *Political Writings* (Cambridge: Cambridge University Press, 2002). The highly structured *Summa Theologiae* contains Parts Ia, IIa, and IIIa; Part II is subdivided into two parts which are usually cited as IaIIae and IIaIIae. The presentation of the argument proceeds by means of numbered topics. Each topic is discussed in several articles and each article begins with a question and what seems to be the obvious answer, followed by

various specific arguments and counter-arguments, and then ends with Thomas's own response that also includes specific answers to the arguments. *Summa* in its entirety is available on the Internet in the original Latin: <http://www.corpusthomisticum.org/iopera.html> and in English: <http://www.intratext.com/X/ENG0023.HTM>.

9. *Summa*, Ia 96, 4.

10. *De Regimine Principium*, Chapter I, para. 3.

11. *De Regimine*, I, 4.

12. *De Regimine*, I, 4.

13. *De Regimine*, I, 1.

14. *De Regimine*, I, 5.

15. *De Regimine*, I, 15.

16. *Summa*, Ia, IIae, 90, 1.

17. *Summa*, Ia, Iiae, 90, 2.

18. *Summa*, Ia, IIae, 96, 1; *negotia* would be translated better as negotiations = activities, and hence as the entire range of practical life.

19. *Summa*, Ia, IIae, 97, 3; similarly Aristotle, *Politics*, 1287b1.

20. Edmund Burke, *Reflections on the Revolution in France*, 1790, ed. Connor Cruise O'Brien (London: Penguin, 1986), 183.

21. *Summa*, Ia, IIae, 95, 4; also 105, 1.

22. *Summa*, Ia, IIae, 90, 3,

23. *Summa*, Ia, IIae, 90, 2.

24. *Summa*, Ia, Iiae, 105, 1.

25. *Summa*, Ia, IIae, 96, 5.

26. *Summa*, Ia, IIae, 91.

27. *Summa*, Ia, IIae, 91, 1.

28. *Summa*, Ia, IIae, 91, 2.

29. *Summa*, Ia, IIae, 95, 4.

30. *Summa*, Ia, IIae, 91, 4.

31. *Scripta super libros sententiarum*, Book II, Distinction 44, Question 3; Lombard's Sentences were the authoritative textbook of theology when Thomas was assigned to teach it at the beginning of his career in Paris.

32. In his 1525 (?) pamphlet, "Against the Robbing and Murdering Hordes of Peasants," Luther refers to the same passage, albeit taking it from Luke 20:25.

33. *Summa*, Ia, 96, 4. In fact, Thomas relied on a translation of *Politics* commissioned by William of Moèrbeke, 1215-86, himself a distinguished scholar of the time, who translated that "man is by nature a social and political animal" (*naturale autem est homini ut sit sociale et politicum*). This is the translation Thomas uses more literally *in De Regimine*, I, 4.

34. Hannah Arendt, *The Human Condition* (Chicago: University of Chicago Press, 1998), 23-24.

35. Jürgen Habermas, *Theorie und Praxis* (Frankfurt: Suhrkamp, 1974), 54-55, without proper acknowledgment of his reliance on Arendt.

36. *Politics*, 1254a28; "where one man rules and another is ruled."

37. *Summa*, Ia, 96, 4.

38. *Summa*, Ia, IIae, 105, 1.

39. R.W. Dyson, "Introduction" to *Political Writings*, by Aquinas (Cambridge: Cambridge University Press, 2002), xxxv.

40. *Nicomachean Ethics*, 1140a30.

41. *Summa*, IIa, IIae, 50, 2.

42. *Summa*, IIa, IIae, 104, 1.

43. *Summa*, Ia, 108, 4.

44. Most of what we do know about Marsilius has been competently summarized by Cary J. Nederman, *Community and Consent* (Lanham: Rowman & Littlefield, 1995), 9-14.

45. There is a highly romantic painting of Ludwig of Bavaria's 1328 coronation in Rome by A. Kreling that contains an image of Marsilius, but it was painted in 1859. It hangs in the corridor of the Bavarian *Landtag* (Parliament) in Munich.

46. Quoted in Alan Gewirth, *Marsilius of Padua: The Defender of Peace*, vol. 1 (New York: Columbia University Press, 1951), 20.

47. Marsilius of Padua, *Defensor Pacis* (New York: Columbia University Press, 2001); the Latin original is easily available in a German edition still in print: Marsilius von Padua, *Defensor pacis*, 2 vols. (1932; reprint, Hannover: Hahnsche Buchhandlung, 1933).

48. *Defensor Pacis*, Discourse I, Chapter XIX, para. 12-13.

49. The underlying issue was who among the two swords had the right of "investiture," being the appointment of bishops who were both spiritual leaders and territorial princes and as such involved in the king's election.

50. Marsiglio of Padua, *Defensor minor and De Translatione Imperii* (Cambridge: Cambridge University Press, 1993).

51. Nederman, *Community and Consent*, 13-14.

52. The same pope, Leo XIII, who effectively made Thomas the official church philosopher in his encyclical *Aeterni Patris* (On the Restoration of Christian Philosophy, 1879), also issued *Immortale Dei* (On the Christian Constitution of States, 1891) in which he declared, very much in Aristotelian-Thomist fashion, that "every body politic must have a ruling authority, and this authority, no less than society itself, has its source in nature, and has, consequently, God for its Author. Hence, it follows that all public power must proceed from God." The English encyclical texts are available at <http://www.papalencyclicals.net/Leo13/>.

53. Alan Gewirth, *Marsilius of Padua: The Defender of Peace*, vol. 2 (New York: Columbia University Press, 1956); see Nederman, *Community and Consent*, 1.

54. The only recent exception seems to be David Boucher and Paul Kelly, eds., *Political Thinkers: From Socrates to the Present* (Oxford: Oxford University Press, 2003). Outstanding among the older texts is George Sabine, *A History of Political Theory*, rev. Thomas L. Thorson, 4th ed. (Hinsdale: Dryden Press, 1973).

55. For example by Otto [von] Gierke, *Political Theories of the Middle Age*, trans. Frederic W. Maitland (Cambridge: Cambridge University Press, 1958), 46; Maitland's influential book contained parts of Gierke's third volume of *Genossenschaftsrecht* (1868).

56. See Nederman, *Community and Consent*, 20.

57. See Habermas, *Theorie und Praxis*, 56-62.

58. The Gewirth translation is now available as Marsilius of Padua, *Defensor pacis* (New York: Columbia University Press, 2001).

59. *Defensor Pacis*, III, I; this exclusive assignment of blame is of course polemical because it entirely chooses to ignore strife and warfare that were rampant among secular powers as much as between those and the pope.

60. *Defensor Pacis*, I, I, 3; see Sabine, *A History of Political Theory*, 274.

61. *Defensor Pacis*, I, IX, 2; note the more literal use of words by Marsilius: the human establishment of government and its institutions is *conceded* in such a way that it can be considered as *arbitrary* with regard to whatever the divine will may be (the discovery of which, as Marsilius asserts in the same passage, is a matter of faith and therefore beyond demonstration).

62. See Marsilius's similar discussion of different laws, *Defensor Pacis*, I, X, 3.

63. *Defensor Pacis*, I, X, 1; and especially II, VIII, 5.

64. *Defensor Pacis*, I, XIX, 6.

65. *Defensor Pacis*, II, X, 2.

66. *Defensor Pacis*, II, 20, 2, and XXII, 5.

67. *Defensor Pacis*, II, XXII, 9.

68. Richard Scholz, "Einleitung," to *Defensor pacis*, by Marsilius von Padua (Hannover: Hahnsche Buchhandlung, 1932), LXIX.

69. *Defensor Pacis*, I, XVIII; Scholz, "Einleitung."

70. For a different interpretation, see especially Nederman, *Community and Consent*.

71. *Defensor Pacis*, I, IV, 3; Marsilius quotes Aristotle directly, here, from the Latin translation by William of Moerbeke; see *Politics*, 1253a29.

72. *Defensor Pacis*, I, IV, 1; compare again *Politics*, 1252b27.

73. *Defensor Pacis*, I, IV, 3; see especially Nederman, *Community and Consent*, 53, 70.

74. Johannes Althusius, *Politica* (1614; reprint, Indianapolis: Liberty Fund, 1995), I, 2-3.

75. *Defensor Pacis*, I, IV, 1-2.

76. *Defensor Pacis*, I, V, 2-3; see *Politics*, 1332b3-10.

77. *Defensor Pacis*, I, V, 5-6.

78. *Defensor Pacis*, I, VIII, 2.

79. *Defensor Pacis*, I, VIII, 3.

80. Ibid.

81. *Defensor Pacis*, I, XIII, 3.

82. *Defensor Pacis*, I, XIII, 4.

83. *Defensor Pacis*, I, V, 7.

84. *Politics*, 1281b30.

85. *Defensor Pacis*, I, XII, 3; Marsilius's reference is to *Politics*, Book III, Chapter 6, which is Book III, Chapter 11 in modern editions.

86. On the whole, compare Gewirth, *Marsilius*, vol. 1, 169-72.

87. *Defensor Pacis*, I, XII, 3.

88. Ibid.

89. See for instance Nederman, *Community and Consent*, 143.

90. *Defensor Pacis*, I, XII, 4.

91. *Defensor Pacis*, I, V, 1.

92. *Defensor Pacis*, I, VIII, 3.

93. Machiavelli, *Istorie Fiorentine* (History of Florence), Book III, Chapters 11 and 13; compare *Politics*, 1297a5-10 where Aristotle remarks that "the encroachments of the rich are more destructive to the constitution than those of the people."

94. *Defensor Pacis*, I, VIII, 1.

95. *Defensor Pacis*, I, XI, 4.

96. *Defensor Pacis*, I, IX, 7.

97. *Defensor Pacis*, I, XVII.

98. *Defensor Pacis*, I, XIII, 8.

99. *Defensor Pacis*, I, XII, 2.

100. We are back to the central passage of *Defensor Pacis*, I, XII, 3.

101. See Nederman, *Community and Consent*, 86.

102. Largely following what is still the most competent interpretation, Gewirth, *Marsilius*, vol. 1, 182-99.

103. *Defensor Pacis*, I, XII, 3.

104. *Defensor Pacis*, I, XII, 4.

105. *Politics*, Book VI, Chapters 2-3 in the modern edition (1318a3-33); Aristotle means by qualification a weighting of votes according to property assessment. According to Gewirth, Marsilius probably simply took it to be a weighting between the honourable and common class because Willliam of Moerbeke translated the Greek word for "assessed property" with "honorabilitas;" see Gewirth, *Marsilius*, vol. 1, 198-99.

106. Sheldon. S. Wolin, *Politics and Vision: Continuity and Innovation in Western Political Thought* (Princeton: Princeton University Press, 2004), 122-28.

107. Joseph Canning, *A History of Medieval Political Thought, 300-1450* (New York: Routledge, 1996), 132.

108. See Christopher Hill, *The Century of Revolution* (New York: Norton, 1980).

109. See Perry Miller, *The New England Mind* (Cambridge: Harvard University Press, 1962).

110. See Janet Coleman, *Political Thought From the Middle Ages to the Renaissance* (Oxford: Blackwell, 2000), 166.

111. See Hedley Bull, *The Anarchical Society: A Study of Order in World Politics* (New York: Columbia University Press, 1977).

112. See Robert D. Putnam, *Making Democracy Work: Civic Traditions in Modern Italy* (Princeton: Princeton University Press, 1993).

Chapter 5: Class Politics

1. See Dante Germino, "Was Machiavelli a 'Spiritual Realist'?" (paper presented at the 16th Annual Meeting of the Eric Voegelin Society, Washington, DC, September 1-2, 2000).

2. Niccolo Machiavelli, *The Prince* (London: Penguin, 1961); the Italian original is available at <http://www.libromania.it/>.

3. Niccolo Machiavelli, *The Discourses* (London: Penguin, 1970); the Italian original is available at <http://www.libromania.it/>.

4. Harvey C. Mansfield, *Machiavelli's Virtue* (Chicago: The University of Chicago Press, 1998), 125.

5. Thus reported by Machiavelli, in *History of Florence*, Book VII, Chapter 1 (5); the Italian original is available at <http://www.libromania.it/>. The number given in parentheses refers to the paragraphs of each book (rather than the chapter) in the Italian text. Note that on occasion I significantly depart from the English version.

6. Machiavelli refers to him as a "man of almost supernatural genius" (*uomo quasi che divino*); *History of Florence*, VIII, 7 (36).

7. Pico della Mirandola, "Oration on the Dignity of Man" (*Oratio de hominis dignitate*), 1486, in *The Civilization of the Italian Renaissance: A Sourcebook*, ed. Kenneth R. Bartlett (Lexington: D.C. Heath, 1992), 131; the original Latin text is available at <http://www.brown.edu/Departments/Italian_Studies/pico/>.

8. *History of Florence*, VII, 1 (6).

9. For an instructive biography of Machiavelli, see Maurizio Piroli, *Niccolo's Smile* (New York: Hill and Wang, 2002).

10. See <http://www.gruppoitalianovini.com/machiavelli_it.htm>.

11. Machiavelli, "Letter 208," in *Machiavelli and His Friends*, ed. James B. Atkinson and David Sices (DeKalb: Northern Illinois University Press, 1996), 225; Machiavelli's letters are available in the original Italian at <http://www.classicitaliani.it/index090.htm>; I have changed "talk about politics" in the English version to "reason about politics" — it is not only closer to the original but also conveys better Machiavelli's dilemma: he has to say about politics what (his) reason tells him to say, and not what might be politically correct or convenient.

12. *The Prince*, Chapter IX; "*grandi*" is variably translated as "nobles" or "upper classes." What Machiavelli has in mind here is the distinction of a higher class of wealthy merchants, bankers, etc., also known as the "fat people" (*populo grasso*), from the lower-class crafts people and workers known as the "petty people" (*populo minuto*).

13. *The Prince*, XXVI.

14. *The Prince*, IX.

15. *The Prince*, XV.

16. *History of Florence*, Books VII and VIII, respectively.

17. *History of Florence*, VIII, 1 (3); "flushed with youth and power" in the English edition.

18. *History of Florence*, VII, 5 (28).

19. *History of Florence*, VIII, 7 (36).

20. *History of Florence*, VII, 1 (6).

21. *History of Florence*, VII, 1 (1).

22. *History of Florence*, VII, 1 (2).

23. The following summary, first published in Thomas O. Hueglin, "Machiavelli Revisited in the Neoconservative Age," *Journal of History and Politics* VIII (1990): 130, mainly relies on Gene Brucker, *Renaissance Florence* (New York: John Wiley, 1969), 133-60.

24. See also Nicolai Rubinstein, *The Government of Florence Under the Medici, 1434-1494* (Oxford: Oxford University Press, 1966), esp. 221-23.

25. *The Prince*, XXVI.

26. Thus the caption of Book I, of *The Discourses*.

27. *The Prince*, III.

28. *The Prince*, IX.

29. *Politics*, 1297a5-10.

30. *The Prince*, XV. Again, I deviate from the English version here; to translate "*buono*" with "virtuous" as the Penguin edition does is misleading because what Machiavelli calls "virtue" (*virtù*) includes to be good and not to be good as necessity requires — see below.

31. Jürgen Habermas, *Theorie und Praxis* (Frankfurt: Suhrkamp, 1972), 56.

32. Thucydides, *The Peloponnesian War* (New York: Modern Library, 1934), Book V, Chapter XVII (105); see Chapter 3.

33. Marsilius, *Defensor Pacis*, Discourse I, Chapter XIX, para. 11; see Chapter 4.

34. *The Prince*, XVIII.

35. Ibid.

36. *The Prince*, XVII; note that Machiavelli writes "safer" (*più securo*) and not "better" as is translated in the Penguin edition.

37. Ibid.; note again that contrary to the impression given by the English translation ("his subjects and citizens"), Machiavelli appears to make a deliberate distinction between "citizens" (*cittadini*) and "subjects" (*sudditi*): the Machiavellian prince can also be the executive head of a constitutional form of government — in fact, this is Machiavelli's preference; see *The Prince*, IX.

38. Ibid.

39. *The Prince*, XV; see above, endnote 30.

40. *The Prince*, XXV.

41. See *The Prince*, XVIII.

42. *The Discourses*, Book III, Chapter 8.

43. *The Discourses*, III, 9.

44. *The Prince*, IX.

45. Ibid.

46. *The Prince*, I; I am abstaining from using the Penguin translation of *virtù* as "prowess" because it strikes me as too limited — see below. As exemplary for the literature on these terms, see esp. Mansfield, *Machiavelli's Virtue*, and the classical study by Hanna F. Pitkin, *Fortune is a Woman* (Chicago: University of Chicago Press, 1984/1999).

47. *The Prince*, XXV.

48. *The Prince*, XV.

49. This in itself is hardly surprising. The quote may simply be a careless reflection of, and reference to, Machiavelli's own libidinous love life, which at some point even got him accused of sodomy; see Piroli, *Niccolo's Smile*, 153-69.

50. *The Prince*, XXV.

51. *The Prince*, XXVI.

52. Habermas, *Theorie und Praxis*, 61.

53. *The Prince*, IX.

54. *The Prince*, IX.

55. *The Discourses*, I, Preface.

56. *The Discourses*, I, 2.

57. *The Discourses*, I, 2.

58. See the section on Polybios in the most elaborate recent study on the idea of the mixed constitution in the history of political thought: Alois Riklin, *Machtteilung* (Darmstadt: Wissenschaftliche Buchgesellschaft, 2006), 77.

59. See Chapter 3 of this book.

60. *The Discourses*, I, 5.

61. *The Discourses*, I, 6.

62. *The Prince*, IX.

63. *The Discourses*, I, 4.

64. The most brilliantly convincing interpretation of Machiavelli in this sense is Frank Deppe, *Niccolo Machiavelli: Zur Kritk der reinen Politik* (Köln: Pahl-Rugenstein, 1987); see Thomas O. Hueglin, "Actuality and Illusion in the Political Thought of Machiavelli," review article, *Journal of Early Modern History* 2, no. 4 (1998): 395-99.

65. *The Discourses*, II, Preface; similarly *The Discourses*, I, 6.

66. Karl Marx, *Manifesto of the Communist Party*, 1848, "I. Bourgeois and Proletarians."

67. *History of Florence*, III, 3 (11).

68. *The Discourses*, I, 4.

69. See again *The Prince*, IX, and *The Discourses*, I, 4.
70. *The Discourses*, I, 4.
71. *The Discourses*, I, 17.
72. *History of Florence*, VII, 1 (2); also VII, 1 (1).
73. *History of Florence*, III, 3 (13).
74. *The Discourses*, I, 5.
75. *The Discourses*, I, 55; that honest work is part of republican virtue also constitutes a considerable redefinition of the Aristotelian notion of citizenship.
76. *The Discourses*, I, 6.
77. *The Discourses*, I, 17.
78. *The Discourses*, I, 18.
79. *The Discourses*, III, 29.
80. *The Discourses*, I, 17.
81. *The Discourses*, I, 34.
82. See again Rubinstein, *The Government of Florence*, 221-23.
83. *The Discourses*, I, 17.
84. See also Deppe, *Machiavelli*, 224.
85. *The Discourses*, I, 58.
86. *The Discourses*, III, 9.
87. See most recently, Quentin Skinner, *Machiavelli: A Very Short Introduction* (Oxford: Oxford University Press, 2000). One of the reasons for Machiavelli's obsession with the idea that a militia system of domestic defense should replace the Florentine practice of hiring mercenary armies was that he saw the latter as a prime source of financial ruin and corruption.
88. Sheldon S. Wolin, *Politics and Vision* (Princeton: Princeton University Press, 2004), 200.
89. Bernard Crick, "Introduction" to *The Discourses*, by Machiavelli (London: Penguin, 1970), 14; as in the case of Marsilius, a good deal of affinity can be found with a more recent and controversial attempt at identifying civic culture or "human capital" as a prime variable of political success and failure. See Robert D. Putnam, *Making Democracy Work* (Princeton: Princeton University Press, 1993).
90. Crick, "Introduction," 65, 67.
91. Riklin, *Machtteilung*, 83.
92. This interpretation is particularly prevalent in Deppe, *Machiavelli*.
93. *History of Florence*, III, 3 (13).
94. Antonio Gramsci, *Selections from the Prison Notebooks* (New York: International Publishers, 1983).
95. Edward S. Herman and Noam Chomsky, *Manufacturing Consent* (New York: Pantheon, 2002).
96. See Alexander Hamilton, John Jay, and James Madison, *The Federalist* (New York: The Modern Library, without year); the central argument that "society itself will be broken into so many parts" that there will be "little danger from interested combinations of the majority," is in *The Federalist*, nr. 51.

Chapter 6: Sovereignty

1. Thomas Hobbes, *Leviathan* (1651), Chapter 13 (62). The edition used is (Cambridge: Cambridge University Press, 1992); pagination of the original 1651 edition in parentheses.

2. The Latin version was published a few weeks before Hobbes's death in 1679. The English translation was published in 1680 as *The Life of Mr. Thomas Hobbes of Malmesbury, Written by himself In a Latine Poem And now Translated into English* (reproduction, University of Exeter, 1979). By trying to emulate the rhymed form, this translation sometimes digresses significantly from the Latin original.

3. "Diet" is an old-fashioned word for the assembly of the imperial estates. It goes back to the ancient Greek word for the payments that the lower classes received in order to be able to attend assemblies and public office.

4. Harold J. Laski, "Historical Introduction" to *A Defence of Liberty Against Tyrants*, a translation of *Vindiciae Contra Tyrannos* anonymously published under the pseudonym of Junius Brutus in 1579 (1924; reprint, New York: Burt Franklin, 1972), 22.

5. The most influential of these was *Vindiciae Contra Tyrannos* cited in the previous endnote.

6. Jean Bodin, *Les Six Livres de la République*, 1576, Book I, Chapter 8; the English translation is based on the Latin edition by Richard Knolles (1606) as Jean Bodin, *The Six Bookes of a Commonweale*, ed. Kenneth D. McRae (Cambridge: Harvard University Press, 1962). The introduction to the book written by McRae contains valuable comparisons of Bodin's different definitions in French and Latin.

7. See Christopher Hill, *The Century of Revolution 1603-1714* (New York: Norton, 1980), 103.

8. Ibid., 235-37.

9. A recent biography is A.P. Martinich, *Hobbes: A Biography* (Cambridge: Cambridge University Press, 1999).

10. The second of altogether three continental tours was undertaken in the service of another gentleman, Sir Gervase Clifton of Nottinghamshire.

11. *Leviathan*, 18 (93).

12. *Leviathan*, 18 (92). There is no clear evidence that Hobbes had read Bodin; see above, endnote 6.

13. *Leviathan*, 42 (300).

14. See Chapter 2 of this book.

15. Quoted in Noel Malcolm, "Hobbes," in *The Cambridge History of Political Thought 1450-1700*, ed. J.H. Burns (Cambridge: Cambridge University Press, 1991), 533.

16. Thomas Hobbes, *On the Citizen* (Cambridge: Cambridge University Press, 1998), Epistle dedicatory (1); the original was written in Latin as *De Cive* (Oxford: Oxford University Press, 1983).

17. *Leviathan*, 13 (62).

18. C.B. Macpherson, *The Political Theory of Possessive Individualism* (Oxford: Oxford University Press, 1962), esp. 65-66.

19. *On the Citizen*, Chapter I, para. 2.

20. *Leviathan*, 2 (4).

21. See Sheldon S. Wolin, *Politics and Vision: Continuity and Innovation in Western Political Thought* (Princeton: Princeton University Press, 2004), 570-75.

22. *On the Citizen*, X, 12.

23. *On the Citizen*, VII, 4; see also *Leviathan*, 29 (172).

24. *Leviathan*, 21 (111).

25. Macpherson, *Political Theory*, 66, again quoting from *Behemoth*.

26. *On the Citizen*, I, 2; note that Hobbes neither uses "education" nor "training" but the harsher word "discipline" in order to describe how civil society must be achieved.

27. *On the Citizen*, Epistle dedicatory.

28. *Leviathan*, 17 (87).

29. *Leviathan*, 18 (88).

30. *Leviathan*, 18 (90).

31. Hobbes points to self-preservation as the motive for moving from a state of nature to civil society; but, as the history of all wars and conflict shows, and as Hobbes himself knew full well, self-preservation is overridden by ignorance and misguided passion more often than not.

32. *Leviathan*, 18 (87).

33. Richard Tuck, "Introduction" to *Leviathan*, by Thomas Hobbes (Cambridge: Cambridge University Press, 1992), xviii.

34. *Leviathan*, 17 (87).

35. *Leviathan*, 18 (88).

36. *Leviathan*, 18 (88-92).

37. *Leviathan*, 18 (90).

38. Tuck, "Introduction," xviii.

39. *Leviathan*, 21 (109).

40. *Leviathan*, 46 (367).

41. *Leviathan*, 19 (95).

42. *Leviathan*, 19 (97).

43. *Leviathan*, 18 (93).

44. And with Aristotelian roots: in *Politics* 1286b30-35 Aristotle speaks of a limited monarchy where "the king must have such force as will be more than a match for one or more individuals, but not so great as that of the people."

45. At the reform council of Basel (1431-49), the formula that the pope is superior in the church (*maior in ecclesia*) but not of the church (*maior ecclesia*) gave expression to the same idea. See Hasso Hofmann, *Repräsentation* (Berlin: Duncker & Humblot, 1974), 278.

46. Especially in *Vindiciae*, see endnote 4.

47. Samuel Rutherford, *Lex, Rex* (1644), (Harrisonburg: Sprinkle Publications, 1982), Question 5; see also online at <http://www.constitution.org/sr/lexrex.htm>.

48. Quentin Skinner, "Hobbes on Representation," *European Journal of Philosophy* 13, no. 2 (2005): 155-84; esp. 158-59.

49. *Leviathan*, 18 (93).

50. Rutherford, *Lex, Rex*, Question 28.

51. Johannes Althusius, *Politica Methodice Digesta* (1614; facsimile reprint, Aalen: Scientia, 1981). The last of five editions of *Politica* appeared in 1654. An abridged English translation is Johannes Althusius, *Politica* (Indianapolis: Liberty Fund, 1995), translated and introduced by Frederick S. Carney.

52. Althusius, *Politica*, Chapter XXXVIII, Section 30-31 (Rutherford, in the English text of *Lex, Rex*, erroneously cites Chapter XXVIII). This passage is not in the abridged English translation cited in endnote 51.

53. Biographical knowledge about Althusius remains sketchy. See the only published book-length treatment of Althusius in English: Thomas O. Hueglin, *Early Modern Concepts for a Late Modern World: Althusius on Community and Federalism* (Waterloo: Wilfrid

Laurier University Press, 1999). Much of the following has been adapted from that book.

54. The most succinct summary of the argument can be found in *Vindiciae*; see endnote 4.

55. Again, I am not always following the English translation.

56. The 1603 preface (*Praefatio*) is included in the English translation of the 1614 edition. The Latin original can be found in Carl Joachim Friedrich, ed., *Politica Methodice Digesta of Johannes Althusius* (Cambridge: Harvard University Press, 1932; reprint, New York: Arno Press, 1979).

57. The translation of "*Respublica*" with "commonwealth" is correct because Althusius uses it in the literal classical understanding: *res publica* = what is in the public or common domain.

58. See above, endnote 6.

59. A fourth edition of *Politica* in 1625 essentially remained unchanged, and the fifth and last edition appeared after his death in 1654.

60. Emden had become the "mother church" for exiled Calvinists during the Dutch Revolt against Spain.

61. It had no such status, and Althusius went to great lengths making the de facto argument by describing Emden as a major metropolis in its own right; see *Politica*, V, 76, and VI, 1-6.

62. Thus the concluding assessment in the only scholarly source for Althusius's life and political activities in Emden: Heinz Antholz, *Die politische Wirksamkeit des Johannes Althusius in Emden* (Köln: Leer, 1954).

63. *Politica*, IX, 19.

64. Ibid.

65. *Politica*, IX, 12-15.

66. *Politica*, IX, 3.

67. *Politica*, IX, 18.

68. See Robert Derathé, *Jean-Jacques Rousseau et la science politique de son temps* (Paris: Vrin, 1950), 98.

69. *Politica*, XXXIII, 20.

70. Thus, Jügen Habermas, *Theorie und Praxis* (Frankfurt: Suhrkamp, 1974), 68.

71. *Politica*, I, 31-32; Althusius says that man is a "more civil animal" (*animal civilius*) than the bee or other creatures.

72. See Chapter 2 of this book; on Althusius's Ramist methodology, see Frederick S. Carney, "Translator's Introduction" to *Politica*, by Johannes Althusius (Indianapolis: Liberty Fund, 1995), xii-xv.

73. Carney, "Translator's Introduction," xiv.

74. *Politica*, XXXIX, 84.

75. *Politica*, I, 1-2; the English edition translates "*consociatio*" with "association" rather than "consociation." This is somewhat misleading because the Althusian consociation is more like a fellowship or community than an interest association in the modern sense.

76. *Politica*, I, 7.

77. *Politica*, VI, 18-26.

78. *Politica*, VI, 28-29.

79. *Politica*, I, 10.

80. *Politica*, I, 21.

81. *Politica*, I, 10; this is an example of Althusius's adoption of yet another Ramist

inheritance: to split up arguments in endless chains of dichotomizing for which he also provides a graphic "Scheme of Politics" (*Schema Politicae*) at the outset of the book.

82. *Politica*, I, 11.

83. *Politica*, I, 19.

84. See again Habermas, *Theorie und Praxis*, 68.

85. See above, endnote 6.

86. *Politica*, II-VIII.

87. *Politica*, III, 42.

88. *Politica*, VIII, 50.

89. See again *Politica*, XXXIII, 20.

90. *Politica*, XVIII, 60.

91. *Politica*, XVIII, 111.

92. *Politica*, XVIII, 62.

93. The institution of the ephors is adapted from a similar institution in ancient Sparta that found its way into Calvin's *Institutes of the Christian Religion* (originally *Institutio Christianae Religionis*, 1536); see John Calvin, *Institutes of the Christian Religion*, 2 vols., ed. John T. McNeill (Philadelphia: The Westminster Press, 1977), Book IV, XX.31.

94. He uses "confederation" (*confederatio*) when he describes how one commonwealth might merge with another; see *Politica*, XVII, 24-31.

95. Pius XI, *Quadragesimo Anno* [Encyclical letter of His Holiness Pope Pius XI on social reconstruction, 1931], in Helmut Schnatz, ed., *Paepstliche Verlautbarungen zu Staat und Gesellschaft* (Darmstadt: Wissenschaftliche Buchgesellschaft, 1973), 401-17.

96. Maastricht Treaty, Article 3b (1993); see the official website of the European Union at <http://europa.eu/abc/treaties/index_en.htm>.

97. J.F. Goeters, ed., *Die Akten der Synode der Niederländischen Kirchen zu Emden vom 4.-13. Oktober 1571* (Neukirchen-Vluyn: Neukirchener Verlag, 1971), 79-83; own translation.

98. *Politica*, IV, 20, and similarly XVII, 60.

99. *Politica*, VIII, 70; the entire passage in this chapter concerns provincial administration, but similar formulations can be found about the decision-making process in colleges, cities, and in the universal commonwealth.

100. *Politica*, XIX, 49.

101. See Thomas O. Hueglin, "From Constitutional to Treaty Federalism: A Comparative Perspective," *Publius: The Journal of Federalism* 30, no. 4 (Fall 2000): 137-52.

102. Montesquieu, *The Spirit of the Laws* (Cambridge: Cambridge University Press, 2005), Book XI, Chapter 6.

103. Alexis de Tocqueville, *The Old Régime and the Revolution* (Chicago: Chicago University Press, 1998), Part 3, Chapter 1.

104. Charles Lindblom, *Politics and Markets* (New York: Basic Books, 1977).

105. Wolin, *Politics and Vision*, 255.

106. Macpherson, *Political Theory*.

107. Thomas Mann, *Reflections of an Unpolitical Man* (New York: F. Ungar, 1982).

108. Otto von Gierke, *Johannes Althusius und die Entwicklung der naturrechtlichen Staatstheorien* (1880; reprint, Aalen: Scientia, 1958).

109. Friedrich, *Politica Methodice Digesta*.

110. See Hueglin, "From Constitutional to Treaty Federalism," 137-38.

111. Among the few exceptions: Robert Nisbet, *The Social Philosophers* (New York: Washington Square Press, 1983).

112. See Ken Endo, "The Principle of Subsidiarity: From Johannes Althusius to Jacques Delors," *Hokkaido Law Review* 44, no. 6 (1994): 652-553 [*sic*].

113. Giuliano Amato, "Plenary Speech," in *Federalism in a Changing World*, ed. Raoul Blindenbacher and Arnold Koller (Montreal: McGill-Queen's University Press, 2003), 577-81. Adoption of the European Constitution was stalled by the outcome of two negative referendums, in France, and in the Netherlands (2005). The Althusian principles of (con)federalism and subsidiarity, however, are just as manifest in the extant treaty framework that for now remains the basis of European Union governance.

114. *Leviathan*, A Review, and Conclusion (395).

115. See Max Weber, *The Protestant Ethic and the Spirit of Capitalism* (London: George Allen and Unwin, 1930).

116. See Sheldon S. Wolin, "Calvin and the Reformation: The Political Education of Protestantism," *American Political Science Review* LI (1957): 435-53.

Chapter 7: State and Society

1. Quoted in Christopher Hill, *The Century of Revolution 1603-1714* (New York: Norton, 1982), 234.

2. This and the following are largely based on Rudolf Braun, "Taxation, Sociopolitical Structure, and State-Building: Great Britain and Brandenburg-Prussia," in *The Formation of National States in Western Europe*, ed. Charles Tilly (Princeton: Princeton University Press, 1975), esp. 280-90.

3. See also Hill, *Century of Revolution*, 137.

4. Ibid., 263.

5. Ibid., 264.

6. Ibid., 111.

7. Leon Radzinowicz, *A History of English Criminal Law*, vol. 1 (London: Stevens & Sons, 1948), 4-5; see Robert Hughes, *The Fatal Shore* (New York: Vintage Books, 1986), 29.

8. John Locke, *Two Treatises of Government*, Treatise II, para. 3.

9. Radzinowicz, *A History*, 231-33.

10. Ibid., 34. Radzinowicz is identifying the Williams quote as from volume 11 of the *Oxford History of England*.

11. Montesquieu, *The Spirit of the Laws*, Book 6, Chapters 19 and 13, respectively; quoted in Radzinowicz, *A History*, 270-71.

12. C.B. Macpherson, *The Political Theory of Possessive Individualism: Hobbes to Locke* (Oxford: Oxford University Press, 1962); see also Braun, "Taxation," 289.

13. Quoted in Hill, *Century of Revolution*, 265.

14. John Locke, *An Essay Concerning Human Understanding*, Book IV, Chapter XX.

15. John Locke, "Some Considerations of the Consequences of the Lowering of Interest and Raising the Value of Money," in *Several Papers Relating to Money, Interest and Trade, &c.* (1696; reprint, New York: Augustus M. Kelley, 1968), 34, 100; obviously, I have been pointed in the direction of these citations by the work of Macpherson, *Political Theory*.

16. The authoritative biography is Maurice Cranston, *John Locke, A Biography* (London: Longmans, 1957); I am mainly relying on the summary in Paul E. Sigmund,

"Introduction" to Paul E. Sigmund, ed., *The Selected Political Writings of John Locke* (New York: Norton, 2005), xi-xxxix.

17. A brief excerpt providing an overview is available in Sigmund, *Selected Political Writings*, 262-69.

18. *Two Treatises*, II, 1.

19. *Two Treatises*, II, 222 and 225.

20. See Sigmund, "Introduction," xv-xvi.

21. *Two Treatises*, II, 4 and 6.

22. *Two Treatises*, II, 8.

23. *Two Treatises*, II, 11.

24. *Two Treatises*, II, 22.

25. *Two Treatises*, II, 23; Locke regarded the capturing of slaves in Africa as a legitimate and just state of war.

26. *Two Treatises*, II, 89.

27. *Two Treatises*, II, 97.

28. *Two Treatises*, II, 102.

29. See also *Two Treatises*, II, 211, where Locke distinguishes the dissolution of government from the dissolution of political society.

30. *Two Treatises*, II, 149.

31. *Two Treatises*, II, 143.

32. *Two Treatises*, II, 220.

33. Althusius, *Politica*, Chapter VIII, Section 92.

34. *Two Treatises*, II, 95.

35. *Two Treatises*, II, 98. Apparently, according to Peter Laslett, "Introduction," to *Two Treatises of Government*, by Locke (Cambridge: Cambridge University Press, 1988), 71, Locke lent out his only copy of *Leviathan* in 1674 and did not get it back until 1691 — some things never seem to change.

36. He first published a Latin version of his famous *A Letter Concerning Toleration* in 1685 in response to the revocation of the Edict of Nantes (1598), which had granted religious toleration to the Huguenots. Like the *Two Treatises*, the English translation of *A Letter Concerning Toleration* appeared anonymously in 1689; see Sigmund, "Introduction," xviii, who also reports that Locke was spied on by agents of the English monarchy while working on both *A Letter Concerning Toleration* and *An Essay Concerning Human Understanding* in Dutch exile.

37. *Two Treatises*, II, 222.

38. See James Tully, "Locke," in *The Cambridge History of Political Thought 1450-1700*, ed. J.H. Burns (Cambridge: Cambridge University Press, 1991), 616-52.

39. See the representative overview in the "Interpretations" section in Sigmund, *Selected Political Writings*, 271-398.

40. Macpherson, *Political Theory*, 261.

41. *Two Treatises*, II, 154.

42. *Two Treatises*, II, 155-56.

43. Hill, *Century of Revolution*, 37.

44. Ibid., 255

45. *Two Treatises*, II, 157.

46. See Laslett's comments in Locke, *Two Treatises of Government*, 372-73 (footnotes).

47. *Two Treatises*, II, 158.

48. Ibid.

49. See *Two Treatises*, II, 140; compare Macpherson, *Political Theory*, 249.

50. *Two Treatises*, II, 25-51.

51. *Two Treatises*, II, 28.

52. *Two Treatises*, II, 36.

53. *Two Treatises*, II, 37.

54. *Two Treatises*, II, 49.

55. *Two Treatises*, II, 50.

56. *An Essay Concerning Human Understanding*, IV, XX.

57. See the excerpt from James Tully, *A Discourse on Property: John Locke and his Adversaries* (Cambridge: Cambridge University Press, 1980), in Sigmund, *Selected Political Writings*, esp. 326.

58. *Two Treatises*, I, 42.

59. See Sigmund, "Introduction," xxii.

60. *Two Treatises*, II, 123.

61. *Two Treatises*, II, 3.

62. Radzinowicz, *A History*, 45-47; "without benefit of clergy" meant that a traditional right to a lesser sentence for first offenders was excluded.

63. Macpherson, *Political Theory*, 262.

64. Hill, *Century of Revolution*, 111.

65. Montesquieu, *The Spirit of the Laws*, Book 6, Chapter 6; in French see *De l'esprit des lois* (1748), in Montesquieu, *Œuvres Complètes*, vol. 2 (Paris: Gallimard, 1958).

66. Montesquieu, *Pensées* in *Œuvres Complètes*, vol. 2 (Paris: Nagel, 1950), nr. 1760.

67. *Pensées*, nr. 647.

68. *Pensées*, nr. 2084.

69. The authoritative biography is Robert Shackleton, *Montesquieu: A Critical Biography* (Oxford: Oxford University Press, 1961).

70. *Lettres persanes* (1721), in Montesquieu, *Oeuvres Complètes*, vol. 1 (Paris: Gallimard, 1958); English: *Persian Letters* (London: Penguin, 2004).

71. Montesquieu, *Considerations on the Causes of the Greatness of the Romans and their Decline* (Indianapolis: Hackett, 1965); the French original is available online at <http://classiques.uqac.ca/classiques/montesquieu/montesquieu.html>.

72. Montesquieu, *The Spirit of Laws* (trans. Thomas Nugent, 1750), available as *The Spirit of Laws by Montesquieu* (Berkeley: University of California Press, 1977); this translation was based on the first edition of 1748 and did not contain a number of revisions and extensions incorporated into later editions.

73. On this and the following see C.J. Betts, "Introduction" to *Persian Letters*, by Montesquieu (London: Penguin, 2004), 17-33.

74. Ibid., 19.

75. The main function of the *Parlement* was the administration and adjudication of legal matters.

76. See Chapter 2 of this book.

77. See Shackleton, *Montesquieu*, 114-16.

78. Montesquieu, *Considerations*, Chapter IX.

79. Compare Shackleton, *Montesquieu*, 167-69.

80. *Considerations*, XVIII.
81. *Considerations*, XXII.
82. Ibid.
83. *The Spirit of the Laws*, Book 1, Chapter 1.
84. *The Spirit of the Laws*, 2, 1.
85. *The Spirit of the Laws*, 2, 2.
86. Ibid.
87. *The Spirit of the Laws*, 2, 3.
88. *The Spirit of the Laws*, 2, 4.
89. Ibid.
90. Ibid.
91. *The Spirit of the Laws*, 2, 5.
92. *The Spirit of the Laws*, 11, 6.
93. James Madison, Alexander Hamilton, and John Jay, *The Federalist Papers* (1787-88; reprint, London: Penguin, 1987), nr. 47.
94. *The Spirit of the Laws*, 19, 27.
95. Ibid.
96. Shackleton, *Montesquieu*, 301.
97. *The Spirit of the Laws*, 11, 6.
98. *Pensées*, nr. 1960.
99. *Pensées*, nr. 1760.
100. *The Spirit of the Laws*, 11, 6; note that I am not entirely following the translation in the new Cambridge edition.
101. *The Spirit of the Laws*, 9, 1.
102. Shackleton, *Montesquieu*, 18.
103. *The Spirit of the Laws*, 9, 1.
104. *The Spirit of the Laws*, 8, 19-20.
105. *The Spirit of the Laws*, 9, 1.
106. *The Spirit of the Laws*, 9, 2-3.
107. See Thomas O. Hueglin, "Federalism at the Crossroads: Old Meanings, New Significance," *Canadian Journal of Political Science* 36, no. 2 (June 2003): 275-94.
108. *The Spirit of the Laws*, 5, 8; Montesquieu's wife was a Huguenot, though.
109. *The Spirit of the Laws*, 9, 3.
110. See the previous chapter in this book.
111. *The Spirit of the Laws*, 9, 1.
112. Shackleton, *Montesquieu*, 286.
113. Ibid., 276.
114. See Louis Desgraves, ed., *Catalogue de la Bibliothèque de Montesquieu* (Genève: Librairie Droz, 1954).
115. Shackleton, *Montesquieu*, 234.
116. Ibid., 271.
117. *The Spirit of the Laws*, 5, 14.
118. *The Spirit of the Laws*, 1, 2; note that again I am not entirely following the translation of the new Cambridge edition.
119. *The Spirit of the Laws*, Books 14-31, the entire and larger second part of the work.
120. *The Spirit of the Laws*, Book 10, Chapter 3.

121. *The Spirit of the Laws*, 15, 3.

122. *The Spirit of the Laws*, 15, 5.

123. *The Spirit of the Laws*, 15, 6-7.

124. *The Spirit of the Laws*, 15, 3.

125. Compare Judith N. Shklar, *Montesquieu* (Oxford: Oxford University Press, 1987), 88.

126. *The Spirit of the Laws*, 11, 6.

127. Ibid.

128. *The Spirit of the Laws*, 6, 9.

129. *The Spirit of the Laws*, 6, 13.

130. See again Radzinowicz, *A History*, 270-71.

131. *The Spirit of the Laws*, 6, 9.

132. *The Spirit of the Laws*, 6, 13.

133. *The Spirit of the Laws*, 6, 9.

134. *The Spirit of the Laws*, 7, 1.

135. *The Spirit of the Laws*, 7, 2.

136. *The Spirit of the Laws*, 7, 1.

137. *Two Treatises*, II, 220.

138. See Sheldon S. Wolin, *Politics and Vision: Continuity and Innovation in Western Political Thought* (Princeton: Princeton University Press, 2004), 277.

139. Tully, "Locke," 618.

140. Macpherson, *Political Theory*.

141. Compare Wolin, *Politics and Vision*, 529-56.

142. *Two Treatises*, II, 58.

143. See differently and, in my view, mistakenly, Shklar, *Montesquieu*, 86.

144. *The Spirit of the Laws*, 11, 3.

145. Madison, Hamilton, and Jay, *The Federalist Papers*, nr. 51.

146. See Hueglin, "Federalism at the Crossroads."

147. See again *Pensées*, nr. 1760.

Chapter 8: Power of the Majority

1. On the following see Maurice Cranston, *The Noble Savage: Jean-Jacques Rousseau 1754-1762* (London: Penguin, 1991), 323-62.

2. Alexis de Tocqueville, *The Old Regime and the Revolution* (Chicago: The University of Chicago Press, 1998), Book II, Chapters 10, 9. By comparison with this new translation by Alan S. Kahan, which I have used in this chapter, the widely used older edition, Alexis de Tocqueville, *The Old Régime and the French Revolution* (Garden City: Doubleday, 1955), provides a much more freely translated text that makes side-by-side presentation with the French original next to impossible; the French text is available at <http://classiques.uqac.ca/classiques/De_tocqueville_alexis/de_tocqueville.html>.

3. *The Old Regime*, II, 7.

4. *The Old Regime*, II, 10.

5. See Maurice Cranston, *Jean-Jacques: The Early Life and Work of Jean-Jacques Rousseau 1712-1754* (London: Penguin, 1983), 279-91.

6. See the classic study of Alfred Einstein, *Mozart: His Character, His Work* (Oxford: Oxford University Press, 1962), esp. 154-55.

7. Jean-Jacques Rousseau, *A Discourse on the Arts and Sciences*; in French: *Discours sur les sciences et les arts*. Note: English translations appear to take considerable liberty with the exact title of the discourses. When talking about Rousseau's first discourse in this chapter, I have stuck with the "sciences and the arts" rather than the common English phraseology of "arts and sciences."

8 Cranston, *Noble Savage*, xiii.

9. *Discourse on the Arts and Sciences*, Part I.

10. *Discourse on the Arts and Sciences*, II.

11. Ibid.

12. Ibid.

13. *A Discourse on the Origin of Inequality*; in French: *Discours sur l'origine et les fondements de l'inégalité parmi les hommes*.

14. *Origin of Inequality*, Part I.

15. *Origin of Inequality*, I.

16. *Origin of Inequality*, II.

17. Ibid. (In Book III of *The Social Contract*, Rousseau does engage in an extended discussion of different forms of government, but this discussion is ultimately not central to his main argument.)

18. Ibid.

19. *The Social Contract*; in French: *Du contrat social*.

20. See G.D.H. Cole, "Introduction" to *The Social Contract and Discourses*, by Jean-Jacques Rousseau (London: Fitzhenry & Whiteside, 1986), ix.

21. See Maurice Cranston, "Introduction" to *The Social Contract*, by Jean-Jacques Rousseau (London: Penguin, 1968), 27.

22. *The Social Contract*, Book I, Chapter 1.

23. *The Social Contract*, I, 6.

24. *The Social Contract*, I, 7.

25. See as a particularly thoughtful example, Brian R. Nelson, *Western Political Thought* (Englewood Cliffs: Prentice Hall, 1982), 232-33.

26. *The Social Contract*, I, 7.

27. Ibid.

28. *Origin of Inequality*, II.

29. *The Social Contract*, III, 4. There is, however considerable discrepancy between theory and practice in Rousseau's political thought; in *The Social Contract*, IV, 3, he seems to endorse majority decisions as practicable.

30. *The Social Contract*, III, 15.

31. *The Social Contract*, IV, 3.

32. See esp. *The Social Contract*, II, 3.

33. Jean-Jacques Rousseau, "A Discourse on Political Economy," in *The Social Contract and Discourses*, trans. G.D.H. Cole (London: Fitzhenry & Whiteside, 1986), (Part I).

34. See Karl Marx, "Critique of the Gotha Program," in *The Marx-Engels Reader* (New York: Norton, 1972), Part I (531); since the *Marx-Engels Reader* will be used throughout this chapter, I am giving the page number in parentheses.

35. *The Social Contract*, II, 7.

36. *The Social Contract*, II, 6.

37. The text is available at <http://www.china.org.cn/english/features/49109.htm#1>.

38. See Nelson, *Western Political Thought*, 242.
39. *The Social Contract*, II, 3
40. See above, endnote 29.
41. *The Social Contract*, II, 3.
42. Ibid.
43. Ibid.
44. See Manfred G. Schmidt, *Demokratietheorien* (Opladen: Leske + Budrich, 1997), 73.
45. James Madison, Alexander Hamilton, and John Jay, *The Federalist Papers* (1787-88; reprint, London: Penguin, 1987), nr. 71; see also Chapter 7 in this book.
46. *The Social Contract*, IV, 2.
47. In *The Social Contract*, II, 3; in a footnote Rousseau cites Machiavelli on the mixed blessings of "divisions"; however, he does so only to underscore his own negative view of them.
48. See the useful chronology of Tocqueville's life in Alexis de Tocqueville, *Democracy in America and Two Essays on America*, trans. Gerald E. Bevan (London: Penguin, 2003), vii-viii; a compelling recent account of Tocqueville's life and work is André Jardin, *Tocqueville: A Biography* (New York: Farar, Straus, Giroux, 1988).
49. See endnote 48. I prefer the Penguin translation by Gerald E. Bevan to that of Harvey C. Mansfield and Delba Winthrop: Alexis de Tocqueville, *Democracy in America* (Chicago: University of Chicago Press, 2000); the latter edition, however, has the advantage of a very useful index. In French: Alexis de Tocqueville, *De la démocratie en Amérique*, 2 vols. (Paris: Gallimard, 1961).
50. Alexis de Tocqueville, *Selected Letters on Politics and Society* (Berkeley: University of California Press, 1985), 115-16; in French: Alexis de Tocqueville, *Œuvres et correspondance inédites*, ed. Gustave de Beaumont (Paris: Michel Lévy Frères, 1861), 72-73.
51. Parts of this speech are cited in J.P. Mayer, *Alexis de Tocqueville* (Gloucester: Peter Smith, 1966), 41-42; in French: Alexis de Tocqueville, *Œuvres Complètes, Tome III, Écrits et Discours Politiques* (Paris: Galimard, 1985), 745-58.
52. Isaac Kramnick, "Introduction" to *Democracy in America and Two Essays on America*, by Alexis de Tocqueville (London: Penguin, 2003), xxxix.
53. Cited in Mayer, *Alexis de Tocqueville*, 62.
54. See above, endnote 2.
55. *The Old Regime*, III, 8.
56. See above, endnote 2.
57. Mayer, *Alexis de Tocqueville*, 62-63.
58. He also forayed briefly into what was then called Lower and Upper Canada.
59. John Stuart Mill's review of *Democracy in America* appeared in the *Edinburgh Review*, 1840; cited in Schmidt, *Demokratietheorien*, 84.
60. See among many, Seymour M. Lipset, *American Exceptionalism* (New York: Norton, 1996), 17-18.
61. *Democracy in America*, Volume I, Author's Introduction.
62. Ibid.
63. *Democracy in America*, Volume I, Part 1, Chapter 3.
64. Ibid.
65. *Democracy in America*, Author's Introduction.
66. *The Social Contract*, III, 4.
67. The following is largely owed to Schmidt, *Demokratietheorien*, 80-81.

68. *Democracy in America*, I, 1, 4.

69. Ibid.

70. *Democracy in America*, I, 2, 1; the italics in the English translation are not in the French original.

71. *Democracy in America*, I, 1, 5.

72. Ibid.

73. Ibid.

74. Ibid.

75. Ibid.

76. Ibid.

77. See Thomas O. Hueglin and Alan Fenna, *Comparative Federalism* (Peterborough: Broadview Press, 2006), 156.

78. *Democracy in America*, I, 1, 5.

79. *Democracy in America*, I, 2, 9.

80. *Democracy in America*, I, 1, 8.

81. Ibid.

82. Ibid.

83. *Democracy in America*, I, 2, 2-4.

84. *Democracy in America*, I, 2, 5.

85. See Schmidt, *Demokratietheorien*, 94.

86. *Democracy in America*, I, 1, 4.

87. *Democracy in America*, I, 2, 5.

88. Ibid.

89. Ibid.

90. Ibid.

91. For example, see Plato, *Politeia*, 481e; see Chapter 3 of this book.

92. *Democracy in America*, I, 2, 5.

93. Ibid.

94. Ibid.

95. Ibid.

96. See above, endnote 70.

97. *Democracy in America*, II, 1, 2.

98. Ibid.

99. *Democracy in America*, I, 2, 7.

100. Ibid.

101. *On the Citizen*, Chapter VII, para. 4; see Chapter 6 of this book.

102. *Democracy in America*, I, 2, 7.

103. Ibid.

104. *Politics*, 1281a40-b1; see Chapter 3 of this book.

105. *Democracy in America*, I, 2, 5.

106. *Democracy in America*, I, 2, 7.

107. *Democracy in America*, I, 1, 2.

108. *Democracy in America*, I, 2, 7.

109. Ibid.

110. *Democracy in America*, I, 1, 2.

111. *Democracy in America*, I, 2, 10.

112. *Democracy in America*, I, 1, 2.
113. John Locke, *Two Treatises of Government*, Treatise II, para. 95; see Chapter 7 of this book.
114. *Democracy in America*, II, 4, 8.
115. Ibid.
116. Ibid.
117. Plato, *Politeia*, 481e.
118. Ibid.
119. Harvey C. Mansfield and Delba Winthop, "Editors' Introduction" to *Democracy in America*, by Alexis de Tocqueville (Chicago: University of Chicago Press, 2000), xvii.
120. Kramnick, "Introduction," ix.
121. *Democracy in America*, II, 4, 7.
122. *Democracy in America*, I, 2, 9.
123. *Democracy in America*, II, 2, 12.
124. *Democracy in America*, I, 2, 9.
125. *Democracy in America*, II, 3, 16.
126. *Democracy in America*, I, 2, 9.
127. See James A. Henretta, David Brody, and Lynn Dumenil, *America: A Concise History* (Boston: Bedford, 2006), 309-14.
128. *Democracy in America*, II, 2, 20.
129. *Democracy in America*, II, 3, 5.
130. *Democracy in America*, II, 3, 7.
131. See Lipset, *American Exceptionalism*.
132. Sheldon S. Wolin, *Politics and Vision: Continuity and Innovation in Western Political Thought* (Princeton: Princeton University Press, 2004), 561.
133. See Schmidt, *Demokratietheorien*, 79.
134. *The Discourses*, Book I, Chapter 4; see Chapter 5 of this book.
135. *The Social Contract*, IV, 2.
136. *Democracy in America*, II, 4, 7.
137. Wolin, *Politics and Vision*, 605-06.

Chapter 9: Human Rights
1. Veit Valentin, *Knaurs Weltgeschichte* (Droemersche Verlagsanstalt: München, 1959), 692; own translation.
2. See Conor Cruise O'Brien, "Introduction" to *Reflections on the Revolution in France* by Edmund Burke (London: Penguin, 1986), 68.
3. So labelled by writer and politician Horace Walpole (1717-97); quoted in Miriam Brody, "Introduction" to *A Vindication of the Rights of Woman* by Mary Wollstonecraft (London: Penguin, 1992), 13.
4. Diana H. Coole, *Women in Political Theory* (Boulder: Lynne Rienner, 1988), 34-35; the passage in question is *Politeia*, 502d-e, which in most translated editions reads less ominously as having "adequately dealt with" the "subject of women and children." See Plato, *Complete Works* (Indianapolis: Hackett, 1997), or similarly Plato, *The Republic* (London: Penguin, 1987).
5. *Politeia*, 458c-d.

6. *Politics*, 1254b10-15; see Coole, *Women in Political Theory*, 44.

7. Coole, *Women in Political Theory*, 47.

8. *Politica*, Chapter II, paras. 40-46.

9. *The Prince*, Chapter XXV.

10. Hanna F. Pitkin, *Fortune is a Woman* (1984; reprint, Chicago: University of Chicago Press, 1999).

11. The following is largely inspired by, but not entirely in agreement with, Coole, *Women in Political Theory*, 71-102.

12. *Leviathan*, Chapter XX (102); the number in parentheses again refers to the original pagination of the 1651 edition.

13. Ibid.

14. *Leviathan*, XXX (185).

15. See again Coole, *Women in Political Theory*, 92-94.

16. John Locke, *Two Treatises of Government*, Treatise II, para. 124.

17. *Two Treatises of Government*, II, 72.

18. *A Discourse on the Origin of Inequality*; in French: *Discours sur l'origine et les fondements de l'inégalité parmi les hommes*.

19. *Origin of Inequality*, Part II.

20. *A Discourse on Political Economy*, Part I.

21. Ibid.

22. Ibid.

23. *Origin of Inequality*, II.

24. *Émile: Or Treatise on Education*, trans. William H. Payne (Amherst, NY: Prometheus, 2003). The French version is available at <http://projects.ilt.columbia.edu/pedagogies/rousseau/>; note inconsistencies in the progression of the two texts.

25. *Émile*, Book V.

26. Ibid.

27. Ibid.

28. Ibid.

29. See Valerie Bryson, *Feminist Political Theory* (Houndmills: Macmillan, 1992), 11-35.

30. Bryson, *Feminist Political Theory*, 1.

31. See for example, Dale Spender, *Women of Ideas* (Melbourne: ARK, 1983).

32. See Joan K. Kinnaird, "Mary Astell: Inspired by Ideas," in *Feminist Theorists*, ed. Dale Spender (New York: Random House, 1983), 28-39.

33. See Christine de Pizan, *The Book of the Body Politic* (Cambridge: University of Cambridge Press, 1994), and Renate Blumenfeld-Kosinski, ed., *The Selected Writings of Christine de Pizan* (New York: Norton, 1997).

34. Bonnie S. Anderson and Judith P. Zinsser, *A History of Their Own*, vol. 1 (New York: Harper & Row, 1988), 105.

35. See Natalie Zemon Davis, *Women at the Margins* (Cambridge: Harvard University Press, 1995).

36. See Brody, "Introduction," 18-19.

37. Quoted in D.L. Macdonald and Kathleen Scherf, "Introduction" to *The Vindications*, by Mary Wollstonecraft (Peterborough: Broadview Press, 1997), 14.

38. Ibid.

39. Quoted from Wollstonecraft, *The Vindications*, 353; the French version of the

Declaration is available at <http://www.justice.gouv.fr/textfond/ddhc.htm>; note that *"droits de l'homme"* has been translated with "human rights" rather than "rights of man" — both meanings are possible in French, and the *Declaration* ambiguously oscillates between both.

40. Mary Wollstonecraft, *A Vindication of the Rights of Men*, 35; since *The Rights of Men* was written unstructured as a public letter to Burke, citations are identified by page numbers in the Broadview edition of *The Vindications*, fully cited in endnote 37.

41. Burke, *Reflections*, 153; again, since the *Reflections* are written as one long unstructured epistle, it is impossible to cite other than by the page numbers of one particular edition (the Penguin edition, as fully cited in endnote 2).

42. See Harvey C. Mansfield, "A Sketch of Burke's Life," in Mansfield, ed., *Selected Letters of Edmund Burke* (Chicago: University of Chicago Press, 1984), 29-35.

43. Edmund Burke, *A Philosophical Enquiry into the Origin of Our Ideas of the Sublime and Beautiful* (Oxford: Oxford University Press, 1998).

44. Burke, *Reflections*.

45. Cited in L.G. Mitchell, "Introduction" to *The Writings and Speeches of Edmund Burke*, by Edmund Burke, vol. 8 (Oxford: Clarendon Press, 1989), 13.

46. Edmund Burke, *The Writings and Speeches of Edmund Burke*, vol. 2 (Oxford: Clarendon Press, 1981), 406-63.

47. *Writings and Speeches*, vol. 8, 102-69.

48. See Macdonald and Scherf, "Introduction," 25.

49. Mitchell, "Introduction," vol. 8, 2-4.

50. Burke, *Reflections*, 150-53.

51. *Reflections*, 153.

52. *Reflections*, 183.

53. *Reflections*, 206.

54. See Chapter 2 of this book.

55. Giambattista Vico, *On the Study Methods of Our Time* (Ithaca: Cornell University Press, 1990); the original Latin text can be found in Giambattista Vico, *Opere di Giambattista Vico*, vol. 1 (Naples: Fulvio Rossi, 1972), VII.

56. *The New Science of Giambattista Vico* (Ithaca: Cornell University Press, 1984), 141; see the Italian text in Giambattista Vico, *Opere*, vol. 2 (Naples: Fulvio Rossi, 1972).

57. *New Science*, 1101.

58. *Reflections*, 188.

59. *Reflections*, 195.

60. *Reflections*, 280.

61. See Mansfield, "A Sketch of Burke's Life," 34-35.

62. "A Sketch of Burke's Life," 34.

63. *Reflections*, 206.

64. *Reflections*, 372.

65. *Reflections*, 138.

66. *Reflections*, 140.

67. See Chapter 7 of this book.

68. See *Two Treatises of Government*, II, 37 and 50.

69. *Two Treatises*, II, 158.

70. *Two Treatises*, II, 157-58.

71. *Reflections*, 146.
72. *Reflections*, 141.
73. *Reflections*, 147.
74. *The Rights of Men*, 53-54.
75. Macdonald and Scherf, "Introduction," 10.
76. See Brody, "Introduction," 3-20; also see the moving account of Wollstonecraft's life by her husband, William Godwin, in *Memoirs of the Author of "A Vindication of the Rights of Woman"* (1798; reprint, Peterborough: Broadview Press, 2001).
77. See Macdonald and Scherf, "Introduction," 9-10.
78. See the dedicatory preface to M. Talleyrand-Périgord in Mary Wollstonecraft, *A Vindication of the Rights of Woman*, in *The Vindications* (Peterborough: Broadview Press, 1997).
79. See again Macdonald and Scherf, "Introduction," 14.
80. Macdonald and Scherf, "Introduction," 12-14.
81. See *The Works of Mary Wollstonecraft*, ed. Janet Todd and Marilyn Butler, 7 vols. (New York: New York University Press, 1989).
82. Percy Bysshe Shelley, *The Masque of Anarchy* (1819).
83. *The Rights of Men*, 38.
84. *A Vindication of the Rights of Woman*, Chapter I (125); since *The Rights of Woman* is structured by chapters, citations will be identified by the chapter number followed by the page number of the Broadview edition of *The Vindications* in parentheses (see endnote 37 for citation of Broadview edition).
85. *The Rights of Woman*, I (125).
86. *The Rights of Men*, 54.
87. *The Rights of Woman*, IV (171).
88. *Origin of Our Ideas*, Part I, Section 7.
89. *Origin of Our Ideas*, II, 6.
90. *Origin of Our Ideas*, I, 10.
91. *Origin of Our Ideas*, III, 27.
92. *The Rights of Men*, 35.
93. *The Rights of Men*, 85.
94. *The Rights of Woman*, II (131).
95. *The Rights of Men*, 40.
96. Charles Tilly, "Western State-Making and Theories of Political Transformation," in *The Formation of National States in Western Europe*, ed. Charles Tilly (Princeton: Princeton University Press, 1975), 635.
97. *Reflections*, 183.
98. *The Rights of Woman*, V (Section IV, 226).
99. *The Rights of Men*, 38.
100. *The Rights of Men*, 44.
101. *The Rights of Woman*, IX (281).
102. Rudolf Braun, "Taxation, Sociopolitical Structure, and State-Building: Great Britain and Brandenburg-Prussia," in *The Formation of National States in Western Europe*, ed. Charles Tilly (Princeton: Princeton University Press, 1975), 287.
103. *Two Treatises of Government*, II, 28.
104. *The Rights of Men*, 47.

105. *The Rights of Woman*, IX (282).

106. *The Rights of Woman*, IX (277).

107. *Reflections*, 186.

108. *The Rights of Men*, 67.

109. *The Rights of Men*, 57.

110. *Reflections*, 161.

111. *Reflections*, 169.

112. *Reflections*, 164-65.

113. *The Rights of Men*, 62.

114. *The Rights of Men*, 62.

115. *The Rights of Woman*, II (129).

116. *The Rights of Woman*, Introduction (109).

117. *The Rights of Woman*, I (125).

118. *The Rights of Woman*, I (117).

119. *The Rights of Woman*, II (145).

120. *The Rights of Woman*, III (151-52).

121. *Symposium*, 192a-b.

122. *Politeia*, 460c-d.

123. *The Rights of Woman*, III (165).

124. *The Rights of Woman*, IX (283).

125. *The Rights of Woman*, XII (298-323).

126. *The Rights of Woman*, IX (286-87).

127. *The Rights of Woman*, IX (287).

128. Cited in Brody, "Introduction," 30.

129. *The Rights of Woman*, IX (285).

130. See James Trager, *The Women's Chronology* (New York: Henry Holt, 1994), 414-19.

131. *The Rights of Woman*, VIII (275-76).

132. *The Rights of Woman*, IX (282).

133. *Politica*, I, 7; see Chapter 6 of this book.

134. *Leviathan*, XXX (185).

135. *The Rights of Woman*, III (153).

136. See *Émile*, V.

137. *The Rights of Woman*, V (204-05).

138. *The Rights of Woman*, IV (179).

139. David Boucher and Paul Kelly, "Introduction," in *Political Thinkers: From Socrates to the Present*, ed. David Boucher and Paul Kelly (Oxford: Oxford University Press, 2003), 13.

140. *Reflections*, 280.

141. *Reflections*, 146.

142. *The Rights of Woman*, I (125).

143. See the previous chapter in this book.

144. Charlotte Perkins Gilman, *Women & Economics* (New York: Harper & Row, 1966), 207.

145. See for instance Zillah R. Eisenstein, *The Radical Future of Liberal Feminism* (Boston: Northeastern University Press, 1993), 89-112.

Chapter 10: Modernity and Beyond

1. See Karl Polanyi, *The Great Transformation* (1944; reprint, Boston: Beacon Press, 1957).

2. *The Great Transformation*, 166.

3. Cited in Helmut Quaritsch, *Staat und Souveränität* (Frankfurt: Athenäum, 1970), 11.

4. *The Gay Science*, Book III, para. 125; all German citations are taken from Friedrich Nietzsche, *Kritische Studienausgabe*, 15 vols. (München: Deutscher Taschenbuch Verlag, 1999). All references to Nietzsche's work are given by his own numbering of paragraphs rather than page numbers. His main works in German are available at <http://gutenberg. spiegel.de/autoren/nietzsch.htm>.

5. See Chapter 8 of this book.

6. *The Gay Science*, V, 343.

7. *Manifesto of the Communist Party*, "I. Bourgeois and Proletarians," 476. All English citations are from *The Marx-Engels Reader*, 2nd ed., ed. Robert C. Tucker (New York: Norton, 1978). All citations in German are taken from Karl Marx and Friedrich Engels, *Studienausgabe*, 5 vols. (Berlin: Aufbau, 2004). Online German texts are available at <http://www.mlwerke.de/me/default.htm>.

8. See Rüdiger Safranski, *Schopenhauer und die wilden Jahre der Philosophie* (Frankfurt: Fischer, 2001).

9. *Schopenhauer*, 375.

10. *Philosophy of Right*, para. 258 and addition 152.

11. *Philosophy of Right*, Preface; see Safranski, *Schopenhauer*, 377.

12. Cited in: Safranski, *Schopenhauer*, 376; own translation.

13. *Der Hessische Landbote* (*The Hessian Messenger*); own translation.

14. *Deutschland, Ein Wintermärchen* (*Germany, A Winter's Tale*); own translation.

15. Veit Valentin, *Knaurs Weltgeschichte* (München: Droemersche Verlagsanstalt, 1959), 748.

16. *Die Schlesischen Weber* (*The Silesian Weavers*); own translation.

17. Friedrich Engels, *The Condition of the Working Class in England* (New York: Macmillan, 1958), 278-84.

18. *Twilight of the Idols*, "Skirmishes of an Untimely Man," 40.

19. The best account of Nietzsche's life is Rüdiger Safranski, *Nietzsche* (München: Hanser, 2000). Most editions of Nietzsche's various works contain brief biographical essays and/or life chronologies.

20. *The Birth of Tragedy* (*Die Geburt der Tragödie*, 1872).

21. On the whole episode see Safranski, *Nietzsche*, 256-63.

22. *Human, All Too Human* (*Menschliches, Allzumenschliches*, 1878-80).

23. *The Gay Science* (*Die fröhliche Wissenschaft*, 1882).

24. *Thus Spoke Zarathustra* (*Z; Also sprach Zarathustra*, 1883-85).

25. *Beyond Good and Evil* (*Jenseits von Gut und Böse*, 1886).

26. *On the Genealogy of Morals* (*Genealogie der Moral*, 1887).

27. *The Anti-Christ* (*Der Antichrist*), *Ecce Homo* (*Ecce Homo*); *Twilight of the Idols* (*Götzendämmerung*); *The Case of Wagner* (*Der Fall Wagner*); *Nietzsche contra Wagner* (*Nietzsche contra Wagner*); all in Nietzsche, *The Anti-Christ, Ecce Homo, Twilight of the Idols, and Other Writings*, trans. Judith Norman (Cambridge: Cambridge University Press, 2005).

28. *The Will to Power* (*Der Wille zur Macht*); the notes are found in volumes 7-13 in the German *Kritische Studienausgabe*.

29. Cited in Walter Kaufmann, "Translator's Introduction" to *Zarathustra*, by Nietzsche (New York: Modern Library, 1995), xx.

30. The following account is based on Safranski, *Nietzsche*, 326-32; 387-89.

31. *The Will to Power*, Book I, Part I, "Nihilism," para. 25; *Kritische Studienausgabe*, Volume 12, Part 9, para. 123.

32. *The Birth of Tragedy*, Section 1.

33. *The Birth of Tragedy*, Section 15.

34. *Kritische Studienausgabe*, Volume 1, page 541. This lecture is not subdivided into paragraphs. I am therefore providing the page number in the *Kritische Studienausgabe*; own translation.

35. Probably influenced by Schopenhauer, Nietzsche had considerable sympathy for Buddhism.

36. It should be clear that "gay" is to be understood here in its original meaning as "joyful."

37. Zarathustra, Prologue, para. 3.

38. *The Gay Science*, Book IV, para. 283.

39. *Kritische Studienausgabe*, Volume 9, Part 11, para. 141; own translation. On the following I am indebted to, but not strictly following, Safranski, *Nietzsche*, 231-44.

40. *The Gay Science*, III, 109.

41. *The Gay Science*, IV, 285.

42. *Kritische Studienausgabe*, 9, 11, 159; own translation.

43. *Kritische Studienausgabe*, 9, 11, 160; own translation.

44. *Kritische Studienausgabe*, 9, 11, 161; own translation.

45. *Zarathustra*, Part IV, "The Drunken Song," para. 10; the German title of this section is *Das Nachtwandler-Lied*, which correctly translates as "sleepwalker's song." In the German language, there is the idiomatic expression of someone moving along with the sure-footedness of a sleepwalker. Once man has found eternity in his own existence, Nietzsche seems to suggest, he can follow his path of life with unerring confidence.

46. *The Gay Science*, III, 121.

47. *Twilight of the Idols*, "Skirmishes of an Untimely Man," para. 39.

48. Ibid.

49. Ibid.

50. *The Gay Science*, V, 349.

51. *The Will to Power*, Book I, Part II, "European Nihilism," para. 120; *Kritische Studienausgabe*, 12, 10, 53.

52. *The Gay Science*, I, 4.

53. See *The Gay Science*, IV, 335.

54. *Beyond Good and Evil*, Part 9, para. 260.

55. *The Gay Science*, I, 2.

56. *The Discourses*, Book I, Chapter 16; the Italian original is available at <http://www.libromania.it/>.

57. See Chapter 5 of this book.

58. *The Gay Science*, III, 116.

59. *The Gay Science*, III, 149.

60. *Twilight of the Idols*, "Skirmishes of an Untimely Man," para. 39.

61. Ibid.

62. Ibid., 38.

63. *Human, All Too Human*, Volume I, para. 473.

64. *The Gay Science*, III, 174.

65. *The Gay Science*, I, 42.

66. *The Gay Science*, I, 38.

67. Ibid.

68. *Human, All Too Human*, I, 475.

69. See Liah Greenfeld, *Nationalism and Capitalism* (Boston: Harvard University Press, 2001).

70. *Beyond Good and Evil*, 8, 244.

71. *The Gay Science*, 5, 348.

72. *Human, All Too Human*, I, 475.

73. Ibid.

74. *Human, All Too Human*, II, "Assorted Opinions and Maxims," 318.

75. *On the Jewish Question*, *The Marx-Engels Reader*, 48.

76. Closest in *From the Afterword to the Second German Edition* (of *Capital*, Volume 1), *The Marx-Engels Reader*, 302; like Ingrid Bergman in *Casablanca*, Marx never quite said it.

77. Preface to *A Contribution to the Critique of Political Economy*, *The Marx-Engels Reader*, 4.

78. The following is based on the classical and thorough biography, David McLellan, *Karl Marx: His Life and Thought* (London: Macmillan, 1973); as well as the more recent and refreshingly irreverent account by Francis Wheen, *Karl Marx: A Life* (New York: Norton, 2000).

79. In 1890 an English translation of *Das Kapital* seemed to have sold well mainly because it was advertised to Wall Street bankers as a book on "how to accumulate capital"; Wheen, *Karl Marx: A Life*, 385.

80. *Germany, A Winter's Tale.*

81. See Karl Korsch, *Marxismus und Philosophie* (1923; reprint, Frankfurt: Europäische Verlagsanstalt, 1966), esp. 123-24 and 139; I owe this Korsch reference to Iring Fetscher, "Einleitung" to *Studienausgabe*, vol. 1, by Karl Marx and Friedrich Engels, 17.

82. *Manifesto of the Communist Party*, opening paragraph and "I. Bourgeois and Proletarians," *The Marx-Engels Reader*, 473.

83. *From the Afterword to the Second German Edition*, *The Marx-Engels Reader*, 301.

84. Preface to *A Contribution to the Critique of Political Economy*, *The Marx-Engels Reader*, 4.

85. *The German Ideology*, Part I (Feuerbach), Section A, "2. Concerning the Production of Consciousness,"*The Marx-Engels Reader*, 172.

86. *The Grundrisse* (Foundations of the Critique of Political Economy), "E. Pre-Capitalist Property and Production," *The Marx-Engels Reader*, 266.

87. *Manifesto of the Communist Party*, "I. Bourgeois and Proletarians," *The Marx-Engels Reader*, 474.

88. *Twilight of the Idols*, "Skirmishes of an Untimely Man," para. 40. .

89. *Economic and Philosophic Manuscripts of 1844*, "Private property and Communism," *The Marx-Engels Reader*, 84.

90. *Manifesto of the Communist Party*, "I. Bourgeois and Proletarians," *The Marx-Engels Reader*, 476.

91. Ibid., 477.

92. My interpretation of the *Communist Manifesto* as a modernist document is greatly influenced by Marshall Berman, *All That Is Solid Melts Into Air* (New York: Penguin, 1988).

93. *Manifesto of the Communist Party*, "I. Bourgeois and Proletarians," *The Marx-Engels Reader*, 476-77.

94. Ibid., 476. The metaphoric beauty of the language ("all that is solid …") is in fact more pronounced in the English version, which stems from the 1888 edition by Engels, than in the German original; see the introductory note by Robert C. Tucker in *The Marx-Engels Reader*, 469.

95. William Shakespeare, *Julius Caesar*, Act 3, Scene 2.

96. *Manifesto of the Communist Party*, "I. Bourgeois and Proletarians," *The Marx-Engels Reader*, 475.

97. *Capital*, Volume I, *The Marx-Engels Reader*, 413.

98. Albert Hüglin, *Der Tarifvertrag zwischen Arbeitgeber und Arbeitnehmer* (Stuttgart: Cotta, 1906), 7. My grandfather Albert Hüglin wrote this dissertation on the development and legal justification of collective agreements under the supervision of Lujo Brentano, one of the most progressive economists at the time who later served briefly as minister of trade in Kurt Eisler's revolutionary Bavarian government of 1918. Because of this dissertation, my grandfather was invited for a year to work, as private secretary, for Hugo Stinnes, one of the wealthiest German industrialists at the time, a member of the Weimar Republic's parliament, and the German industry's spokesperson for negotiations with the trade unions.

99. See *Capital*, I, *The Marx-Engels Reader*, 329-36.

100. *The Grundrisse*, "C. The Dynamics of Capitalism," *The Marx-Engels Reader*, 247-50.

101. Isaac Newton had formulated one of the basic axioms of physics according to which action equals reaction; see Chapter 6 of this book.

102. *The Grundrisse*, *The Marx-Engels Reader*, 249.

103. *Manifesto of the Communist Party*, "I. Bourgeois and Proletarians," *The Marx-Engels Reader*, 479.

104. Ibid.

105. *Economic and Philosophic Manuscripts*; for the following see especially the section on "Estranged Labour" (*Die Entfremdete Arbeit*), *The Marx-Engels Reader*, 70-81.

106. *Manifesto of the Communist Party*, "I. Bourgeois and Proletarians," *The Marx-Engels Reader*, 481.

107. Ibid., 479.

108. Ibid., 479-80.

109. Ibid., 478; Marx obviously borrowed the idea from Goethe's famous poem, *The Sorcerer's Apprentice*.

110. Ibid.

111. See "Crisis Theory," Chapter 17 of *Theories of Surplus Value*, *The Marx-Engels Reader*, 443-65.

112. *Manifesto of the Communist Party*, "I. Bourgeois and Proletarians," *The Marx-Engels Reader*, 478.

113. Ibid.

114. Ibid.

115. Alain Lipietz, *Mirages and Miracles* (London: Verso, 1987), 36.

116. Ibid.

117. *Manifesto of the Communist Party*, "I. Bourgeois and Proletarians," *The Marx-Engels Reader*, 475.

118. *On the Jewish Question*, Part 1, *The Marx-Engels Reader*, 33-34.

119. *Manifesto of the Communist Party*, "II. Proletarians and Communists," *The Marx-Engels Reader*, 490.

120. Ibid.

121. Ibid., 491.

122. *The Anti-Christ*, 3.

123. Stuart Sim, ed., *The Icon Critical Dictionary of Postmodern Thought* (Cambridge: Icon Books, 1998), 325.

124. Sheldon S. Wolin, *Politics and Vision: Continuity and Innovation in Western Political Thought* (Princeton: Princeton University Press, 2004), 481, 483.

125. See Stephen K. White, *Political Theory and Postmodernism* (Cambridge: Cambridge University Press, 1994), 119.

126. See Leslie P. Thiele, *Thinking Politics* (New York: Chatham House, 2003), 152-53.

127. See Ernesto Laclau and Chantal Mouffe, "Post-Marxism Without Apologies," *New Left Review* 166 (1987): 79-106.

128. Chantal Mouffe, "Democratic Politics Today," in *Dimensions of Radical Democracy*, ed. Chantal Mouffe (London: Verso, 1992), 3.

129. As reported by Friedrich Engels, in a letter to the German socialist/Marxist Eduard Bernstein, November 2/3, 1882; Marx made this remark to his son-in-law, Jenny's husband, Paul Lafargue; cited in Marx and Engels, *Studienausgabe*, vol. 1, back cover.

130. Cited in Safranski, *Nietzsche*, 355 (trans. T.H.).

131. See Wolin, *Politics and Vision*, 457-58.

132. *Twilight of the Idols*, "Skirmishes of an Untimely Man," para. 39.

133. *Zarathustra*, Part I, "On Little Old and Young Women."

134. Iris Marion Young, *Justice and the Politics of Difference* (Princeton: Princeton University Press, 1990), 239.

135. Wolin, *Politics and Vision*, 464.

136. *The Will to Power*, Book I, Part I, "Nihilism," para. 12; *Kritische Studienausgabe* Volume 13, paras. 46-47; see Wolin, *Politics and Vision*, 475.

137. Justin Rosenberg, *The Follies of Globalisation Theory* (London: Verso, 200), 35-36.

138. Thus, the main tenor of a 1997 special edition of *The New Yorker*; cited in Wheen, *Karl Marx: A Life*, 5.

139. *Two Treatises of Government*, Treatise II, para. 37; see Chapter 7 of this book.

140. John Rawls, *A Theory of Justice* (Cambridge: Harvard University Press, 1971), 60; see also modifications, 82-83 and 302-03.

141. *History of Florence*, Book III, Chapter 3 (13); see Chapter 5 of this book.

142. Wolin, *Politics and Vision*, 532.

143. *On the Jewish Question*, Part 1, *The Marx-Engels Reader*, 33-34.

144. See above, endnote 93.

Bibliography

Althusius, Johannes. *Politica.* 1614. Translated by Frederick S. Carney. Indianapolis: Liberty Fund, 1995.

————. *Politica Methodice Digesta.* Herborn, 1614; facsimile reprint, Aalen: Scientia, 1981.

Amato, Giuliano. "Plenary Speech." In *Federalism in a Changing World.* Edited by Raoul Blindenbacher and Arnold Koller, 577-81. Montreal: McGill-Queen's University Press, 2003.

Anderson, Bonnie S., and Judith P. Zinsser. *A History of Their Own: Women in Europe from Prehistory to the Present,* vol. 1. New York: Harper & Row, 1988.

Antholz, Heinz. *Die Politische Wirksamkeit des Johannes Althusius in Emden.* Cologne: Leer, 1954.

Aquinas, Thomas. *De Regimine Principium.* In *Political Writings.* Edited by R.W. Dyson. Cambridge: Cambridge University Press, 2002.

————. *Political Writings.* Edited by R.W. Dyson. Cambridge: Cambridge University Press, 2002.

————. *Scripta super libros sententiarum.* In *Political Writings.* Edited by R.W. Dyson. Cambridge: Cambridge University Press, 2002.

————. *Summa Theologiae.* c. 1270. In *Political Writings.* Edited by R.W. Dyson. Cambridge: Cambridge University Press, 2002. Online Latin edition, Corpus Thomisticum, 2006. <http://www.corpusthomisticum.org/sth0000.html>. Online English edition, IntraText, n.d. <http://www.intratext.com/X/ENG0023.htm>.

Arendt, Hannah. *The Human Condition.* Chicago: University of Chicago Press, 1998.

Aristotle. *The Complete Works of Aristotle: The Revised Oxford Edition.* Edited by Jonathan Barnes. 2 vols. Princeton: Princeton University Press, 1995.

————. *Nicomachean Ethics.* Translated by Martin Ostwald. Indianapolis: Bobbs-Merrill, 1962.

————. *The Politics.* Translated by T.A. Sinclair. London: Penguin, 1981.

————. *Topics.* In *The Complete Works of Aristotle: The Revised Oxford Translation,* vol. 1. Edited by Jonathan Barnes. Princeton: Princeton University Press, 1995.

Aron, Raymond. *Introduction to the Philosophy of History.* London: Weidenfeld & Nicolson, 1961.

Augustine. *The City of God.* Translated by Marcus Dods. New York: Modern Library, 1993.

Ball, W.W. Rouse. *A Short Account of the History of Mathematics.* New York: Dover, 1960.

Beck, Ulrich. *World Risk Society*. London: Polity Press, 1999.

Berman, Marshall. *All That Is Solid Melts Into Air: The Experience of Modernity*. New York: Simon & Schuster, 1982; reprint, New York: Penguin, 1988.

Betts, C.J. "Introduction" to *Persian Letters*, by Montesquieu. Translated by C.J. Betts. London: Penguin, 2004.

Black, Anthony. *Political Thought in Europe, 1250-1450*. Cambridge: Cambridge University Press, 2000.

Bloom, Allan. "Interpretive Essay." In *The Republic of Plato*. 2nd ed. Translated by Allan Bloom. New York: Basic Books, 1991.

Blumenfeld-Kosinski, Renate, ed. *The Selected Writings of Christine de Pizan*. New York: Norton, 1997.

Bodin, Jean. *The Six Bookes of a Commonweale*. 1576. Edited with an introduction by Kenneth D. McRae. Cambridge: Cambridge University Press, 1962.

Boucher, David. *Texts in Context*. Dordrecht: Nijhoff, 1985.

Boucher, David, and Paul Kelly, eds. *Political Thinkers: From Socrates to the Present*. Oxford: Oxford University Press, 2003.

Braun, Rudolf. "Taxation, Sociopolitical Structure, and State-Building: Great Britain and Bradenburg-Prussia." In *The Formation of National States in Western Europe*. Edited by Charles Tilly, 243-327. Princeton: Princeton University Press, 1975.

Brody, Miriam. "Introduction" to *A Vindication of the Rights of Woman*, by Mary Wollstonecraft. London: Penguin, 1992.

Brucker, Gene. *Renaissance Florence*. New York: John Wiley, 1969.

Bryson, Valerie. *Feminist Political Theory: An Introduction*. Houndsmills, UK: Macmillan, 1992.

Büchner, Georg. *Der Hessische Landbote [The Hessian Messenger]*. In Büchner, *Werke und Briefe*. München: Deutscher Taschenbuch Verlag, 1965.

Bull, Hedley. *The Anarchical Society: A Study of Order in World Politics*. New York: Columbia University Press, 1977.

Burke, Edmund. *A Philosophical Enquiry into the Origin of Our Ideas of the Sublime and Beautiful*. Edited by Adam Phillips. Oxford: Oxford University Press, 1998.

———. *Reflections on the Revolution in France*. 1790. Edited by Connor Cruise O'Brien. London: Penguin, 1986.

———. *The Writings and Speeches of Edmund Burke*. Vol. 2, *Party, Parliament and the American Crisis, 1766-1774*. Edited by Paul Langford. Oxford: Clarendon Press, 1981.

———. *The Writings and Speeches of Edmund Burke*. Vol. 8, *The French Revolution, 1790-1794*. Edited by L.G. Mitchell. Oxford: Clarendon Press, 1989.

Burke, Peter. *Vico*. Oxford: Oxford University Press, 1985.

Calvin, John. *Institutes of the Christian Religion [Institutio Christianae Religionis]*. 1536. Edited by John T. McNeill. 2 vols. Philadelphia: Westminster Press, 1977.

Canning, Joseph. *A History of Medieval Political Thought, 300-1450*. New York: Routledge, 1996.

Carney, Frederick. "Translator's Introduction" to *Politica*, by Johannes Althusius. Translated by Frederick S. Carney. Indianapolis: Liberty Fund, 1995.

Chianti Classico Niccolò Machiavelli, see <http://www.gruppoitalianovini.com/machiavelli_ it.htm>.

Chinese Communist Party, General Program, at <http://www.china.org.cn/english/features/ 49109.htm#1>.

Cole, G.D.H. "Introduction" to *The Social Contract and Discourses*, by Jean-Jacques Rousseau. Translated by G.D.H. Cole. Revised by J.H. Brumfitt and John C. Hall. London: Fitzhenry & Whiteside, 1986.

Coleman, Janet. *Political Thought from the Middle Ages to the Renaissance*. Oxford: Blackwell, 2000.

Coole, Diana H. *Women in Political Theory*. Boulder, CO: Lynne Rienner, 1988.

Cottingham, John. "General Introduction" to *Mediations on First Philosophy*, by René Descartes. Edited and translated by John Cottingham. Cambridge: Cambridge University Press, 2005.

———. "Translator's Preface" to *Principles of Philosophy*, by René Descartes. In *The Philosophical Writings of Descartes*, vol. 1. Edited and translated by John Cottingham, Robert Stoothoff, and Dugald Murdoch. Cambridge: Cambridge University Press, 1985.

Cottingham, John, Robert Stoothoff, and Dugald Murdoch, eds. *The Philosophical Writings of Descartes*, vol. 1. Cambridge: Cambridge University Press, 1985.

Cranston, Maurice. "Introduction" to *The Social Contract*, by Jean-Jacques Rousseau. Translated by Maurice Cranston. London: Penguin, 1968.

———. *Jean-Jacques: The Early Life and Work of Jean-Jacques Rousseau, 1712-1754*. London: Penguin, 1983.

———. *John Locke, A Biography*. London: Longmans, 1957.

———. *The Noble Savage: Jean-Jacques Rousseau, 1754-1762*. London: Penguin, 1991.

Crick, Bernard. "Introduction" to *The Discourses*, by Niccolò Machiavelli. Edited by Bernard Crick. Translated by Leslie J. Walker. London: Penguin, 1970.

Davis, Natalie Zemon. *Women at the Margins*. Cambridge: Harvard University Press, 1995.

Pico della Mirandola, Giovanni. "Oratio de Hominis Digitate" [Oration on the Dignity of Man]. 1486. Online Latin edition, Pico Project (Brown University), n.d. <http://www. brown.edu/Departments/Italian_Studies/pico/>.

———. "Oration on the Dignity of Man." 1486. In Kenneth R. Bartlett, *The Civilization of the Italian Renaissance: A Source Book*. Lexington, MA: D.C. Heath, 1992.

Deppe, Frank. *Niccolò Machiavelli: Zur Kritik der reinen Politik*. Cologne: Pahl-Rugenstein, 1987.

Derathé, Robert. *Jean-Jacques Rousseau et la Science Politique de son Temps*. Paris: Vrin, 1950.

Descartes, René. *Discours de la méthod* [*Discourse on the Method*]. 1637. Online French edition, Malaspina University-College, n.d. Translated by Ian Johnston. <http://www.mala.bc.ca/~johnstoi/descartes/Discours.htm>.

———. *Discourse on the Method*. 1637. In *The Philosophical Writings of Descartes*, vol. 1. Edited and translated by John Cottingham, Robert Stoothoff, and Dugald Murdoch. Cambridge: Cambridge University Press, 1985.

———. *Meditationes de Prima Philosophia* [*Meditations on First Philosophy*]. 1641. Online Latin edition, Wright State University, 1996. <http://www.wright.edu/cola/descartes/medl.html>.

———. *Meditations on First Philosophy*. 1641. Edited and translated by John Cottingham. Cambridge: Cambridge University Press, 2005.

———. *Les Passions de l'âme* [*The Passions of the Soul*]. 1649. Online French edition, Académie de Toulouse, 2001. <http://pedagogie.actoulouse.fr/philosophie/phpes/descartes.htm>.

———. *The Passions of the Soul*. 1649. In *The Philosophical Writings of Descartes*, vol. 1. Edited and translated by John Cottingham, Robert Stoothoff, and Dugald Murdoch. Cambridge: Cambridge University Press, 1985.

———. *The Philosophical Writings of Descartes*, vol. 1. Edited and translated by John Cottingham, Robert Stoothoff, and Dugald Murdoch. Cambridge: Cambridge University Press, 1985.

———. *Principles of Philosophy*. 1644. In *The Philosophical Writings of Descartes*, vol. 1. Edited and translated by John Cottingham, Robert Stoothoff, and Dugald Murdoch. Cambridge: Cambridge University Press, 1985. French available at <http://visualiseur.bnf.fr/Visualiseur?Destination=Gallica&O=NUMM-94260>.

———. *Regulae ad Directionem Ingenii* [*Rules for the Direction of the Mind*]. 1684. Online Latin edition, Académie de Toulouse, 2001. <http://pedagogie.actoulouse.fr/philosophie/descregulae.htm>.

———. *Rules for the Direction of the Mind*. 1684. In *The Philosophical Writings of Descartes*, vol. 1. Edited and translated by John Cottingham, Robert Stoothoff, and Dugald Murdoch. Cambridge: Cambridge University Press, 1985.

Desgraves, Louis, ed. *Catalogue de la Bibliothèque de Montesquieu*. Geneva: Librairie Droz, 1954.

Dyson, R.W. "Introduction" to *Political Writings*, by Thomas Aquinas. Edited by R.W. Dyson. Cambridge: Cambridge University Press, 2002.

Einstein, Alfred. *Mozart: His Character, His Work*. Oxford: Oxford University Press, 1962.

Eisenstein, Zillah R. *The Radical Future of Liberal Feminism*. Boston: Northeastern University Press, 1993.

Endo, Ken. "The Principle of Subsidiarity: From Johannes Althusius to Jacques Delors." *Hokkaido Law Review* 44, no. 6 (1994): 652-553 [*sic*].

Engels, Friedrich. *The Condition of the Working Class in England*. New York: Macmillan, 1958.

Fetscher, Iring. "Einleitung" [Introduction] to *Studienausgabe*, vol. 1, by Karl Marx and Friedrich Engels. Edited by Iring Fetscher. Berlin: Aufbau, 2004.

Friedrich, Carl Joachim, ed. *Politica Methodice Digesta of Johannes Althusius*. Cambridge: Harvard University Press, 1932; reprint, New York: Arno Press, 1979.

Germino, Dante. "Was Machiavelli a 'Spiritual Realist'?" Paper presented at the 16th Annual Meeting of the Eric Voegelin Society, Washington DC, September 1-2, 2000.

Gewirth, Alan. *Marsilius of Padua: Defender of Peace*. 1324. 2 vols. New York: Columbia University Press, 1951-56.

Gianturco, Elio. "Translator's Introduction" to *On the Study Methods of Our Time*, by Giambattista Vico. Translated by Elio Gianturco. Ithaca: Cornell University Press, 1990.

Gierke, Otto von. *Johannes Althusius und die Entwicklung der Naturrechtlichen Staatstheorien*. 1880; reprint, Aalen: Scientia, 1958.

———. *Political Theories of the Middle Age*. Translated by Frederic W. Maitland. Cambridge: Cambridge University Press, 1958.

Godwin, William. *Memoirs of the Author of "A Vindication of the Rights of Woman."* 1798. Peterborough, ON: Broadview Press, 2001.

Goeters, J.F. "Die Akten der Synode der Niederländischen Kirchen zu Emden vom 4.-13. Oktober 1571." Neukirchen-Vluyn: Neukirchen Verlag, 1971.

Gramsci, Antonio. *Selections from the Prison Notebooks*. Edited and translated by Quintin Hoare and Geoffrey Nowell-Smith. New York: International Publishers, 1983.

Granatstein, J.L. *Who Killed Canadian History?* Toronto: HarperCollins, 1998.

Greenfeld, Liah. *Nationalism and Capitalism*. Boston: Harvard University Press, 2001.

Habermas, Jürgen. *Technik und Wissenschaft als 'Ideologie'*. Frankfurt: Suhrkamp, 1969.

———. *Theorie und Praxis*. Frankfurt: Suhrkamp, 1974.

Hallowell, John H., and Jene M. Porter. *Political Philosophy: The Search for Humanity and Order*. Scarborough, ON: Prentice Hall, 1997.

Hamilton, Alexander, John Jay, and James Madison. *The Federalist: A Commentary on the Constitution of the United States*. New York: Modern Library, 2001.

Hegel, G.W.F. *The Philosophy of Right*. 1820. Translated by T.M. Knox. Oxford: Clarendon Press, 1965.

Heine, Heinrich. *Germany, A Winter's Tale* [*Deutschland, Ein Wintermärchen*]. In Heine, *Gedichte*. Frankfurt: Insel Verlag, 1968. Online English and German editions, <http://helios.hampshire.edu/~jjwSS/projects/winterstale//index.html>.

———. *Die Schlesischen Weber* [*The Silesian Weavers*]. In Heine, *Gedichte*. Frankfurt: Insel Verlag, 1968.

Held, David, and Anthony McGrew, "The Great Globalization Debate." In *The Global Transformation Reader*. Edited by David Held and Anthony McGrew. Cambridge: Polity Press, 2004.

Henretta, James A., David Brody, and Lynn Dumenil. *America: A Concise History*. Boston: Bedford, 2006.

Herman, Edward S., and Noam Chomsky. *Manufacturing Consent: The Political Economy of the Mass Media*. New York: Pantheon, 2002.

Hill, Christopher. *The Century of Revolution, 1603-1714*. New York: Norton, 1980.

Hobbes, Thomas. *De Cive.* 1642. Edited by Howard Warrender. Oxford: Oxford University Press, 1983.

———. *Leviathan.* 1651. Edited by Richard Tuck. Cambridge: Cambridge University Press, 1992.

———. *The Life of Mr. Thomas Hobbes of Malmesbury, Written by himself In a Latine Poem And now Translated into English.* 1680; facsimile reprint, Exeter, UK: University of Exeter Press, 1979.

———. *On the Citizen.* 1642. Edited by Richard Tuck and Michael Silverthorne. Cambridge: Cambridge University Press, 1998.

Hofmann, Hasso. *Repräsentation.* Berlin: Duncker & Humblot, 1974.

Hösle, Vittorio. "Einleitung" to *Prinzipien einer neuen Wissenschaft über die Gemeinsame Natur der Völker,* vol. 1, by Giovanni Battista Vico. Hamburg: Felix Meiner, 1990.

Hueglin, Thomas O. "Actuality and Illusion in the Political Thought of Machiavelli." Review of *Machiavelli* by Herfried Muenkler, and *Niccolò Machiavelli* by Frank Deppe. In *Journal of Early Modern History* 2, no. 4 (1998): 395-99.

———. *Early Modern Concepts for a Late Modern World: Althusius on Community and Federalism.* Waterloo, ON: Wilfrid Laurier University Press, 1999.

———. "Federalism at the Crossroads: Old Meanings, New Significance." *Canadian Journal of Political Science* 36, no. 2 (June 2003): 275-94.

———. "From Constitutionalism to Treaty Federalism: A Comparative Perspective." *Publius: The Journal of Federalism* 30, no. 4 (Fall 2000): 137-52.

———. "Machiavelli Revisited in the Neoconservative Age." *Journal of History and Politics* 8 (1990): 123-52.

Hueglin, Thomas O., and Alan Fenna. *Comparative Federalism.* Peterborough, ON: Broadview Press, 2006.

Hughes, Robert. *The Fatal Shore.* New York: Vintage, 1986.

Hüglin, Albert. *Der Tarifvertrag zwischen Arbeitgeber und Arbeitnehmer.* Stuttgart: Cotta, 1906.

Jardin, André. *Tocqueville: A Biography.* New York: Farrar, Straus & Giroux, 1988.

Kant, Immanuel. *Fundamental Principles of the Metaphysics of Morals.* 1785. In *Basic Writings of Kant.* Edited by Allen W. Wood. Translated by Thomas K. Abbott. New York: Modern Library, 2001.

———. *To Eternal Peace.* 1795. In *Basic Writings of Kant.* Edited by Allen W. Wood. Translated by Carl J. Friedrich. New York: Modern Library, 2001.

Kaufmann, Walter. "Translator's Introduction" to *Thus Spoke Zarathustra,* by Friedrich Nietzsche. Translated by Walter Kaufmann. New York: Modern Library, 1995.

Kinnaird, Joan K. "Mary Astell: Inspired by Ideas." In *Feminist Theorists: Three Centuries of Key Women Thinkers.* Edited by Dale Spender. New York: Random House, 1983.

Korsch, Karl. *Marxismus und Philosophie.* 1923. Frankfurt: Europäische Verlagsanstalt, 1966.

Kramnick, Isaac. "Introduction" to *Democracy in America and Two Essays on America,* by Alexis de Tocqueville. Translated by Gerald E. Bevan. London: Penguin, 2003.

Laclau, Ernesto, and Chantal Mouffe. "Post-Marxism Without Apologies." *New Left Review* 166 (1987): 79-106.

Laski, Harold J. "Historical Introduction" to *A Defence of Liberty Against Tyrants: A Translation of the "Vindiciae Contra Tyrannos,"* by Junius Brutus [Hubert Languet]. New York: Burt Franklin, 1972.

Laslett, Peter. "Introduction" to *Two Treatises of Government*, by John Locke. Edited by Peter Laslett. Cambridge: Cambridge University Press, 1988.

Leo XIII. *Immortale Dei* [*On the Christian Constitution of States*]. 1885. Online edition, Papal Encyclicals Online. <http://www.papalencyclicals.net/Leo13/l13sta.htm>.

Lewis, Ewart. *Medieval Political Ideas*. New York: Cooper Square, 1976.

Lindblom, Charles. *Politics and Markets: The World's Political-Economic Systems*. New York: Basic Books, 1977.

Lipietz, Alain. *Mirages and Miracles: The Crises of Global Fordism*. London: Verso, 1987.

Lipset, Seymour M. *American Exceptionalism*. New York: Norton, 1996.

Locke, John. *A Letter Concerning Toleration*. 1685. Edited by James Tully. Indianapolis: Hackett, 1983.

————. *An Essay Concerning Human Understanding*. 1689. 2 vols. New York: Dover Books, 1959.

————. "Some Considerations of the Consequences of the Lowering of Interest and Raising the Value of Money." 1691. In Locke, *Several Papers Relating to Money, Interest and Trade*. 1696; reprint, New York: Augustus M. Kelley, 1968.

————. *Two Treatises of Government*. 1690. Edited by Peter Laslett. Cambridge: Cambridge University Press, 1988.

Luther, Martin. "Against the Robbing and Murdering Hordes of Peasants." 1525. In *Martin Luther: Documents of Modern History*. Edited by E. Gordon Rupp and Benjamin Drewery, 121-26. London: Edward Arnold, 1970. Online edition, Trinity & All Saints, n.d. <http://www.leedstrinity.ac.uk/histcourse/reformat/maincore/rupp6213.htm>.

Maastricht Treaty. European Union. See document at <http://europa.eu/abc/treaties/index_en.htm>.

Macdonald, D.L., and Kathleen Scherf. "Introduction" to *The Vindications*, by Mary Wollstonecraft. Edited by D.L. Macdonald and Kathleen Scherf. Peterborough, ON: Broadview Press, 1997.

Machiavelli, Niccolò. *Discorsi sopra la prima deca di Tito Livio* [*The Discourses*]. 1525. Online Italian edition, LibroMania, 1998. <http://libromania.it>.

————. *The Discourses*. 1520. Edited by Bernard Crick. Translated by Leslie J. Walker. London: Penguin, 1970.

————. *History of Florence and the Affairs of Italy: From the Earliest Times to the Death of Lorenzo the Magnificent*. 1525. New York: Walter Dunne, 1901.

————. *Istorie Fiorentine* [*History of Florence*]. 1525. Online Italian edition, LibroMania, 1998. <http://libromania.it>.

——. "Letter 208." 1513. In *Machiavelli and His Friends*. Edited by James B. Atkinson and David Sices. DeKalb: Northern Illinois University Press, 1996.

——. "Lettere" [Letters]. Edited by Mario Martelli. Online Italian edition, Biblioteca dei Classici Italiani, 1996. <http://www.classicitaliani.it/index090.htm>.

——. *The Prince*. 1513. Translated by George Bull. London: Penguin, 1961.

——. *Il Principe* [*The Prince*]. 1525. Online Italian edition, LibroMania, 1995. <http://libromania.it>.

Macpherson, C.B. *The Political Theory of Possessive Individualism: Hobbes to Locke*. Oxford: Oxford University Press, 1962.

Madison, James, Alexander Hamilton, and John Jay. *The Federalist Papers*. 1787-88. London: Penguin, 1987.

Malcolm, Noel. "Hobbes." In *The Cambridge History of Political Thought, 1450-1700*. Edited by J.H. Burns, 530-44. Cambridge: Cambridge University Press, 1991.

Mann, Thomas. *Reflections of an Unpolitical Man*. Translated with an introduction by Walter D. Morris. New York: F. Ungar, 1982.

Mansfield, Harvey C. *Machiavelli's Virtue*. Chicago: University of Chicago Press, 1998.

——. "A Sketch of Burke's Life." In *Selected Letters of Edmund Burke*. Edited by Harvey C. Mansfield, 29-38. Chicago: University of Chicago Press, 1984.

Mansfield, Harvey C., and Delba Winthop. "Editor's Introduction" to *Democracy in America*, by Alexis de Tocqueville. Chicago: University of Chicago Press, 2000.

Marsiglio of Padua. *Defensor Minor and de Translatione Imperii*. c. 1342. Edited by Cary J. Nederman. Cambridge: Cambridge University Press, 1993.

Marsilius of Padua. *Defensor Pacis*. 1324. Translated by Alan Gewirth. New York: Columbia University Press, 2001.

Marsilius von Padua. *Defensor Pacis*. 1324. 2 vols. Hannover: Hahnsche Buchhandlung, 1932-33.

Martinich, A.P. *Hobbes: A Biography*. Cambridge: Cambridge University Press, 1999.

Marx, Karl. *Capital*, vols. 1, 3. 1873-94. In *The Marx-Engels Reader*. 2nd ed. Edited by Robert C. Tucker. New York: Norton, 1978.

——. *Capital*, vol. 2. 1885. Translated by Samuel Moore and Edward Aveling. London: Allen & Unwin, 1949.

——. *Crisis Theory*. From *Theories of Surplus Value*. 1862. In *The Marx-Engels Reader*. 2nd ed. Edited by Robert C. Tucker. New York: Norton, 1978.

——. *Critique of the Gotha Program*. 1875. In *The Marx-Engels Reader*. 2nd ed. Edited by Robert C. Tucker. New York: Norton, 1978.

——. *Economic and Philosophic Manuscripts of 1844*. In *The Marx-Engels Reader*. 2nd ed. Edited by Robert C. Tucker. New York: Norton, 1978.

——. *From the Afterword to the Second German Edition*. 1873. In *The Marx-Engels Reader*. 2nd ed. Edited by Robert C. Tucker. New York: Norton, 1978.

——. *The German Ideology*. 1845. In *The Marx-Engels Reader*. 2nd ed. Edited by Robert C. Tucker. New York: Norton, 1978.

————. *The Grundrisse [Foundations of the Critique of Political Economy]*. 1857. In *The Marx-Engels Reader*. 2nd ed. Edited by Robert C. Tucker. New York: Norton, 1978.

————. *On the Jewish Question*. 1843. In *The Marx-Engels Reader*. 2nd ed. Edited by Robert C. Tucker. New York: Norton, 1978.

————. *Preface to A Contribution to the Critique of Political Economy*. 1859. In *The Marx-Engels Reader*. 2nd ed. Edited by Robert C. Tucker. New York: Norton, 1978.

Marx, Karl, and Friedrich Engels. *The Marx-Engels Reader*. 2nd ed. Edited by Robert C. Tucker. New York: Norton, 1978.

————. *Studienausgabe*. Edited by Iring Fetscher. 5 vols. Berlin: Aufbau, 2004. Online German texts available at MLwerke, "Stimmen der proletarischen Revolution." <http://www.mlwerke.de/me/default.htm>.

Marx, Karl, with Friedrich Engels. *Manifesto of the Communist Party*. 1848. In *The Marx-Engels Reader*. 2nd ed. Edited by Robert C. Tucker. New York: Norton, 1978.

Mayer, J.P. *Alexis de Tocqueville*. Gloucester, UK: Peter Smith, 1966.

McKillop, A.B. "Who Killed Canadian History? A View From the Trenches." *Canadian Historical Review* 80, no. 2 (June 1999).

McLellan, David. *Karl Marx: His Life and Thought*. London: Macmillan, 1973.

McRae, Kenneth D. "Ramist Tendencies in the Thought of Jean Bodin." *Journal of the History of Ideas* 16 (1955): 306-23.

Miller, Perry. *The New England Mind*. 2 vols. Cambridge: Harvard University Press, 1962.

Montesquieu. *Considerations on the Causes of the Greatness of the Romans and their Decline*. Translated by David Lowenthal. Indianapolis: Hackett, 1965.

————. *Considérations sur les causes de la grandeur des Romains et de leur décadence*. 1721. Online edition, Université du Québec à Laval, "Les Classiques des Sciences Sociales," n.d. <http://classiques.uqac.ca/classiques/montesquieu/montesquieu.html>.

————. *De l'esprit des lois*. 1748. In *Oeuvres Complètes*, vol. 2. Paris: Gallimard, 1958.

————. *Lettres Persanes [Persian Letters]*. 1748. In *Oeuvres Complètes*, vol. 2. Paris: Gallimard, 1958.

————. *Pensées*. In *Œuvres Complètes*, vol. 2. Paris: Nagel, 1950.

————. *Persian Letters*. 1721. Translated by C.J. Betts. London: Penguin, 2004.

————. *The Spirit of Laws by Montesquieu*. Translated by Thomas Nugent. London: Nourse, 1750; reprint, Berkeley: University of California Press, 1977.

————. *The Spirit of the Laws*. 1748. Edited by Anne Cohler, Basia Miller, and Harold Stone. Cambridge: Cambridge University Press, 2005.

Monumenta Germaniae Historica. Electronic access at <http://www.dmgh.de>.

Mouffe, Chantal. "Democratic Politics Today." In *Dimensions of Radical Democracy*. Edited by Chantal Mouffe, 1-14. London: Verso, 1992.

Munn, Mark. *The School of History: Athens in the Age of Socrates*. Berkeley: University of California Press, 2000.

Nederman, Cary J. *Community and Consent: The Secular Political Theory of Marsiglio Padua's "Defensor Pacis."* Lanham, MD: Rowman & Littlefield, 1995.

Nelson, Brian R. *Western Political Thought*. Englewood Cliffs, CA: Prentice Hall, 1982.

Nietzsche, Friedrich. *The Anti-Christ*. 1888. In Nietzsche, *The Anti-Christ, Ecce Homo, Twilight of the Idols, and Other Writings*. Edited by Aaron Ridley. Translated by Judith Norman. Cambridge: Cambridge University Press, 2005.

———. *The Anti-Christ, Ecce Homo, Twilight of the Idols, and Other Writings*. Edited by Aaron Ridley. Translated by Judith Norman. Cambridge: Cambridge University Press, 2005.

———. *Beyond Good and Evil*. Translated by Walter Kaufmann. New York: Vintage, 1966.

———. *The Birth of Tragedy*. 1872. In *Basic Writings of Nietzsche*. Edited and translated by Walter Kaufmann. New York: Modern Library, 2000.

———. *The Gay Science*. 1882. Translated by Walter Kaufmann. New York: Vintage, 1974.

———. *Human, All Too Human*. Translated by R.J. Hollingdale. Introduction by Richard Schacht. Cambridge: Cambridge University Press, 1986.

———. *Kritische Studienausgabe*. Edited by Giorgio Colli and Mazzino Montinari. 15 vols. Munich: Deutscher Taschenbuch Verlag, 1999. Online German texts available at Project Gutenberg. <http://gutenberg.spiegel.de/autoren/ nietzsch.htm>.

———. *On the Genealogy of Morals*. 1887. In *Basic Writings of Nietzsche*. Edited and translated by Walter Kaufmann. New York: Modern Library, 2000.

———. *Thus Spoke Zarathustra*. 1885. Translated by Walter Kaufmann. New York: Modern Library, 1995.

———. *Twilight of the Idols*. In Nietzsche, *The Anti-Christ, Ecce Homo, Twilight of the Idols, and Other Writings*. Cambridge: Cambridge University Press, 2005.

———. *The Will to Power*. 1901. Edited by Walter Kaufmann. Translated by Walter Kaufmann and R.J. Hollingdale. New York: Vintage, 1968.

Nisbet, Robert. *The Social Philosophers: Community and Conflict in Western Political Thought*. New York: Thomas Y. Crowell, 1973; reprint, New York: Washington Square Press, 1983.

O'Brien, Connor Cruise. "Introduction" to *Reflections on the Revolution in France*, by Edmund Burke. London: Penguin, 1986.

Ostwald, Martin. "Introduction" to *Nicomachean Ethics*, by Aristotle. Translated by Martin Ostwald. Indianapolis: Bobbs-Merrill, 1962.

Perkins Gilman, Charlotte. *Women & Economics*. New York: Harper & Row, 1966.

Piroli, Maurizio. *Niccolò's Smile*. New York: Hill and Wang, 2002.

Pitkin, Hanna F. *Fortune is a Woman: Gender and Politics in the Thought of Niccolo Machiavelli*. Chicago: University of Chicago Press, 1999.

Pius XI. "Quadragesimo Anno" [Encyclical Letter of His Holiness Pope Pius XI on Social Reconstruction]. 1931. In *Paepstliche Vertautbarungen zu Staat und Gesellschaft*. Edited by Helmut Schnatz. Darmstadt, Germany: Wissenschaftliche Buchgesellschaft, 1973.

Pizan, Christine de. *The Book of the Body Politic*. Cambridge: University of Cambridge Press, 1994.

Plato. *Gorgias*. Translated by Donald J. Zeyl. In *Plato: Complete Works*. Edited by John

M. Cooper. Indianapolis: Hackett, 1997.

———. *Laws*. Translated by Trevor Saunders. In *Plato: Complete Works*. Edited by John M. Cooper. Indianapolis: Hackett, 1997. *

———. *Plato: Complete Works*. Edited with an introduction by John M. Cooper. Indianapolis: Hackett, 1997.

———. *Politeia* [*The Republic*]. Translated by G.M.A. Grube. Revised by C.D.C. Reeve. In *Plato: Complete Works*. Edited by John M. Cooper. Indianapolis: Hackett, 1997.

———. *Politikos* [*Statesman*]. Translated by C.J. Rowe. In *Plato: Complete Works*. Edited by John M. Cooper. Indianapolis: Hackett, 1997.

———. *Protagoras*. Translated by Stanley Lombardo and Karen Bell. In *Plato: Complete Works*. Edited by John M. Cooper. Indianapolis: Hackett, 1997.

———. *The Republic*. Translated by Desmond Lee. London: Penguin, 1987.

———. *The Republic of Plato*. 2nd ed. Translated by Allan Bloom. New York: Basic Books, 1991.

———. *Seventh Letter*. Translated by Glenn R. Morrow. In *Plato: Complete Works*. Edited by John M. Cooper. Indianapolis: Hackett, 1997.

———. *Symposium*. Translated by Alexander Nehamas and Paul Woodruff. In *Plato: Complete Works*. Edited by John M. Cooper. Indianapolis: Hackett, 1997.

Polanyi, Karl. *The Great Transformation: The Political and Economic Origins of Our Times*. 1944; reprint, Boston: Beacon Press, 1957.

Putnam, Robert D. *Making Democracy Work: Civic Traditions in Modern Italy*. Princeton: Princeton University Press, 1993.

Quaritsch, Helmut. *Staat und Souveränität*. Frankfurt: Athenäum, 1970.

Radzinowicz, Leon. *A History of English Criminal Law*, vol. 1. London: Stevens & Sons, 1948.

Rawls, John. *A Theory of Justice*. Cambridge: Harvard University Press, 1971.

Riklin, Alois. *Machtteilung*. Darmstadt: Wissenschaftliche Buchgesellschaft, 2006.

Robinson, Jancis. *The Oxford Companion to Wine*. Oxford: Oxford University Press, 1999.

Rosenberg, Justin. *The Follies of Globalisation Theory*. London: Verso, 2002.

Rousseau, Jean-Jacques. *Discours sur l'économie politique*. French text available at <http://www.ac-nice.fr/philo/textes/Rousseau-Emile.htm>.

———. *Discours sur les sciences et les arts*. In Rousseau, *Discours sur l'origine et les fondements de l'inégalité parmi les hommes, Discours sur les sciences et les arts*. Paris: Flammarion, 1962.

———. *Discours sur l'origine et les fondements de l'inégalité parmi les hommes*. In Rousseau, *Discours sur l'origine et les fondements de l'inégalité parmi les hommes, Discours sur les sciences et les arts*. Paris: Flammarion, 1962.

———. *Discours sur l'origine et les fondements de l'inégalité parmi les hommes, Discours sur les sciences et les arts*. Paris: Flammarion, 1962.

———. "A Discourse on Political Economy." In *The Social Contract and Discourses*. Translated by G.D.H. Cole. Revised by J.H. Brumfitt and John C. Hall. London: Fitzhenry & Whiteside, 1986.

————. *A Discourse on the Arts and Sciences*. 1750. In *The Social Contract and Discourses*. Translated by G.D.H. Cole. Revised by J.H. Brumfitt and John C. Hall. London: Fitzhenry & Whiteside, 1986.

————. *A Discourse on the Origin of Inequality*. 1755. In *The Social Contract and Discourses*. Translated by G.D.H. Cole. Revised by J.H. Brumfitt and John C. Hall. London: Fitzhenry & Whiteside, 1986.

————. *Du contrat social ou Principes du droit politique* [*Social Contract*]. 1762. Strasbourg: F.G. Levrault, IVe année de la République, 1796.

————. *Émile*. 1762. Online French edition, Columbia University, n.d. <http://projects.ilt. columbia.edu/pedagogies/rousseau/>.

————. *Émile: Or Treatise on Education*. Translated by William H. Payne. Amherst, NY: Prometheus, 2003.

————. *The Social Contract*. Translated by Maurice Cranston. London: Penguin, 1968.

Rubinstein, Nicolai. *The Government of Florence Under the Medici, 1434-1494*. Oxford: Oxford University Press, 1966.

Rutherford, Samuel. *Lex, Rex*. 1644. Harrisonburg, VA: Sprinkle Publications, 1982. Online edition, Constitution Society, edited by Jon Roland, 2002. <http://www.constitution. org/sr/lexrex.htm>.

Sabine, George. *A History of Political Theory*. 4th ed. Revised by Thomas L. Thorson. Hinsdale, IL: Dryden Press, 1973.

Safranski, Rüdiger. *Nietzsche*. Munich: Hanser, 2000.

————. *Schopenhauer und die wilden Jahre der Philosophie*. Frankfurt: Fischer, 2001.

Schmidt, Manfred G. *Demokratietheorien*. Opladen: Leske + Budrich, 1997.

Scholz, Richard. "Einleitung" to *Defensor Pacis*, vol. 1, by Marsilius von Padua. Hannover: Hahnsche Buchhandlung, 1932.

Schopenhauer, Arthur. *The World as Will and Idea*, vol. 1. 1819. Edited by R.B. Haldane and John Kemp. London: Routledge and Kegan Paul, 1957.

Shackleton, Robert. *Montesquieu: A Critical Biography*. Oxford: Oxford University Press, 1961.

Shakespeare, William. *Julius Caesar*. Oxford: Clarendon Press, 1984.

Shelley, Percy Bysshe. *The Mask of Anarchy*. 1819. Available at <http://www.online-literature. com/view.php/complete-works-of-shelley/9?term=masque>.

Shklar, Judith N. *Montesquieu*. Oxford: Oxford University Press, 1987.

Sigmund, Paul E., ed. *The Selected Political Writings of John Locke*. With an introduction and interpretations by Paul E. Sigmund. New York: Norton, 2005.

Sim, Stuart, ed. *The Icon Critical Dictionary of Postmodern Thought*. Cambridge, UK: Icon Books, 1998.

Skinner, Quentin. "Hobbes on Representation." *European Journal of Philosophy* 13, no. 2 (2005): 155-84.

————. *Machiavelli: A Very Short Introduction*. Oxford: Oxford University Press, 2000.

Spender, Dale. *Women of Ideas and What Men Have Done to Them: From Aphra Behn to Adrienne Rich*. Melbourne: Ark, 1983.

Stoothoff, Robert. "Translator's Preface" to *The Passions of the Soul*, by René Descartes. In *The Philosophical Writings of Descartes*, vol. 1. Edited and translated by John Cottingham, Robert Stoothoff, and Dugald Murdoch. Cambridge: Cambridge University Press, 1985.

Supreme Court, United States of America. *Schenck v. U.S.* 249 U.S. 47 (1919).

Thiele, Leslie P. *Thinking Politics: Perspectives in Ancient, Modern, and Postmodern Political Theory*. 2nd ed. New York: Chatham House, 2003.

Thomas Aquinas, see Aquinas, Thomas.

Thucydides. *The Peloponnesian War*. In *The Complete Writings of Thucydides*. Translated by Richard Crawley. New York: Modern Library, 1934.

Tilly, Charles. *Durable Inequality*. Berkeley: University of California Press, 1998.

———. "Western State-Making and Theories of Political Transformation." In *The Formation of National States in Western Europe*. Edited by Charles Tilly, 601-38. Princeton: Princeton University Press, 1975.

Tilly, Charles, ed. *The Formation of National States in Western Europe*. Princeton: Princeton University Press, 1975.

Tocqueville, Alexis de. *L'Ancien Régime et la Révolution*. 1856. Paris: Gallimard, 1952. Online edition, Université du Québec à Laval, Les Classiques des Sciences Sociales, n.d. <http://classiques.uqac.ca/classiques/montesquieu/montesquieu.html>.

———. *De la démocratie en Amérique*. 1840. 2 vols. Paris: Gallimard, 1961.

———. *Democracy in America*. 1840. Edited and translated by Harvey C. Mansfield and Delba Winthrop. Chicago: University of Chicago Press, 2000.

———. *Democracy in America and Two Essays on America*. Translated by Gerald E. Bevan. London: Penguin, 2003.

———. *Œuvres Complètes*, Tome III, *Écrits et discours politiques*. Paris: Gallimard, 1985.

———. *Œuvres et correspondance inédites*. Edited by Gustave de Beaumont. Paris: Michel Lévy Frères, 1861.

———. *The Old Régime and the French Revolution*. 1856. Translated by Stuart Gilbert. Garden City, NY: Doubleday, 1955.

———. *The Old Regime and the Revolution*. 1856. Translated by Alan S. Kahan. Chicago: University of Chicago Press, 1998.

———. *Selected Letters on Politics and Society*. Berkeley: University of California Press, 1985.

Trager, James. *The Women's Chronology: A Year-By-Year Record from Prehistory to the Present*. New York: Henry Holt, 1994.

Trudeau, Pierre E. *Federalism and the French Canadians*. Toronto: Macmillan of Canada, 1968.

Tuck, Richard. "Introduction" to *Leviathan*, by Thomas Hobbes. Edited by Richard Tuck. Cambridge: Cambridge University Press, 1992.

Tully, James. *A Discourse on Property: John Locke and his Adversaries*. Cambridge: Cambridge University Press, 1980.

————. "Locke." In *The Cambridge History of Political Thought, 1450-1700*. Edited by J.H. Burns, 616-52. Cambridge: Cambridge University Press, 1991.

Valentin, Veit. *Knaurs Weltgeschichte*. Munich: Droemersche Verlagsanstalt, 1959.

Vico, Giambattista. *The New Science of Giambattista Vico*. 1744. Translated by Thomas Bergin and Max Fisch. Ithaca: Cornell University Press, 1984.

————. *On the Most Ancient Wisdom of the Italians*. 1710. Translated by L.M. Palmer. Ithaca: Cornell University Press, 1988.

————. *On the Study Methods of Our Time*. 1709. Translated by Elio Gianturco. Ithaca: Cornell University Press, 1990.

————. *Opere di Giambattista Vico*. 2 vols. Naples: Fulvio Rossi, 1972.

Viroli, Maurizio. *Niccolò's Smile: A Biography of Machiavelli*. Translated by Antony Shugaar. New York: Farrar, Straus and Giroux, 2000; reprint, New York: Hill and Wang, 2002.

Walker, R.B.J. *Inside/Outside: International Relations as Political Theory*. Cambridge: Cambridge University Press, 1993.

Weber Max. *The Protestant Ethic and the Spirit of Capitalism*. London: George Allen & Unwin, 1930.

Wheen, Francis. *Karl Marx: A Life*. New York: Norton, 2000.

White, Stephen K. *Political Theory and Postmodernism*. Cambridge: Cambridge University Press, 1994.

Williams, Bernard. "Introductory Essay" to *Meditations on First Philosophy*, by René Descartes. Edited and translated by John Cottingham. Cambridge: Cambridge University Press, 2005.

Williams, Melissa. "Toleration, Canadian-Style: Reflections of a Yankee-Canadian." In *Canadian Political Philosophy*. Edited by Ronald Beiner and Wayne Norman. Don Mills: Oxford University Press, 2001.

Wolin, Sheldon S. "Calvin and the Reformation: The Political Education of Protestantism." *American Political Science Review* 51 (1957): 435-53.

————. *Politics and Vision: Continuity and Innovation in Western Political Thought*. Princeton: Princeton University Press, 2004.

Wollstonecraft, Mary. *A Vindication of the Rights of Men*. In Wollstonecraft, *The Vindications*. Edited by D.L. Macdonald and Kathleen Scherf. Peterborough: Broadview Press, 1997.

————. *A Vindication of the Rights of Woman*. Edited by Miriam Brody. London: Penguin, 1992.

————. *A Vindication of the Rights of Woman*. In Wollstonecraft, *The Vindications*. Edited by D.L. Macdonald and Kathleen Scherf. Peterborough: Broadview Press, 1997.

————. *The Vindications*. Edited by D.L. Macdonald and Kathleen Scherf. Peterborough: Broadview Press, 1997.

————. *The Works of Mary Wollstonecraft*. Edited by Janet Todd and Marilyn Butler. 7 vols. New York: New York University Press, 1989.

Young, Iris Marion. *Justice and the Politics of Difference*. Princeton: Princeton University Press, 1990.

Index

absolute power, 45, 101-02, 135
absolute sovereignty, 95, 101, 106, 115-16
Montesquieu's opposition to, 133, 140
absolute truth, 1-3, 22, 27, 37
absolutism, 4, 97, 114, 123
abstract knowledge. *See* knowledge
abstract reason, 5, 24-28
Adams, John, 131
age of men, 26
Age of Reason, 28
age of the gods, 26
Albertus Magnus (Albert the Great), 51-52
Alexander the Great, 38
alienation, 222-23, 227
Althusius, Johannes, 4-5, 9-10, 13-14, 116, 140, 144, 154, 174, 179
chief administrative officer, 105
common will, 107
definition of sovereignty, 106-07, 109-10, 113
Dicaeologica libris tres, 106
ephors, 112
federal (or confederal) political system, 111-12, 114
law of consociation and symbiosis, 110
Politica Methodice Digesta, 103-05, 109, 115, 139
political science as separate discipline, 105
political theory, 108-09, 112-14, 125
private/public separation, 197

on the right of resistance, 106
on source of government authority, 110
Amato, Giuliano, 116
American Civil War, 164
American democracy
crass commercialism, 172, 204
"equality of social conditions," 160
extreme forms of spiritualism, 172, 204
American exceptionalism, 160, 172
American Federalists, 91, 136, 139, 145, 156, 165
American political system, 162-64, 172
American Revolution, 127, 145, 147, 184, 189
amour-propre, 151, 154
Analytical Review, The, 189
Anti-Christ, The (Nietzsche), 207
anti-Semitism. *See* Jews; race and racism
antipopes, 58, 61
Arendt, Hanna, 56
aristocracy, 30, 36, 41-42, 63, 65, 134. *See also* nobles; oligarchy; rule of few
Aristotelian-Christian synthesis, 57, 69-70
Aristotelian ideas, 169
Aristotelian logic, 52
Aristotelian method of inquiry, 17, 20, 41, 63
rejected by Descartes, 19-20
Aristotelian separation of public and private, 198
Aristotle, 5, 10, 13, 37, 43, 53-54, 56, 68, 84, 88, 144

analytical scientist, 38
comparison of regimes, 41-42
Constitution of Athens, 38
criticism of Plato, 42
definition of citizenship, 40-41, 43
Eudemian Ethics, 39
faith in collective practical wisdom, 44, 99
Hobbes's criticism of, 16
on justice, 40-41
Latin translations, 9, 51
man as political animal (*zoon politikon*), 39, 56, 62, 108
Marsilius's adaptation of, 61
on middle class, 85, 127
mixed polity, 41-42
Nicomachean Ethics, 39-41
Pierre de la Ramée's criticism, 16
political economic perspective, 42
political thought, 39-41
Politics, 39-41, 45, 60, 67
rediscovery, 47, 49-51
on rich *vs.* poor, 79
separation of legislative and ordinary business, 40, 63-64
sociological and political realism, 45
sociology, 41
Topics, 17
on universal suffrage, 166
Ashby v. White, 126
Astell, Mary, 182-83
Athenian democracy. *See* Greek democracy
Athens, 29-31, 35, 43

283

Augsburg Religious Peace
  Treaty, 94, 106
Augustine, St., 49
  City of God, The, 46
Augustinian sense of order,
  54
Aurich, 106
autarkeia, 62
Averroes (Ibn Rushd), 51-52

Bacon, Francis, 22-23, 96
balance of power, 164
balie, 78
Bastien and Bastienne
  (Mozart), 150
Behemoth (Hobbes), 98
Berth, Edouard, 204
Beyond Good and Evil
  (Nietzsche), 207
Bible, 104
Birth of Tragedy, The
  (Nietzsche), 207-08
Birth of Venus, The
  (Botticelli), 84
blacks, 165, 170
Bodin, Jean, 95, 97, 110
Boniface VIII, pope, 58
Botticelli, Sandro, *Birth of*
  Venus, The, 84
Brunelleschi's dome, 74, 83
Bruno, Giordano, 16, 22, 97
Büchner, Georg, 205
Burke, Edmund, 6, 13-14,
  53-54
  civil society as "fixed
    compact," 186
  closed class system, 187
  conservatism, 188, 199
  contribution to history
    of political thought,
    198
  Member of Parliament,
    184-85
  member of Whig Party,
    184
  Philosophical Enquiry,
    184, 191
  practical wisdom, 185
  prejudice, 185
  preservation of property,
    186-88
  prudence, 185
  Reflections on the
    Revolution in France,
    177, 184-85, 189
  scholarship, 185

speeches on "American
  Taxation," 184
Wollstonecraft's criti-
  cism, 190-93, 199

Calvin, John, 155
Calvinism, 94, 106, 150
  political Calvinism, 104,
    139
  right of resistance against
    rulers, 104, 106
Calvinist political theory,
  124-25. *See also*
  Althusius, Johannes;
  Locke, John
Capital (Marx), 221
capital punishment, 121,
  129-30, 142
capitalism, 172, 221, 230
  expanded use of machin-
    ery, 224
  isolation from political
    accountability, 115
  overproduction/under-
    consumption theory,
    224
  social legislation and,
    223
capitalist exploitation, 221-
  22
Cartesian principles, 149.
  See also Descartes, René
Case of Wagner, The
  (Nietzsche), 207
Catholicism, 123, 150. *See*
  also popes
  papacy, 58, 60, 66, 70,
    131
Cavendish, William, 96
centralization, 148, 159
  decentralization, 164
  "division of classes," 149
  Tocqueville on, 163
Charlemagne, 50
Charles I, king of England,
  95-96, 119
Charles II, king of England,
  96-97, 120, 123
Charles V, emp., 94
Charles VIII, king of
  France, 78
Charles X, king of France,
  157
checks and balances, 84,
  89, 136, 145, 165
Chianti Classico Niccolò

Machiavelli (wine), 75
Chinese Communist Party,
  155
Chomsky, Noam, 91
Christian, Count Rudolf,
  106
Christian religion, 209. *See*
  also Catholicism;
  Protestantism
Christina, queen of
  Sweden, 18, 20
church and state, 60. *See*
  also religious wars
church as intermediator,
  16. *See also* Catholicism
Church of England, 61, 69-
  70, 95
Ciompi-riot, 65, 86-87, 90
cities, 49, 111. *See also* individual cities
city-states, 29
  as third estate, 68
Citizen (Hobbes), 97
citizenship, 29, 33, 45, 61,
  65-69, 167. *See also*
  democracy; franchise
  Aristotle's definition, 40-
    41, 43
  inclusion of common
    multitude, 66
  Machiavelli on, 89
  Marsilius on, 65, 68
  qualification, 147, 165
    (*See also* property)
City of God, The
  (Augustine), 46
civic virtue, 90
  or "active citizenship," 89
  republican, 86
  teachability, 33
civil society, 124, 159, 185,
  204. *See also* public-private separation
  "fixed compact," 186
  transnational forces and, 2
class, 67, 84, 96, 121, 126,
  148-49, 226. *See also*
  inequality; Übermensch
  closed class system, 187
  English ruling class, 137
  "honourable class," 65, 67
  interests, 135
  justice, 141
  labouring classes, 44, 122,
    158, 172, 223, 225
  lower social classes, 169

mass class, 65, 67
middle class (See middle
  class)
new bourgeois class of
  monied men, 119
political classes, 29
propertied classes, 230
  (See also property)
separation of classes, 35
class struggle, 27, 73-74,
  218, 221
  liberty and, 85-86
classical canon, 1, 3-4, 15,
  177
  in globalizing world, 2
  historical context, 6-7
  translations, 7-9
classification of regimes.
  See regime types
Cleisthenes, 29-30
Clemens V, pope, 58
Clinton, Hillary, It Takes a
  Village, 171
"cogito, ergo sum," 18
collective decision making,
  46
collective effort, 231
collective practical wisdom,
  5, 44, 99, 169-70
commodification of labour,
  222-23, 229
common good, 128, 211
common law (lex commu-
  nis), 110
common sense through his-
  torical learning, 16, 23,
  25, 28, 71. See also collective practical wisdom;
  historical learning
commonwealth construction,
  105
  covenant for, 113
communism, 28
communist internationalism,
  2, 227
Communist Manifesto
  (Marx), 85, 204, 217-19,
  223, 225-26
communitarian group iden-
  tity, 71
Condition of the Working
  Class in England
  (Engels), 206
confederal federalism, 116,
  139
consensus, 144

consent, 100, 113, 125, 187
conservatism, 13-14, 177,
  199
  Burke, 188, 199
  twenty-first century, 201
Considerations
  (Montesquieu), 131-33
consociations, 111
Constitution of Athens
  (Aristotle), 38
constitutional government,
  42-43
constitutional monarchy,
  120
constitutional order (Greek
  democracy), 29
constitutionalism, evolu-
  tionary, 199
Contrat social (Rousseau),
  107
Coole, Diana, 178
Cooper, Anthony Ashley.
  See Shaftesbury,
  Anthony Ashley Cooper,
  Earl of
Copernican system, 16
corporate elites
  reaction to Machiavelli,
  73, 87
corporate governance, 68, 70
corporate power, 114
corruption, 86, 88, 90
covenant, 105, 113
covenanted federalism
  Althusian origins of, 115
craft guilds, 65, 68, 86, 111
Cranston, Maurice, 152
Crick, Bernard, 89
crime and punishment, 121,
  129-30, 142
crimes against humanity, 93
Critias, 32
Cromwell, Oliver, 95-97, 120
Cromwell, Thomas, 61
cultural relativism, 133, 140
custom, 53-54

David (Michelangelo), 84
De antiquissima Italorum
  sapientia. See On the
  Most Ancient Wisdom
  of the Italians (Vico)
De Cive. See On the
  Citizen (Hobbes)
De nostri temporis studio-
  rum ratione. See On the

Study Methods of Our
  Time (Vico)
De Regimine Principium
  (Aquinas), 52-53
death penalty. See capital
  punishment
Declaration of the Rights
  of Man and of the
  Citizen, 3, 147, 179, 183
Defensor Minor
  (Marsilius), 59
Defensor Pacis (Marsilius),
  58-61, 64, 67-68, 70
Delors, Jacques, 116
democracy, 42, 44, 64-65,
  134, 160. See also
  majority rule; universal
  suffrage
  Aristotle's view of, 41
  direct democracy, 30,
    154, 161
  England's move towards,
    199
  France, 200
  Greek, 29-31, 37, 45
  "imagination"(immagi-
    nazione) of, 91
  Machiavelli on, 90
  manipulation of ignorant
    masses, 33-34, 167
  Marcilius on, 63
  means to an end, 30
  mediocre middle-class
    rule, 167
  Nietzsche and, 212-13
  Plato's critique of, 33,
    36-37
  plural interest group, 156
  political form of mass
    culture, 212
  "radical democracy,"
    227
  regime of collective wis-
    dom, 32
  representative govern-
    ment, 134, 161-62
  Rousseau on, 152
  Socrates's view of, 32
  Tocqueville's under-
    standing of, 161-62,
    165, 167, 173, 175
Democracy in America
  (Tocqueville), 157, 159,
  165, 173
  American exceptionalism,
    160, 172

cited by American presidents, 171
J.S. Mill's review of, 160
democratic equality
as most developed form of human condition, 171
social inequality and, 172
democratic majority rule. *See* majority rule
Descartes, René, 5
"clear and certain" knowledge, 25, 28
Discourse on the Method, 17-18, 21
faith in abstract reasoning, 25, 27-28
Meditations on First Philosophy, 19-20
method of inquiry, 18-22, 27-28
Passions of the Soul, 19
Principia philosophiae, 19, 22
rejection of classical core, 28
Rules for the Direction of the Mind, 18, 20
World, The, 18
despotism, 134, 142, 160. *See also* tyranny
Dicaeologica libris tres (Althusius), 106
Dickens, Charles, 129
dictatorship (in modern world), 90. *See also* princely rule; tyranny
Dijon Academy, 150-51
direct democracy, 30, 154, 161
Discourse on Political Economy (Rousseau), 155
Discourse on the Method (Descartes), 17-18
Discourse on the Sciences and Arts (Rousseau), 150
Discourses, The (Machiavelli), 13, 73-74, 76, 82
optimism, 91
on republican liberty, 89
superiority of republican over princely government, 84
divine law, 54-56, 61

Domville, William, 136
Du contrat social. See Social contract (Rousseau)
East India Company, 184, 186
Ecce Homo (Nietzsche), 207
Economic and Philosophic Manuscripts (Marx), 223
Économie politique. See Discourse on Political Economy (Rousseau)
education, 23, 38-39, 206
Aristotle's view of, 43
free public education for all children, 226
Plato on, 37
education of women, 181-82, 194-96
Rousseau's position on, 189
Wollstonecraft's views on, 189
educational methods. *See On the Study Methods of Our Time* (Vico)
eigentlich, 6
ekklesia, 29
Elazar, Daniel J., 115
Elements of Law (Hobbes), 97-98
Elizabeth, Princess of Bohemia, 20
Elizabeth I, Queen, 95
Emden, 105-06
church synod of, 113
Émile (Rousseau), 148, 194, 198
emperor. *See* rulers
empirical observation, 15-16, 22, 26, 122, 159
Engels, Friedrich, 216-17
Condition of the Working Class in England, 206
England, 119, 121, 130, 163
class, 148
English Civil War, 95, 97, 100, 114, 119
evolutionary constitutionalism, 199
Glorious Revolution, 22, 96, 120-21
inequality, 122
Interregnum, 120

liberal climate post-French Revolution, 189
Long Parliament, 119-20
"possessive individualism," 121
property/taxation, 119
Protectorate of Oliver Cromwell, 120
Reformation, 95
religious wars, 95-96
Rump Parliament, 95
England, Commonwealth of, 95
Enlightenment, 15, 22
Ephialtes, 30
ephors, 112, 139
episteme, 35, 44, 99
equality, 131, 146-47, 155, 159. *See also* inequality; social inequality
democratic, 171-72
formal, 230
of opportunity, 45
political equality, 160
Rousseau's understanding of, 147, 155
of social condition, 137, 160, 172
Tocqueville's view of, 160
universal equality, 211
as unstoppable, 160
Essay Concerning Human Understanding, An (Locke), 123
Ethica. See Nicomachean Ethics (Aristotle)
ethics, 23-24, 28, 39
in education system (*See On the Study Methods of Our Time* [Vico])
Eudemian Ethics (Aristotle), 39
European Constitution, 116
European Union, 113, 116
excessive social inequality, 89-90, 130
exchange value, 221
exploitation, 214, 221-22
factions, 87, 111, 156, 193
false consciousness, 201
families and clans, 111
"federal theology," 104
federalism, 6, 135, 137, 145, 165

American Federalists, 91,
136, 139, 145, 156, 165
confederal, 116, 139
covenanted, 115
as organized plurality, 3
feminism, 182, 190, 200.
See also women
Filmer, Robert, *Patriarcha*,
123
Florence, 74-76, 78
emergency governments
(*galie*), 88
*Florentine Histories. See
History of Florence*
(Machiavelli)
Florentine republicanism,
75-77
factiousness and instability, 78-79
reasons for failure, 84
scrutiny (*squittino*), 78
special governing coun-
cils (*balie*), 78
"Fordism," 225
*Formation of National
States in Western
Europe, The* (Tilly), 12
forms of government. *See*
regime types
fortune, 82
Four Books of Sentences
(Lombard), 55
framework legislation, 113,
116
France. *See also* French
Revolution
age of absolutism, 114
Calvinism, 94
centralization, 148-49,
159, 163
class barriers, 148
Fronde, 100
music, 149-50
political and social
unrest, 100
religious wars, 95
franchise, 126-27. *See also*
citizenship
universal suffrage, 165-67
women, 197
Frankenstein (Godwin),
190
Franklin, Benjamin, 189
Frederic II, Emperor (1194-
1250), 50
French Revolution, 3, 147,

153, 161, 173, 200, 203-
05
bourgeois revolution, 218
Burke's attacks on, 183-
86
Richard Price's defence
of, 189
right of property and,
158
women and, 183
Friedrich, Carl Joachim, 115
Fuseli, Henry, 189

"gallant" *vs.* "learned,"
149, 173
Galileo Galilei, 16, 20, 22,
97-98
Gay Science, The
(Nietzsche), 207
gender inequality, 177, 192-
93, 205
Genealogy of Morals
(Nietzsche), 207
*General Theory of
Employment, Interest
and Money* (Keynes), 225
general will, 151, 153-56,
168, 173, 200
collective expression of a
superior moral power,
154
equality and, 155
Geneva, 103, 107, 131, 148,
150, 154-55, 173
German Empire, 163
Germany
Thirty Years War, 94, 106
Gewirth, Alan, 59
Gierke, Otto von, 115
Gilman, Charlotte Perkins,
200
Gingrich, Newt, 171
globalization theories, 1-2,
47, 160
globalizing forces, 175, 224
Glorious Revolution, 22
bourgeois revolution, 120
protection of property
and, 121
victory of traditional
class interests, 96
God, 16, 60, 186, 204-05,
209, 227
Descartes's explanation,
19
universal knowledge, 25

God, Moses, and the tribes
of Israel, 104
Godwin, Mary
Wollstonecraft,
Frankenstein, 190
Godwin, William, 183
Memoirs, 189
good life, 39, 45, 62
Gorgias (Plato), 33
governance, 49, 64
beyond the state, 5
for the common good, 63
corporate, 68, 70
global society, 70-71
human mind as cause of,
61
inclusion of common
multitude, 66
medieval Europe, 50
mixed regime of divided
governance, 70
separation of legislative
and executive func-
tion, 69
vs. government, 2
government types. *See*
regime types
Gramsci, Antonio, 90-91
Great Depression, 224-25
"great Leviathan," 101. *See
also* absolute sovereignty
greed, 90, 100, 103, 143,
151, 209
as deadly sin, 129
Greek democracy, 29-31, 40,
45
active participation in
public affairs, 29, 37
based on utility, 30
direct public participa-
tion, 30
Gregory VII, pope, 58
Grotius, Hugo, 22-23
Grundrisse, The (Marx), 222
Guicciardini, Luigi, 65, 86
guilds. *See* craft guilds

Habeas Corpus
Amendment Act (1679),
101
Habermas, Jürgen, 22, 80,
110
Theorie und Praxis, 11
Hambacher Fest, 205
Hamilton, William Gerard,
185

Hanging, Not Punishment Enough, 121
Hastings, Warren, 186
Hegel, G.W.F., 203-04, 218
  Philosophy of Right, 205
Heine, Heinrich, 205, 217
heliaia, 29
Henry IV, emperor of Germany, 58
Henry VIII, king of England, 61, 95
"herd instinct," 212
heroic age, 26
Hickes, George, 122
"higher human beings" (*die höhren Menschen*), 212
Hill, Christopher, 120
historical learning, 5-7, 16, 23, 25-28, 71
  Hobbes's rejection of, 102
historical or practical reasoning "getting along," 15
history as history of class struggle, 218, 221
History of Florence (Machiavelli), 65, 75-77
History of Political Theory, A (Sabine), 4
Hobbes, Thomas, 3-5, 13-14, 27, 69, 82-83, 93, 110-11, 114, 145, 154, 192, 198
  absolute sovereignty, 4, 101, 115-16, 228
  Behemoth, 98
  On the Citizen, 16, 96-98
  contract of state, 101
  criticism, 151
  Elements of Law, 97-98
  Leviathan, 16, 27, 96-99, 151
  on mixed government, 169
  monarchism, 97
  pessimistic view of human nature, 98, 100-01
  renunciation of Aristotelian heritage, 91, 97, 99, 101, 115
  scientific conversion, 98
  on social conflict, 99-100
  on sovereignty, 103
  turncoat theory, 97
Hohe Schule, Herborne, 104

"Holland, Germany, and the Swiss leagues," 137, 139
Holt, Chief Justice, 126
Holy Roman Empire, 139
House of Lords, 188
Huguenots, 95, 103
Human, All Too Human (Nietzsche), 207
human law, 55, 61
human nature, 89, 98
  Althusius's view of, 108
  Hobbes's understanding of, 98, 100-01 (*See also* state of nature)
  Machiavelli's views of, 86, 91
  man as microcosm, 16-17, 97
  man as political being (*zoon politikon*), 39, 56, 62, 108
  Rousseau's view of, 151
  ultimate human goal, 213
human rights, 177, 185
humanism, 141

Ibn Rushd, known as Averroes, 51
Imlay, Gilbert, 189-90
Imperial Diet at Worms, 94
imperialism, 214
India, 184, 186
individual citizenship, 68-69
individual human ingenuity, 93
individual (vernacular) Christian conscience, 94
individualism, 71, 99, 121, 125
  liberal, 126
  Whiggish, 124
Industrial Revolution, 204, 221
industrialization, 119
inequality, 151, 214. *See also* equality
  class structures and, 230
  "durable inequality," 45-46
  England, 121-22, 130
  Locke's justification for, 127-28
  moral issue, 230
  politics of, 191
  Rousseau on, 152

social, 87, 90, 126-28, 143, 172, 177, 192, 201, 218
  vs. equality of citizenship, 45
Inquisition, 16, 22, 93
Ireland, 184-85
Ireton, Henry, 121, 130
iron law of supply and demand, 99
Istorie Fiorentine. See History of Florence (Machiavelli)
It Takes a Village (Clinton), 171
Italian fascism, 90
Italian Renaissance, 74, 83

Jacobin terror, 153, 199
James II, king of England, 120, 123
Jefferson, Thomas, 131, 184
Jews, 214-15
Johan the Elder, Count of Nassau-Dillenburg, 104
Johnson, Joseph, 189
Joyce, James, 25
judiciary, 135, 138, 141-42
juris communio, 110
jury-courts, 30, 40
justice, 33, 40-41, 63, 141
  most important virtue, 35
  social justice, 90, 141

Kant, Immanuel, 31
Keynes, John Maynard, *General Theory of Employment, Interest and Money*, 225
Keynesian welfare state, 225
knowledge, 33, 40. *See also* historical learning
  abstract, 44
  clear and certain, 25, 28
  individual master thinker, 21
  universal, 25
  Vico's views on, 25
Korsch, Karl, 217

labour. *See also* workers
  commodification of, 222-23, 229
  wage labour, 127
labouring classes, 44, 158, 172, 230

Laski, Harold, 95
law, 35-37, 41, 64, 66, 68, 122, 135. *See also Spirit of the Laws* (Montesquieu)
  appropriate for a monarchy, 134
  common law, 110
  depositories, 134
  divine law, 61
  eternal and natural, 55
  global, 71
  highest law of the land (Althusius), 113
  human law, 61
  "institution of magistracy," 152
  "lawgiver," 155
  legislator/ruler distinction, 66
  mutability, 54
  primary human legislator, 64
  Roman, 50
  rule of, 30, 36, 101, 124
  source of, 64, 85, 124, 155
  specific law, 110
  "supreme" art of, 40
  Thomas on, 54-55, 57
Law and the Prince, The (Rutherford), 103
Laws. See Nomoi (Plato)
legislation. *See* law
leisure, 44, 46, 65, 67, 166
Leo III, pope, 50
Leo XIII, pope, 52
Letters (Plato), 33
Lettres persanes. See Persian Letters (Montesquieu)
Leviathan (Hobbes), 16, 27, 96-99, 151
Lex, Rex. See Law and the Prince, The (Rutherford)
lex consociationis & symbiosis, 110
liberalism, 2, 9, 11, 45, 102, 148
  American, 172
  fear of mass culture, 212
  liberal state, 230
  Rawlsian liberalism, 12
  separation of political state and society, 115
  undermining of will to power, 213

liberty, 90, 130, 133, 135-36, 140, 142
  categorical rights and obligations, 145
  equality and, 137, 146, 159
  harsh penal systems and, 142
  negative, 143
  republican political, 138
  result of class struggle, 85-86, 99
  as security of property, 192
  social justice and, 90, 141
Lindblom, Charles, 114
Lipietz, Alain, 225
Livius, Titus (Livy), 83-84, 88
Locke, John, 1, 3-4, 10, 13-14, 44, 145, 154, 180, 192
  An Essay Concerning Human Understanding, 122
  on Board of Trade and Plantations, 122-23, 129
  Calvinist background, 122-23
  common good, 127-28
  definition of political power, 121
  empiricism, 122
  Essay Concerning Human Understanding, An, 123
  on franchise reform, 127
  influence on British parliamentary tradition, 125
  liberal individualism, 6, 125-26, 129
  popular sovereignty, 126, 144
  representative government, 126
  separation of legislative authority from executive power, 125, 135, 141
  state as night watchman, 143
  theorist of social inequality, 126-29, 230
  theory of property and

representation, 187
  trickle-down theory of economics, 128-29
  Two Treatises of Government, 123-24
logic, 52, 214
Lombard, Peter, *Four Books of Sentences*, 55
Louis-Philippe, king of the French, 157-58
Louis XIV, king of France, 132, 163
Louis XVI, king of France, 157
Louis XVII, king of France, 157
Ludwig of Bavaria, 58-59, 61
Luther, Martin, 55, 69, 94

M-C-M formula, 221, 224
Machiavelli, Niccolo, 6, 68, 79, 144, 157, 212
  anticipation of Marx, 85
  Aristotelian view, 91
  career as public servant, 75, 78
  on corruption and inequality, 90, 100
  critique of Medici rule, 78-79
  dialectical reasoning, 86, 89, 91
  Discourses, The, 13, 73-74, 76, 82-88, 91
  on excessive social inequality, 87
  on good and bad forms of government, 79, 84, 88, 90
  History of Florence, 65, 75-77
  on human condition, 86, 91
  on liberty and class struggle, 86, 90, 99
  Mandragola, 75
  misogyny, 179
  modernity, 86
  political theory, 84, 86, 88-90
  on popular *vs.* noble support, 79, 88
  on power and wealth, 230
  Prince, The, 5, 13, 69,

73, 76, 79-83, 85, 87-89
Principe, Il, 84
realpolitik, 81, 89, 91, 228
republican theory, 88, 90
Seven Books on the Art of War, 75
Macpherson, C.B., 98, 115, 121, 144
Political Theory of Possessive Individualism, 11
Madison, James, 131
Magna Charta, 99
majority, 30
majority rule, 68, 102, 113, 125, 143-44, 156, 173-74
attack on intelligence, 169
citizenship qualification and, 147
class divisions and, 170
unassailability, 169-70
"universal suffrage," 165
worst form of government except all others, 170
Malesherbes, Chrétien Guillaume de Lamoignon de, 148, 157
man as microcosm, 16-17, 97
man as political animal (*zoon politikon*), 39, 56, 62, 108
Mandragola (Machiavelli), 75
Mann, Thomas, *Reflections of an Unpolitical Man*, 115
market capitalism. *See* capitalism
Markievicz, Constance, 197
marriage
Nietzsche's view of, 212-13, 229
suspension of women's legal existence, 197
women's inroads into men's world and, 183
Marsilius of Padua, 3, 5, 9, 13, 57, 80, 85, 88, 144, 179
Aristotelian heritage, 59, 61-63, 65-66

attack on papacy, 58, 60, 66, 70
Defensor Minor, 59
Defensor Pacis, 58-61, 64, 67-68, 70
distinction between faith and reason, 61
on law, 61, 64, 66, 68
legislator/ruler distinction, 66
mixed regime of divided governance, 70
on Papal Index, 131
secular political theory, 59-61, 70
separation of legislative and executive function, 69
treatment of plurality, 59
well-tempered polity, 65, 68
Marx, Karl, 3, 5-6, 13, 28, 152, 201, 203, 206, 214
on alienation of workers, 222-23, 227
belief in collective effort, 231
belief in progress, 229
biography, 216
Capital, 221
Communist Manifesto, 85, 204, 217-19, 223, 225-26
contribution to history of political thought, 228
critique of bourgeois society and ideology, 217
critique of capitalism, 218, 221, 223-24, 229-30
Economic and Philosophic Manuscripts, 223
exile, 205
Grundrisse, The, 222
historical dialectics, 85
On the Jewish Question, 225
journalistic activities, 217
on potential of modernity, 215, 231
on profit, 222
on social inequality, 230

"standing Hegel on his feet," 215, 218
"universal interdependence of nations," 220
utopia of social harmony and freedom, 226
Marxism, 46
critical Marxists, 225
"post-Marxism without apologies," 227
Marxism-Leninism, 228
mass class, 66-67
mass society, 66-67, 170, 174
"master morality" (*Herren-Moral*), 211
master-servant relationship, 219
master-slave relationship, 152, 212
materialism, 204
Medici, Cosimo de', 74-77
Medici, House of, 75-76
bribery and political pressure, 78, 87 (*See also* corruption)
reaction to *Prince, The*, 76
Medici, Lorenzo de', 75-76
Medieval Christian Platonism, 46
Meditations on First Philosophy (Descartes), 19-20
Memoirs (Godwin), 189
Merian, Sbylla, 183
method of inquiry, 15-28
Althusius, 109
Aristotelian, 17, 19-20
Descartes, 18-22, 27-28
historical and sociological, 133
Hobbes, 97
Montesquieu, 133
Tocqueville, 159
Vico, 23-26, 28
Wollstonecraft's questions on, 191
Metternich, Klemmens von, 177
Michelangelo Buonarroti, *David*, 84
Middle Ages, 46-47, 50
overlapping plurality of rule, 50, 53-55
rivalry between pope and emperor, 49-50

middle class, 85, 90, 127, 167, 223
Aristotle's idea of, 43-44, 46
new class of women, 182, 200-01
Wollstonecraft's criticism, 191
Mill, John Stuart, 160, 212
Minor Defender. See Defensor Minor (Marsilius)
misogyny, 179, 229
mixed constitution, 147
mixed polity, 41, 53, 63, 68, 74, 84, 169
Aristotle's use of, 85
Marsilius's description, 70
pragmatic (reciprocal and proportional), 42
Thomas's acceptance of, 53-54, 56
Tocqueville's view of, 169
mixed republic
Hobbes's rejection of, 99
modernism
commitment to scientific certitude and progress, 21
modernists (17th C.), 17
modernity, 6, 86, 203, 211, 215, 219, 231
promise of, 200
monarchical absolutism, 123-24. *See also* rule of one; tyranny
monarchomachs, 95
monarchy, 96
constitutional, 120
hereditary *vs.* elective, 66
Hobbes's view of, 102
need for intermediate powers, 134
Thomas on, 53
Monde, Le. See World, The (Descartes)
money, 119, 128, 131. *See also* wealth
monism *vs.* pluralism, 13
Montesquieu, Charles de Secondat, baron de, 3, 6, 13-14, 28, 114, 130, 148, 168, 174, 179
American Federalists and, 136

checks and balances, 145
Considerations, 131-33
on crime and punishment, 121-22
cultural relativism, 133, 140
elected to French Academy, 131-32
on English party politics, 136
federalism, 135, 137-40, 145
forms of government, 134-35, 140
historical and sociological method of inquiry, 133
as judge, 132, 142
on judiciary, 142
on liberty, 135, 141, 145
"On the Constitution of England," 135
opposition to despotic government, 135, 140
Papal Index, 131
Persian Letters, 131-32
political liberty/social justice link, 141
political plurality and social diversity, 140, 144
on popular tumults, 133
redistribution policies, 143
separation of powers, 135, 141, 145
on small nations, 164
Spirit of the Laws, 8, 131, 133, 135-36, 138, 140, 142
"Thoughts," 131
moral certainty, 211
moral relativism, 228, 231
Mozart, Wolfgang Amadaeus, 149
Bastien und Bastienne, 150
multiculturalism, 12
music, 149-50

Napoléon III, 158
nation states. *See* state
national banks, 226
nationalism
Marx on, 220
Nietzsche's opposition to, 214

Native peoples, 170
crimes against, 93
universal suffrage and, 165
natural law, 122
Nazi ideology, 207-08, 215, 227-28
Nazi state, 115
necessity, 81-82
negroes. *See* blacks
New Science (Vico), 25-26, 133
new scientism, 133
New World, 93
New York Daily Tribune, 217
Newton, Isaac, 98
Nicomachean Ethics (Aristotle), 39-41
Nietzsche, Friedrich, 3-4, 6, 13, 28, 201, 204
Anti-Christ, The, 207
antipolitical, 208
Beyond Good and Evil, 207
beyond good-and-evil formula, 228
Birth of Tragedy, The, 207-08
Case of Wagner, The, 207
contempt for mass culture, 212, 227
criticism of modernity, 211
critique of Western civilization and Christian morality, 210
on democracy, 212-13
disciple of Hegel's idealism, 215
dismissal of parliamentary plurality, 213
Ecce Homo, 207
Gay Science, The, 207
Genealogy of Morals, 207
hierarchy of strong over weak, 213
Human, All Too Human, 207
iconic status, 227-28
idea of eternal recurrence, 210
idea of "mixed European race," 228

moral relativism, 228, 231
Nazi ideology and, 207-08, 215, 227-28
Nietzsche contra Wagner, 207
nihilism, 6, 28, 208, 229
opposition to idea of race, 228
opposition to nationalism, 228
opposition to socialism, 228
philosopher's philosopher, 208
relationship with Lou Salomé, 207
Thus Spoke Zarathustra, 207, 209, 215
Twilight of the Idols, 207
on ultimate human goal, 213
on universality, 211
views on women, 229
warrior-philosophers, 215
Will to Power, The, 207
Nietzsche contra Wagner (Nietzsche), 207
nihilism, 6, 28, 208, 229
Nisbet, Robert, *Social Philosophers, The*, 12
"noble" lie or falsehood, 34, 49
nobles, 82. *See also* aristocracy
as intermediate power, 134
out to dominate and oppress, 83
Nomoi (Plato), 33, 36, 89

"Ode of Joy" (Schiller), 200
Old Regime and the Revolution, The (Tocqueville), 158
oligarchy, 36, 41-42, 121. *See also* aristocracy; nobles; rule of few
On Kingship. See De Regimine Principium
On the Citizen (Hobbes), 16, 96, 98
"On the Constitution of England" (Montesquieu), 135

On the Jewish Question (Marx), 225
On the Most Ancient. Wisdom of the Italians (Vico), 24
On the Origin and Foundations of Inequality Among Men (Rousseau), 151
On the Study Methods of Our Time (Vico), 23
"overman." *See* Übermensch

Paine, William, 189
papacy. *See under* Catholicism
Papal Index, 131
Parliament, 95, 120, 126
British parliamentary tradition, 125
legislative control, 124
privileged upper class, 121
Parliamentarism, 213
particularism, 14
Passions of the Soul (Descartes), 19
Patriarcha (Filmer), 123
payment of public officials, 30
Peloponnesian War, 30-31, 38
Pensées. See "Thoughts" (Montesquieu)
Pergolesi, Giovanni Battista, *Serva Padrona, La*, 149
Pericles, 30, 33
Persian Letters (Montesquieu), 131-32
personal is political, 190, 198
personal liberty/social equality tension, 159
persuasion, 33
Philadelphia Convention, 139
philosopher, the. *See* Aristotle
philosopher-kings, 34-36, 41, 45, 56
Philosophical Enquiry into the Origin of Our Ideas of the Sublime and Beautiful (Burke), 184, 191

philosophy as a "gay science," 209
philosophy of knowledge (*episteme*), 35, 44, 99
Philosophy of Right (Hegel), 205
phronesis, 41, 44, 99
Pico della Mirandola, Giovanni, 75
Pitkin, Hanna, 179
Pius XI, pope, 112
Pizan, Christine de, 182-83
Plato, 3-8, 12-13, 23, 145, 152, 155
on democracy, 34, 44
on education, 195
Gorgias, 33
justice, 35
Letters, 33
Nomoi, 33, 36, 89
philosopher-kings, 34-36, 56
philosopher's philosopher, 44
Politeia, 33-34, 36, 41, 89
political thought, 33-37
Politikos, 33, 35-36
Protagoras, 33, 35
science of truth, 44
Seventh Letter, 32
Symposium, 195
Plato's Academy, 32
Plato's noble lie, 34, 49
plural interest group democracy, 156
plurality, 1-3, 11, 44, 88, 91, 108, 116
Althius's theory of, 108-09, 125
and decentralization, 14
Marsilius of Padua's treatment, 59
organized, 111
and particularity, 14
political, 140
of rule, 111
social, 66
Pocock, J.G.A., 6
Polanyi, Karl, 203
polis, 29, 38-39, 41
Politeia (Plato), 33-34, 36, 41, 89
Politica Methodice Digesta (Althusius), 103-04, 115, 139

political Calvinism, 104, 139
political corruption. *See*
    corruption
political culture, 159
"political fixity," 12-13
"political insight," 41
political leadership (princes).
    See princely rule
political liberty. *See* liberty
political participation. *See
    also* citizenship; democ-
    racy
    on basis of property and
    wealth, 203
    Plato's political thought
    on, 44
political philosophy, 6-8,
    37, 44, 47, 53
political science, 51, 161
    practical wisdom, 39-40
    as separate discipline,
    104-05
political survival, 82-83
*Political Theory of
    Possessive Individualism*
    (Macpherson), 11
Politics and Vision (Wolin),
    12
Politics (Aristotle), 39-41,
    45, 60, 67
Politika. See Politics
    (Aristotle)
politike koinonia, 43
Politikos (Plato), 33, 35-36
polity, 41, 43, 62. *See also*
    mixed polity
Polwhele, Richard, 183
Polybios, 84
popes, 56, 58, 61, 95, 132.
    See also individual popes
    antipopes, 58, 61
    rivalry with emperor, 47,
    49-50
popular sovereignty, 64, 67,
    152, 161, 168. *See also*
    democracy
postmodernism, 5, 11, 229
power
    absolute, 45, 101-02,
    135
    gained by force or fraud,
    87, 230
    between men and
    women, 192
practical wisdom, 5, 40,
    44, 99, 169-70

prejudice, 141, 185
Price, Richard, 189
Prince, The (Machiavelli),
    69, 73, 79-83, 85, 89
    concentration on politi-
    cal survival, 82
    as footnote to
    Discourses, 74, 87-88
    princely rule in, 76
princely rule, 68, 73, 76
    fox and lion argument,
    81
    popular support or
    nobles' support, 76,
    79
    private method, 77
    public way, 77-78
    as restoration of order,
    86, 88, 90
principalities, 82, 88
Principia philosophiae
    (Descartes), 19, 22
private/public linkage or
    separation, 115, 197-98
private property. *See* prop-
    erty
professional colleges, 65,
    68, 111
progress, 122, 201
    human, 189
    Marx's belief in, 229
    modernism and, 21
    progressive facade of the
    bourgeois revolution,
    220
    technical progress, 28
    toward perfection, 22
    Wollstonecraft's faith in,
    200
property, 192
    male control, 197
    preservation of, 121,
    130, 186
    private, 127, 144, 151,
    226
    requirement for fran-
    chise, 126
    right of inheritance, 226
    women and, 180
property-based taxation,
    119, 127, 187
property qualifications,
    147, 165
property rights, 4, 122,
    151, 158
proportionality, 40-41

Protagoras (Plato), 33, 35
Protestantism, 93. *See also*
    Calvinism; Reformation
prudence, 23-25, 185
public-private separation,
    115, 197-98. *See also*
    personal is political
public good, 187
public opinion, 29
public system of communi-
    cation and transporta-
    tion, 226
pure or technical reasoning
    "getting it right," 15
Puritan Revolution, 70
Puritans, 95

Quadragesimo Anno (Pope
    Pius XI), 112

race and racism, 214, 228
Radzinowicz, Leon, 121
Raffaello Sanzio (Raphael),
    School of Athens, The,
    51
Rameau, Jean-Philippe, 149
Ramée, Pierre de la, 16, 109
Rawls, John, 145
    theory of justice, 230
Rawlsian liberalism, 12
Re, Paul, 229
realpolitik, 81, 89, 91
reciprocity, 40-41
reconciliation, 46
redistributive public poli-
    cies, 43, 143. *See also*
    welfare state
    targeted sectional relief,
    225
*Reflections of an Unpoliti-
    cal Man* (Mann), 115
*Reflections on the Revo-
    lution in France* (Bruce),
    177, 184-85
    Wollstonecraft's reply
    to, 189
Reformation, 47, 61, 69, 95
    new age of individual
    conscience, 15
regime types, 36, 54, 64,
    77, 79, 82-83. *See also*
    democracy; state
    classification, 41-42
    despotism, 134, 142, 160
    good and bad forms of,
    79, 84, 88, 90

government by assembly, 102

government contract, 105

inequality and, 151

mixed (*See* mixed polity)

Montesquieu on, 134-35, 140

principalities, 82, 88

representative government, 67

Rousseau on, 151

rule of few, 42, 64, 90, 147

rule of many, 42-43, 53, 64

rule of one, 36, 42, 64

"well-tempered" regimes, 62-65, 68

Regulae ad Direction Ingenui. See Rules for the Direction of the Mind (Descartes)

religion, 191, 225. *See also* Catholicism; church and state; Protestantism

conflict in political affairs, 70

religious fundamentalism (21st C.), 70

use by conservatives, 193

religious dissent, 95

religious toleration, 101, 125

religious wars, 93. *See also* Thirty Years War

Renaissance, 61, 69

new critical consciousness, 15

rediscovery of Aristotle, 47

republican governance, 74, 76, 78, 88

republicanism, 84, 134, 137-38

checks and balances, 84, 89, 91

civic virtue, 86

Florence, 77, 88

Rome, 84, 88

social, 130

republics *vs.* principalities, 82, 88

revolution. *See also* American Revolution; French Revolution

workers against bourgeois capitalists, 218

revolutionary elites, 155

rex imperator in regno suo, 50

right of resistance or revolution, 104, 106, 124, 143

Riklin, Alois, 90

Roman Empire, 46

Roman law, 50

Rousseau, Jean-Jacques, 3-4, 6, 13-14, 27, 146, 174, 179, 193-94

"back to nature," 151-52

Calvinism, 150

Catholicism, 150

Contrat Social, 107

different forms of government, 151

discourse on inequality, 152

Discourse on Political Economy, 155

Discourse on the Sciences and Arts, 150

on education of women, 181, 194

Émile, 148, 194, 198

general will, 154, 156, 168, 173, 200, 228

idealism, 152

inspiration for French Revolution, 153

"lawgiver" ("extraordinary man"), 155

On the Origin and Foundations of Inequality Among Men, 151

patriarchy, 188

on popular sovereignty, 168

rejection of majority rule, 156, 173

Social Contract, 27, 147-48, 152-53, 155

social contract theory, 173

support for galant style, 149

views on women, 180-81, 194

Wollstonecraft's criticism, 191, 198, 200

yearning for harmony, 157, 174

rule of few, 42, 147. *See also* oligarchy

hegemonic control, 90

rule of law, 30, 36, 101, 124

rule of many, 42-43. *See also* democracy

Thomas on, 53

rule of one, 42. *See also* princely rule

Plato's account of, 36

rulers, 50. *See also* princely rule

legislator/ruler distinction, 66

Marsilius on, 62

Rules for the Direction of the Mind (Descartes), 18, 20

ruling classes. *See* rule of few

Rutherford, Samuel, *Law and the Prince, The,* 103

Sabine, George, *History of Political Theory, A,* 4

Salomé, Lou, 207, 213, 229

"satanic mill," 203

Schiller, Friedrich, "Ode of Joy," 200

School of Athens, The (Raffaello), 51

science

during Italian Renaissance, 74

modernism and, 21

New Science, 25-26, 133

new science of Galileo and Descartes, 97

Plato *vs.* Aristotle on, 44

politics as "master science," 39

separation from politics and ethics, 28

scientific exactitude and rational choice, 15, 99, 141

Scienza nuova. See New Science (Vico)

scrutiny (*squittino*), 78

secular power, 55, 61. *See also* two swords, doctrine of

self-interest/public interest dichotomy, 154

separation of powers, 135, 145

Serva Padrona, La (Pergolesi), 149-50

sette. See factions

Seven Books on the Art of War (Machiavelli), 75
Seventh Letter (Plato), 32
Shackleton, Robert, 139-40
Shaftesbury, Anthony Ashley Cooper, Earl of, 122-23, 126
Shelley, Percy Bysshe, 190
Sidney, Algernon, 139
Silesian weavers uprising, 205
Skinner, Quentin, 89
"slave morality" (*Sklaven-Moral*), 211
slavery, 45, 65, 170
  Montesquieu's opposition to, 140-41
Smith, Adam, 186
social conflict, 86. *See also* class struggle
  Hobbes on, 99-100
  Montesquieu on, 133
  Tocqueville's acceptance of, 175
Social Contract (Rousseau), 27, 148, 152-53
  political, economic, and social equality, 147
social contract theories, 27, 100-01, 109, 124, 145, 173
social inequality, 172, 177, 201, 218. *See also* equality
  excessive, 87, 90
  John Locke's theories, 126-28
  link with punishment regime, 143
  Wollstonecraft's criticism, 192
Social Philosophers, The (Nisbet), 12
socialism, 213
Socrates, 33, 37, 209
  elitism, 32
  "noble" lie or falsehood, 34
Solon, 29
sophists, 33, 38, 167
sovereign territorial state. *See under* state
sovereignty
  absolute, 95, 101, 106, 115-16, 133, 140
  Althusius's definition,

106-07, 109-10, 113
  general will and, 154
  Hobbes's definition of, 97, 103, 106
  Locke on, 124
  of the people, 107, 160
  from realm or commonwealth and people, 105-06
  right of, 107
  state sovereignty, 2, 69, 114
Soviet Union, 227
Spanish Armada, 93, 96
Sparta, 31
special governing councils (*balie*), 78
specific law (*lex propria*), 110
spirit of the laws, 134, 142
Spirit of the Laws (Montesquieu), 8, 131, 133, 136, 138, 140, 142
  separation of powers, 135
squittino, 78
St. Barholomew Day Massacre, 95, 103, 109
Stalinism, 228
state, 5, 41, 203
  corporate powers and, 114
  Hegel's account of, 204-05
  intervention, 225
  liberal, 230
  Marx's view of, 225
  Nazi, 115
  as night watchman, 143
  Plato's description of, 33, 37
  separation from privatized society, 115
  sovereign territorial state, 2, 47, 59, 69, 94, 114, 119
  welfare, 203, 225
state of nature, 98, 100, 140, 151, 180
  transition from, 124
Statesman. See Politikos (Plato)
status quo, 177
Study Methods (Vico), 25
subsidiarity, principle of, 111-13, 116
sufficiency, 62

Summa Theologiae (Aquinas), 52-54, 57
  adaptation of Aristotle, 69
"supreme magistrate," 139
Swift, Jonathan, 119
Symposium (Plato), 195

Tacitus, 23
Talleyrand-Périgord, Charles-Maurice, 189
taxation, 4, 120, 127
  excise, 120
  Monthly Assessment, 120
  progressive income tax, 226
  property-based, 119, 127, 187
  without representation, 184
territory/political power link, 2. *See also* state
Theorie und Praxis (Habermas), 11
Thirty Years War, 94, 106
Thomas, Aquinas, Saint, 3, 5, 8, 13, 51
  Aristotelian-Christian synthesis, 57, 69-70
  church philosopher (*See* Thomism)
  commentary on Aristotle's *Ethics*, 52
  De Regimine Principium, 52-53
  discussion of law, 54-55, 57
  endorsement of mixed regime, 54, 56
  forms of government, 54
  man as "social animal," 53, 56
  Summa Theologiae, 52-54, 56-57, 69
  synthesis of faith and reason, 52-53, 69
Thomism, 52, 59-60
"Thoughts" (Montesquieu), 131
Thucydides, 80
Thus Spoke Zarathustra (Nietzsche), 207, 209, 215
Tilly, Charles, 45
  Formation of National

*States in Western
  Europe, The*, 12
Tocqueville, Alexis de, 3, 6,
  9, 13-14, 28, 114, 144,
  146, 149, 152, 179, 204,
  212
  acceptance of dissension
    and disturbances, 175
  Althusian arguments,
    162-63
  Aristotelian,
    Machiavellian tradi-
    tion, 174
  on class in England, 148
  contribution to history
    of political thought,
    173-74
  Democracy in America,
    157, 159, 165, 171,
    173
  on effects of universal
    suffrage, 166
  on mixed government,
    169
  *Old Regime and the
    Revolution, The*, 158
  public career, 158
  "sovereignty of the peo-
    ple," 160
  tyranny of the majority,
    157
totalitarian communist
  regimes, 227
translation, 7-9, 62
Trudeau, Pierre, 14
truth, 40, 151
  absolute, 1-3, 22, 27, 37
  immutable Truth, 102
  "real truth," 76
  true historical meaning, 6
  Vico's views on, 24
Tully, James, 129
Twilight of the Idols
  (Nietzsche), 207
two swords, doctrine of,
  50, 55. *See also* church
  and state
*Two Treatises of
  Government* (Locke),
  123-24
types of government. *See*
  regime types
tyrannicide, 95
tyranny, 41, 102-03, 152
tyranny of the majority, 53,
  157, 168, 173

Tyranny of the Thirty, 31-
  32, 34

Übermensch, 209-10, 215
Unam Sanctam (Boniface
  VIII), 58
universal equality, 211
universal suffrage, 166
  mediocre leaders, 167
  Tocqueville's under-
    standing of, 165
universality, 2, 25, 28, 185,
  211
University of Cologne, 103
University of Naples
  church free, 50-51
utility, 211-12

Valentin, Veit,
  Weltgeschichte, 12
verum/factum principle,
  26-27
Vico, Giambattista, 5, 22,
  140
  historical common
    sense, 23, 25, 28, 133
  method of inquiry, 23-
    26, 28
  *On the Most Ancient
    Wisdom of the
    Italians*, 24
  New Science, 25-26, 133
  profit and loss account,
    22, 24
  prudence *vs.* abstract sci-
    entific knowledge,
    23-24
  separation of science from
    politics and ethics, 28
  *On the Study Methods
    of Our Time*, 23, 25
  synthesis of old and new,
    26
  three historical ages, 26
  truth as relative concept,
    24
Vienna Congress, 177
*Vindication of the Rights of
  Men, A* (Wollstonecraft),
  189
*Vindication of the Rights of
  Women, A*
  (Wollstonecraft), 189,
  192, 194
Virginia Declaration of
  1776, 147

virtue, 35
  civic, 33, 86, 89-90
  in Machiavelli's works,
    82, 88
vulgus, 66-67, 170, 174

Wagner, Richard, 207, 214
wealth, 42, 122, 203
  distribution, 137
  by force or fraud, 87,
    230
Weber, Max, 117
welfare state, 203, 225
"well-tempered" regimes,
  62-65, 68
Weltgeschichte (Valentin),
  12
Westminster system, 136
Westphalian Peace Treaties,
  94
what touches all approved
  by all, 50, 113. *See also*
  Roman law
Whig Party, 177, 184-85
Whigs, 120, 122, 126
  indifference to social
    evils, 121
  individualism, 124
will, 27, 60
  common will, 107
  free will, 75
  general, 151, 153-56,
    168, 173, 200
  reduce all to one, 100-01
will to power, 211, 213
Will to Power, The
  (Nietzsche), 207
William and Mary, king
  and queen of England,
  120, 123
William of Orange, 104
Williams, Basil, 121
Wolin, Sheldon, 117, 175,
  229
  Politics and Vision, 12
Wollstonecraft, Mary, 3-4,
  6, 13, 181, 193
  attack on patriarchy, 198
  on education of women,
    189, 194-96
  faith in progress, 200
  first female author in
    classical canon, 177-
    78
  gender-specific predica-
    ments, 190

in history of political
thought, 182, 199
married William
Godwin, 183, 190
on middle class, 191
on modernity, 200
Newington Green, 188
reaction to Rousseau,
200
scholarship, 185
on social inequality, 201
"unwomanly" intrusion
into male domain, 177
*Vindication of the
Rights of Men, A*, 189
*Vindication of the
Rights of Women, A*,
189, 192, 194
on women's rights, 189,
192, 194-98
writing career, 188
women, 3, 5, 65, 188, 192,

206. *See also* feminism
Aristotle's views, 45, 178
in Christian Middle
ages, 179
equality, 177, 192, 205
Hobbes on, 180
Machiavelli's view of, 82
Nietzsche's views on, 229
Plato's view of, 35, 178
political representation,
200
political rights, 179, 182,
197
property control and, 181
rank trumps gender, 179,
193
role in politics and society, 178-79, 194-95,
197-98
Rousseau on, 180-81
sexual control, 181
as societal gatekeepers

(triage position), 195
as supreme rulers, 179
vote, 165, 197
workers
acceptance of capitalist
system, 225
alienation, 222-23
revolution against capi-
talism, 218
working classes, 44, 158,
172, 230
World, The (Descartes), 18
*World History. See
Weltgeschichte*
(Valentin)
"world literature," 220

Young, Iris Marion, 229

zoon politikon, 39, 56, 62,
108
Zweig, Stefan, 207